A Political History of Western Europe
Since
1945

A POLITICAL HISTORY OF WESTERN EUROPE
SINCE
1945
Fifth Edition

DEREK W. URWIN

LONGMAN
London and New York

Addison Wesley Longman Limited
Edinburgh Gate,
Harlow, Essex CM20 2JE,
United Kingdom
and Associated Companies throughout the world.

*Published in the United States of America
by Addison Wesley Longman Inc., New York*

© Longman Group UK Limited 1968, 1972, 1981, 1989
Fifth Edition © Addison Wesley Longman Limited 1997

The right of Derek W. Urwin to be identified
as author of this Work has been asserted by
him in accordance with the Copyright,
Designs and Patents Act 1988.

First published 1968
Second Edition 1972
Third Edition 1981
Fourth Edition 1989
Fifth Edition 1997

ISBN 0 582 31618 9 CSD
ISBN 0 582 25374 8 PPR

British Library Cataloguing-in-Publication Data

A catalogue record for this book is available from the British Library

Library of Congress Cataloging-in-Publication Data

Urwin, Derek W.
A political history of Western Europe since 1945 / Derek W. Urwin.
— 5th ed.
p. cm.
Includes bibliographical references and index.
Summary: Describes political developments in Europe from the
aftermath of World War II to the decline of the Soviet empire.
ISBN 0–582–31618–9 (csd.). — ISBN 0–582–25374–8 (pbk.)
1. Europe—Politics and government—1945– —Juvenile literature.
[1. Europe—Politics and government—1945–] I. Title.
D1051.U785 1997
940.55—dc20
96–35274
CIP

Set by 35 in 10/12 pt ITC Garamond Light
Produced by Longman Singapore Publishers (Pte) Ltd.
Printed in Singapore

CONTENTS

LIST OF MAPS

PREFACE AND
ACKNOWLEDGEMENTS

Space precludes a complete listing of all those who have been my mentors: it must suffice to say that I am indebted to both the many students and practitioners of contemporary politics who have offered in print their thoughts and conclusions on European affairs, and to my departmental colleagues, past and present, at Strathclyde, Bergen, Warwick and Aberdeen Universities for giving me the benefit of their expertise and knowledge. The final synthesis and interpretation is, of course, my responsibility alone. To cover in a few hundred pages five decades of European history during a period which has witnessed dramatic and far-reaching socioeconomic and political change is a daunting task. Selection and condensation are unavoidable. I have therefore concentrated upon those events and themes which seem to me to be of the most value for an understanding of the rich vein of postwar Western European politics as a whole. By so doing, I hope that I have not confused the issue further.

Derek W. Urwin
Aberdeen, March 1996

LIST OF ABBREVIATIONS

APO	Extra-Parliamentary Opposition (Federal Republic of Germany)
BR	Red Brigades (Italy)
CAP	Common Agricultural Policy
CDU	Christian Democratic Union (Federal Republic of Germany)
CIS	Commonwealth of Independent States
CND	Campaign for Nuclear Disarmament (Britain)
COMECON	Council for Mutual Economic Assiatance
COREPER	Committee of Permanent Representatives
CSCE	Conference on Security and Cooperation in Europe
CSU	Christian Social Union (Federal Republic of Germany)
DC	Christian Democrat Party (Italy)
DDR	German Democratic Republic
EC	European Communities
ECSC	European Coal and Steel Community
ECU	European Currency Unit
EDC	European Defence Community
EEA	European Economic Area
EEC	European Economic Community
EFTA	European Free Trade Association
EMS	European Monetary System
EMU	Economic and Monetary Union
END	European Nuclear Disarmament
EP	European Parliament
EPC	European Political Community
EPC	European Political Cooperation
EPU	European Payments Union
ERM	Exchange Rate Mechanism
ETA	Euskadi Ta Askatasuna (Basque Homeland and Freedom)
EU	European Union
EURATOM	European Atomic Energy Community
FDP	Free Democrat Party (Federal Republic of Germany)
G–7	Group of Seven
GATT	General Agreement on Tariffs and Trade

ICBM   Intercontinental ballistic missile
IEA   International Energy Authority
IGC   Intergovernmental Conference
IMF   International Monetary Fund
IRA   Irish Republican Army
MBFR   Mutual and Balanced Force Reductions
MFA   Armed Forces Movement (Portugal)
MLF   Multilateral Force
MRP   Popular Republican Movement (France)
NATO   North Atlantic Treaty Organisation
NORDEK   Nordic economic union
NPD   National Democrat Party (Federal Republic of Germany)
OECD   Organisation for Economic Cooperation and Development
OEEC   Organisation for European Economic Cooperation
OPEC   Organisation of Petroleum Exporting Countries
PASOK   Panhellenic Socialist Movement (Greece)
PCI   Italian Communist Party
RAF   Red Army Faction (West Germany)
RPF   Rally of the French People
RPR   Rally for the Republic (France)
SALT   Strategic Arms Limitation Talks
SDI   Strategic Defence Initiative
SDS   Socialist German Student Alliance
SEA   Single European Act
SNP   Scottish National Party
SPD   Social Democrat Party (Federal Republic of Germany)
START   Strategic Arms Reduction Talks
UCD   Union of the Democratic Centre (Spain)
UDF   Union for French Democracy
UN   United Nations
UNESCO   United Nations Educational, Scientific and Cultural
              Organisation
UNRRA   United Nations Relief and Recovery Agency
VAT   Value Added Tax
WEU   Western European Union
WTO   World Trade Organisation

For Patricia

CHAPTER 1

PARAMETERS AND PERSPECTIVES

We have learned, whether we like it or not, that we live in one world, from which world we cannot isolate ourselves. We have learned that peace and well-being cannot be purchased at the price of peace or the well-being of any other country. (*James F. Byrne, 1946*)

On 7 May 1945, in a schoolhouse near the French city of Rheims, Admiral Friedeburg and General Jodl accepted on behalf of Germany the Allied terms of unconditional surrender. At midnight of the following day, silence fell over Europe. Adolf Hitler's Thousand Year Reich had failed in its thrust for European and world domination: in the end it had lasted for only twelve years, or two years less than its maligned democratic predecessor, the Weimar Republic. Three months later the world entered the nuclear age when atomic bombs were dropped on the Japanese cities of Hiroshima and Nagasaki, bringing to an end the war in the Pacific and the Far East.

For six years the continent of Europe had been a battleground for Nazi Germany and the Allies. The Second World War had been all-embracing. The development of military technology had ensured that battle was not restricted to front lines or trench warfare: there had been many fronts, and civilian populations had suffered as much as the military forces. In addition, in every country the national economy, civil liberties and social life had all been subordinated to the exigencies of war on an unprecedented scale. The impact of the second world conflict of the twentieth century was traumatic for the individual, for European politics and for international relations. It was decisively to transform the face of the continent for decades to come, but while it was widely accepted in 1945 that the peace marked the beginning of a new reality, the true nature of that reality was as yet less immediately apparent or appreciated.

It seemed as if another chapter of history had been closed. Officially, the world in 1945 was at peace. With strategic imperatives reduced in urgency or dismissed altogether, the nations of Europe could turn to the problem of putting their own houses in order. Old protagonists renewed with greater vehemency their debates about the kind of society they desired, and about the kind of Europe that would or should rise out of the ashes of war. After the First World War many people had believed in 1918 that all that was needed to be done was simply to pick up the threads of prewar life. In 1945 the inevitability of change was widely accepted. The prime question raised, and one which had been debated throughout the hostilities by many of those concerned with the future, was the extent of the change – political, social and economic – which should occur. Yet while the necessity and unavoidability of change may have been widely accepted, not many could grasp that the Europe which had largely been forged in the nineteenth century had already expired.

The question of Europe's future was not to be the concern of Europeans alone. The summer months of 1945 did not herald a new era of peace; rather, they were a brief interlude between the struggle against Hitler and Nazism and the commencement of a new and different type of conflict. The new Cold War was to be another struggle for world influence, even supremacy, between two incompatible political faiths and value systems, epitomised by the United States of America and the Soviet Union. For different reasons, both these states had previously remained somewhat aloof from international affairs. Thrown temporarily together by their opposition to Hitler, both had drawn upon the vast resources of a continent, to such an extent that they could, if they wished, have a decisive voice in the fate of Europe. The continent's future was no longer mainly in the hands of the European states themselves.

This was obvious even in 1945. Of the former leading European powers, Germany had been destroyed, Italy had proved to have a brittle façade, France was still suffering from the psychological and economic consequences of military and moral collapse in 1940, while Britain was economically and financially exhausted by the years of war. None had the ability or the means to profit from or fill the vacuum that was the direct consequence of the disintegration of Nazi hegemony on the continent. The several meetings of American and Soviet troops – on the Elbe, in Czechoslovakia, and elsewhere – during the dying days of the Reich symbolised the future role which these two quasi-European powers would play in European affairs.

Indeed, it was already apparent that Europe, particularly the smaller states, would be subjected to a traditional 'spheres of influence' policy. In the wartime Allied conferences Joseph Stalin, the Soviet leader, had already forcefully indicated that such a policy was central to his view of how the Allies should participate in the political functioning of the postwar world. Eastern Europe, it was expected, would be claimed by the Soviet Union as its sphere of influence. What was perhaps not expected was the rigorous and exclusive way in which the Soviet Union would interpret and apply a sphere-of-influence policy. Notwithstanding the fact that the wartime victors might continue their cooperation in the Security Council of the newly formed United Nations (UN) and in the Allied Control Councils of occupied Germany and Austria, to all intents and purposes there were two Europes in existence more or less immediately after the cease-fire, one obliged to look towards the Soviet Union, the other with increasing urgency looking towards and across the Atlantic. Their expected meeting places, the UN and the Control Councils, were to be transformed into undeclared battlegrounds.

The intention of this book is to look at the postwar events in Western Europe, or that Europe which looked towards the Atlantic. To avoid becoming bogged down in problems of definition, it will suffice to describe Western Europe as that part of the continent which after 1945 found itself outside the Soviet sphere of influence, to the west of Winston Churchill's 'iron curtain'. This specifically post-1945 political definition has the merit of at least imposing a boundary that reflects a postwar reality that survived and structured European affairs for over four decades. The iron curtain may never have been impermeable, but the reality of a divided continent persisted until the dramatic events of 1989 which brought down the Communist regimes of the East. The demise of the Soviet Union itself in 1991 seemingly brought down the final curtain on the European settlement that emerged in 1945. However, in many ways – politically and economically – the East–West divide persisted after 1989. After the first flush of enthusiasm about the new possibilities afforded by the fall of Communism, more sober reflection and the experiences of the East European states indicated that stability, democratisation and an effective market economy would not be automatically or easily gained, that a true pan-European convergence could not be realised quickly. Hence, while in the 1990s the governments of Eastern Europe may have embraced democracy and market reforms, and while they may have sought membership of Western organisations such as the European Union and the North Atlantic Treaty Organisation, their situation was such that to a considerable degree they remained different, and might continue to remain so for some time, from the world of Western Europe that was fashioned politically and economically by and during the events and practices of the postwar decades.

Even with the definition outlined earlier, it would be impossible to examine within a single volume the myriad politics, policies and problems of all the Western states other than very summarily. Without implying that they are somehow less interesting or relevant, the discussion of the smaller democracies of Western Europe will be limited to those aspects of their domestic politics which have a bearing upon the wider themes examined. More attention will be paid to Britain, France, the Federal Republic of Germany and Italy: their demographic size gave them dominance in many ways, making it reasonable to regard them as the core states of Western Europe. Their problems and policies could more readily have important consequences outside their own territory, both within and beyond Europe.

The countries of Western Europe are nevertheless not alike in every respect. But nor is each unique in every respect. There is a broad consistency in their experiences across the decades since 1945: economic reconstruction and the development of a welfare state, their involvement in an increasing and interlocking network of international organisations, increasing prosperity and affluence in the 1950s and 1960s, growing pressures upon government and a more pessimistic appraisal after the 1970s of what is reasonably and economically possible, leading to a heightened uncertainty and scepticism. Yet while Western Europe can be reviewed as an entity on such a broad canvas, its inner diversity should never be neglected. Over the centuries it has displayed a richness of variety unmatched by other parts of the world. That pervasive diversity offers a multitude of viewpoints from which the region can be and has been examined.

Historically, attempts to integrate the territory within one political system never came near to success. However, the idea of unity never died. It resurfaced again during and after the war to force politicians and citizens to consider whether they should seek to defend the retention of the independent state or, alternatively, attempt to achieve some unification of state practices that in time might lead to a comprehensive European political community embracing as many countries as possible. Since 1945 Western Europe has moved, albeit hesitatingly and sporadically, along the road to unity. Unlike the past, however, it was a road constructed out of consent and consensus rather than upon military conquest.

While the theme of European unity is a profitable framework within which postwar events can be examined, the forces for and against integration cannot be fully understood without some consideration of politics within the various states or of the relationship of European politics to the wider world stage. So we return to the questions of the independence of states and international politics. It is the individual politics of the several states which most decisively set the tone of, or hindered, movements towards European integration. Furthermore, so much of what has happened in Western Europe since 1945 has been conditioned by world politics that the region cannot be isolated from the rest of the globe. The war may have hastened the end of the imperialist phase of European states, yet the continent remained central to world politics, not least because the confrontation between the two new imperialist 'superpowers' was sharpest in Europe. Because the United States has played such a large role in Europe since 1945, and because much of postwar European politics was a reaction to the policies, real and imagined, of the Soviet Union, Western Europe could not be totally divorced from the competition for world influence between the super-powers.

Within this broader setting, arguments were renewed in the 1940s as to what would be the postwar shape of things in Western Europe. Attitudes and opinions were many and varied, but very generally we can speak of an opposition between two broad viewpoints which in the immediate postwar years carried on a long and relentless debate on European organisation and arrangements of power. The first may be loosely termed 'traditional' national self-interest, espoused by those who preferred to place their trust in the validity of tested institutions and practices. Opposing them were people committed to the establishment of a new order of international collaboration and integration. During these first peacetime months and years, reform was packaged in what might be called the ideology and vision of the national Resistance movements, which by and large sought a complete change in the political, social and economic structures of the European states. The ideals espoused by these movements were not only supported by men and women who had actively fought against Nazi hegemony; they attracted all those who sought a new moral climate of man's responsibility to man, as well as that minority of prophets who in the pre-1939 wilderness had preached against the stultifying effects of materialism and nationalism.

If we disregard for the moment the wider implications of international politics, it is not too unreasonable to view political activity during the first few years of peace as centring upon the contest of national self-interest and reform for the allegiance of the public and for control of the institutions of power. By 1950, when international considerations had intruded more persistently upon the European consciousness, the forces for change, earlier so much in the ascendant, appeared to be in retreat, with the realisation of a European political community at best pushed back to a much more distant future. But it was not a complete defeat. The experiences of war and occupation, of mobilisation and destruction – along with the dawning of a postwar reality fraught with danger – had radically altered perceptions of the world. While delusions of restoring former imperial grandeur might persist, it had become painfully obvious to all except the most blinkered that the boundaries of Europe's ambition had contracted dramatically. It is within this psychological context that one should consider the wartime Resistance movements. Because, through the prestige it had acquired from its wartime role, it was a potentially powerful newcomer on the political stage and because much political activity in these first years revolved around its political ideas and proposals, the Resistance is an appropriate starting point for an account of the politics of postwar Western Europe.

CHAPTER 2

THE RESISTANCE IN THE POSTWAR WORLD

A movement without doctrine, without coherence, without definite outlines, destined to attract much support . . . but not to achieve strong and
disciplined action.   (*Vincent Auriol*, Le Populaire, *27 October 1944*)

The philosophy of the Resistance embraced, and was willing to embrace, all
those who felt that a new spirit should be injected into European reconstruction. Its recipe for the future was revolutionary, its leaders nearly all leftist
in inclination and favouring radical solutions to socioeconomic problems. Politically, the several national Resistance movements were dominated by three
major currents of thought: Communism, Socialism and Social Catholicism. In
some areas there could also be found those who advocated a marriage between
Liberalism and Socialism, stressing egalitarian values and the public good while
rejecting Marxist determinism. Brought together during the war by the necessity of fighting a common enemy, men and women from all these political
persuasions and from all walks of life seemed genuinely determined to forget
their differences in the fight for a common, peaceful and harmonious future.

There were, of course, differences of opinion, even distrust. In particular,
some Resistance leaders were suspicious of and hostile to their Communist
associates: fearing the possibility of a Communist takeover of an integrated
Resistance organisation, they sought to prevent Communists from achieving
positions of influence within the movements that could be used as spring-
boards for exerting strong political pressure at the war's end. While such attitudes were an augury of what was to come, during the war the vast majority
of Resistance participants saw no necessity for discrimination. The Italian
Committees of National Liberation, which contained representatives of all the
anti-Fascist parties, were typical of the dominant wartime mood, conveying an
image of a broad-ranging and generous camaraderie, of sharing the same risks
and responsibilities in the fight against German occupation.

The Resistance dream was that this camaraderie would persist into the postwar
world to encompass the whole of society. The scenario for postwar reconstruction drawn up by the Resistance movements was all-embracing. Not only
did they seek a radical overhaul of the institutional structure of the state; a new

morality and a new belief in the dignity and value of all humanity had to permeate the whole of society. The blueprint for the future prepared in 1944 by the French National Resistance Council was typical in its insistence upon the need for a new morality in human affairs, upon regarding social and economic rights as being as important as those political rights which had for long been accepted as essentials of parliamentary democracy.

Central to the overall vision and programme of the Resistance was the pre-war idea of the Popular Front, previously expounded by such men as Léon Blum, the veteran French Socialist, and Aneurin Bevan, the fiery Welsh radical. The core of the Front would be a Communist–Socialist alliance, though it would nevertheless be open to any other political movement desiring the same goals. These two parties had collaborated closely in Italy since the 1930s, and for a short while in 1936 the Communists had supported a Popular Front coalition government in France. It was felt that the common ground shared by these two ideologies had been broadened and strengthened by common involvement in Resistance activities. Certainly the two seemed close everywhere, and in Norway there was even talk in 1945 of a party merger.

For many, however, this was too much of a class construct. The dilution of class was provided by the third strand of Social Catholicism. Despite the seemingly equivocal position of Pope Pius XII *vis-à-vis* right-wing authoritarianism during the war, Catholic opposition to Nazism had gradually hardened, and Catholics played a leading role in Resistance activities. Catholic political inspiration was derived ultimately from the two basic encyclicals of the Church, *Rerum Novarum* (1891) and *Quadragesimo Anno* (1931) which stressed social justice while rejecting both dogmatic Socialism and unbridled free competition. At the heart of Catholic belief was a commitment to class conciliation. Christian Democracy sought to unite two alienated groups, the working classes and practising Catholics, and bring them into the mainstream of political life from which, at least in Catholic Europe, they had largely been excluded. Christian Democracy also considered social and economic rights to be as important as political rights, but argued that these applied across the whole community, that one class should not gain at the expense of others.

Whatever the ideological inheritance, all were profoundly affected by their common involvement in anti-Nazi activities. In that sense, one should not underestimate the importance of the Resistance movements in bridging the gap both between state and society and between the industrial and rural masses. In two major countries, at least, the working classes had largely been consigned to a social and political ghetto (admittedly partly of their own choosing) far removed from the centre of gravity of national political life. But in Italy, for example, there were in 1945 around 250,000 combatants in the northern partisan groups, and it was virtually the first time in modern Italian history that the peasants had been associated with other social groups in a political activity. Elsewhere, as in Belgium and the Netherlands, the electoral and organisational strength of Socialist parties may have prevented them from being totally marginalised, yet society and politics had nevertheless remained highly segmented and Socialist parties had only rarely participated in government. Even Britain might be said to have undergone a similar experience, with national mobilisation as an equivalent of Resistance participation. Only perhaps in Scandinavia had the working classes been accepted to some extent as an integral part of the political system.

Together, all these forces would work for a new society in which there would be benefits for all and an end to hardship, privation and insecurity. But if this brave new world was to come about, then those ideologies and movements which, in the eyes of the reformers, were old and discredited could not be allowed to regain control and influence in the postwar world. The best way, many argued, to ensure victory was a grand alliance of all progressive movements, an alliance that would possess sufficient strength and popular support to achieve electoral success: if there was, after all, a common purpose, then it made sense also to have a common organisation. Thus there was born the idea of a single Resistance party of all those who had worked for the liberation of Europe.

But in its optimism the ideology of the Resistance did not stop at national boundaries. The new spirit of reconciliation which it advocated was concerned not only with the creation of a new society, but also to ensure that never again would Europe be engulfed by war. Not just capitalism and material self-interest, but also nationalism and national pride, were identified as root causes of past conflicts on the continent. Discussions on the future therefore paid attention not only to the pressing needs of socioeconomic reconstruction after the ravages of war, but also to the need to transcend historic national state boundaries, dismissed as discredited and artificial, in order to achieve a revitalised and genuinely European community.

Declarations to this effect were made long before the end of the war. During 1944 several French Resistance groups had begun to argue for some supranational structure in Europe, built along federal lines, to replace the old system of independent states. Similar views held even greater credence within Italian Resistance movements, where some even went so far as to insist that national reconstruction should cede first priority to the urgency of establishing a new federal Europe. In Geneva, in July 1944, leaders of Resistance movements in several countries, including France, Italy and the Netherlands, appended their signatures to a declaration stating that a completely new federal and democratic governmental structure was required for the whole of Europe. The Geneva declaration, however, was apparently not signed by the representatives from Denmark and Norway.

In the Netherlands, however, a return to the prewar political system seemed to be favoured by most people. Sentiment for a unified Dutch Resistance political party had weakened considerably by 1945, and some politicians were arguing that leaders of an underground Resistance organised along quasi-military lines would not necessarily be the people best qualified to operate a peacetime political system. Similarly, while the political parties in Norway had all agreed upon a Common Programme of long-term planning for reconstruction and development, none had thoughts about allowing itself to be absorbed within a broader political organisation.

Nevertheless, the Geneva statement and similar documents were widely publicised in Resistance circles. Taken as a whole, the movements did possess a fairly comprehensive vision of a future Europe. Many of their leaders would be content with nothing short of total reconstruction since the historic national state had proved utterly incapable of preventing wars. In the eyes of the Resistance, the prewar political leaders and the political and social systems they represented had been found wanting. The reformers believed that the wholesale victories of the Nazi juggernaut had proved an opportunity to recast Europe in an entirely new guise.

The impetus for a new world did not come only from Resistance movements. In so far as it had thought about the future, much official American opinion looked rather favourably upon European union. The Soviet Union did not seem to be averse to the notion: at least Communists were following orders from Moscow to present a cooperative face to other groups. Britain also was seen as a sympathetic supporter. There was little reason for these pan-Europeans to foretell the result of the 1945 British general election: they simply expected Winston Churchill to continue in office after the war, and assumed that he would pursue a policy along the lines of his dramatic offer to France in 1940 that 'there shall no longer be two nations, but one Franco-British Union'. Confident that they had the blessing, tacit or expressed, of the Allies and that, because of their leadership and sacrifices in the fight for liberation, they would gain the electoral gratitude of their own populations, men of the Resistance groups looked towards the postwar world with increasing optimism.

THE FIRST POSTWAR ELECTIONS

For all the countries which had been affected by the war, one of the most pressing needs was to hold an election as soon as possible in order to establish or reconfirm legitimacy. These elections gave further encouragement to those in the Resistance organisations who were seeking a new form of society. The tone was set by the British election of 1945. A massive Conservative majority in Parliament disappeared overnight in a landslide victory for the Labour Party. For the first time in its history, Labour was able to form a one-party government with an assured majority. This was the most surprising electoral outcome of the immediate postwar years. Churchill, as war supremo and Conservative leader, commanded a massive popularity in the country. The wartime national government, which many Europeans had misleadingly identified solely with Churchill, had issued its own plans for social reconstruction in the Beveridge Plan of 1942, which some have called Britain's Resistance charter. The Beveridge Plan, in fact, was a primary source of the programmes and charters later announced by continental Resistance movements. Few, if any, therefore expected Churchill to be defeated.

Notwithstanding any specifically British reasons for the Labour victory, the same swing to the left was apparent in most other European democracies. In France the two elections of 1946 were dominated by the three mass parties of the left: on both occasions the Communists and Christian Democrats each received about one-quarter of the votes, with the Socialists not far behind. A similar tripartite pattern emerged in Italy in 1946: there, however, in the first free election since 1921, the Christian Democrats easily outstripped their two Marxist rivals. In Belgium and the Netherlands also, these three parties or their counterparts were the major electoral beneficiaries, with the Communists emerging as a serious party for the first time. An identical pattern appeared in liberated Scandinavia, though in Denmark Communist gains were partly at the expense of the dominant Social Democrats, who had to bear some of the opprobrium for heading the wartime coalition government under the German occupation. In Norway the change was more decisive: not only did the Communists register large gains, the Labour Party also won its first absolute parliamentary majority. Neutral Sweden also fitted into the general picture: while the dominant Social Democrats lost votes and seats in 1944, mainly to the Communists, this hardly disturbed their pre-eminence in Swedish politics.

When the smoke had cleared, it seemed that the spirit of the Resistance had won a great victory. Left-wing parties with their programmes for radical social reform could claim to have received an electoral mandate. Western Europe had rejected any return to the prewar system. Together with the Communist and Socialist parties, new or revived 'social' Catholic movements had been the major beneficiaries. Later developments, however, revealed that Christian Democracy had been lured into a false position. In some instances it received the support of large numbers of liberals or conservatives who felt the need for some change, but who could not endorse the more extreme Marxist alternatives. Liberal and conservative parties were the chief losers, partly because of their association in the interwar years with depression and unemployment, and conservatism also because of its silence over or seemingly tacit acceptance of right-wing authoritarianism.

It was obvious that there was an almost universal yearning for social reform along the lines proposed by Resistance propaganda, prompted by the emotional fears of insecurity coming out of the war and the memories of the economic crises of the 1920s and 1930s. On the surface, therefore, the way seemed open for Resistance groups to realise at least some of their aims. Yet these first postwar elections, while seeming to vindicate the optimism of Resistance reformers, proved that they had been defeated in one of their objectives. At the same time, the elections carried the seeds of destruction for their other plans and hopes for the future.

THE RESISTANCE PARTY

For many in the Resistance, the keystone of any political reorganisation was to be the creation of a new and comprehensive Resistance party incorporating all progressive elements of society. It was soon evident that this proposal had very little chance of success. Many political parties had managed to maintain some form of organisation in functioning order during the war. Others, especially Communists, had actually strengthened and extended their organisation. This was particularly true of French and Italian Communism. The party membership in Italy, only around 10,000 in 1944, had leapt to over one million by 1946. In France it was estimated that about half the active participants in the Resistance belonged to the Communist Party. Their activities allowed them to seize a strong foothold among the peasantry. Building on a meagre prewar base in rural France, the party gradually achieved an impressive organisational structure buttressed by a network of Committees of Peasant Defence and Action. In addition, the war and noticeable middle-class support for the Vichy Government gave the Communists an outstanding opportunity to strengthen their influence within the trade union movement. Middle-class support for Vichy suggested that the working classes and their 'true' representatives, the Communists, should be the new rulers of France.

The spirit of comradeship may have been strong among those party activists who had remained in the occupied territories: however, governments and party leaders in exile had kept alive the thought and traditions of the old party structure. Almost without exception they were loath to be merged with other political forces. In the Netherlands, for example, most leaders welcomed the decision of the monarch to involve Resistance leaders in discussions about the formation of a new government, but nevertheless regarded a possible Resistance party as being completely out of the question. Here, as in almost all the smaller democracies, the revival of the old party system was accepted more or less as a matter of form. But in these smaller countries the old parties did not seem to stand accused of so many faults and inadequacies as their counterparts in the larger countries, and so did not have to face so much criticism. The basic problems essentially involved parties in France, Italy and Germany.

It was the return of former party leaders, from exile, semi-retirement or concentration camp, that more or less finally ended the hopes of Resistance organisations for a single comprehensive party. Men of an older generation, they were well versed in the arts required of party leaders. Resistance activists often proved incapable of opposing them effectively on this very different type of battlefield: in this context they were essentially innocents abroad. Partisans survived the broils of peacetime political in-fighting only if they possessed previous experience or, as it were, compromised themselves by joining a traditional political party. Only outstanding forceful personalities, such as General de Gaulle, could be exceptions to this seemingly inexorable law. For some, particularly Catholics, adaptation was virtually impossible because of their quite different reasons for participating in the Resistance: religion, as well as nationalism, had been the basis of their opposition to Nazism.

It was not long before Communists also contributed to the difficulties of the Resistance unifiers. During the war, when minds were occupied with the day-to-day necessities of guerrilla fighting and sabotage, it had appeared that Communism had changed. Local Communist leaders were often young men who, because of the dictates of war, usually acted on their own initiative, and willingly in collaboration with others, according to their judgement of the local situation. To their partisan companions, it may well have appeared that their prime concern was with general welfare rather than with Moscow's wishes. After 1945, however, Moscow sought to regain total influence over Western

European Communism and to force it into the rigid code of Communist aims. The return to Soviet suzerainty was symbolised by the return from their years of exile in Moscow of older Communist leaders such as Maurice Thorez and Palmiro Togliatti, who sought a tight centralised control of local organisations. The Communist parties were determined, though perhaps not much more than other parties, not to renounce their independence to any Resistance party unless certain that they themselves would control it. Since it quickly became evident that this would not be the case, the Communists returned to a policy of building up their own monolithic party structure, a state within the state. Consequently, an open and irreconcileable breach in Resistance homogeneity soon opened between Communists and the rest.

Even during the war there had been obvious signs that the prospects for a Resistance party were not auspicious. What was desired was not the postwar perpetuation of something that already existed. National Resistance movements were in reality little more than uneasy coalitions of people with different political allegiances and interests who were unwilling to forfeit that distinctiveness. In many areas, partisan activity was associated with only one or two political parties. In some rural areas of France, for example, resistance was the Communist Party. The Italian situation is more instructive. In northern Italy the partisan armies were organised along party lines and owed their allegiance primarily to the party: the best organised were the Communist Garibaldi brigades. Given such circumstances, which fostered some degree of mutual suspicion and competitiveness during the war, it is difficult to see how any effective union could have been achieved in the more relaxed atmosphere of peacetime. The presence of parallel but separate party-related resistances was a product of countries where social divisions and cleavages ran deep, and where it simply was not possible for old prejudices to disappear overnight. By contrast, in countries with a more homogeneous society and a more integrated culture, there already was a high degree of consensus, and so also a feeling that it was not necessary for existing parties to merge their identities within an umbrella Resistance party.

Perhaps only two parties were to a great extent directly created out of the Resistance experience – the French Christian Democrats (MRP or Mouvement Républicain Populaire) and the Italian Action Party. The MRP, however, claimed an intellectual inheritance in the Catholic religion: strictly speaking, its ideology was not obtained directly from Resistance experience or aspirations. The Action Party, on the other hand, may be described as the Resistance party *par excellence*. It owed its origin to no other clear source. Under the leadership of Ferruccio Parri, it set out to expound the demands of the Resistance, including a 'European Federation of free democratic states' in a political and ideological framework of 'liberal socialism'. It hoped to provide the leadership and common meeting ground of the Marxist and non-Marxist left.

The portents for the Action Party were at first favourable. The pressure for change had forced the resignation of the government of liberated Italy that had been appointed by the King after the collapse of Mussolini's regime. The two great forces of Catholicism and Marxism (the Communist and Socialist parties having pursued a common course for some years) were too evenly matched for a leader of one to be acceptable to the other. In between lay the Action Party. Parri was nominated and commissioned to form a government. However, he did not survive for long. The direct cause of his fall was a realignment of political parties, due to the growing self-confidence of the right and the strategy pursued by Alcide de Gasperi, the Christian Democrat leader, which was to keep his party at the centre of the political spectrum. The Italian economy was in turmoil and social conditions desperate. The working classes and peasantry were committed to Marxist or Catholic loyalties, while the middle classes hesitated to travel into unknown territory and accused the Resistance of turning into a Communist conspiracy. Fearing Parri's proposals for extending the purge of Fascism and its supporters into state and private industry, his plans to break up monopolies and his intense republicanism, the middle classes retreated back to traditional values where they felt safe. While Parri's own lack of political experience compounded his problems, the essential point was the lack of a central pillar of popular support. The Action Party remained a party of leaders agreed on principle but without any significant mass following. Speculation ended in November 1945 when first the Liberals and then the Christian Democrats withdrew their support of the government: Parri was forced to resign as premier.

This was the death knell of the Action Party, and could be taken as the final indication that the ideals of the Resistance could not be implemented or translated into a secure electoral base, not just in Italy, but in the whole of liberated Europe. A similar situation occurred in France. Sectional political parties were increasing in strength, and none was willing to renounce its distinctive identity for an uncertain future as part of a larger movement. Only General de Gaulle had the authority and prestige to attempt an organisation that cut across traditional cleavages and loyalties. This he was unwilling to do, though he was prepared to accept the leadership of a movement emerging 'spontaneously' from the people. Equally, all the parties moved to oppose de Gaulle's views on a variety of issues.

In the smaller countries a traditional party system quickly re-established itself almost as a matter of course. A pattern of politics different from that envisaged by the Resistance dreamers, but one symbolised by the election results of 1945 and 1946, was to determine the course of events in Western Europe during the crucial first postwar years. If any of the ideals of the Resistance were to be achieved, they would be engineered by political forces motivated primarily from a different base. Furthermore, these forces would subsequently be able to claim the credit for social and economic reform.

THE PURGES

Not only were the Resistance movements defeated in the field of practical politics; they also failed to accomplish the most symbolic policy of their drive for a new morality in Europe. They had wanted to purify the atmosphere of the virulent hate and inhumanity of the previous years, above all by instituting and implementing an effective judicially based purge of Fascists and collaborators from public life. This proved to be an impossible task. Too much political passion had been generated during the years of occupation. Emotions were still too strong for any rational system to be devised for punishing the guilty and awarding damages to the victims. What constituted guilt varied greatly from country to country: in the Netherlands, to have eaten in public with a German could easily lead to an accusation of collaboration.

The illiberal tone was instituted at the outset by Resistance partisans themselves, either individually or through self-appointed kangaroo courts. In nearly all the liberated countries, summary justice was meted out by elements of the Resistance before the Allied authorities and the returning exiled governments were able to establish effective control. In France, for example, the number of summary executions was estimated at 5,000, or about the same as the number of death sentences (out of 170,000 cases) later decreed by the judicial courts. In northern Italy, several thousand Fascists were executed by the partisans. Mussolini himself was captured and executed after a brief and highly irregular 'trial'.

Unfortunately, revenge was not simply directed against the more malevolent Fascists. The guise of patriotism and outraged morality provided an excellent excuse also for dealing once and for all with old enemies for personal or political satisfaction or gain. Criminal elements, who had been quite prominent in the partisan movements, were especially guilty of such acts. Communists also seized the opportunity of eliminating both potential adversaries and ex-Communists who had resigned from the party. Whether or not the victims had joined the Resistance or had collaborated was of no account: what mattered was that they were a possible source of embarrassment. While nowhere did the total number of executions approach the scale of mass murder practised by the Nazis, the Resistance had stained its character even before it embarked on its ambitious moral programme, alienating many, especially in countries like France where the degree of collaboration had been quite high, who might otherwise have been at least tacit supporters.

Once government of some kind had been established in the liberated states, a regularised purge was inaugurated under normal judicial procedures. The burden of supervising this vast cleansing operation fell on bureaucrats and judges, who conscientiously strove to achieve the intended aims. A series of penalties was devised, ranging from discharge and debarment from public office up to the extreme of the death penalty. This ambitious programme, however, soon foundered in a welter of recriminations, accusations and counter-accusations. While there was perhaps little argument over who were major war criminals, no consensus was achieved over the minor actors and what their punishment ought to be. In retrospect, much of the initial legislation might seem unduly harsh: even so, the Resistance often criticised it for being too lenient. And that criticism increased as the courts steadily moderated their judgments because of the enormity of the task before them.

Nowhere was the dilemma more apparent than in Germany, where the purge and denazification procedures were directed by the Allied occupation authorities. Germany was the most monumental problem, for instead of a minority of the population being involved, nearly every adult had been connected in some way with the Nazi regime. Some eight million had been party members, many simply because possession of a party card had been the only guarantee of secure employment. The exposure of the Nazi death camps discovered during the Allied advance towards the heart of Germany had given greater urgency and even greater complexity to the questions of complicity and punishment. The occupation authorities drafted lengthy questionnaires which Germans had to complete. Even so, it proved to be impossible to determine with any great exactitude who was responsible for a particular crime or incident. Given the complex, intertwining and often chaotic nature of the structure and machinery of both the Reich and the Nazi Party, nearly everyone could confuse the issue by finding a reasonably valid excuse for claiming that responsibility for a particular action had in fact belonged to someone else.

The mood of Germany with regard to the purge changed comparatively rapidly from wariness to more or less open hostility. Few Germans could see any sense or application of justice in the whole affair. They preferred to draw a veil over the unsavoury past rather than have it paraded in full public view. Given the complex nature of the problem, it had proved easier for the Allies to try the minnows first: their cases could be dealt with simply and quickly. More senior Nazis often had greater resources that enabled them to throw many red herrings across the path of the inquisitors, or to take new identities and disappear into obscurity either abroad or within a totally disorganised German society. This strategy meant that the Allies, instead of meting justice, stood accused of committing an injustice. For as they became aware of the magnitude of their appointed task and of their inability to deal with it satisfactorily, they gradually moved to wind down the denazification procedures. The problem was more acute for the American and, to a much lesser extent, the British authorities who, unlike France and the Soviet Union (which tended to focus more on major war criminals), had attempted to be completely methodical. In the end many delayed cases were never taken up, amnesties were granted to categories yet to be investigated and to some individuals already sentenced, and punishments became less severe. Although trials of people accused of war crimes persisted through to the 1990s – for example the trial of personnel associated with the infamous Auschwitz death camp began only in 1963 – this trend became even more marked after the Allies resigned this duty in favour of constituted German authorities. Thus many minor offenders who had been sentenced first received relatively harsh penalties. It was not calculated to endear the purge to the ordinary German.

At the heart of Allied policy in Germany, endorsed by the Resistance, was the desire to demonstrate to Germany and the world the magnitude of the wrongs committed in the name of Nazism. The symbol of this punitive lesson was to be the Nuremberg trials of major war criminals held between November 1945 and September 1946. Much time and thought had gone into the preparations for the trials. There was to be an international board of nine judges presided over by a British Lord Justice, while a member of the American

Supreme Court acted as chief prosecutor. The charges against the defendants were 'crimes against humanity' and conducting an aggressive war. The penalty demanded was death. Most of the leading Nazis were on trial, except Hitler, Goebbels and Himmler who had all committed suicide, and Martin Bormann, the party secretary, and Heinrich Müller, the Gestapo chief, both of whom had disappeared.

Of the twenty-two Nazis who stood trial, only three were acquitted. These acquittals were perhaps the only verdicts which came as a surprise to Germany. Of the remainder, seven were given prison terms and twelve were sentenced to death. All the sentences were carried out except that on Hermann Goering who committed suicide in his cell. Elsewhere, the same fate awaited other prominent Nazi collaborators. Vidkun Quisling, whose name gave a new word to the English language, was sentenced to death and executed in Norway, as was William Joyce (Lord Haw Haw) in London. In France the two outstanding leaders of the Vichy Republic, Pierre Laval and Marshal Pétain, were also condemned to death, although Pétain's sentence was later commuted to life imprisonment by General de Gaulle.

In Germany the Nuremberg Trials were received with apathy and cynicism. They seemed merely to confirm evidence from the other denazification procedures that justice was not being done. The Allies had failed to communicate their high moral purpose to the Germans. To the latter, the sentences delivered at Nuremberg, coupled with the fact that Soviet and French judges were also participants, were merely further indications that the whole policy was no more than an act of revenge carried out by the victorious nations on the vanquished, as had been done by all victors in past wars.

A similar effect was noticeable in the liberated countries. The trials of Laval and Pétain in France were the scene of much virulent invective, poisoning the atmosphere further. The general public lost interest in the proceedings. The precarious economic situation obliged people to pay more attention to their own pressing immediate needs. The trials and the purges, perhaps inevitably, had been conducted in a political, not a moral, atmosphere. The anxiety of Resistance reformers to lead a great moral crusade appeared to the average onlooker to have degenerated into acts of personal revenge upon political opponents; whereas Germans saw denazification as the retribution imposed by some nations on another, in the liberated countries many were worried that the purge of collaborators had become just the revenge of some political groups which sought to destroy the credibility of their opponents.

Even if we take into account the many obstacles facing the prosecutors and the virtual impossibility of implementing any other workable course of action, the postwar purges still marked a second important failure for Resistance thinking. The ordinary European had not seen justice carried out; he was more likely to believe that injustice had been done. Many innocents had suffered at the hands of stronger political adversaries, while many who were less implicated with Hitler's drive for domination had been punished more severely than more serious offenders. This was partly a consequence of the postwar situation, where unified and firm political direction and social cohesion were somewhat lacking. However, an equally important reason lay in the nature of the action itself. The greatest problem had been to construct a scale of punishment compatible with the crimes committed. And it was here that the whole operation faltered from the beginning. No one could determine easily to which grade of collaboration a crime should be ascribed. Above all, the gigantic, almost superhuman scale of Nazi persecution defied any normal efforts of retribution that might repair or equal the damage already committed. Public resentment at Resistance extremism in trying to force the issue to a definite conclusion may well have harmed the overall Resistance programme.

THE FEDERAL UNION OF EUROPE

The third major Resistance proposal was the plan to create a great new federal union of Europe. It had been believed that this step could be taken when the Resistance movements became the governments of their respective countries. The return to traditional political and parliamentary life and the failure of Resistance leaders to thrive in this alien environment meant that unless a majority of the parties in a country were agreed, not only upon the goal, but also upon its details and the methods necessary to achieve it, the likely outcome would be deadlock and the shelving or abandonment of the dream. Only in Belgium, the Netherlands and Luxembourg, whose governments in exile had agreed in principle to a postwar customs union between the three states, did there appear to be some chance of a more limited objective being achieved.

Old issues which had previously kept parties apart, such as the historic hostility between Socialists and Catholics, returned to drive further divisions between the various segments of the Resistance, while Communists were totally opposed to European union unless it was under their control. In any case the federal commitment varied from country to country: the Danish and Norwegian Resistance movements had always been distinctly lukewarm about the idea. Moreover, the new governments of Western Europe found and believed that bread-and-butter problems such as supplies of food and fuel were more urgent. Solutions to these problems were what the electorates were expecting and demanding. Economic reconstruction perforce took priority over ambitious plans for European union. While Jean Monnet, in many ways the leading architect of the union that was to come in the next decade, and others had for some time conceived of a union based upon an Anglo-French core, there was no resurrection of Churchill's 1940 proposal. Indeed, that idea had not perhaps been a serious suggestion, but a plea, as Churchill confessed later, that might persuade a wavering French government to continue as a belligerent.

Plans for European union therefore disappeared rapidly from governmental agendas. They now had to be sponsored by private associations. These could count parliamentarians and even government ministers as members and patrons, but that support could not be said to reflect the unequivocal policy of their governments. To the more ardent supporters of the Resistance ideals in these first postwar months, it seemed that the vision of a great new society, born of high moral hope, had died of despair, intrigue and political pettiness.

AN ASSESSMENT

At first glance, it would seem that the Resistance vision failed to exert a positive impact on Europe; nowhere was it able to assert a moral authority over practical politics. Some partisans argued that they had been ruthlessly tricked and suppressed by unscrupulous political manipulators and by the self-interest of short-sighted officialdom. Its opponents countered that its conception of human society was essentially unrealistic and politically impossible under existing circumstances, that it advocated only a few generalised ideas but failed to present any extensive list of practical policy proposals. As with most things, the truth probably lies somewhere between these two claims.

The Resistance recipe for the future had only one complete failure – its inability to establish a comprehensive radical party. There was only one definitely major arrival on the party scene in Europe in 1945, the West German Christian Democratic Union, but while interdenominational in design and character, its roots lay in the pre-Nazi Catholic Centre Party. Like other Christian Democrat parties, it soon abandoned pretensions to radicalism and adopted a moderate conservative profile. Perhaps the one radical experiment associated with postwar Christian Democracy was the worker–priest policy pursued by the French Catholic Church. This was a move to woo the working classes back to religion through the activities of priests who would first work incognito in the factories as ordinary labourers. Their task was to win the workers' confidence: once that barrier was overcome, they could reveal their true identity and begin their proper evangelical mission. However, isolated from the Church, some priests became receptive to Marxist ideas, and the Vatican intervened to limit, and eventually in 1959 to end, the experiment. All other 'Resistance' parties disappeared or were unable to break out of narrow confines. By the 1950s, except in Britain and Scandinavia, Christian Democrat parties dominated Western Europe.

The moral aim of purging Europe of Fascism had only a limited success. The spontaneous judgments and trials generated much resentment at the time, most noticeably in Germany and Austria. In the latter only 9,000 were pursued; by contrast, Belgium, a state of similar size, investigated 87,000 cases. And in Italy the end result was little more than the removal of a few bureaucrats. Moreover, even limited success carried a hidden sting. Many eminent jurists were doubtful about the value of using due legal process to try the Nazi leaders for war crimes, suggesting that the trials at Nuremberg and elsewhere set a dangerous precedent that could be used by a victor in any future war to justify placing the defeated leaders on trial. In the longer run, however, Nuremberg and denazification did have an impact upon Germany. By the 1960s many Germans were prepared to accept the reality of the country's recent past. In other countries, memories of Nazi atrocities barely faded. In the Netherlands, for instance, proposals in the 1980s to release convicted war criminals from life imprisonment were abandoned in the face of strong public outcry. Trials of those accused of war crimes persisted through to the 1990s in Germany and elsewhere. One enduring consequence, however, was that protection of human rights was made an important issue that after 1950 was to be enshrined as a fundamental principle of democratic life in Western Europe.

In its attempt to create a federal European union, the Resistance also failed, yet not entirely. Its views at least helped to pave the way for the establishment of several European institutions such as the Council of Europe, which began to function in 1949. They also indirectly helped to inspire both the loose association of Scandinavian states within the Nordic Council and the more intense experiment of economic union of Belgium, the Netherlands and Luxembourg known as Benelux. Above all, the Resistance can claim some credit for the establishment of the European Economic Community in 1957. Admittedly, it would be foolish to suggest that these attempts at supranational cooperation and integration arose directly and solely from the Resistance experience. The latter, however, did take an issue which before 1939 had been relegated to the fringes of politics and contributed towards it being taken much more seriously by governments.

The legislative provisions passed by postwar parliaments were also influenced by Resistance ideas. For example, the French Resistance Charter of 1944 had, in calling for a 'more just social order', demanded a rational reorganisation of the national economy for the benefit of the general interest, socio-economic guarantees for workers, a comprehensive social security system, the nationalisation of many private monopolies, and the right of workers to participate in economic policy-making within industries. French legislation between 1945 and 1950 was heavily influenced by these views. Comparable legislation, also influenced by the native Resistance movements, was realised in other liberated countries.

Where new constitutions were adopted, the ideas of the Resistance also made their mark. The French Resistance Charter had been very largely socialist in its inspiration, and the new French constitution, although finally the result of compromises, showed much of the thinking of the Charter. In Italy, while some provisions of the constitution were derived from Communist proposals, much of what the Action Party, the epitome of Resistance 'ideology', had advocated was incorporated as principles in the new document. Something similar might be said about the West German constitution of 1949, deeply influenced as it was by Christian and moral ideas and precepts.

Moreover, Resistance adherents had the satisfaction of seeing incorporated into the new constitutions clauses which provided for the abrogation of national sovereignty in favour of supranational authorities. Statements to this effect can be found in the French, Italian and West German constitutions. While such clauses clearly reflected the hopes that in 1945 had been placed in the newly formed United Nations, they also symbolised the fact that Europe had become smaller. What was new was a willingness to recognise that viable international and European associations provided perhaps a more satisfactory means of advancing world, European and national interests. This recognition continued beyond the immediate postwar years, illustrated, for example, by similar provisions in the new constitution ratified in Denmark in 1953.

In view of all this, perhaps the Resistance did not fail completely in the years of reconstruction. Although it proved impossible to generate a broad consensus on ideology and organisation, it was perhaps a symbol of how the world had changed in 1945, in ways which it had not in 1918. The Resistance in that sense reflected the changed mood of public opinion and the shifting structures of politics. The *status quo* of prewar days, which for long had remained relatively undisturbed, could not be regained. That was to be further stressed by the hardening of the Cold War. The rejection of traditional liberal democracy with its emphasis upon political rights, and the acceptance of the need for a social democracy that would also stress social and economic rights, were forged by the experiences of war and occupation. By their efforts during these years, Resistance participants played an important role in conditioning people to the new social way of thinking. In that sense, the Resistance contributed towards the establishment and consolidation of the welfare state. Despite the problems of a tense international situation, the postwar hopes were reinforced by more than a decade of satisfaction and prosperity. Sheltering behind a belief in economic growth, the cost of welfare provision was not to be seriously challenged until the 1970s, when economic stagnation and decline coincided with problems of structural economic change and a questioning of the extent of the social role of government.

CHAPTER 3

PROBLEMS OF RECONSTRUCTION

The truth of the matter is that Europe's requirements for the next three or four years of foreign food and other essential products – principally from America – are so much greater than her present ability to pay that she must have substantial additional help or face economic, social and political deterioration of a very grave character.   (*George C. Marshall, 1947*)

The primary task awaiting Western Europe and its leaders after 1945 was to pick up the scattered threads of economic life and knit them together in some viable whole. Government ministers were quickly made painfully aware that the toll reaped by the war upon the continent seemed to be vastly greater than had been imagined. Their hopes and plans for a better future were contingent upon solving urgent economic and political problems of reconstruction: many feared that failure to do so might well result in a fracturing of the socioeconomic fabric more severe in its consequences than that which had occurred during the war.

THE CATALOGUE OF DAMAGE

In 1918 when the First World War ended, only the battlefields of Belgium and northern France lay in ruins. In 1945 the situation was entirely different. Military and technological development had made war almost universal: very few areas of Europe had remained immune to severe damage of some kind, and the outlook everywhere appeared bleak. The development of air warfare had laid even the British Isles open to destruction. Only the neutral states of Sweden and Switzerland retained a semblance of material normality. The devastation of northern France between 1914 and 1918 may have been more intense, but what the Second World War may have lacked in intensity, it made up for in quantity.

The economic consequences were highly visible. Industrial production on the continent had slumped. In 1945 and 1946 it stood at only one-third of the 1938 figure. In the factories and mines, the surviving machinery had been overworked or not maintained satisfactorily. Replacement parts were not easily available, and supplies of raw materials had been disrupted. Cities had been severely damaged, and there was an acute housing shortage in many of the great urban centres of Europe. Agriculture had also suffered: production was down to half the prewar level. Millions of acres of valuable farming land had been rendered useless, not only from being battlefields, but also through overcropping and the general unobtainability of commercial fertilisers. Livestock had been decimated to the point where it would take time for breeding rates to bring herds back to normal levels. Europe was no longer in a position to feed itself. Food rationing not only persisted after the war: many governments found it necessary to reduce allowances below even the meagre wartime levels.

There were other reasons why economic reconstruction after the war started off at a great disadvantage. The war had disrupted and destroyed communications networks. The Allies had placed a high priority on the destruction of communication lines: bridges, railways, marshalling yards and shipping facilities had been major targets for both bombers and saboteurs. Similarly, rather than allowing such links to fall into the hands of the advancing enemy, the German military had attempted to destroy them whenever possible. At the extreme, at the war's end two of Western Europe's major rivers, the Rhine and the Elbe, were each spanned by only one serviceable bridge.

In Britain, damage was largely restricted to the larger cities and ports. Nevertheless, the pressure of serving the war machine for six years had left little scope for investment. Overseas assets had been liquidated to pay for the war. One-quarter of the merchant fleet had gone, and much machinery was exhausted and outdated. France, which had never really recovered from the drain of manpower and resources inflicted twenty-five years earlier, was once again critically affected. Several cities were badly damaged, with some of its ports in ruins. Nearly one-fifth of France's houses and two-thirds of its railway stock had been destroyed or rendered useless, while about one-half of the country's livestock had been killed. Summing up the extent of the damage, the French War Damage Commission gloomily estimated the cost at 45 per cent of the country's total wealth.

In Italy the spread of destruction reflected the various stages of the Allied advance northwards through the peninsula and the degree of intensity of German resistance. Damage was greatest in those areas where the Allied push had been halted by adverse winter conditions and entrenched enemy positions. Although the large conurbations of Milan and Turin, and several ports, had been hit by bombing raids, the industrial core of northern Italy escaped relatively unscathed; the more poverty-stricken south had suffered more heavily. Even so, it was estimated that, overall, one-third of Italy's assets had been destroyed.

The picture in northern Europe seemed rather brighter. Neither Denmark nor Norway had been the scene of much fighting and were still (bar the far north of Norway) occupied by German troops at the end of the war. Norway's resistance, however, had cost the country dear. In the far north, German forces, retreating before the Red Army, had pursued an effective scorched-earth policy:

there, postwar social and economic conditions were particularly acute. In addition, Norway had lost half of its economically important merchant fleet. Conditions in Denmark may not have been so adverse, yet the country was virtually bankrupt. Even Sweden had not escaped entirely: while its neutral status had enabled it to avoid the ravages of war, it had been placed on a permanent war footing during the hostilities and so had to face similar problems of adjustment to peacetime.

Belgium too had fared rather better than its neighbours, due partly to the rapidity of the Allied advance through the country and its consequent speedy liberation. The road back to normality was also made somewhat easier because of its giant colonial possession of the Congo. During the war the Congo became one of the main suppliers to the Allies of raw materials and minerals, especially uranium. The exiled government in London was able to accumulate substantial credit which could be used to arrange for food, clothing, shelter and new machinery once it was able to return to Brussels. Yet notwithstanding its relatively good fortune, Belgium still had to introduce the same stringent measures of control as other democracies. The Netherlands had not been so fortunate. Dutch opposition to Nazi domination had been vigorous from the outset. As the Allied advance approached the country's borders, both German troops and Dutch partisans played the deadly game of breaching the dykes and flooding the countryside. Much valuable land was agriculturally useless in 1945, and food supplies extremely scarce. A government survey estimated that one-third of Dutch housing had been destroyed and that the total loss was more than three times the country's annual income.

There remained Germany itself. On the surface the country appeared to have been obliterated by the Allies' determined advance against a stubborn resistance. The American Strategic Bombing Survey claimed that two-fifths of the buildings in the fifty largest cities had been destroyed. Very little survived of Frankfurt, over 90 per cent of Düsseldorf was thought to be uninhabitable, while Berlin, the scene also of vicious street-by-street fighting between German and Soviet troops, was described by the playwright, Bertolt Brecht, as 'the rubble heap near Potsdam'. Despite the obvious destruction, this surface appearance was somewhat illusory. Much of Germany had been spared, not only its agriculture but also its industry. Allied bombing raids, for example, had been more successful in scoring hits on private dwellings and public buildings than on industrial plants.

Nevertheless, the damage and dislocation in Germany, as elsewhere, was extensive. Coal output in the Ruhr was only a small fraction of the prewar level and, in 1946, industrial production was still only one-third of the 1936 figure. In France, industrial output at the beginning of 1945 had not reached 50 per cent of the 1938 volume of production. Similar statistics could be produced more or less throughout Western Europe. It was this overall gloomy outlook which seemed to give credence to the pessimistic assertions that European recovery would take the best part of twenty to twenty-five years. In the event, the process of reconstruction was well under way within five years, and virtually completed within ten.

These analyses of the various economic systems were based only on catalogues and assessments of material damage. No forecast of the time-span necessary for future development could easily take into account the effect of the great loss in human life and expertise. France had been bled of its young manhood in the First World War; and again the country had suffered greatly. Over two million French citizens had been transported to Germany, there to be placed in detention camps or to be used as forced labour. Many had died from exhaustion and starvation or had been executed. Of those who returned, many more were physically or mentally crippled, unable to participate fully in social and economic activities. A similar story was reported by the other belligerent and occupied countries. On the other hand, military losses were not as great as they had been between 1914 and 1918; only Germany lost more fighting men in the Second World War than in the First. Nearly four million German soldiers had been killed or reported missing. In addition, another one and a half million were prisoners of war. Many of those who had been captured on the Eastern Front were destined never to return home from the Soviet Union.

It was this drain of human resources as much as the material destruction which gave rise to the pessimism about any speedy economic recovery. The conflict had been more total than the First World War. Civilians as well as the military had been involved. Nations had given virtually their all, in spirit as well as in goods, and a feeling of exhaustion was universal. The question had to be asked whether Europeans were psychologically and physically capable of the task of economic reconstruction. This general fatigue and the psychological aftermath of defeat, collaboration and suffering must be set as counterbalances to the unbounded optimism of the Resistance vision.

A further important factor was the complete disruption of international trade and payments, and the economic dominance of the United States, which by the war's end held some two-thirds of the world's gold stock. Even before the war, the balance of economic as well as political power had begun to shift away from Western Europe, not only to the United States, but also to the Soviet Union and the Pacific states. The war merely hastened this trend by enforcing a radical change upon Europe's pattern of markets and commerce. Nowhere was the effect greater than in Britain. Although its political and economic reach was in decline before the war, it remained the second largest creditor in the world in 1939: the war turned Britain into the largest debtor as it liquidated one-third of its overseas assets to meet the costs of the conflict.

In short, economic dislocation had spread far beyond the land area of the old continent. Invisible sources of earning foreign currency, especially dollars, had disappeared, merchant shipping had been decimated, and overseas foreign insurance schemes and investments had been plundered to finance the war. The rather abrupt economic change created a vacuum which was largely filled by the United States. By 1945, American exports had soared to nearly three times the 1938 total. This created a new problem for Europe: the dollar gap. The United States could supply Europe with more than its requirements. On the other hand, American imports were extremely low and did not balance the exports. In any case, Europe did not possess the necessary credit or cash to purchase the American products that were available.

It was the extent of economic dislocation and the need to rebuild the national economies that contributed, as much as anything, to the failure of Resistance schemes for integration. In many instances, economic disruption meant individual unemployment and privation. Many had lost most or all of their personal belongings. The average citizen was more acutely aware of individual economic wants and needs than of the high moral aims of the Resistance idealists. People's horizons were more likely to be defined by bread-and-butter issues.

PROPOSED SOLUTIONS

Initially, progress seemed to be slow and results minimal, which accorded with the pessimistic view of the vastness of the task that governments thought lay before them. To restore the supply of essential services, government efforts centred around rebuilding communications systems and power supplies. Although this was the general pattern everywhere, the methods employed to restore the economy varied considerably. Once again the debate took place as to whether one should pursue the *laissez-faire* policies that had characterised the prewar world or impose government direction with, for example, stringent control over prices and wages. Generally speaking, four main themes were advocated: that reconstruction should occur within comprehensive national economic plans under rigid government control; that basic industries should be nationalised; that landholding systems should be reformed and modernised; and that social security systems should be introduced or greatly extended.

The notion of complete national government control was not popular. It reminded people of Nazi rule and of the formula which the Soviet Union was introducing in Eastern Europe. A few countries, most notably France, produced a reasonably comprehensive national economic plan, but there was to be no question of coercion. Governments had to be content with direction gained primarily through influence and persuasion rather than by diktat.

However, the principle of planning and of government involvement in the economy was widely accepted. This was not a new idea. Many European states had industrialised on the basis of a close liaison between government and industry: the notion was radical perhaps only in Britain, the home of the first, and perhaps the only spontaneous, industrial revolution. The principle of planning took second place to *laissez-faire* doctrines perhaps only in West Germany: on the other hand, the widespread publicity given to the social market nature of the West German economy after 1948 concealed the considerable extent of government planning and supervision that did exist. What was important everywhere was the more or less unquestioned acceptance of governmental involvement in the economy, to produce a new version of capitalism that essentially mixed private and governmental activity within a broad framework of free enterprise.

The importance of planning increased when American aid, which eventually was deemed essential for recovery to proceed at a satisfactory rate, was made available on the condition that the recipient European states present both a plan for the use of foreign aid and some institutional bodies to administer it. In addition to the Organisation for European Economic Cooperation, established as the main organ of the overall scheme known as the European Recovery Programme, states set up their own planning organisations: France had its General Planning Council; Belgium a Central Council of the Economy; and Italy a Committee of Reconstruction. These bodies were given the task of supervising the proposals to overhaul and modernise industrial plants, to reach self-sufficiency in production, to boost exports, and to develop a new pattern of markets made necessary in some instances in the late 1940s by the disappearance of traditional outlets in Central and Eastern Europe.

Hence the state became a prime factor in the various national economies. Nearly everywhere, some measure of public ownership was thought necessary, especially in energy and communications. The motives for nationalisation depended upon the circumstances of each case. In some instances, as in Italy, it came about because of the need to rescue failing but vital industries by injections of government aid, and from aid it was but a short step to ownership. In other instances, it was simply because only the government had the capacity to undertake and underwrite reconstruction programmes. In Britain, the Labour Party implemented nationalisation schemes because the policy was an integral part of its ideological belief system. This was also true in France, but there, in addition, the government felt compelled to nationalise the mines to bring an end to severe industrial unrest, while other industries – for example, the Renault car firm – were appropriated because their previous owners had collaborated closely with the German occupation authorities.

The pressure for nationalisation diminished after the first burst of enthusiasm in 1945 and 1946. Strong sentiment in favour survived only among a few Socialist parties, as in Britain where it remained an article of faith to the Labour Party's left wing. Generally, there was a preference for limiting the use of nationalisation to economic situations where private ownership clearly could not function satisfactorily. In Norway the Labour government preferred a system of private ownership operating within government-designed and directed economic plans, an arrangement typical of Scandinavia. The Socialist members of the Belgian coalition government opted for a policy of economic reforms which could be operated by private initiative. Already possessing a tradition of close collaboration between state and industry, Italy preferred to continue the old system to one of outright nationalisation. In West Germany the prospects for nationalisation were poor. When Germans themselves were given the opportunity for administering their own country, they rejected government control as being too reminiscent of the Nazi era and the desperate situation under rationing between 1945 and 1947. Instead, they pursued a course of allowing, within fairly liberal limits, market forces a looser rein, encouraging investment by means of generous tax concessions.

Several decades later, any assessment of the postwar nationalisation policies is still likely to generate some political passion, nowhere perhaps more so than in Britain. Their supporters and apologists have asserted that this kind of large-scale government intervention in the control of the economy permitted a more speedy programme of redevelopment and investment, and that private control could not have achieved the same effect in so short a period of time. It was equally clear, however, that state ownership created nearly as many problems as those it was intended to resolve. It was certainly not the panacea some of its ardent advocates believed it would be, but it was not until the 1980s that the pendulum began to swing firmly in favour of privatising state-owned industries. In many ways, however, the debate over the virtues of nationalisation was and is rather sterile. There may have been valid reasons for nationalising specific industries, as with Renault, or because it was deemed a necessary social service, but in general there was no necessary virtue attached to state ownership, and after the 1970s it became identified more with stifling ministerial interference and rigid inefficient bureaucratic control.

The essential point was not state ownership, but state control, a point grasped and practised perhaps most clearly by the Scandinavian Social Democrat parties, which were instrumental in setting up a dense web of institutional arrangements whereby employers and trade unions collaborated and liaised with government, but always under the latter's direction. This was easier in most continental countries where ever since the industrial revolution there had been a close relationship between government and industry. It was most difficult in Britain because of a deep attachment to *laissez-faire* principles. There the picture tended to be painted symbolically in black and white: either large-scale state ownership or unchecked market forces.

However, even the British Conservative Party accepted that government had to play a more active economic role. That role was essentially determined not by an ideological commitment to nationalisation, but by an acceptance and application of Keynesian economic theory. In his *The General Theory of Employment, Interest and Money*, published in 1936, John Maynard Keynes was in favour of macroeconomic policies that would enable the market economy to work more productively. He argued that an active government role was inevitable, that the time of individualism and free enterprise was over. Control should go beyond traditional policies of balancing the budget, to regulation of the economy by manipulation of both supply and demand. Writing at the height of the great depression, Keynes argued that the main purpose of government was to ensure full employment as the way to greater productivity, demand and consumption. Such government direction would not necessarily generate inflation: government intervention could check rising prices and control the boom–slump cycle typical of capitalism. Many observers thought that Sweden had already adopted Keynesian principles in the 1930s and that this was the reason for the subsequent sharp turnaround of the Swedish economy. Certainly, Keynesian economics, embraced by the European left after 1945, had by the 1950s been adopted by more or less all political parties. The age of Keynes lay more in the decade or so after 1948, but it was seeded in the immediate years after the Second World War.

The economic situation in 1945 was ripe for some of the ideas expounded by Keynes. Much of Western Europe's industrial plant had not been severely damaged or destroyed. The stumbling block was perhaps more a loss of self-confidence. Moreover, productivity potential had expanded greatly during the war. Even in Germany it was estimated that there had been a marked increase in the fixed assets of industry even after the costs of destruction and of those plants dismantled and transported elsewhere were taken into account. The capacity to rectify the shortage of goods therefore existed: what was needed was the financial injection. Moreover, where factories had been totally destroyed, if investment was forthcoming, it permitted the building of new plants with modern cost-effective equipment. Even the wholesale razing of cities had a beneficial aspect: rebuilding offered considerable employment prospects in the construction trades. What Western Europe was in greatest need of during these first postwar years was capital: that was to come from the United States.

There was much more agreement on the need to boost agricultural production, although the means adopted varied a great deal. Production grants, guaranteed prices and heavy taxation on fallow land that could be productive made it profitable for landowners to cultivate their property wherever possible. If there was a general bias, it was in favour of small farmers. France, with a limited degree of success, introduced schemes to rationalise its patchwork system of smallholdings, while Italy attempted to redistribute the agricultural land of inefficient large estates in favour of the small peasant through compulsory purchase and improvement grants. Such measures, where they occurred, helped to consolidate the conservative mood of the countryside. In many countries, farmers and peasants formed a substantial segment of the electorate: with their support, conservative parties began a slow electoral comeback in the late 1940s.

Finally, social security systems were introduced or improved beyond their rudimentary prewar levels with very little argument. The British Beveridge Report of 1942, with its implications of cradle-to-grave security for at least the most unfortunate groups in society, served in many ways as the basic inspiration of security and welfare schemes. In general, concentration was first upon social legislation and improved social insurance within a framework designed to make medical and health facilities accessible to all irrespective of income, and to provide a safety net for low-income groups so as to mitigate hardship. With these provisions of widespread social insurance, Western Europe launched the era of the welfare state.

THE THREAT OF INFLATION

When politicians and economists had considered during the war what was likely to occur after its end, they drew a lesson from 1918. They assumed that again there would be an intense but short-lived boom brought about by the launching of reconstruction programmes, followed by depression. That the predicted upswing was underway was evident in 1946, as the level of demand steadily increased. This, however, brought other problems to the attention of governments. One was the need to restrict the circulation of currency outside essential reconstruction programmes. Another was to control or destroy the black market which had sprung up everywhere because the supply of goods, still largely subject to rationing, could not match demand.

The level of currency in circulation had increased greatly during the war, but usually strict goverment control prevented it from causing enormous rises in prices. The social climate after the war was less conducive to rigorous controls, and prices began to rise. The pressure from consumers yearning for scarce products was reinforced by manufacturers who wanted high prices in order to finance investment and modernisation programmes. The vicious circle was made complete when workers inevitably began to demand more substantial wage increases to maintain their standard of living.

This inflationary spiral appeared everywhere. It was perhaps less noticeable in Scandinavia, where a broader national consensus on social equity prevailed, and in Britain which pursued, with some success, an austere rationing system. Nevertheless, inflation and the inability to force its exports up to a level where they could match imports were two reasons which contributed to the decision in 1949 to devalue sterling. Governments worried about inflation not least because it threatened that long-term investment deemed necessary to hoist industrial production up to and beyond its prewar level. On the other hand, it seemed to many to be a natural complement of other economic policies, and so something which, at least in the short term, had to be lived with.

A precondition of any action against inflation and the black market was strong government and strong government measures. On the continent, this was forthcoming most readily in Scandinavia and the Low Countries where fully legitimate governments in exile had returned to ease the transition to peacetime conditions. Postwar governments had been quickly constituted, and they were at least able to tackle reconstruction and its attendant economic problems without being trammelled by political debates over their legitimacy and the type of political regime the country should possess. Inflation may not have been destroyed, but it was prevented from reaching unacceptable levels.

Elsewhere, the picture was not so bright. Germany, Italy and France found it more difficult to curb the mushrooming of inflation and the inevitable black market. In all three countries the old regimes had been destroyed or discredited. Arguments over legitimacy and constitutions, over what the rules of the political game should be, tended to occupy much attention, allowing for little common ground from which a concerted attack could be made on economic problems. Government regulations were often ineffective: the black market flourished, and the value of money as a medium of currency steadily decreased. The problem was perhaps greatest in Germany where, for a while, cigarettes replaced money as the medium of exchange. The threat of total ruin through hyperinflation such as that which disrupted the country in 1923 was again very real. In France the exchange rate of the franc multiplied nearly six-fold between 1944 and 1948. During the same period, the rate for the Italian lira multiplied five times: between 1938 and 1948 prices had increased fiftyfold. If unchecked, the consequences of such inflation would have been an almost total drain on individual savings, the reduction to poverty of those living on fixed incomes, and the disappearance of the small investor. That this did not occur was due to several factors: the strength of the economic boom, the continued application by governments of their interpretation of Keynesian economic theory and, above all, the political interests of the United States.

RECONSTRUCTION AND FOREIGN AID

By the end of the decade the struggle against economic deprivation was succeeding. A severe financial squeeze in Italy had helped production to climb past the prewar level. In France the investments of the immediate postwar years were beginning to have an effect. In short, the rate increase in Western European economic productivity was amazing, confounding the earlier pessimistic forecasts. Overall, industry was back at its prewar level by 1948: agriculture took only two years more, despite the extremely harsh winter of 1947 and the widespread droughts of 1949. Recovery, however, did not mean that Western Europe had regained its former world position. The immediate objective had been economic reconstruction, not expansion beyond the prewar base. The rest of the world had not been standing still: despite the great advances made, production and incomes in Western Europe still lagged, relatively speaking, behind those of several other countries. In particular, it was the relationship with the United States, not domestic inflation or the previously predicted recession, which was to threaten an economic crisis.

Considering the difficulties which had to be overcome, the rate of reconstruction was little short of miraculous. A good railway network did not appear until 1947, while a further three years were required for shipping to regain its feet. The basis of industry, coal production, was something of a problem: there was an overall shortage of miners and up-to-date equipment, while in France, for example, a militant miners' union also hindered progress. Indeed, old class hostilities had not disappeared, despite views about the communality of mankind and the predominance of left-wing parties in government. Workers and management remained suspicious of each other, especially in France and Italy with their large Communist parties.

The new stress on social democracy was in some ways a further hindrance. Social security and insurance benefits were inflationary in their effect, but most governments were hesitant to curb them for this reason alone. The general policy of seeking a more equitable wages structure produced a similar inflationary pressure. Again, the postwar governments were committed to a policy of full employment whether or not this was justified by the economic situation. Where governments instructed firms not to dismiss workers, even where there was overmanning, inefficiency resulted. Prices remained high to cover costs, introducing a risk of stagnation in productivity and investment. States were placed in a position where purely monetary methods of controlling inflation and regenerating the economy were insufficient.

Yet notwithstanding these problems, the European economies had experienced a remarkable turnaround by 1947. Why then were there persisting worries about their viability and such pessimism as that expressed by George Marshall, the American Secretary of State, and his concern about Europe's requirements and a possible deterioration that would be extremely grave in its consequences? To understand such worries, we have to turn away from the minutiae of the domestic economies to look at the international economic system. Quite simply, Western Europe was finding it difficult to maintain any reasonable balance of payments.

Western Europe needed to export its products, but could do so only if it acquired new equipment and raw materials from abroad. However, its ability to pay for imports was severely limited. Governments, through their own policies and because of factors outside their control, were finding it very difficult to bridge the dollar gap. They had been reasonably successful in setting their own houses in order, yet did not possess the level of financial resources necessary to purchase raw materials from abroad. Furthermore, they were faced also with problems of trade dislocation. Old markets had disappeared, even within Europe. The fall of Germany and its relatively tardy recovery was gradually accepted as something that seriously inhibited the redevelopment of European trade.

The efforts of European governments in attaining prewar levels of economic activity may have been praiseworthy, but none was content to stop there. All were deeply affected by the experience of mass unemployment in the 1930s; to stabilise the economy at 1938 levels was simply not acceptable. The policies of high output, full employment, a greater tempo of industrialisation and modernisation, and expanding foreign trade were not just admirable; they had become immutable tenets of political faith which had been sold to the electorate. Because it was politically impossible, or at least dangerous, for any government to seek to renege upon this expansionary programme, Western Europe was heading by 1947 towards an external payments crisis. In time it might have recovered without outside help, but progress would have been slow and painful. In addition, the prospect of political turmoil and instability could not have been ruled out. In the event, it was injections of foreign aid from the United States which averted the impending crisis and enabled Western Europe to move smoothly from the immediate postwar boom into a period of steady growth and prosperity that lasted for two decades. The economic turbulence that followed upon the ending of the First World War was not to be repeated.

During the war, American aid had taken the form of the Lease-Lend programme initiated in 1941 by President Roosevelt, which provided material for the war against Germany: Britain had been the prime beneficiary. Europe may have expected something like this assistance to continue, but once Germany capitulated, its original justification had gone, and Lease-Lend was summarily ended. However, American aid in the form of food and necessary supplies had to be provided on the continent to combat the emergency situation prevalent immediately after liberation. But by 1946 only Germany, still under military occupation, was a beneficiary of this kind of aid. The rest of Europe was expected to stand on its own feet.

A measure of assistance was provided by an organ of the newly constituted United Nations (UN), the United Nations Relief and Recovery Agency (UNRRA), and by American grants to specific states. Anticipating the creation of the UN, UNRRA was formed in 1943 to combat the expected shortages of food, shelter and clothing. It was UNRRA which took the lead in distributing supplies after liberation and in resettling and tracing displaced individuals. Overall, it handled some twenty-five million tons of supplies, the vast bulk of which came from the United States. However, it was mainly concerned with Central and Eastern Europe since the American Congress insisted that states (which meant most of Western Europe) which still possessed some foreign assets should be excluded from the programme.

Every country and government accepted that if economic growth and full employment were to be achieved, then the world could not return to the international system of the 1930s. At a conference held in 1944 at Bretton Woods in America, representatives from several states had agreed upon a new monetary system based upon fixed exchange rates and backed by two reserve currencies, the dollar and sterling. The intention was to make currencies convertible for payments on current account, so enabling multilateral trade between countries, while stable exchange rates would avoid the need for devaluation. In addition, an International Bank for Reconstruction and Development (more usually known as the World Bank) was set up to lend money to war-ruined countries, while the main aims of the system were to be aided by an International Monetary Fund (IMF), into which members would pay, which could issue loans to states plagued by an imbalance of payments. Inevitably, the United States was by far the largest donor.

These new international organisations did play a useful role in the tortuous process of adaptation to peacetime conditions, but none proved sufficient to cope with Western Europe's inability to boost its economic position internationally, especially *vis-à-vis* the United States. The major difficulty related perhaps to the assumptions which underlay the Bretton Woods agreements. In retrospect, they did not possess the clarity of purpose with which they were attributed at the time. Bretton Woods fundamentally assumed that the problems of international trade and payments that would arise at the end of the war would only be short-lived. Their resolution would come about by dollar-financed relief programmes, such as those operated under the aegis of UNRRA, after which the world would move swiftly to a pattern of multilateral trade and payments buttressed by a system of fixed exchange rates. It is debatable whether the Bretton Woods model ever functioned satisfactorily in the immediate postwar years. By 1947 it was badly out of kilter, with a massive outflow of capital from Western Europe, so jeopardising the continent's international position, with possible severe consequences for the domestic economies.

Given this situation, it may well have been the case that a massive injection of American aid would have been forthcoming anyway. Particularly in Britain and France, there was a tacit assumption that there was no need to change their policies because in the end the United States, whose economy had expanded greatly during the war, would have to come to the aid of Western Europe to secure markets for its own products. In addition, by 1947 the United States was concerned about the worsening political situation and the effect upon its own strategic interests. Antagonism and competition between it and the Soviet Union were intensifying rapidly, and Western Europe seemed an obvious target for Communist expansion. Like other Western governments, the American administration did not wish a return to the destructive economic climate of the 1930s. If, as a governmental report in Denmark pointed out, a shortage of foreign exchange in Europe threatened domestic reconstruction programmes, then the real worry was not old-fashioned economic autarky, but political unrest that might destabilise democracy. In American eyes, only the Soviet Union could benefit from such a scenario.

The shift in American policy that led to further economic aid for Europe is conventionally dated to a report prepared in May 1947 by an American official, who wrote upon his return from Europe that 'Europe is steadily deteriorating. The political position reflects the economic. One political crisis after another merely denotes the existence of economic distress. Millions of people in the cities are slowly starving.' There may have been severe political problems in France, Greece and Italy, but elsewhere in Western Europe one could hardly identify anything remotely approaching a revolutionary situation. Similarly, rationing may have been endemic on the continent, but this was not the same as starvation. Western Europe did have an economic problem, but it was one caused to some extent by the surprising success of the postwar years and governmental anxiety to push for even more economic growth. It was in America's interest to help Europe out of its payments crisis by providing additional capital, yet that crisis did not seem to bear any relationship to the hyperbole of the 1947 State Department memorandum. That was designed for domestic consumption, to persuade American congressmen that financial aid for Western Europe was necessary, not just to halt the drift towards a break-down in international trade, but also to prevent possible Communist gains on the continent. In other words, the United States came to Western Europe's assistance in part as a result of its own strategic interests.

In June 1947 George Marshall outlined the policy of proposed American aid that was to bear his name. The offer was nevertheless couched in strictly humanitarian language: Marshall Aid was offered to all states, 'directed not against country or doctrine, but against hunger, poverty, desperation, and chaos'. Not surprisingly, the East European states under Soviet influence rejected the offer, even if, like Czechoslovakia and Poland, they were originally favourably disposed towards the scheme. In general, Western Europe welcomed the Marshall Plan wholeheartedly, with Britain taking the lead. Thus, because of Soviet hostility – a predictable stance, and one which must have been taken into account by American officialdom when it unveiled the scheme – the Marshall Plan, or the European Recovery Programme to give its formal title, was limited to Western Europe. The only formal proviso attached by the United States was that the recipient states should coordinate their economic activities to achieve the maximum benefit. A new body, the Organisation for European Economic Cooperation (OEEC), was formed to help the administration of the Marshall Plan and the channelling of its funds to the most appropriate objectives.

The introduction and implementation of the Marshall Plan was the catalyst which eventually enabled the Western and international economies to function more effectively, even though there was nothing innovatory about the programme. By 1947 the United States had already donated more than 15 billion dollars of aid to Europe. Under the Marshall Plan a further 23 billion dollars were funnelled into Western Europe between 1947 and 1952. The significance of Marshall Aid was perhaps more its psychological effect rather than its quantitative input. In addition, by 1947 the Western European economies were much stronger than in 1945, and from this firmer base they were able to use Marshall Aid to generate their own financial resources. By 1950, Western Europe had largely overcome the obstacles to development. It had achieved a higher gross national product than that of 1938, and a much larger proportion of this product was being reinvested. By 1952, production was more than 200 per cent above prewar efforts. The same general success story was true of all Western European countries irrespective of their degree of central planning and direction. The breakthrough had been achieved. In the 1950s, productivity increased more rapidly in export-oriented industries. By the middle of the decade the volume of European trade had doubled, and the continent felt strong enough largely to dispense with discriminatory measures against American imports.

CHAPTER 4

THE REVIVAL OF POLITICAL COMPETITION

Equal opportunities to participate in the development of greater prosperity
and a richer life.   (*Norwegian Labour Party Programme, 1949*)

Never before . . . such flagrant civil war within a government.
                    (*Gordon Wright*, The Reshaping of French Democracy,
                                            London, 1950, p. 222)

The principal political task after 1945 was to re-establish an effective governmental and political structure. In each country this had to be adapted
to meet the altered condition of European parliamentarianism and the prevailing mood of public opinion. For the three major continental powers, the
problem was more difficult: France, Italy and Germany had to construct a
completely new governmental and political structure.

THE RESTORATION OF PARLIAMENTARY DEMOCRACY

The end of hostilities saw a general reversion to parliamentary democracy
throughout Western Europe, except in Spain and Portugal where right-wing
dictatorships remained in force. This was true even of Britain, Ireland, Sweden
and Switzerland where the imperatives of war had in each case entailed severe
restrictions on normal political and constitutional life, though the three neutral
states had continued to hold scheduled elections throughout the war. In Britain, however, the parliament elected in 1935, which should have been dissolved by 1940, was extended by annual legislation, with an electoral truce
between the major parties. In all these countries there had been but a patina
of normality: government powers were far greater (in Britain almost dictatorial) than in normal circumstances.

In the liberated countries, apart from France which had witnessed the utter
collapse of the Third Republic and the compromised regime of Vichy, the
governments which had fled into exile returned to their old offices and authority, and to superintend new elections. Since in most countries the regimes had
been representative of a long democratic tradition and had not been compromised by right-wing authoritarianism, very little dislocation was involved in

35

the transition from occupation to freedom. One general clash of opinion that did occur was that between the exiled politicians and the impatient dynamism of Resistance activists. Because this only occasionally involved a difference in fundamentals, compromise and adjustment were sometimes possible. But the experience of the older politicians was usually decisive; their hand was strengthened by the first elections which confirmed the survival of traditional party systems.

Scheduled elections were even held in Greece in 1946, despite the country being in the midst of a civil war. The pro-royalist parties won a majority and later in the year, a referendum indicated overwhelming support for the restoration of the monarchy. The Greek election and referendum, however, did not guarantee political stability, even though the Communist guerrillas were eventually defeated. Republic versus monarchy, left versus right, had for decades generated deep cleavages in Greek politics, which were not to be satisfactorily bridged for some time to come.

In Belgium also, the major issue was the fate of the monarchy. King Leopold III had refused to leave his country in 1940, and, although he had been interned for most of the war, had subsequently been suspected of sympathising and collaborating with the occupying German forces, giving extra ammunition to the earlier bitter accusations that the King, as commander-in-chief of the Belgian forces, had surrendered in 1940 before defeat was obvious, so facilitating the German sweep into France. The debate over whether Leopold should abdicate in favour of his son resolved itself along the deep-rooted cleavage of language, which was buttressed also by regional separation and religious differences. It was in French-speaking Wallonia, more left-wing and secular, that the demand for abdication had greatest force, while Flanders, more conservative and religious, was behind the King. For a long time the government refused to allow Leopold to resume his royal role. When he did return to Belgium in July 1950, after a narrow referendum endorsement, continuing protests and riots threatened to stretch to breaking point the delicate balance between Flemings and Walloons. The only way out of the impasse was for Leopold to abdicate: this he did only a few days after his resumption of office.

There remained the problems of France and Italy and the question mark hanging over Germany. In the two defeated Axis powers, democracy had disappeared more than a decade earlier: even before then, it had operated under grave disabilities, opposed by influential groups either indifferent towards its survival or actively striving for its overthrow. A successful democracy after 1945 could not be taken for granted. The same point could be made about France, even though the Third Republic (1870–1940) had lasted longer than any other of the numerous attempts at constitution-making since 1789. However, from Boulangism to Fascism, the Third Republic had faced several challenges from rightist movements which had never been prepared to accept parliamentary democracy.

Of all the French political forces in 1945, only the Radicals, who had benefited enormously from it, favoured the return of the Third Republic. De Gaulle, the Resistance activists and the three large parties of the left all preferred a new and different constitutional system. Their arguments were endorsed by a 1945 referendum which decisively rejected the resurrection of the Third Republic. A Constitutional Assembly elected at the same time therefore had full authority to search for a new constitutional formula. The longer it debated, however, the more obvious it was that the gulf between left and right was as great as ever. The right argued that state authority must not be subservient to public opinion; following Jacobin tradition, the left argued for popular control of government through an all-powerful parliament.

Together, the Communists and Socialists commanded a slight majority. Claiming a direct descent from the revolutionaries of 1793, they forced through a draft constitution that would allow a popularly elected National Assembly to be the only source of authority in the political system. This proposal was anathema to conservatives. De Gaulle, who favoured more government authority, was opposed, as was the Popular Republican Movement (MRP). In the event, a referendum in 1946 rejected ratification by a small majority. France therefore had to start again, with a new Constituent Assembly. This lacked any coherent majority: any formula would inevitably be a compromise resulting from complex and protracted bargaining. However, while the new draft was less radical than the first, it was still far from being acceptable to conservatives. In a further referendum it was passed by a small majority: however, one-third of the electorate abstained. Hence the constitutional basis of the Fourth Republic was not approved by a majority of the electorate, a weakness that was to be reflected in the future.

The crux of the success or fall of the new constitution would revolve around the question of political stability. The premier was nominated by the president, but before the nomination could be approved by parliament and a government installed, the candidate had to present and defend a policy programme before the National Assembly. If approval of the programme was withheld, France would remain without a government until a presidential nominee could persuade the Assembly to endorse both him and his programme. This new technique was never successful. If anything, it made the operation of government more hazardous than in the Third Republic. Prime ministers failed to sustain themselves with monotonous regularity, while deadlocks in the search for a successor were commonplace. Gradually, more moderate and conservative forces, many of which never really endorsed the Republic, showed a willingness to take over the system and work it for their own advantage. More generally, large sections of the population were alienated from the system, with widespread cynicism about the whole procedure whereby governments were the result of byzantine negotiations among several political parties, some of which lacked any homogeneity and internal discipline. One corollary of this cynicism was that the parties became divorced from the electorate.

In Italy the existing constitution was rejected even more decisively than that in France. It had been drawn up a century earlier and, with its provisions for a monarchy with extensive powers and a large measure of control over the government, was anachronistic and totally unacceptable to the parties of the left. Mussolini had merely suspended it (as Hitler did with the Weimar Constitution).

Resurrected in 1943, it served as the basis of Italian government until the election of a Constituent Assembly in 1946, when a referendum also voted for the replacement of the monarchy by a republic. After nine months the Assembly produced a lengthy document which included several radically new proposals, for example on guaranteeing individual rights. However, it proved impossible to reconcile these novel moves with the traditions and practice of Italian politics. Very few radical changes were made in the structure of government. Several provisions, however, did bear a Communist imprint. The party had worked hard in the Assembly to produce a design that would be amenable to a Communist government when it came to power. However, it was never given the opportunity. The shrewdness of the Christian Democrat leader, Alcide de Gasperi, supported by the middle classes and the Church, barred the way to power for the Communists. In its functioning after 1948 the new constitution seemed little different from its predecessor. As in France, government and politics became somewhat divorced from the public, who saw it as a game pursued by a closed and self-interested circle.

QUESTIONS OF POLITICAL STABILITY

The first postwar elections generated single-party majorities only in Britain and Norway, though a similar majority was gained in Ireland in 1944. In Sweden the Social Democrats won exactly one-half of the parliamentary seats in 1944. Elsewhere government had to be by coalition. The extent to which coalition governments proved durable depended not just on the degree to which the participants were in harmony with each other on a range of issues, but also on the political traditions and culture of each country. In the event, this proved to be a major problem only in France and Italy, and to some extent in Finland and Greece.

Britain stood out from the rest in that, partly because of its retention of a first-past-the-post electoral system, it was totally dominated by two parties (though this was also true of Austria). Indeed, for the first time since the Irish Home Rule issue had split the Liberals in the 1880s, Britain possessed a genuine two-party system. This political arithmetic, along with the traditional gladiatorial style of debate, ensured that politics remained highly competitive. The Labour programme of 1945 was drawn from three basic inspirations: the Socialist tenets of its 1918 Constitution, Keynesian economic theory, and the Beveridge Report. The parties may have argued about details on the latter, but underneath there was a fundamental agreement on the direction to be followed in, for example, education and health. It was on the introduction of Socialist-inspired legislation, particularly the nationalisation programme, that the Conservative Party found itself in bitter opposition to the government. Even so, the Conservatives found it difficult to mount a sustained rejection of the principle. For some ailing industries, it was hard to find a legitimate argument for opposing their transfer into public ownership. The issue for the Conservatives therefore became one of whether an industry had already proved itself to be viable under private ownership. On these grounds, it was the nationalisation of road transport and steel which the Conservatives opposed most strongly.

The steel issue became probably the most acrimonious point dividing the parties, and one that remained symbolically important through to the 1970s, no matter how out-dated the argument. It became the symbol of the debate over the type of economic structure Britain should possess: many Labour members considered that the party's whole political strategy would be judged by its performance in this one industry. The battle was long and bitter, and involved a constitutional debate which led to a reduction in the delaying powers of the House of Lords, which was dominated by Conservatives. All this meant that steel passed into public ownership only towards the end of Labour's full term of office. By 1951 the Labour Party was out of government, the nationalised industry had scarcely begun to function, and it was relatively easy for the new Conservative government to carry out its avowed intention of denationalising steel without causing too much dislocation. On the whole, however, the new government accepted the nationalisation measures of the 1940s and the whole welfare system.

The Conservatives, therefore, moved leftwards and implicitly accepted a government's responsibility to regulate and intervene in large areas of economic and social life. The effect of the 1945–51 period on the Labour Party was perhaps more traumatic. Its term of office had been especially notable for carrying out to the letter its massive programme of 1945. In some quarters it raised a question which had no straightforward answer: what should the party do now? On the other hand, the party had been reformist, not revolutionary. Its approach had been pragmatic and cautious, favouring short-term solutions to immediate problems. While it had achieved some economic success, it had failed to eradicate the nuances and expressions of social difference and in-equality. While this was a possible path to follow towards the new Jerusalem, the party suffered from becoming associated with the heavy hand of central-isation and bureaucratic direction, and from being tarred with the brush of austerity and high taxation. These were to be heavy burdens for Labour to bear in the 1950s as the economy recovered and the country began to enjoy unprecedented levels of prosperity.

Similar problems did not afflict Social Democracy in Scandinavia to the same extent. Opposition to the Social Democrats was divided among several parties, most of more or less equal strength, which were kept apart from each other by the possession of distinctive electoral clienteles and by historical memories of mutual antagonisms. In addition, except in Finland, the Social Democrats had become electorally dominant, particularly in Norway and Sweden. The task of government by the left was made easier by the existence in Scandinavia of a more egalitarian political culture, to which all the parties were more or less committed. In Norway, for example, all the parties had put their name in 1945 to a common programme of reconstruction, which to a considerable degree formed the policy base of the subsequent Labour government. In both Norway and Sweden, Social Democracy had not been a purely urban phenom-enon: a substantial rural support gave the left something in common with the

Agrarian parties, which in fact in the 1930s had helped to sustain minority left governments in return for favourable agricultural policies. This kind of compromise remained possible in the postwar world, with the Social Democrats able to 'divide and rule'. It would be some time before the non-Socialist parties would seriously entertain the notion of a bourgeois coalition, and some time before Social Democracy would face a serious challenge to its predominance.

Indeed, the major worry of the late 1940s was the vastly improved strength of Communism but, as in most other countries, this proved to be short-lived, as world tension increased. In the wake of the Communist purges in Eastern Europe, many Western Communist parties were obliged, under Soviet instruction, to expel some of their leaders, and in Norway the party tore itself apart in a paroxysm of ideological conflict. Communist success had been much more marked in Finland where the party, after being illegal since 1930, returned to capture one-quarter of the votes. Here too, however, the Social Democrats and Agrarians, who had reached a *modus vivendi* in the 1930s, were able to provide, with a few disruptions, a continuity in government and to resist an attempted Communist coup in 1948. Equally important was the role of the presidency, which possessed considerable constitutional powers, and the aftermath of defeat by the Soviet Union, which forced most of the political spectrum towards consensus. The first postwar president, Juho Kusti Paasikivi, skilfully played a role that would ensure political stability internally and establish a reputation for trust in Moscow that would permit Finland the maximum amount of manoeuvrability and flexibility in its dealings with the rest of Western Europe.

Uniquely in Scandinavia, the Danish Social Democrats, falling far short of a majority, did not form the government after the first elections. Seemingly worried by Communist gains, the party moved somewhat to the left, making it difficult to attract possible alliance partners on its right. Consequently, Denmark's first postwar government was a minority Liberal administration backed by parties of the right. Inherently fragile and lasting only until 1947 when it was replaced by the Social Democrats, it proved to be the first of several minority governments. Even so, it had a social–reformist outlook, and pursued policies that were largely acceptable to the parties of the left. Similarly, the new Social Democracy government, as a minority, was obliged to abandon its radical stance of 1945 to follow a moderate course not too far removed from that of its predecessor. The Danish Social Democrats were not to move back to the left for several decades.

Further south, coalition governments were the norm. However, it was disputable here whether Social Democracy was the dominant force, for politics were not so clearly focused on the left–right cleavage as in Scandinavia or Britain. The complicating factor was Christian Democracy, which possessed a tradition of effective organisation and activity in the Low Countries, Austria and Switzerland, and which had emerged after 1945 with heightened vigour in France, Italy and Germany. Christian Democracy was an amalgam of cautious conservatism and social reform derived from the papal encyclicals, *Rerum Novarum* and *Quadragesimo Anno*, which criticised equally capitalist and

Marxist materialism. In those countries with a large Catholic population, the Church was part of politics because of its conceptions of the role it should play in social life and the rights it should possess. Historically, this had brought it into conflict with the secularising tendencies of states, which had sought to eliminate Church privileges. One consequence had been the emergence of political parties of religious defence. Perhaps the major unresolved policy area of concern to the Church was education. While this issue had been settled in the Netherlands in 1918, it remained a potentially explosive factor in France and Belgium until at least the end of the 1950s.

Christian Democrats found themselves, albeit as an important party, only one actor in a multiparty system. Majority governments could often be constructed only through the willingness of several parties to collaborate with each other. This proved less of a problem in the smaller countries, where party forces had for long been equally balanced. In addition, Communist electoral popularity was more limited in 1945 and the leading parties felt less obligation to take cognisance of the far left. While it might take time to reach agreement on a coalition government, the latter, once established, tended to be quite durable and effective. There was a consolidation (introduction in the case of Austria) of a tradition of collaboration and consultation with all important political parties, irrespective of whether they were in government. This practice of consultation with all in order to achieve a political consensus on any one issue became known as consociational democracy, a style of politics marked by a deep and positive interaction of party elites which reached a pinnacle in the 1950s and early 1960s. In Austria under the Grand Coalition of its two big parties between 1945 and 1966, and persistently in Switzerland, this consensual style was institutionalised by the incorporation of all parties deemed important into the government. In Switzerland, it may be said that neither elections nor post-election bargaining decide government, since the same four parties have, with one brief exception, been in government since 1943 (in the case of the Radicals, since 1848!).

The serious problems arose in France and Italy. At least three reasons may be mentioned: political cleavages, especially between left and right, were deeper and more ideological; there was a weaker tradition of compromise; and the place of the Catholic Church was more problematic. And Communism had emerged in 1945 as a leading electoral contender, posing thorny problems for the Socialist parties. In France the three major parties – Communists, Socialists, Christian Democrats – were more or less equal in strength, though remaining suspicious of each other. In Italy, while the numbers of Christian Democrats were much larger, they had to contend with a united front to their left.

In both countries, political expediency, electoral arithmetic and whatever memories of Resistance harmony lingered on suggested a government of all three. Between 1945 and 1947 both France and Italy were ruled by tripartite governments – two years of trial and tribulation. Generally, the two Marxist parties came together on economic policies, while questions of individual liberties often found the Communists isolated. In addition, since the parties had divided ministries among themselves, each attempted to control and consolidate its own share of the spoils of office without brooking any interference from its partners, though their increasingly mutual hostility limited the significance of this. In the end, perhaps the most outstanding point about tripartism was that it was able to function at all.

In France the tripartite government had to face another potential threat: the shadow of the man who had effectively hijacked the symbol of the Resistance. General de Gaulle had headed an interim government after liberation. His policies of contributing to the Allied war effort and economic reconstruction were based upon his interpretation of France's collapse in 1940 and the need to re-establish the country's credentials as a world power. Impatient of, even hostile to, political parties, de Gaulle became increasingly isolated in government. He clung on after the initiation of tripartism, even though profoundly disagreeing with the constitutional structure that was emerging. The final break came over the issue of increased military expenditure, which the parties opposed. Seeing no way out of the impasse, de Gaulle resigned in January 1946 to retire for the first time to his country home, there to wait for a call to office. While de Gaulle was willing to establish a government and republic of his own liking only by constitutional means, he remained a permanent reminder to France and the parties that an alternative was available.

Italy lacked such a dominant personality. The link between Resistance and peace was Parri and his Action Party. While Parri lacked any mass support, the Marxist left was unwilling to deliver a *coup de grâce*, feeling that their ends would be better advanced by a persisting governmental crisis. It was the conservative forces which brought down Parri late in 1945. He was replaced by the Christian Democrat leader, Alcide de Gasperi. The rise of de Gasperi in Italy offered a strong contrast with the departure of de Gaulle in France, which introduced a period of comparative confusion. De Gasperi remained premier throughout the tripartite period: given his party's parliamentary strength, no government could survive without its support. De Gasperi's aim was to free his party from the straitjacket of the left and make it the nucleus of a broad democratic centre. This entailed wooing small conservative parties and abandoning the strict anti-Fascist policy of the Resistance alliance and Action Party. Tripartism saw little in the way of significant legislation: that would come later when de Gasperi felt Christian Democrat policy could not be blocked by Communist and Socialist interference.

By contrast, the legislative record of French tripartism was reasonably impressive, closely following the social and economic demands of the Resistance Charters. On the political front, however, there was persistent instability and conflict: prime ministers came and went, and political life became affected by a deep malaise. The equal strength of the three parties and their mutual hostility could always guarantee a negative majority: one for the government was much more difficult to construct.

The climax of tripartism came in May 1947. The break came first in France, where the other government parties decided to dispense with Communist support, ostensibly for supporting a strike in the car industry. The Communists had been fomenting unrest for some time, and believing that they would shortly be returned to office and that no government could function without them, they left confidently; but it was to be more than thirty years before they tasted power again. The Cold War contributed to Communist exclusion, not least because of the party's unyielding pro-Soviet stance. Later, President Truman's intervention in the 1948 Italian election campaign indicated that American foreign policy would assist the regime against collapse, and would not tolerate a Communist takeover in France.

In the same month, de Gasperi made his long-expected move against the Italian Communists. The catalyst was dissension within the Socialist Party where a moderate minority, unhappy with the close liaison with the Communists, broke away to form a new Social Democrat Party. Although a stable government of the centre could not be guaranteed, this schism gave de Gasperi more opportunity to forge a majority coalition. Consequently he dissolved the Cabinet, thus creating the fourth government crisis in two years; the Communists went into an opposition which proved permanent.

The relegation to an isolated position of the two largest Communist parties in Western Europe emphasised a growing conservative trend throughout the continent. Except for Scandinavia, the left would play only a subsidiary role in the politics of the 1950s. Wherever it was present, it was Christian Democracy that was to have the decisive voice in policy formulation, a factor that was crucial for the future development of European integration. Tripartism was in part a casualty of the Cold War. It had had more than its fair share of skirmishes, but afterwards France and Italy had to face up to an even sterner ideological conflict within their own boundaries, as their Communist parties, freed from the shackles of government, launched a campaign of direct action to discredit and hopefully destroy the fragile republics.

POSTWAR PARLIAMENTARY DEMOCRACY

With the establishment of a West German state in 1949, parliamentary democracy had been established everywhere, except in the Iberian peninsula. The important point about this restoration was the universal return to old and tried political systems and methods, even in France, Italy and West Germany. The trend simply illustrated that each country had its own interpretation of parliamentary democracy, one that was deeply coloured by its own historical experience. Radical innovations were often shelved, or assimilated and converted by tradition.

Nevertheless, parliamentary democracy in Western Europe had changed somewhat. There was a more general acceptance that governments should play a more extensive and active role in the economy. By the end of the decade, even conservative parties, after an initial resistance, had accepted this position: indeed, many took pains to stress that they would be more efficient managers of the emerging welfare state. The heightened role of government implied an end to classical parliamentarianism (if that had ever existed). Henceforth, parliaments would be more clearly relegated to a secondary position. The seeming decline of parliamentary influence over government eventually brought with it accusations of government bureaucratisation, and raised the question of how governments could be curbed and held responsible for their actions.

This was accompanied by the even greater prominence of political parties and a greater stress upon party organisation and loyalty. The first successes of the more regimented Socialist and Communist parties forced others to think along the same lines. But whereas regimentation, particularly on the left, had previously meant that parties were confined within narrow ideological limits, there was now, partly because of the desire to secure stable government, partly because of the increasing complexity of society, a greater concern for the mass party with a large national following over and above sectarian claims such as class or religion.

This trend led to the belief that the number of national parties would decrease. Britain after 1945 was even more of a two-party system than before the war. West Germany emerged in 1949 with two parties clearly superior to all others. France and Italy seemed to be dominated by only three parties. Elsewhere, where multipartyism remained, especially in Norway and Sweden, the imperatives of politics – that one party was substantially greater than all others – often meant that the several parties were obliged to commit themselves to one or the other of only two coalition blocs, usually left versus right. In most of Western Europe, therefore, there came into force a variety of pseudo-two-party politics.

The other side of the coin was that with increased regimentation, the parties often tended to become fossilised and bureaucracy-ridden. Decisions were made more within the parties, with which ordinary people felt little relation, rather than through parliament or the electoral process. The party manipulations and manoeuvring in several countries, that was part and parcel of forming coalition governments, gave extra weight to a feeling of alienation from politics and political decision-making. In some instances, for example in the Netherlands, Belgium and Switzerland, the parties seemed to encourage an absence of mass involvement in politics other than providing electoral fodder. When such attitudes were added to the belief that too great a commitment to political ideology could be disastrous, the danger was a relatively massive withdrawal from association with politics and a growth of apathy and scepticism about the sincerity of party argument and activity.

This process of depoliticisation did not, obviously, apply equally to all countries: it was, for example, less marked in Britain, with its adversarial political style, and in Scandinavia. Nevertheless, it could perhaps be valid to say that it became a characteristic of Western European politics after 1950. In some ways this withdrawal was a consequence of the parties compromising whatever ideological bases they possessed in the search for broader electoral support. But in the long run it also generated a decline in party membership. The problem of finding new voters was paralleled by that of retaining existing members, if for no other reason than trying to preserve a healthy financial base.

Virtually the only major ideological cleavage that seemed to remain by the end of the decade was that between Communism and western democracy.

This cleavage, intensified by the Cold War, more or less dominated European political thinking for almost a decade. Only when people had, as it were, learned to accept the threat of thermonuclear war as either a normal state of affairs or an unlikely event did there occur a revival of concern for 'domestic' ideologies. In addition, the intensification of the Cold War at least accelerated the revival of conservative parties. In this respect, 1948 would seem, in retrospect, to have been the turning point in European politics. It marked the isolation of Communist parties and a general weakening of the left in the major continental countries. The more pragmatic Scandinavian Social Democrat parties survived in strength for much longer, though the British Labour Party lost its parliamentary majority in 1951. Except in Scandinavia, the politics of the 1950s were to be dominated by conservative parties. On the continent it was the Christian Democrat parties which were left as victors: dominant in West Germany, the key to government stability in the Low Countries and Austria, essential to government in Italy, and providing much of the continuity of policy-making in France. The Christian Democrat hegemony was to prove significant not just for the generation of national styles of politics and policies, but also for the movement that occurred in the field of European integration.

CHAPTER 5

COLD WAR AND ATLANTIC ALLIANCE

We really believed in our hearts that this was the dawn of the new day. The Russians had proved that they could be reasonable and far-seeing and there wasn't any doubt in the minds of the President or any of us that we could live with them and get along with them peacefully for as far into the future as any of us could imagine.

(*Harry Hopkins quoted in R.E. Sherwood*, Roosevelt and Hopkins: An Intimate History, *New York, 1948, p. 870*)

From Stettin in the Baltic to Trieste in the Adriatic an iron curtain has descended across the continent.   (*Sir Winston Churchill, 1946*)

The United States emerged from the war as undisputedly the strongest military power. The Democrat administration under Presidents Roosevelt and Truman, along with many of the country's most influential politicians, had accepted that the traditional policy of isolationism had to be abandoned, that the United States had global responsibilities which could not be evaded. However, there would be finite limits to how far those responsibilities should extend. There would be collaboration with the Soviet Union, symbolised by the participation of both in the UN, while a peace settlement would establish normality in Europe. But by 1947 the United States was locked into an enduring European involvement and fearful of the Soviet Union which, shrouded in a secrecy designed to obscure its relative military weakness, was regarded as having embarked upon a crusade of Communist expansion.

AMERICAN FOREIGN POLICY: THEORY AND REALITY

The foreign policy beliefs formulated by American leaders during the war about the future pattern of world relationships received little sustenance from postwar reality. For President Roosevelt, the belief that the United States should accept a more active world role did not mean involvement in any place at any time. The United States wanted world responsibilities to be shared with the Soviet Union and the major states of Western Europe.

America's wartime allies were all assigned strategic roles in this world model:

Britain would resume its role as policeman of the Mediterranean and the Middle East, France would be dominant in continental Western Europe, while the Soviet Union would have a hegemony of influence in Eastern Europe. The four powers would be united in Europe in their guard over Germany, while in the world at large they would, along with China, take the lead within the UN. Roosevelt may have been pragmatic in his understanding of American public opinion and its moods, but his assessment of the globe was sadly naïve. Lulled by a false belief in the innate goodness of humanity, many Americans regarded themselves as participants in a story which had come to an end: good had triumphed over evil, and everyone would live happily ever after in a moral utopia. The United States was soon obliged to undergo a painful period of reappraisal and readjustment.

American policy was based on two erroneous assumptions, both of which had serious consequences for postwar international affairs. The first was that the Allies would continue to cooperate in the postwar world. The first indication that this would not be so came in disagreements over the occupation of Germany, which very quickly came to resemble four distinct areas with four distinct policies. Germany was to be merely a microcosm of the new world alignment of political power. The second assumption arose from an overestimation of the strength of the Western European powers and an underestimation of the wartime toll on their resources. Britain found that all efforts had to be directed towards the economy and its empire: few resources could be diverted to the Mediterranean role. When Britain asked for American help to subdue Communist guerrillas in Greece early in 1947, it indicated that Britain could not fulfil the role assigned to it in American thinking, a fact that had perhaps been apparent for some time. Simultaneously, the United States had to recognise that France had never been in a position to assume the leadership of Western Europe. Threatened internally by a strong Communist Party steadily displaying an aggressive hostility to the Fourth Republic, worried by the right-wing challenge under the possible leadership of General de Gaulle, riddled by social cleavages that may have been irrelevant and historical, but still deep and irreconcilable, France was to have problems in ensuring its own government stability. Abroad, it could hardly maintain adequate supply lines for the colonial wars in which it was already heavily engaged. On the other hand, Roosevelt's acceptance of a spheres-of-influence policy, which had accommodated the demands of Stalin at Yalta, had given the Soviet Union a free hand in Eastern Europe: the hegemony of influence offered at Yalta soon became a hegemony of power.

American conceptions became illusions. Britain and France were too weak to play a distinctive role. With Germany prostrate, a power vacuum had opened between the United States and the Soviet Union. If America did not wish to become isolated and confined to its own continent, steps had to be taken to consolidate its presence in Europe. Wartime camaraderie had definitely evaporated by the early months of 1947. Events of the following two years strengthened the Western conviction that the Soviet Union was probing for signs of weakness preparatory to a major ideological, and possibly military, advance westwards. Guerrilla warfare in Greece, Communist attempts at political and industrial sabotage in France and Italy, Soviet conditions imposed upon Finland, arguments over Germany, the Communist coup in Czechoslovakia, the Berlin blockade – all followed swiftly on one another's heels. Whether they were all part of a calculated grand design is irrelevant; they all seemed to aim for Soviet hegemony in Europe. If any further proof was needed, they gave added emphasis to the military and economic weakness of Western Europe. Reluctantly but inexorably, the United States was sucked further into European affairs. Some form of American guarantee or intervention came to be thought of as necessary, for the security and economy of the United States as well as those of Western Europe. A Soviet victory in Europe would give Communism control of one of the largest industrial concentrations in the world, leaving the United States excluded on the other side of the Atlantic.

THE ROLE OF THE UNITED NATIONS

The UN was to be the major symbol of the new moral order. But the disruption of the wartime alliance meant that it was never given the chance of functioning in the way America had conceived; it ran the risk of becoming completely ineffective and deadlocked by the world cleavage. It retained some importance, however, for apart from the short-lived Allied Control Council in Germany, it was the only body in which American and Soviet representatives could meet, even if only to engage in stylised verbal warfare. More significantly, once its teething troubles were over, the UN proved to have some values, unforeseen by its founders, which were created by the changed world situation and balance of power.

The foundation of the UN in 1944 had a precedent in the old League of Nations of 1919. The drafters of the new charter modelled their creation fairly closely upon this predecessor, taking into account its good and bad points. It was obvious that the UN could succeed only if it became a world organisation: the old League had been little more than an institutionalisation of the European balance of power. The organisation was to have two general functional bodies. First, based upon the old League structure, there was a General Assembly where each state was allowed one representative and one vote. Above this was a Security Council with eleven seats, but with permanent membership for five powers: the United States, the Soviet Union, Britain, France and China. The remaining six seats were filled at two-yearly intervals by election from the other members of the General Assembly. In addition, several specialised agencies and committees were established to provide coordination and assistance in various socioeconomic and cultural fields. The UN steadily proved itself to be truly international as, with decolonialisation, new Asian and African members added to its world character.

One fundamental difference from the old League of Nations was the constitutional recognition of special privileges for the major powers. Something like this had been demanded at Yalta by Stalin as a necessary precondition for Soviet participation. Stalin's views, however, were not divergent from the opinion of the other leaders, especially Churchill. Accordingly, the Security Council, because of the permanent representation of the major states, was intended to be the centre of the UN. Here, the great powers would thrash out their differences without being distracted by too many other states, and prosecute their postwar aims. The major powers strengthened the Security Council and their own position in it in three ways, again based on the Yalta agreements: the Council rather than the General Assembly was given primary responsibility for maintaining world peace; the major powers were guaranteed permanent representation on the Council; and, perhaps most important, each of the permanently represented states was given the right of veto on Council decisions. Normally, no action could be taken against the opposition of any one of the big five. This was perhaps no more than a formal recognition that the major powers would, veto or not, place their own national interests first, even though the agreement had been that the veto would be used only in specific situations and not as a normal part of Council business.

The functioning of the UN did not take the direction planned for it: the changes occurred within the Security Council. It had already been debatable whether China should have been given permanent representation. China proved to be the sick man of the Council. The corrupt government of Chiang Kai-Shek was engaged in a losing battle with the Communists under Mao Zedong. The issue was resolved in 1949 when the Communists ousted the Nationalist armies from the Chinese mainland, but Chiang Kai-Shek and his successors, although confined to the island of Formosa (Taiwan), were to hold the Council seat until 1971. The Soviet Union pursued an increasingly negative course: the Soviet delegate in the Council routinely used the veto on almost every issue that arose. The other three powers tended to band together, as if unanimity was necessary as a symbol of their alliance.

The inability of the Security Council to fulfil its assigned role forced more limelight and responsibility on the General Assembly. Here resolutions were relatively easier to adopt (though not to implement). No veto was permitted, since unanimous decisions were not necessary; all that was required was a two-thirds majority. The Assembly could often act when the Security Council could not. As the number of members rose, this role of the Assembly correspondingly grew in importance. The Afro-Asian states and the neutrals demanded attention, and received it because of the polarisation between the two super-powers. The influence and prestige of the Secretary-General of the UN, despite the vendetta waged against the first occupant, Trygve Lie of Norway, by the Soviet Union, illustrated that the new world body did possess some authority, and was far better able to arbitrate in disputes than the old League of Nations.

But the UN found itself powerless to intervene or arbitrate effectively in matters intimately affecting the security of the two super-powers, as events in Hungary in 1956 or in Cuba in 1962 illustrated. The European continent also fell into this category of exclusion. The global polarisation took its most crystallised form in Europe. Limited wars for ideological and strategic supremacy could be fought in Korea, Vietnam and elsewhere, where there was a kind of 'no man's land' situation. In Europe the dividing line was clearly demarcated: the continent had been carefully separated into two opposing camps, where any transgressions could not be concealed and where, along the boundary between the two worlds – the Central Front – there could be found after 1949 the most intense concentration of troops and armaments in the world. Only the traditional neutral states of Sweden and Switzerland, or those in precarious positions (Finland, Austria, and perhaps Yugoslavia) could avoid having to make a firm choice. Europe, therefore, was not a major concern of the UN: the 'keep off' signs were unmistakeable. Its most important actions lay elsewhere – for example in Israel in 1948, Korea in 1950, Suez in 1956, the Congo in 1960, or the Indian subcontinent in 1965. During the Cold War its only European involvement was as a peacekeeping barrier between the Greek and Turkish communities in Cyprus after 1963, while its post-Cold War involvement in the Balkans after the disintegration of Yugoslavia in 1991 was not a happy experience. Decisions on Europe, it seemed, could be reached only with the mutual consent of the United States, the Soviet Union, and perhaps the continent itself. Since the two sides could not agree even to disagree within the Security Council, it was not surprising that the UN could neither provide the bridging link in Europe nor prevent the two sides from drawing further apart and ignoring any suggestions from what was, after all, their own creation.

THE PEACE TREATIES: NECESSARY OR IRRELEVANT?

A further area where wartime plans for the future failed to materialise was in the Allies' relations with the defeated Axis powers. Quite apart from having to decide the fate of Germany, the victors had to formulate policy towards the other defeated belligerents: Italy, Hungary, Romania, Bulgaria and Finland. At Potsdam it was decided that this responsibility would be delegated to a Council of Foreign Ministers, which first met in September 1945: later meetings incorporated the French foreign minister. Although the details of the peace treaties to be signed with the minor Axis powers were the sole responsibility of the Council, consultations were held with other interested states to solicit their opinions.

Three common features emerged from the treaties: the traditional victor's policy of altering territorial boundaries was followed; reparations were demanded; and the defeated states had limitations imposed upon the size of their armed forces. On the whole, however, the demands were not too exacting, and there was no radical revision of the map of Europe. Apart from problems connected with Italy, the most important point is that the treaties conceded Soviet claims made at Yalta for *de jure* recognition of territory annexed during or after the war: Bessarabia (from Romania) and Karelia and Petsamo (from Finland). The greatest change in the map of Europe, the wholesale westward movement of Poland and the Soviet absorption of the Baltic states of Estonia, Latvia and Lithuania, were regarded by the Soviet Union as *de facto* changes that lay outside the peace treaties. In theory, Poland's new western limits were to be temporary until ratification by an Allied peace treaty with Germany.

Recognition by the West had to wait until 1972, when West Germany signed treaties with East Germany and Poland that accepted the permanence of the latter's western boundary. However, the issue of the Oder–Neisse line as the boundary between Poland and Germany was not fully resolved until after the ending of the Cold War and the reunification of Germany in 1990 when the German Chancellor, Helmut Kohl, formally renounced all claims to those territories, historically German, that lay to the east of the boundary enforced by the Soviet Union in 1945.

Further south, there were problems about Italy's boundaries and the future of its colonies. While France claimed some territorial compensation, the major issue lay on Italy's eastern frontier, in a confrontation with Communist Yugoslavia. Marshal Tito of Yugoslavia and his Soviet supporters were adamant in demanding territorial compensation. The areas in dispute, long a bone of contention between Slavs and Italians, were Trieste and its Istrian hinterland. The Western Allies conceded the legitimacy of the Yugoslav claim to Istria, whose population was mainly Slav. Trieste, with a large Italian majority, was a different matter. The difficulty of finding an acceptable solution was illustrated by the first formula proposed, that Trieste should become a free city. Given the unfortunate prewar precedent of Danzig, it is not surprising that both Italy and Yugoslavia refused to accept the provisions of the treaty. A settlement was not reached until 1954, by which time Tito had broken with Stalin to embark upon a policy of national Communism within a neutral state: the city of Trieste was to remain with Italy, with Yugoslavia assimilating Istria. The loss of territory was not entirely acceptable to Italy, and questions about it were raised in the Italian legislature as late as 1970. However, the territorial question did not surface during Tito's visit to Italy in 1971, and in 1975 the 1954 settlement, with a few minor boundary adjustments, was confirmed by the Treaty of Osino.

The Allies also failed to agree upon the future of the Italian colonies. The innate anticolonialism of the United States frowned upon them becoming colonies of another state, while no one was anxious to see the Soviet Union acquire a foothold in Africa. The problem was passed to the UN which by 1949, though accepting trusteeship for Somaliland, decided upon independence for Libya. This decision was not to the liking of Britain and France. Independence at some date was more or less inevitable, but by occurring when it did, it helped create a further precedent for the nationalist movements of Asia and Africa which troubled the colonial powers of Europe in the 1950s.

All this lay in the future. The immediate point about the peace treaties is that by the time they were ready for signature, they were largely irrelevant, negated by the changed international climate. The signing of a peace treaty by the West with Hungary, Bulgaria and Romania was meaningless, and Western influence in the subsequent Allied Control Authorities almost less than negligible. Occupied by Russian troops in the closing months of the war, these countries were already integral components of the Soviet defensive system. Only Finland was permitted to retain a precarious neutrality, but one that would acknowledge the special interests of the Soviet Union. The West had to accept, particularly after the April 1948 Treaty of Friendship, Cooperation and Mutual Assistance between the Soviet Union and Finland, which included a provision for reciprocal military aid in the event of invasion, that the latter's freedom to act as an independent state would be extremely limited.

THE TRUMAN DOCTRINE:
TOWARDS A POLITICAL ALLIANCE

The catalyst which may be said to have finally provoked America into positive action was Communist activity in the eastern Mediterranean. Communist guerrillas were again attempting to seize control of Greece. Simultaneously, the Soviet Union was pressing Turkey for some say in the Black Sea straits, especially for the lease of naval and military bases for 'joint defence purposes'. Elsewhere, the Soviet Union was strenuously supporting the Yugoslav claim to Trieste. Further afield, it was still interested in Iran and arguing that it should receive the trusteeship of the former Italian colonies of Tripolitania and Eritrea. In Asia the Communist armies of Mao Zedong were slowly winning the Chinese civil war. The Greek conflict, also because of Western concern at events in Eastern Europe, was therefore not seen as an isolated occurrence in the eastern Mediterranean.

A Communist attempt to control Greece had already been prevented by British troops in 1944. When a new uprising broke out in 1946, the sagging Greek government called for Britain's assistance. The new Communist insurrection was particularly effective, first because it benefited from widespread discontent with the right-wing government and secondly, because of the close proximity of supply bases across the border in the neighbouring Communist states of Albania and Yugoslavia. The plight of Greece could not be ignored by the West. The Communist drive could well be the opening stage of a flanking movement that had both Italy and France, politically two of the more fragile links in the Western armour, lying in its direct path, so making any Allied presence in Germany largely irrelevant.

It soon became obvious that British military support was the major prop of the Greek government. But Britain, the only serious power left in Western Europe, was itself exhausted and incapable of diverting sufficient resources to bring the war to a speedy end. Early in 1947, economic problems and foreign commitments forced the British government to reassess its priorities, including a reduction in military expenditure. The United States was informed that Britain could no longer fulfil its obligations in Greece and would have to withdraw its forces no matter what the consequences would be. Only the United States could occupy the vacuum which even a partial British withdrawal would cause; therefore President Truman accepted responsibility for the area. The significance of his decision went far beyond a simple determination to quell a Communist insurrection in a small country. In committing himself to the governmental cause in Greece, the president was symbolising a re-evaluation of American foreign policy. In March 1947 he outlined what was to be known as the Truman Doctrine.

The Truman Doctrine was a pledge of American support for 'free peoples who are resisting subjugation by armed minorities or by outside pressures'. Stressing the interrelated nature of the democratic world, it emphasised that such subjugation did concern the United States, that world peace was necessary for American security. The Truman Doctrine marked the opening of a more aggressive phase in American foreign policy, giving it a new purpose and crusade. In European affairs this was manifested in a deep concern for the political and economic health of the Western democracies. Previously, despite its words, the United States had been somewhat hesitant, and often reluctant, to intervene abroad so directly. As a first indication of the guarantee, military missions were sent to both Greece and Turkey; military aid also went to Greece to modernise the equipment of the government forces, and military advisers helped plan a systematic campaign against the guerrillas.

The Truman Doctrine was above all a pledge of military aid and a symbol of America's political relationship with the old continent. But that relationship would be much better and much more certain of success if the European democracies were on a sound economic footing that would enable them to reduce domestic dissatisfaction, a potential source of Communist support, and to contribute to their own military capacity to defend themselves. But this the Truman Doctrine did not set out to do. It was these factors, however, which led American leaders to paint such a gloomy picture of the Western European economy in the early months of 1947 and eventually to announce the Marshall Plan.

The Marshall Plan was clearly politically rather than economically motivated. While on the surface it was not obviously part of the Cold War arsenal, its net effect was to escalate the tension. The offer was not limited to those countries with close links with or favourably disposed towards the United States; it was open to all European states, including the Soviet Union. However, the United States must have taken into account that the offer would be rejected by Moscow and its satellites, that its generosity would be interpreted as a tactic designed to wean Eastern Europe away from strict Communist control. The United States could then hope to portray itself as the magnanimous benefactor and accuse the Soviet Union of intransigence.

The Soviet Union was indeed hostile to the Plan, regarding it as a mere variant of the Truman Doctrine. Stalin's loyal lieutenant, Andrei Zhdanov, more or less simultaneously declared that the world was divided into two irreconcilable blocs: that led by the democratic, fraternal Soviet Union was threatened by the one led by the imperialist, warmongering United States. No country which fell within the Soviet orbit would be allowed to avail itself of 'unconditional' American aid, and Czechoslovakia and Poland, which had expressed an interest in doing so, were obliged to retract. The Marshall Plan illustrated again the gulf between East and West. When financial aid first appeared in Europe under its auspices in 1948, it was apparent that to all intents and purposes the programme was the economic complement of President Truman's expressed political intent to organise the West in an ideological alliance against the Soviet Union. The United States, therefore, had an alliance in political and economic terms; the military component was to appear later in the North Atlantic Treaty Organisation (NATO).

In Germany and Greece the Communists were hampered by the presence of British and American military forces. More worrisome, perhaps, were the activities of Western European Communist parties, especially the large ones of France and Italy. These were two states where the legitimacy of the regime was most in question: in both, the end of tripartism in May 1947 and the Communist expulsion from government gave the party a freer hand to attempt to immobilise the political system from without. The prime agent of the Communist assault was to be the trade unions. The Communists had captured the major union movements during and immediately after the war. The federations were a ready-made instrument because historically in both countries they had remained apart from the mainstream political system: never quite accepted as legitimate, they had preferred to retain their independence and had developed the concept of the general strike as a weapon of direct political action against the state.

In September 1947 the relationship between the Western Communist parties and the Soviet Union became clearer when the latter re-established the old Third International. The name was changed from Comintern to Cominform, implying that the new body was no more than a clearing house for reciprocal information. But it was designed to strengthen Soviet control over all Communist movements, and it did criticise the Western Communist parties for too lax a prosecution of the war against capitalism and bourgeois democracy. As a result, a more vigorous Communist line was followed in both France and Italy. The French leader, Thorez, went so far as to claim that French workers would welcome the Soviet army if it 'came to pursue an aggressor on our soil'.

In November, Thorez and his associates attempted to disrupt the economy, calling upon the unions and working classes to rally round a revolutionary general strike that would paralyse all major industries and communications networks: waves of violence and intimidation accompanied acts of sabotage. The young Fourth Republic had to face its severest test. President Vincent Auriol strongly denounced the Communist actions, and the government decided to meet the crisis by matching force with force. It announced that workers who persisted in prolonging the strike would be deprived of all social welfare benefits, and it did not hesitate to deploy army and police forces where necessary to re-establish law and order. It soon became clear that neither the unions nor the Communist Party possessed the resources to sustain a revolutionary challenge in the face of a resolute government. Within a month, many workers had returned to their jobs and the general strike had to be called off.

Having failed in France, the Communist focus turned to Italy. Here the aim was not so much to cripple the country by strike action as to use the threat of it in an effort to win power constitutionally in the April 1948 general election. Communist hopes were high because of the party's great electoral strength and because, unlike in France, the Socialists under Pietro Nenni were happy to join them in a People's Bloc. Opposing them were the Christian Democrats under de Gasperi who led an alliance of the centre and moderate right. The 1948 election campaign still ranks as one of the stormiest in Italian history: Communist militancy was matched by Vatican militancy. President Truman also weighed in, making it clear that the United States would not tolerate a Communist government in Italy. It was the first time that America had actively intervened in an European election. In the event, Western fears proved unfounded. The Christian Democrats alone narrowly missed an absolute majority. Wisely, de Gasperi was content to continue governing in a coalition with his smaller allies. The Italian election was something of a relief for Western Europe: coming shortly after what amounted to a Communist coup in Czechoslovakia in February, it was one of the first visible signs that a seemingly irresistible juggernaut could be halted.

The main Communist thrust had been broken, although an uneasy peace was not obtained for at least another year. In mid-1948 the Italian Communists appeared to be embarrassed by the outbreak of spontaneous strikes that followed an assassination attempt on the party leader, Palmiro Togliatti. In the face of government determination to dispel the insurrectionary atmosphere by force if necessary, the party was unwilling to seek an advantage from the situation. It demonstrated with stark clarity a wide gulf between revolutionary utterances and a real ability to act. One result was a weakening of the Communist grip on the unions, as first Catholics and then Social Democrats broke away to form their own federations. Similar events occurred in France: a Communist summons in the autumn of 1948 to protest against the Marshall Plan received only a lukewarm response, and the party was soon obliged to withdraw its appeal.

As 1948 drew to a close the Communist offensive had been contained by resolute action: there was only a run of failures after the coup in Czechoslovakia. After 1948 the Communist parties in France and Italy were no longer in a position to challenge seriously the constitutional regimes, although their size and presence could hinder the political system from firing on all cylinders. Elsewhere in Western Europe, the Communist parties soon forfeited the popularity they had acquired during the war and, except in Finland, had sunk back to insignificance by the end of the decade. The turbulence of 1947–48 finally pushed some small countries like Denmark, which had hoped to steer clear of power politics, away from neutralism to seek American protection.

Until the theory of Eurocommunism appeared in the 1970s, no new constructive Communist ideas were forthcoming. Retreating to its own fortress, the attitude was 'what we have we hold at any price'. That cost was to be a sacrifice of dynamism and mobility, and a risk of prophesying economic doom when Western Europe was clearly enjoying great prosperity. This rigidity was particularly true in France. Communism became, if anything, more conservative than conservatives. The disciplined following could not be used for revolutionary ends, as a revolutionary situation and the Communists' own ability to exploit it became ever more remote. On the other hand, the Communist leaders did not dare to loosen their hold on their disciples. The parties became introverted, no matter how fantastic their propaganda appeared in the light of solid facts, and caught in a dilemma of stagnation. Committed to a negative policy as the one having the least risk for internal solidarity, they still had to answer to Moscow and the Cominform for failing to be efficient and for allowing 'deviationist' tendencies. At the same time, Western pressure to neutralise them meant that a more active policy might endanger their security and existence, while increased Soviet pressure to follow the Moscow line handicapped any appeals to patriotism and encouraged dissidence among the rank and file. During the 1950s the Communist parties were stretched further on the rack by the post-Stalin profession of competitive co-existence and the later Brezhnev Doctrine, particularly by their most tragic expression, the Soviet interventions in Hungary in 1956 and Czechoslovakia in 1968.

By the end of 1948 the United States was stepping up the European Recovery Programme and had stressed its determination to stay in Germany and Berlin. Short of open war with the United States, the Communist ideological advance could not expand any further westwards. But if open war was inadmissable because of American nuclear supremacy, expansion would have to rely upon the victory of domestic Communism, an increasingly remote possibility. Further east, the American pressure and guarantee had stiffened Turkey's resolve, while the Greek Communist guerrillas were steadily driven back until their final military defeat and surrender in 1949. The guerrillas had been greatly weakened by the decision of Tito to break with the Soviet Union and pursue a more neutralist policy of national Communism. Yugoslavia's expulsion from Moscow's harmony of nations deprived the Greek Communists of their major supply line and base: thereafter they could fight only a rearguard action.

The Cominform never lived up to its original expectations. Rapidly becoming dormant, with little activity and sense of purpose, its influence west of the iron curtain was negligible, and it was officially wound up in 1956 with the establishment of the Warsaw Pact. Although the world situation was still tense, 1949 opened with more promise and hope for Western European security and economic advancement than any Western leader could have dared to hope for one year earlier.

BERLIN: SYMBOL OF POSTWAR REALITY

The iron curtain ran through the middle of Germany. Its division was the most dramatic aspect of the failure of wartime conceptions and of postwar reality. And within Germany, the most dramatic example of the collapse of wartime cooperation was the Soviet blockade of Berlin and the subsequent Allied airlift. Berlin became a symbol of the Western determination to confront and block Soviet aggression.

The Berlin blockade, which began in June 1948, was partly a Soviet reaction to the Western decision to create an independent West German state, partly a reflection of the desire to eliminate the West from its most exposed outpost, a Western fortress in the heart of Soviet-controlled territory. The Soviet decision was also motivated by a fear of Germany, though it seemed unlikely that in the foreseeable future Germany could again almost bring Russia down by virtue of its military capacity. It was rather the fear of what a united healthy Germany could contribute to an alliance focused around the United States, which would give the latter an advanced field position overlooking the main road to Russia. Berlin was the selected battlefield for a test of strength, to see whether American resolve was sufficiently determined to maintain a military force in Europe even at the risk of becoming involved in another war. If the American nerve failed, the way would be open for the Soviet Union to attempt to bring Germany within its own orbit and so increase the opportunity to extend further its influence in Europe.

All road and rail links between the Western-controlled sectors of Berlin and the Allied zones in western Germany were closed. Pressure was brought to bear upon the German city government to concede to Soviet demands. In return, the Soviet authorities promised to restore electric power and food supplies that had previously come from the surrounding Soviet zone. The West's answer was swift: the United States promised to support the city administration, and inaugurated a massive airlift of essential goods and materials – a dangerous move, but with the blockade coming hard on the heels of the Czechoslovakian coup, the West felt that nothing less would demonstrate its credibility. While the airlift was supported unequivocally by the other Allies, only the United States had the capacity to guarantee the supply of planes and provisions necessary to sustain West Berlin as a functioning entity. For almost a year the airlift continued to build up in intensity. Though the cost was enormous, planes arriving at the rate of one every two minutes ensured that the city received adequate quantities of food, raw materials and fuel.

The United States gave every indication of maintaining the airlift for as long as was necessary: this demonstrative action gave Western Europe a huge psychological boost. An economic blockade would not by itself bring about Western evacuation from Berlin. The Soviet Union, unable to use its land military superiority because of American air and nuclear supremacy, admitted defeat. A separate Communist-controlled city council was established in the Soviet sector: Soviet obstruction had already persuaded the elected council to move its offices and agencies to the Western sectors. The blockade was called off in May 1949 as abruptly as it had begun. Thereafter Berlin lived under an uneasy peace punctuated at frequent intervals by the alarums and excursions of a possible Soviet military takeover or the Western abandonment of the city, although it is doubtful whether either was ever seriously mooted as a course of action.

The Berlin blockade, the first real test of strength between East and West in Europe, set three important precedents which were maintained in all subsequent arguments and clashes over the city. The Soviet Union did not use or seriously threaten to use military force to win the whole city, while the Western stand seemed to imply that only military force would compel them to leave Berlin. It was also clear that the Western Allies were not willing to use military means themselves to assert their rights as occupying powers. The use of armed force on the question of Berlin may seem to have been frowned upon by the rules of the game, but what it meant was that the Soviet Union would have to turn to other methods if it wished to force the West out of the city.

While the West may have been reluctant to take any positive action, for example refusing to play an active role during the workers' uprising in East Berlin in 1953, the danger was a gradual erosion of its position in the city. This was apparent in the wake of the most emphatic Soviet action after 1948: the building of the notorious Berlin Wall in 1961. The United States rushed in a token show of extra troops, not to defend the city but to shore up its confidence. President Kennedy emphasised American determination to defend West Berlin, but it was a different *status quo* from that which had existed before the erection of the Wall. Then, movement of people between the two halves of the city had been relatively unrestricted; after 1961 the two were distinct entities with hardly any contact between them. Concerns were expressed that further actions of this kind could endanger the West's position in Berlin.

The events in Berlin were in some ways a microcosm of the larger game played throughout the continent. As the overt threats of the opening years of the Cold War were either thwarted or failed to achieve the desired result, the continent settled down to an uneasy peace between its two halves. The struggle became one of attrition where victories, if any, were the outcome of erosion tactics, perhaps slight in themselves, but significant, at least in terms of propaganda value, for what each of the two blocs saw as the effectiveness of its own security.

NATO: THE MILITARY ALLIANCE

As a further safeguard, Western Europe moved early in 1949 towards the formal military alliance that had been implicit in much of the thought and action of the previous two years. The Truman Doctrine had only been a generalised expression of an American pledge to any individual country under threat, while the European states themselves had advanced little further in the sphere of military cooperation than organising mutual aid treaties with one another, such as the 1947 Treaty of Dunkirk between Britain and France, which in any case was targeted against a revival of German military ambition. The greatest advance was the 1948 Treaty of Brussels, a collective security pact negotiated by Britain, France and the Low Countries: again, however, it was something of an anachronism in that its major concern seemed to be to thwart 'a renewal by Germany of an aggressive policy'. A similar attempt by Sweden at collective security in Scandinavia came to naught with the Soviet-Finnish Treaty of 1948. Norway, followed by Denmark, became more nervous about Soviet intentions, and regarded such a pact as meaningless without American aid. When the United States rejected the Swedish request to supply weapons to a Nordic alliance, the whole notion collapsed.

What was required was a military and defensive equivalent of the Marshall Plan and OEEC. Certainly, the British foreign minister, Ernest Bevin, regarded the Dunkirk and Brussels treaties as interim measures pending the construction by the United States of a collective security system against the Soviet Union.

He and the other Brussels signatories appealed for immediate American provision of 'what they lacked in strength'. In April 1949 the representatives of twelve states signed the Atlantic Pact. The United States and Canada agreed to enter a military arrangement for the mutual defence of Western Europe, along with Britain, France, Italy, Denmark, Norway, the Netherlands, Belgium, Luxembourg, Portugal and Iceland. During the 1950s the new North Atlantic Treaty Organisation (NATO) was extended to embrace Greece, Turkey and the new state of West Germany. Anti-Fascist feeling, especially in Britain, debarred Spain's entry, though an agreement enabled American bases to be established within Spain. Sweden, Switzerland and Ireland preferred to maintain their neutrality, while Finland and, later, Austria, were bound by agreement to eschew military involvement with either side. Those who had desired a definite American commitment in Europe – for the first time in a period of peace – had had their wishes realised.

The new Atlantic alliance was not intended to pursue an aggressive policy; it was a defensive agreement, part of the wider American strategy of containing Communism. Under the terms of the pact the member states promised to provide forces in all three armed services according to their means. It was basically little more than an extension of the previous practice of bilateral treaties, though based upon the core principle that an attack upon one member would be regarded as an attack upon all. However, at first glance, this commitment did not seem to mean a firm guarantee of action. A member state need only take 'such action as it deems necessary', whereas the Brussels Treaty had guaranteed automatic military assistance. The proviso had been included at the insistence of the United States which did not want involvement without discretion. Since American involvement was the objective of the exercise, Western Europe had to defer on this point. In addition, the obligation applied only to the territories of the member states and to their ships and aircraft when operating north of the Tropic of Cancer. Moreover, there was nothing in the agreement which specifically forbade members from decreasing their defence expenditure, or even from using NATO forces for other tasks. Britain's defence policy and colonial commitments in the 1950s, for example, meant that it did not always give NATO the required number of troops, while France's NATO contingents were usually engaged in colonial struggles.

The treaty was not particularly concerned with creating a network of formal institutions. However, these sprang up extensively once it was realised that the alliance would operate most efficiently when there was an institutional framework that permitted continuous military and political consultation. Within a few years NATO had developed a complex network of collaborative bodies, the operation of which proved to be impressive and effective.

A common European or Atlantic army was not the intention, and NATO did not develop a fully and effectively integrated force. Each country would provide its own battalions subject to orders from the NATO chain of command. Since the United States would be providing the most matériel, it was obvious that an American would be the overall military commander. The supreme decision-making body, however, was the political North Atlantic Council: it was accepted that the head of this body would be a European. The core of the grand design for the protection of Western Europe was to be the defence of West Germany, seen as the most obvious Soviet target. American and British troops were therefore to be stationed in West Germany, to act as the nucleus of an overall NATO force.

Given the acknowledged numerical superiority of Soviet ground forces, the Allied commitment in West Germany could not by itself hope to play more than an effective stalling or rearguard action. In essence, it was mainly a symbol of the Western determination to wage an all-out war rather than permit West Germany, the gateway to the West, to become a Communist satrap. The whole of NATO strategy was built upon a belief in the superiority of American air power and its monopoly for some time to come of nuclear weapons. The NATO ground troops were primarily a subsidiary line of defence, a tripwire. It was widely believed that the only war possible in Europe would be a nuclear war and that, until it achieved nuclear and air parity with the United States, the Soviet Union would not launch a full-scale assault.

This strategic design lasted for only a few months. When the Soviet Union exploded its first atomic bomb late in 1949, the United States had to accept that nuclear parity would be achieved sooner than had been expected. When war broke out in Korea in 1950, signs were distressingly clear that the Soviet Union might well be prepared to risk the consequences of total war. Even if one rejected this assumption, the main alternative was equally alarming: that having been baulked in Europe, the Soviet Union was merely shifting the theatre of conflict. One worry was that war in Asia or elsewhere could impose defence priorities on Western Europe that the domestic economies might not be able to sustain; in short, that conflicts elsewhere might still benefit the Soviet Union even in Europe.

In itself the Atlantic alliance could not provide an ideological basis for a Western European political, social and economic federation. But taken together with the Marshall Plan, it did encourage trends in that direction. Official American opinion had also taken a positive stand on European union, encouraging all efforts directed towards this end. President Truman and his administration became more closely involved in European affairs than any other American government before or since. Before, American foreign policy was influenced and checked by isolationist tendencies: in any case, Europe would not have welcomed American interference. Afterwards, American attention was focused more on trouble spots in other parts of the world. In addition, Western Europe became stronger and more sensitive about its independence, making too blunt an American approach inadvisable. That Western Europe was able to turn to the question of integration was due to its healthier political, economic and military situation. In attempting to assist Western Europe out of its payments crisis and by its commitment to the defence of the continent, the United States made an important contribution to political stability. But that stability was also due to the resilience of democratic traditions in Western Europe itself.

CHAPTER 6

THE REBIRTH OF GERMANY

Bonn is not Weimar.
(*F. R. Allemann*, Bonn ist nicht Weimar, *Cologne, 1956*)

We can act like the others. We are a state, an emancipated Government.
(*Willy Brandt, 1971*)

On the whole, the Allies had been circumspect about interfering with the activities and rights of European governments. In the smaller countries there was never any doubt that the exiled governments would simply return and relaunch a democratic system. In France the Allies acted only in a liaison capacity, concentrating upon supply problems. Even Italy, a defeated belligerent, had been allowed its own governments more or less immediately upon the fall of Mussolini, although the Allies did establish a military government to which the Italians were in principle answerable. But the Italian government had a free hand in domestic affairs and, after the signing of a peace treaty, had complete sovereignty in foreign affairs. Germany, however, was classified as occupied territory and placed under a military government. Austria, because of the complete nature of the 1938 *Anschluss*, was treated in the same way.

THE ALLIED DEBATES ON THE FUTURE

The Allies had debated the problem of postwar Germany for some time. The Moscow Conference of foreign ministers in October 1943 took the decision to try individuals for war crimes, but did not reach a firm conclusion on the broader issue of Germany. Several plans had been discussed, but by late 1944 Roosevelt and Churchill appeared to favour a scheme proposed by Henry Morgenthau, the American Secretary of the Treasury. In essence, its solution for the German problem was to destroy the country's industrial capacity. The Ruhr and other industrial areas were to be detached and placed under international control; elsewhere, the population was to practise a purely agricultural economy. In this way, German aggressiveness would be effectively curbed forever.

The Morgenthau Plan was eventually rejected, although the sentiments that lay behind it could still be detected in later discussions. As an economic formula it was unworkable; gradually the Western leaders, despite their desire to placate Stalin who wanted the country dismembered, realised that an agricultural economy could not possibly meet the needs of Germany's large population. The plan was never openly repudiated, but quietly disappeared from official British and American circles. Churchill, already suspicious of Stalin's ambitions, had by the time of the Yalta Conference come down on the side of moderation; Roosevelt remained undecided. What finally emerged at Yalta was extremely ambiguous: the Allies were committed only to the 'complete disarmament, demilitarization and the dismemberment of Germany as they deem requisite for future peace and security'. Not only would this formulation permit scope for future modifications; it essentially gave each a free hand to impose and practise its own interpretation of the decision.

The Soviet Union had a clear attitude towards Germany. Stalin's sole preoccupation was to destroy Germany and, as a corollary, to commandeer as much as possible of German industrial plant and matériel as reparations. For Moscow, the ideal situation would be a Communist revolution that would result in a people's democracy similar to those which were soon to be imposed upon Eastern Europe. Failing that, Stalin would have been quite happy with something akin to the Morgenthau Plan: anything that would destroy German militarism and remove it as a threat to the Soviet Union was acceptable. Moreover, Moscow had definite views about Germany's eastern frontiers. It requested that a substantial area be ceded to Poland, first to compensate the latter for the 1939 invasion and, secondly, to commit Poland more closely to the Soviet Union and allow it to forget the extension of the Soviet frontier westwards at the expense of Polish territory. These ideas met with some sympathy in the West, since the territory involved was part of the historic heartlands of Prussia: many in the Allied camp held 'Prussianism' responsible for German aggressiveness, and the end of Prussia as a political unit was part of their policy.

However, these Soviet demands failed to win acceptance at Yalta, being deferred for a later decision. The Yalta meeting has been heavily criticised: Roosevelt in particular has been charged with selling out to Soviet imperialism. The divergent views at Yalta, not apparent at the earlier Teheran meeting, were due simply to the fact that the Allies had moved on from strategic and military questions to grapple with postwar policies. However, as far as Germany is concerned, any criticism should perhaps be focused more upon the later Potsdam Conference of July 1945.

It was at Potsdam that the West accepted Soviet demands for reparations and boundary changes. It was agreed that the Soviet Union should receive some ten billion dollars in reparations, as well as 25 per cent of dismantled industrial equipment from the Western zones in exchange for food in its own zone. Since neither side could agree on the value of the goods to be exchanged, this arrangement collapsed in mid-1946. Germany's eastern frontier was also to be temporarily fixed on the Oder–Neisse line, bringing some nine million Germans under Polish rule. The West did not see the Oder–Neisse boundary as a necessarily permanent arrangement: the final fate of the transferred region was to be decided by a later peace conference. But for the Soviet Union and Poland, the matter was settled: they took the Oder–Neisse line to be the *de jure* boundary between Germany and Poland. To emphasise the point, almost the whole of the German population was expelled from the region, to join the flood of Germans expelled from the Sudetenland by Czechoslovakia. While the refugee and expellee problem was to be one of the most serious faced by Germany in the postwar years, it ultimately provided the new West German state with a valuable labour reservoir that helped to boost its expanding economy.

It is perhaps not insignificant that at Potsdam, Stalin was the only remaining representative of the wartime alliance. Roosevelt's death had brought Harry Truman to the presidency, while the verdict of the 1945 British election meant that Clement Attlee replaced Churchill midway through the discussions. Being relatively inexperienced, the new Western leaders may have conceded more to Stalin than might otherwise have been the case. Even so, the Potsdam concessions were in the spirit of the previous conferences, though Truman and Attlee closed ranks to refuse the further Soviet demand that the great Ruhr industrial complex should be divorced from the rest of Germany and placed under a joint Allied authority. The West had moved a long way from the Morgenthau Plan.

It was also at Potsdam that the victors settled the general outline of their policy towards Germany: they would themselves take on the responsibility of government under a military occupation. Even without such a decision, the Allies would still have been forced to impose their authority on postwar Germany. No German alternative was available. Invasion and defeat had not only brought about a military collapse: the entire political and administrative structure of the Third Reich also disintegrated almost overnight. The problem was worst in the East where many local officials had joined the flood of humanity fleeing westwards to reach territory controlled by the Western Allies. As far as government was concerned, Germany was a blank cheque: the Allies could write in whatever price they chose. In general, they wished to delay the re-establishment of a national German government for as long as possible. The occupation had no time limit. Having no clear idea of what the future German state would be, they wished to reconstruct the country slowly and to cleanse it of the Nazi past.

THE MILITARY GOVERNMENTS

After hostilities had ceased, Allied forces moved – sometimes having to retreat from positions they had reached – into their previously demarcated zones. The Soviet Union was to govern eastern Germany; Britain had the north-west; and the United States the south plus the ports of Bremen and Bremerhaven. Later, the two Western Allies agreed to admit France as an occupying power, and allotted it a small zone bordering its own territory. This was in addition to the Saar, which was to be administered by France under separate arrangements.

The city of Berlin was excluded from this structure. Because of its symbolic importance as the capital, it was similarly divided into four sectors, even though it lay in the heart of the Soviet zone. The idea was that central administrative agencies would be established in the city, thereby creating a nucleus for some degree of unity. Coordination of activities across the four zones was to be achieved by the Allied Control Authority. A similar body, the Allied Kommandatura, was established to coordinate government in Berlin.

Austria was also treated as occupied territory. The Allies had agreed in principle to the independence of the country but, because of its close ties with Germany since 1938, military government appeared unavoidable. Thus Austria was also divided into four zones, while Vienna was treated in a similar manner to Berlin. There were two important differences between Germany and Austria. The first was the small size of the latter. The rump of the old Habsburg Empire could not present a serious threat to peace or to the major powers. It was therefore easier for the Allies to agree to the creation of a fully sovereign, neutral Austrian state. Secondly, internal administration had not collapsed in Austria. In 1945 a central government was re-established in Vienna: although set up by the liberating Red Army, it was also accepted immediately by the West. The 1920 Constitution was readopted by a government dominated by two parties. Austria proved to be unreceptive to Communism: the party, already negligible, rapidly lost even more ground, leaving government to the People's and Socialist parties which together could harvest more than 90 per cent of the votes. This Grand Coalition, which survived until 1966, was able to present a united front to the outside world on the questions of the ending of occupation and the granting of sovereignty in return for a commitment to neutrality. Stalin did not seem prepared to force the issue in such a small country, and his successors were willing to accept its full sovereignty in 1955.

In Germany the Allied Control Authority never really succeeded in getting off the ground. Although it had been agreed that matters affecting the whole of Germany were to be dealt with by the Authority, it became increasingly difficult for the four occupying powers to concur on what should be classified as all-German concerns. Moreover, a unanimous decision was necessary in the highest organ, the Control Council. In effect, each occupier possessed a veto, and increasingly the military governor in each zone held supreme authority, answerable only to his own government. The tendency of the zones to function independently of each other was strengthened by the practice of withdrawing issues from the Control Council when unanimity could not be obtained.

The Allies began to pay the penalty for not clarifying in greater detail their future course of action before the war ended. France and the Soviet Union in particular held divergent views. France was obsessed by the need to keep Germany weak and divided. Hence French governments tended to drag their heels on reconstruction except in the Saar, which they desired to incorporate into France, while still urging that they receive as reparations substantial supplies of German material, especially coal, to aid in the rebuilding of the French economy. The Soviet Union held quite different views on the meaning of democracy from those of Britain and America. The occupation authorities gave licences in each zone to the Communists, Social Democrats, Christian Democrats and Liberals (Free Democrats). Ideally, Stalin would have preferred Communist superiority to be displayed through free elections. However, in the first acid test of popular support, the all-city election in Berlin in 1946, the Social Democrats won a convincing victory: the Communists went down to ignominious defeat in their pre-1933 stronghold. Thereafter Soviet policy changed course: the use of Soviet force would be the way to a people's democracy. The Social Democrat Party in the Soviet zone was forcibly merged with the weaker Communists in 1946 in a Soviet-dominated Socialist Unity Party. A major step had been taken to retract eastern Germany from Western influence and establish it firmly behind the iron curtain.

Soviet economic policy was also different from that of the West. The United States and Britain tended to give priority to a revitalisation of the economy: after 1946 their main emphasis was upon the need to integrate zonal economies. The Soviet Union, on the other hand, stressed reparations in both theory and practice. Whole factories, industrial material and even railway lines were uprooted and transported eastwards. Current East German production was confiscated as 'reparations exports'. In short, the Soviet zone was operated as a separate and independent economic unit, as indeed was the French zone for a while. This also flouted the Potsdam agreements which had stated that current German production should not be overtapped and that Germany was to be treated as a single economic unit for purposes of foreign trade. The Soviet Union also failed to supply the western regions with food from its zone, as had been agreed.

During its short existence the Allied Control Authority did achieve a limited success, mainly in the area of denazification. However, as the conflict of national interests among the occupying powers became more apparent, Soviet and, to a lesser extent, French obstructionism deprived the Authority of much of its effectiveness. Eventually, the Soviet commander walked out of the Control Council in March 1948. Three months later the Soviet Union withdrew from the Berlin Kommandatura. For Germany the Cold War had started in earnest. The Western Allies were forced to provide an alternative structure for administering their own zones. This was a tripartite Allied Commission, with an extensive network of committees and working parties which had the task of administering German affairs other than local government.

Current developments in Europe were making the Western Allies increasingly uneasy about the Soviet Union and what they feared were its plans for European domination. More hard-line Stalinist regimes had taken control in Eastern Europe, culminating with the successful Communist coup in Czechoslovakia. In June, only two days after the Soviet Union walked out of the Kommandatura, the Berlin blockade began. In this tense atmosphere the United States in particular became convinced of the need to have Germany as an ally. Indeed, the Soviet exit from the Kommandatura and the blockade may have been provoked by the Anglo-American view that it would be futile to await Soviet concurrence on the establishment of a national German government. To that end a six-power conference of Western foreign ministers had been convened in London: the events in Berlin began during that meeting. In turn, Soviet behaviour only helped the West to crystallise its decision to press on with the establishment of a German state out of the three Western zones. The ratchet effect of the Cold War was clearly visible in Germany in the summer of 1948.

At the London conference the Western Allies agreed in principle upon the amalgamation of their zones and to the creation of a central German government covering all three. In order to placate French demands that a guaranteed supply of Ruhr coal was necessary for France's economic recovery, the others agreed to set up an International Ruhr Authority, a body which would control all West German coal production. The new state would be based upon a written constitution drafted by a constituent assembly representative of party strengths in the regional legislatures and subsequently approved both by the Allied representatives in Germany and by popular consent. The Allies would retain some control over German affairs, especially foreign policy. The future relationship between the Allies and the new German government was formalised by the Occupation Statute of April 1949. Under the statute the Allied military government was replaced by a civilian Allied High Commission. During the next few years further agreements extended the competence of legitimate German government and abrogated Allied rights in Germany. Finally, the Paris agreements of 1954 officially brought to an end the period of Western occupation: the Federal Republic of Germany became a fully sovereign state. Berlin was excluded from these discussions. The Western Allies retained their full occupation rights in the city. These remained the basis of the justification of the Allied military presence there until the reunification of Germany in 1991.

Upon their entry into Germany, the occupation forces had had to attend to the immediate needs of the population. The whole German administrative machinery had virtually ceased to function, and there were severe shortages of food, shelter and utilities. To facilitate the establishment of lines of supply, one of the first preoccupations was the reconstruction of local government, which was in line with the Potsdam agreements. The pressing economic situation, however, and the shortage of experienced military personnel probably caused the Allies to move more quickly in this direction.

The search was concentrated upon finding key community leaders who were both competent and untainted by Nazism. Since Nazi control and influence over German public life had been extensive, such people were difficult to find. Many local officials were automatically disqualified because of their association with Nazism. Furthermore, many opponents of Hitler's regime had been in prison for long periods and were too weak, both physically and mentally, to undertake the onus of local government reconstruction. Others who were willing were often only enthusiastic amateurs. Local leaders were eventually found to fill the most important jobs, although increasingly the Allies had to abandon their strict interpretation of Nazi complicity and denazification. When a network of local units had been established, the same processes were adopted to build political units at higher levels until the pyramid was topped with the creation of regional institutions.

These states, or *Länder*, were a revival of the traditional German form of government. Some, like Bavaria, were historical entities with long and proud traditions; others were artificially created by the Allies, mostly out of provinces of the old Prussian state, which they were pledged to destroy. People of confirmed anti-Nazi convictions were appointed to the premierships of the *Länder*. In the absence of a national government, these states became the centre of German political life; they attracted ambitious politicians and became the focal point of all serious discussions on the nature of the new Germany.

Throughout the period of reconstruction the Allies gradually released more authority to German officials, but even in 1948 the country was still highly decentralised. A first unifying move had been made in 1945 when the United States established a Council of States of the *Länder* premiers in its zone. The Council was not intended to possess complete authority over the whole zone; rather, it was meant to act as a coordinating body in those fields of interstate affairs that could not be handled competently at the level of the individual state.

The first steps towards unification had been taken, but these were very far from the resolutions taken at Potsdam. The decision to treat Germany as a single economic unit had been flouted blatantly from the outset. Economic affairs were handled on a zonal basis; interzonal trade was treated as if it were between independent states. Such a situation was clearly unsatisfactory, and in many ways added an extra burden to the already heavy responsibilities of the occupying powers. Finally, in June 1946 the United States invited the other occupying powers to merge the zonal economies, but only Britain was willing to accept the invitation. Plans for the joint administration of the two zones were ready by the end of the year. The new economic unit was named 'Bizonia' and became the real starting point of the development of the future West German state. German joint executive committees were created, composed of the heads of the relevant state ministries. Although policy could be formulated by these committees, implementation could be carried through only by the state governments.

However, where particularist sentiment was strong, as in Bavaria, state cooperation with Bizonia decisions was not always forthcoming. Furthermore, a rapid deterioration in 1947 of the food situation caused additional difficulties. To improve bizonal functioning, an Economic Council was set up in 1947. With its members drawn from the state legislatures, not the governments, the Council was to serve in a legislative capacity, while administrative agencies were established to supervise the execution of its decisions. The following year, the Council was given the right to compel the *Länder* to comply with its decisions, and a German High Court with both original and appellate jurisdiction was established, to enable the bizonal authorities to have access to judicial enforcement of their decisions. The Court was the final touch to the institutional framework. It meant that by the time the Western Allies decided at London to press on with the establishment of a democratic German government in their own zones, a complex structure of political and administrative institutions had already been founded, a pattern, moreover, that followed traditional

German lines and was also roughly the outline of the governmental structure to be adopted by the nascent Federal Republic.

THE GERMAN VIEW

The reaction of most Germans to the total collapse of the Nazi regime had been to withdraw from any form of political activity, to concern themselves primarily with their own private affairs. Political reconstruction was not their business. Many had identified emotionally with the Thousand Year Reich and its programme of national glorification, and felt unable to cope with the transition to the harsh realities of the occupation. The immediate postwar months were dominated by a chronic shortage of food and shelter; inevitably the struggle for survival occupied the attention of most Germans.

Nevertheless there were some who were concerned with the political future and with the particular form it should take. The Allies had permitted groups and associations, in particular political parties, to become active. Politically motivated Germans operated from these organisations. Administrators and politicians had been incorporated into the governmental structures created by the occupation forces and there was, in fact, a strong relationship between party development and the spread of German-directed administration. By the time of the London Conference, the licensed political parties dominated the *Länder* governments and legislatures. Two mass parties, the Social Democrats (SPD) and the Christian Democratic Union (CDU), soon achieved an undisputed superiority over the others.

The origins of the CDU lay in the old Catholic Centre Party of the Empire and Weimar. However, its founders wished to break out of this Catholic ghetto and, by attracting a large Protestant support, to establish a broad interdenominational movement. But the new party still had its strongest roots in Catholic Germany, and its early leaders were predominantly Catholic. Konrad Adenauer was to become the dominating personality of the party and of the new republic. He had served as Lord Mayor of Cologne in the 1920s, but had retired from politics, carefully dissociating himself from the Nazi regime. A shrewd politician, he came forward after 1945 to lead the CDU, first in the British zone and then throughout the country. From chairing the constituent assembly that drafted a constitution for the new state, he went on to become the first chancellor in Germany's second experiment with democracy.

The Social Democrats were one of the oldest parties in Germany, and had kept hope alive during Hitler's rule by maintaining a party organisation in exile. Their leader, Kurt Schumacher, had been interned for much of the Reich. His experiences, and his memories of the SPD failure in the 1920s, had so conditioned him that he had an unbending vision of the future. Believing that the hour of Social Democracy had come, and that his party, because of its impeccable anti-Nazi record, was the sole true representative of Germany, Schumacher argued for a party which would represent the aspirations of the whole German nation, and for nothing less than the reunification of the whole

German nation. Yet his autocratic nature alienated some and, in the long run, he could not dislodge the roots of traditionalism in the party.

Political discussions on the future of Germany tended to revolve around the positions adopted by these two parties. When the Western Allies called upon the *Länder* premiers to set in motion the machinery for forming a constituent assembly that would draft a constitution, the Germans themselves had already put forward several suggestions about the nature of the new state. The collapse of the Third Reich had left a vacuum that was highly conducive for, and receptive to, new ideas. These were diffused by a democratic spirit and Christian principles. The return to fundamentals was linked to a close examination of the lessons offered by German history. Needless to say, the Nazi Reich was universally condemned. Though the Weimar Republic came in for its share of criticism, there was a recognition that its constitution had contained worthy principles which, with the introduction of several safeguards (all reflecting a distrust of mass democracy), could be used as a basis for the future German state. Centralisation was suspect, and there was a general acceptance of a return to a traditional German form of federalism, something which would also meet with Allied prejudices. There was hardly any mention of German *Realpolitik*, but an embracing of the pan-European democratic tradition of the abortive 1848 Frankfurt Assembly. Germans had previously been conditioned to obey a paternalist and authoritarian state, something which stood above society, but which alone could determine what were, and protect, basic freedoms. That concept of the state had been perverted by the Nazis. In its place there had to be a utilitarian organisation that would be part of and answerable to society.

Thus by the time the new Parliamentary Council met in Bonn to consider a new constitution, the German delegates already possessed a framework of ideas which they felt could be made operable in the new Germany. They had broadly accepted a parliamentary, democratic and federal regime based upon traditional German ideas on political organisation. While it is true that the Basic Law which came into effect in 1949 reflected much of Allied policy for the future Germany, it reflected German views on the subject even more. Allied positions were not diametrically opposed to German views. Their suggestions and vetoes merely gave extra support to one of several views already formed in the Council debates; and such situations were rare.

The Parliamentary Council first met in September 1948, shortly after France, under strong American pressure, agreed to merge its zone into Bizonia. Politically, the atmosphere was tense: the Berlin blockade was already in full swing. The economic outlook, however, appeared brighter. A much-needed currency reform in June was beginning to bite. By limiting the supply of money, reforming the debt structure, and progressively removing financial controls, it destroyed the black market and put the German mark on a more stable footing.

The CDU and SPD delegates dominated the Council. Adenauer was elected president; as such, he became the leading German spokesman at the many discussions and negotiations with the three Allied governors. The SPD leader, Schumacher, wanted the new state to be 'as federalistic as possible and as centralised as necessary'; the CDU desired a more decentralised format. On the whole the debates were settled by compromise, though slightly favouring the CDU position. This was again a break with the doctrinal past: the willingness to compromise was a rejection of the previous axiom that only one view could be correct. The strong emphasis in the final draft on federalism reflected the inclination of the whole nature and mood of German politics. There was no central government which could exert pressure upon the Council. Moreover, the Council had rejected that part of the London accord which had laid down that a draft constitution should be ratified by popular approval. Instead it was to be ratified only by the *Länder* legislatures which, irrespective of party, were already jealous of their acquired powers and loath to see them pass into the hands of a central government. If there was a dominant tone to the final document, it was a concern with limitations on power and participation. The memory of the recent past was too overpowering to permit much enthusiasm about an optimistic future.

It had already been agreed that the new constitution should not be known as such. The delegates felt that that would only emphasise the division of Germany and make reunification more difficult. The document was to be known as the Basic Law, leaving a constitution to be ratified by a reunited Germany. Though the document received massive approval, there was opposition from Bavaria which favoured a looser form of confederation. While Bavaria was the only state to vote against acceptance, it did so with the qualification that it would abide by the majority decision of the *Länder*.

The Parliamentary Council then enacted provisions for the first general election, held in August 1949. The result confirmed the lead of the CDU and SPD over the other parties. Konrad Adenauer was nominated as federal chancellor. After lengthy negotiations with some of the smaller parties, he was able to form a coalition government. Germany thus had, as the Federal Republic of Germany, its second chance to function as a parliamentary democracy. Its future operation would be closely monitored, for judgments would be made by comparing it not only with the past, but also with the regime (the German Democratic Republic – DDR) in East Germany created by the Soviet Union in retaliation against the Western Allies' policy. As international concern increased, the Federal Republic was placed under even more pressure to become a committed partner of the Atlantic alliance, a course that would give severe headaches to some of its Western neighbours, as well as making the hope of reunification even more remote. The transition to independence was formalised by a special ceremony at the Allied High Commission headquarters in September 1949. With this ceremony, the Western occupation of Germany ended in practice and the Federal Republic formally began to operate. The date became yet another landmark in the tumultuous and tragic history of Germany.

CONSERVATIVE CONSOLIDATION

Konrad Adenauer was destined to serve as chancellor of the Republic for the next fourteen years. But upon his election in 1949 he was not firmly in the saddle as the CDU leader. The party, although larger than any other, had won only 31 per cent of the popular vote, and it still reflected the factionalism of its decentralised regional origins. However, as chancellor, Adenauer had a great advantage over all his CDU rivals. His was a strong-willed nature linked to acute political shrewdness, and he proved able to combine these qualities with the possibilities for strong executive leadership offered by the Basic Law to create for himself a position of authority which could rarely be challenged over the next decade. In so doing, he very largely shaped West German foreign policy and contributed greatly towards moving the country firmly away from the more radical spirit of the late 1940s.

Upon its formation, the CDU had shared in the general belief that Germany required a completely new beginning. This reforming spirit was captured in its adoption of the Ahlen Programme in 1947, which included a strong critique of capitalism. Ahlen, however, was the high watermark of radicalism within the party. As the CDU gained experience in regional administration and Bizonia, it swung back to an acceptance of a modified capitalism, portraying the notion of the social market economy as an ideal mix of market competitiveness and societal responsibility. In 1949 this was incorporated into a new party programme, and later became almost an article of faith.

The CDU of the 1940s was still a broad church, and after the 1949 election the party's left favoured a grand coalition with the SPD. Adenauer's own inclinations were in a more conservative direction: a coalition with the smaller conservative parties would not just be anti-Socialist, but might also deprive more reactionary groups of benefiting from critiques of the regime similar to those which had been levelled against Weimar after 1918. He was also helped in this course of action by Schumacher (the two were not on the best of terms) who, determined to ensure that the SPD would not again be accused of a lack of patriotism, had married his Socialist convictions with an unbending nationalist stance, emphasising the priority of reunification and rejecting too close a proximity with the capitalist West. Through some adroit manipulation of his colleagues and the exclusion of those on the party's left with whom he profoundly disagreed, Adenauer was able to sell his preferred coalition option and to ensure that his government contained nobody who could offer serious opposition to his policies. He himself took charge of foreign policy, while Ludwig Erhard, the 'father' of the social market economy, was allowed quite a free hand in economic policy. Adenauer's Christian Democrats were to strengthen further their grip on the country's politics: in that way West German developments were typical of the conservative mood which crept over much of Western Europe in the 1950s.

CHAPTER 7

INTEGRATION: THE POSTWAR BEGINNING

Tacit and intellectual consent are insufficient if we are to build Europe. We must have results.

> (*Paul-Henri Spaak*, Council of Europe: The First Five Years, *Strasbourg, 1954, p. 22*)

Nothing is possible without individuals, nothing is durable without institutions.

> (*Jean Monnet*, Mémoires, *Paris, 1976, p. 360*)

Between the world wars, several organisations had sought to promote European unity. The period, however, was still dominated by an intense nationalism which with the rise of Nazism became ever more virulent, and such movements were forced to labour in the wilderness. The turning point came around 1943. The various Resistance movements were elaborating their hopes for the future; prominent among them were schemes for European unification. After the war, European movements proliferated in most countries, including Britain. Internationally, the European Union of Federalists was established in 1946, to be superseded two years later by the European Movement, which had such diverse personalities as Winston Churchill, Léon Blum and Alcide de Gasperi among its patrons – a reflection of the idea's widespread appeal across party divides. However, the onset of the Cold War meant that any moves towards a federation or other form of union would in effect be restricted to the western half of the continent.

OPENING GAMBITS

Motivations for seeking an integrated Europe were varied. In Germany, for example, it was seen as a road by which Germany could win acceptance by its neighbours as an independent, equal and responsible state. In Italy, supporters saw integration as a counterbalance to the possible instability that might arise from the presence of a large Communist party, as well as offering access to broader markets that might enable it to reduce substantially its chronic labour surplus. But for most countries the crucial question was whether Britain would become a committed member of any cooperative European endeavour.

The Scandinavian states were reluctant to enter any organisation without Britain, while France and the Low Countries regarded British participation as an indispensable guarantee of security against a resurgence of German militarism or the threat of the Soviet Union.

Above these narrower national interests were the wider implications of the war. The Soviet Union and the United States had developed into super-powers against which the states of Western Europe could not hope to compete without a high degree of cooperation. Wartime devastation made economic cooperation advisable; and the whole thrust of American foreign policy was also in that direction. Britain's importance was not just a matter of the political prestige gained during the war; it was also economic. For example, after 1945 British steel production was more than two-thirds of the combined total of that of the other European members of the future OEEC, while its coal output nearly equalled that of the other OEEC states.

There was, within the optimism of the immediate postwar years, a European grain of scepticism about the potential value of a world organisation: the projected UN was not hailed as a panacea as the League of Nations had been in 1919. However, there was a belief in the value of approaching world unity in stages: protagonists saw European unity as not only realistic and inherently valuable, but also as an important step towards a world organisation. Finally, there was the perceived looming threat of the Soviet Union. After 1945 the Soviet Union served as a catalyst which helped Western Europe to define itself as an entity with common interests. This element of expediency in European union never entirely disappeared; it perhaps both hindered, and helped Western Europe defer, progress towards political union.

In 1945 the United States, by virtue of its overwhelming military strength and strategic thinking, may have been a European power, but was not and could not be a European state. It could encourage moves towards integration, but could not lead them directly. During the war Britain had provided the European lead, and because of its wartime role was believed to have the reasons and the opportunity to effect some kind of unity. And both inside and outside Britain, the hopes of European federalists were focused upon the charismatic wartime leader, Winston Churchill.

It was accepted that Churchill had been converted to the federalist cause during the war. While leaders of prewar European organisations were forced to spend the war in captivity or exile, Churchill was thought to have kept the flame of union alight. He it was who in 1940, just before the total collapse of France, had dramatically proposed an Anglo-French Union. Throughout the war he had returned to the theme of pan-Europe: in a 1943 broadcast, for example, he emphasised the need for a Council of Europe that would possess an effective network of working institutions, including a common military organisation. Consequently, federalists were shocked and disheartened by the 1945 election result in Britain, since it was doubtful whether the new Labour government would display any enthusiasm for union.

Churchill continued to argue for European integration. In 1946 he stated in Zürich that it was imperative to establish a United States of Europe. This

speech was his most significant review of the question since losing the premiership. It helped spur federalists to greater efforts, stimulated existing bodies
to increase their activities, and inspired the creation of new organisations. All
these groups were distinguished from their prewar predecessors in enjoying
considerable sympathy from parliamentarians, as well as occasionally counting
government ministers among their memberships.

The British Labour government watched this activity cautiously, but the
burst of enthusiasm was too strong to be denied entirely. Still under the aegis
of Churchill, the various organisations agreed in December 1947 to establish
an International Committee of the Movements for European Unity. Its task
was to make arrangements for a congress of all those interested in union, to
impress Europe with the vitality and practicality of their cause. In due course
the Congress of Europe was held in The Hague in May 1948. With over 750
delegates from sixteen states, as well as observers from Canada and the United
States, the Congress was an impressive display of the widespread interest in
the idea, and it passed several resolutions calling for a European union, a
charter of human rights linked to a European court, a common market, and
monetary union. All political persuasions except Communism were represented, though many influential political leaders were conspicuously absent. The
Congress itself was too unwieldy and too disparate to achieve any practical
measure of success, but it did highlight the interest in unification and ways in
which that interest might be advanced. It was at this point that British leadership, symbolised by Churchill, began to disappear from the union movement.

Churchill himself had not been notably concerned with translating the general principle into practical realities. He had, perhaps deliberately, been rather
ambiguous. His speeches had not been fundamentally concerned with 'Britain
cum Europe', but with 'Britain *and* Europe'. Like many British politicians, he
had seen European unity as a valuable ideal. But Britain did not have to be
part of that unity; it could only be associated with it. The fundamental British
attitude had already been summed up nearly twenty years earlier by Churchill
himself when he wrote: 'We see nothing but good and hope in a richer, freer,
more contented European commonalty. But we have our own dream and our
own task. We are with Europe, but not of it. We are linked, but not compromised. We are interested and associated, but not absorbed.' Until at least the
1960s this was the reality of an intransigent British position.

And yet the various movements, brash or hesitating, towards integration in
the late 1940s all looked to Britain for leadership, and all held the hope that
Britain would be absorbed. On the other hand, British political leaders clung
to what Churchill had called their own dream and their own task. These had
two components: the commitment to the Commonwealth, and the 'special'
Anglo-American relationship which had flowered to its fullest between Churchill
and Roosevelt. It is a mistake to regard the development of integration as the
outcome of a continuing argument between Britain and the continent: all
points of view could be found in all countries. Yet in a way it is a simple but
effective way of analysing the subject since Britain was the leading spokesman
for a particular point of view. The essence of the debate, very generally, was

whether people desired a European community or a broader Atlantic community that would include the United States and so, it was argued, provide a more effective bulwark in the ideological struggle against Communism. In this formative period the role of Britain was crucial, for it was the only major protagonist caught between the diverging claims of the Atlantic and the continent.

The official British policy was to establish a number of mutual aid pacts with other European democracies. The first, and in the event the only one, was the 1947 Treaty of Dunkirk with France. Although the pact provided for bilateral economic assistance and cooperation, its justification was primarily military: a guarantee of mutual aid in the face of any future German aggression. As such, it was an inadequate instrument for dealing with the realities of the postwar world. By 1948 the time seemed more propitious for attempting to pull Britain into a pan-European orbit. The Labour government, which had been hostile to British involvement in union because it might hinder what the party considered to be necessary economic controls within Britain, and because it might make accommodation with the East more precarious, appeared to be more willing to listen to European overtures. It had finally abandoned any hope of a working relationship with the Soviet Union. In the House of Commons the Foreign Secretary, Ernest Bevin, declared that further steps should be taken. But the furthest he wished to go was an effective interlocking system of bilateral treaties along the lines of the Treaty of Dunkirk. However, with Germany still an occupied country, only France could enter into a defensive treaty with Britain with some semblance of equality; for the rest, the onus would be on Britain.

The extension of Dunkirk came in a slightly different context. Bevin negotiated a cooperative arrangement with France and the Benelux countries: the result was the 1948 Treaty of Brussels, which Britain saw as a practical basis of cooperation, but not union. Bevin reiterated his warning against what he regarded as excessively ambitious hopes of integration. The Brussels pact was basically military in nature, again with Germany depicted as the possible antagonist, but it also contained provisions for 'economic, social, and cultural collaboration'. The general direction of its affairs would be intergovernmental in nature, the responsibility of a committee of the foreign ministers. It seems clear that the British leaders, at least, did not envisage an institutional body, yet some form of organisation would have been necessary for the proposed tasks to be carried out.

Bevin saw the Brussels agreement gradually being widened, eventually to cover the whole of Western Europe, but each step would have to be thoroughly tested, and the overall character would remain at the level of intergovernmental cooperation. However, there were already signs that the Brussels organisation was running away from the British idea. The enthusiasm aroused by the Hague Congress was one indication that Britain was in danger of becoming rather isolated. At the Congress, ideas and views ranged from those for a weak form of confederation to those demanding a fully sovereign supranational authority. Even within the non-union camp, the British idea of a close association with the United States and American leadership of an Atlantic alliance faced opposition from those who argued for a 'third force', a cooperative European military arrangement without American involvement; General de Gaulle had already made it clear in 1946 that he favoured this path.

Despite British disapproval, ardent federalists of the European movement hoped to utilise the Brussels agreement as a springboard for their ambitions. They were assisted by the changing international atmosphere. The increasing intensity of the Cold War had made the United States even more desirous of a stable and effective Western Europe: integration was thought to be a useful step in the right direction. It is perhaps ironical that Britain was partially responsible for releasing a tiger which ultimately proved uncontrollable. It again resorted to the previously tried formula of a counter-proposal that might serve as a compromise. The suggestion was that European foreign ministers should form a semi-permanent committee that would meet at regular intervals to discuss problems of common concern, except defence and economic matters which would be respectively the province of the proposed military body that became NATO, and the OEEC. It was clear to the pro-Europeans that Britain had not renounced its conviction that anything more than a purely intergovernmental system of cooperation and consultation would be undesirable.

But the force of opinion against Britain and its supporters (notably Ireland and Scandinavia) was gaining strength. By late 1948, Britain had yielded to the pressure for a European Assembly to the extent of reluctantly endorsing the establishment of a study commission on its feasibility. An assembly was regarded as a major step towards full integration, but its supporters were still desirous of British participation. In order to both placate and lure British opinion, the study commission reported three months later that the new organisation could and should have both a consultative and debating assembly and a council of ministers: in that way national governments could be involved. After further discussions, Britain agreed to the proposal. It was finally settled that the ministers should discuss affairs in private, but that assembly debates would be public. These discussions were the nucleus of the Council of Europe.

The British strategy was still, in Bevin's words, to ensure that the proposed structure would be 'as little embarrassing as possible'. In view of the past it is not surprising, and in view of the future it is significant, that Britain still preferred to remain aloof from Europe and to consider itself the link *par excellence* between the continent and the United States. These developments were not simply a confrontation between Britain and Europe, but whereas integrationist sympathies were widespread in many continental states, they had little purchase in Britain which, by virtue of its importance, was the leading opponent of supranationalism. Notwithstanding this opposition, in May 1949, one month after the establishment of NATO, the Statute of the Council of Europe was signed in London, and arrangements were made for the organisation to establish permanent offices in Strasbourg. Its supporters regarded it as a happy augury that on the same day the Soviet Union finally called off the Berlin blockade. With the federalist implications of its aim of achieving 'a greater unity between its Members for the purpose of safeguarding and realising the ideals and principles which are their common heritage and facilitating their economic and social progress', the new body became Western Europe's first postwar political organisation. The original membership of ten (Belgium, Denmark, France, Britain, Ireland, Italy, the Netherlands, Luxembourg, Norway, Sweden) expanded steadily until by the 1980s it embraced almost the whole of non-Communist Europe. In the 1990s the Council of Europe extended its membership eastwards to most of the new democratic regimes in Eastern Europe, with the admission of Russia to its ranks in 1996 symbolising how far old certainties had been swept aside after almost half a century of glaciation.

POLITICAL ASSOCIATION: THE COUNCIL OF EUROPE

In August 1949 the Consultative Assembly of the Council of Europe held its first session in Strasbourg. The ardent federalists immediately set out to make the new body a more effective organ of union than was apparent in its charter. They had two objectives: to develop some semblance of supranational authority, and to strengthen the Assembly *vis-à-vis* the Committee of Ministers. For the creation of the Council of Europe had not in any degree diminished national sovereignty as represented by the ministers. The aims of the Council were to be achieved by 'discussion of questions of common concern and by agreements and common action in economic, social, cultural, scientific, legal and administrative matters and in the maintenance and further realisation of human rights and fundamental freedoms'. Defence was excluded because it was controversial, given the current discussions on an Atlantic alliance and the presence of two neutral states, Ireland and Sweden, as founder members. The Council's aims were therefore generalised. It had a wide field of reference, yet at the same time was limited severely by its Charter. Any international body would minimally agree to a framework of discussion and agreement. The Council of Europe could not itself move forward to a supranational or federalist future. This is not to say that it could not encourage efforts at integration: indeed, this was to be one of its major concerns.

Within the Council there were no surprises or novelties about the Committee of Ministers: it became little more than a conference of foreign ministers meeting twice yearly. In 1952 it adopted the practice of permitting deputies, usually senior diplomats, to stand in for ministers: these became permanent and have usually attended to all business except that deemed to be symbolically important. Most decisions have required unanimity, thus allowing reluctant members, particularly those sceptical about closer union, the right of a veto, though a loophole allows members to pursue a policy without requiring the assent or cooperation of the others: this was not used directly until 1956, with the creation of a European Settlement Fund. The most radical innovations towards integration, like the Coal and Steel Community, were initiated outside the framework of the Council and its Committee of Ministers. In that sense, the Committee has not been a true executive body; nor was it designed to be. In relaying decisions to the member governments, it has only been able to recommend. Committee members could go their own way whenever national concerns dictated a strictly national path.

The Assembly, on the other hand, has been more radical and imaginative. Since 1951 its membership has been determined by the national parliaments, and more or less from the outset delegates displayed a tendency in debates to cluster around political identity rather than nationality. But the Assembly did not acquire powers that matched its functions. The basis of its existence was essentially deliberation. It was permitted only to offer recommendations to the Committee of Ministers, without being able to bind the latter in any way. It did, however, gain some control over its own affairs, and did gain the right to discuss questions of European defence. The essential point is that just as the Committee was not a true executive, so the Assembly was not a true legislature.

Partly because of these restrictions on action and scope, the relationship between the Assembly and the Committee has often been uneasy and strained. Particularly during the early years, the Assembly was populated by delegates interested in Europe and unity, while ministers represented national governments to which they are solely responsible. One frustrated delegate could assert that 'the Council of Europe consists of two bodies, one of them for Europe, the other against it'. Despite the introduction of a liaison committee in 1950, little common ground appeared between the two sides. All this thwarted the Assembly, whose major proposals have involved the notion of greater European unity, and in 1951 Paul-Henri Spaak of Belgium, who had been one of the main instigators of the Council and elected in 1949 as the first President of the Assembly, resigned the office because the limited capacity of the body to effect change and sponsor integration was far less than he wished.

The frustrations and tensions exhibited by the Council must be attributed not only to its structure, but also to the forces which determined it. The design had been influenced greatly by Britain's attitude. The pro-Europeans had reluctantly compromised as much as possible in order to ensure British membership. Britain's willingness to compromise had been far less marked. The end result was that the Council of Europe was in no position to advance by and in itself the concept of European union to any great length. The failure of federal projects within the Council was evident by the time of its second session in 1950. This had several far-reaching effects. First, the British entry into the Council had led some to believe that Britain was prepared to move further along the European path. They were soon disillusioned: Britain still refused to accept anything above a loose intergovernmental structure. The effort to placate Britain came to an end. In the future, attempts to achieve a modicum of unity would go ahead regardless of the British position. Secondly, it tended to downgrade the Council of Europe. Support for it declined fairly rapidly, especially in France, when it was felt that the Council might be little more than a regional version of the UN. Many formerly ardent supporters soon regarded it only as a symbol of unity and of better things to come, with value only as an instrument of and sounding board for public opinion.

The Council of Europe nevertheless survived, and within its limited competence has reason to be proud of the work it has done since its inception. It has always been active on behalf of European integration, and since 1949 has sponsored broad organisational cooperation in a variety of socioeconomic and cultural areas through the production of some 135 non-binding conventions or agreements to which, in fact, most members have appended their signatures. Perhaps the most significant of these was the European Convention for the Protection of Human Rights and Fundamental Freedoms of 1950 and the associated establishment of a European Court of Human Rights, which were to have a deep and direct impact upon ordinary European citizens in the years to come. After the creation of the European Coal and Steel Community (ECSC), which it endorsed, it saw an outlet for its energies in proposing European authorities to coordinate other economic and social policy sectors: transport in 1953, civil aviation in 1954, and agriculture in 1955. After the 1960s its major focus was perhaps more on cultural collaboration and environmental protection. It similarly exerted itself to establish working relationships with other international organisations, so much that the Council became a kind of central clearing house for cooperation and coordination, receiving reports from other European bodies as well as several UN agencies. The first serious challenge to it came with the creation of ECSC outside its boundaries: however, the ECSC states saw no incompatibility between the two bodies, and the Council has remained the organisation with the broadest spread of democratic membership, extending the latter after 1989 into Eastern Europe. Because of this, it has possessed value as a forum where a wide range of ideas and views can be aired for discussion. It is this which has helped to prevent it from being completely submerged by later developments.

Perhaps the major significance of the Council of Europe rests in the fact that it was the first European organisation with a political flavour. As such, it was an important milestone on the road to the closer association of the European Communities, a facet acknowledged by the European Union of Federalists which reported that 'it marked the beginning of a real and organic cooperation between the nations of Europe; it marked the end of the illusion that the aim of European unity can be achieved without political machinery on a supranational level'.

ECONOMIC COOPERATION: OEEC

The honour of establishing the first postwar economic arrangement belongs to Benelux, an economic grouping of Belgium, the Netherlands and Luxembourg. The agreement to come together as an economic unit was reached by the exiled governments during the war. Despite many problems, their decision was put into practice in 1946, and two years later a customs union demonstrated the first fruits of the agreement with the removal of customs duties and the establishment of a common external tariff. During the 1950s the three states pressed on with further economic harmonisation, culminating in an economic union in 1960.

This kind of decision and planning could be introduced without too much difficulty in such a compact and relatively homogeneous area as the Low Countries. The obstacles facing the introduction of a similar scheme across the whole of Western Europe, however, were tremendous. Yet the creation of the Organisation for European Economic Cooperation was an ambitious step in this direction. The roots of OEEC lie in the havoc caused by the Second World War upon domestic economies and the international economic system.

Its beginning lay in the American decision to offer financial assistance to the whole of Europe. Ernest Bevin and Georges Bidault, the British and French foreign ministers, immediately invited their Soviet counterpart to attend discussions on the American offer. This was declined. The Soviet Union wanted each country to negotiate a bilateral economic agreement with the United States, whereas the essence of the American offer was the stipulation that the administration of the relief programme must be collective in order to maximise its benefits. Britain and France therefore invited all other European states, except Germany and Spain, to attend a conference in Paris. Apart from the Communist-dominated states in the East, only Finland, sensitive to the stance of its giant neighbour, did not feel free to accept the invitation. Representatives of fourteen states appeared in Paris to consider the American proposal and to construct a list of European resources and requirements to cover the period from 1948 to 1951. They agreed to meet at intervals to review the situation, and to establish a permanent administration to organise the programme. In April 1948, OEEC came into being.

Its first and immediate preoccupation was the European Recovery Programme, to discover a method of allocating American aid among the recipients. OEEC was reluctant to undertake this chore, since no matter what was decided, some members would receive less than others. Nevertheless, a decision had to be made: the responsibility had to be Europe's since the United States had made it clear that it did not wish to draw up the details itself. The European states eventually found a formula which all, some albeit reluctantly, could accept: aid was to be distributed among OEEC members according to their trade and payment deficits. Those states which possessed a lower standard of living, but had very small deficits, suffered most by the arrangement. But OEEC, with American encouragement, survived this first hurdle to pass on to a wider area of activity.

The basic responsibility for the successful operation of OEEC belonged to the member states themselves; the organisation itself was primarily concerned with questions of cooperation and coordination. Thus, like the Council of Europe, it was only a first step of the movement towards integration, being essentially an intergovernmental body. But the nature of its task necessarily demanded some permanent institutional organs to enable it to perform its allotted functions satisfactorily. The focus of OEEC and its governing body was the Council, where each state had one representative. This body had the power to determine questions of general policy and administration. Its decisions were obligatory on the members, but only because a decision became a decision when everyone had participated in its formulation and had already agreed to adhere to it. On the other hand, OEEC could not force a decision upon a recalcitrant member. Any state had the right to go its own way on any one issue by ignoring or vetoing OEEC suggestions, or by pleading special circumstances. While OEEC was not a supranational body, it was definitely further along that road than the Brussels Treaty from which, like the Council of Europe, it had partly drawn its inspiration.

The OEEC Council could not hope to function successfully in a vacuum. It constructed a complex network of subordinate committees and boards, usually composed of experts, which performed specialised functions. Council recommendations were nearly always based upon reports prepared by these specialist groups. As the workload of OEEC grew, it was forced to decentralise somewhat. The result was the establishment of several separate but related agencies; the best-known and perhaps most successful was the European Payments Union (EPU) of 1950. In 1949 most OEEC currencies had been devalued against the dollar. The EPU was invented to tackle the question of reciprocal credits when Marshall Aid ended. It was essentially a central bank and clearing house processing multilateral intra-European trade and payments. Its major drawback was that its financial settlements discriminated against the dollar, something that was contrary to the Bretton Woods agreement, and so something that would soon have to come to an end.

On paper, the OEEC structure did not appear to possess a great number of possibilities. Undoubtedly it had its drawbacks and liabilities – up to 1952, for example, it disappointed the United States with its failure to develop a comprehensive European Recovery Programme – but on a wider front it succeeded in liberalising trade and payments far beyond what a first glance might suggest. As an example of mutual cooperation, it could hardly be bettered. The right of veto, for instance, was only rarely exercised, and not only because contentious issues were avoided. It was unusual for a member to dare to go against the weight of expertise which the OEEC could command.

Acceptance of the principle of voluntary cooperation undoubtedly helped OEEC to sidestep many of the economic difficulties with which it might have been confronted, especially at a time when states and governments were unfamiliar with, and indeed suspicious of, collaboration. It was helped by the fact that in its formative years it developed a valuable relationship with the Council of Europe. On balance perhaps, given the political situation and attitudes of the late 1940s, no better way could have been formulated for administering Marshall Aid. But OEEC went beyond the European Recovery Programme by inspiring some people to consider ways of achieving closer integration. The founders of the ECSC and European Economic Community (EEC) undoubtedly learnt some important lessons from the OEEC.

It had its limitations. Its work was mostly concerned with the removal or reduction of quota restrictions on European trade. This could not prevent distortions or discrimination in trading patterns. Furthermore, it concentrated, not surprisingly, on easier problems, which meant that progress became increasingly slower as only more difficult questions remained. Again, it concerned itself more with short-term problems than with the long-term difficulty of attempting to settle problems of economic growth and development.

This is perhaps one reason why the founders of the ECSC and EEC preferred to do just that, rather than work through OEEC. But OEEC worked reasonably well within its field of reference. Its ability to tackle other problems was handicapped by the conditions surrounding its birth. Although the United States had desired a maximum degree of economic unity, and while France in particular saw advantages in some degree of supranationality, Britain drew back from any extended plan, desiring only cooperation, not integration. The British attitude was endorsed by some smaller states which feared that their interests might be subordinated to those of their larger neighbours. While cooperation may have won over unity, the true value of OEEC lay in the foundations it established for the future, not least in the fostering of new modes of thinking. By 1959 its original objectives had largely been gained: almost all internal trade had been liberalised and European currencies had generally become convertible, meeting one of the requirements of Bretton Woods, and the EPU was replaced by a more stringent European Monetary Agreement.

OEEC played a major role in driving home the realisation that European economic systems were mutually dependent, and that they prospered or failed together. It survived for twelve years. In many ways its demise was a matter of regret. Strictly speaking, it did not die. In 1960 it was transformed, with all its organs remaining intact, into the Organisation for Economic Cooperation and Development (OECD). The United States and Canada, which had only been associate members of OEEC, now became full members of OECD. The change of name reflected the different purpose and situation. OEEC had been constructed initially to handle the Marshall Aid programme. While it went on into new fields, it remained limited to Europe. By the end of the 1950s, the United States in particular was worried about the possible consequences of the economic division that was developing in Western Europe with the creation of the EEC. OECD was intended to counteract this possible schism by concerning itself with economic coordination and the long-term questions of economic development. With the entry of Japan in 1964, it ceased to be an Atlantic organisation; instead, it became what in many ways had always been a latent rationale, a forum of advanced industrial democracies concerned not only with the effectiveness of the domestic economies of its members, but also with the broader and long-term problems of the international economic system.

ECONOMIC INTEGRATION: THE SCHUMAN PLAN

During the first two years of the Marshall Plan, the European economies responded to American aid, and production rose steadily. The administration of the Marshall Plan through OEEC was giving Western Europe a first lesson in European cooperation. On the other hand, it was clear to the disciples of a united Europe that the Council of Europe and OEEC could have only a limited federal application. If unity were to be achieved, a different path had to be sought. In this the pro-Europeans received encouragement from the Council of Europe and from their own belief that the administration of the Marshall Plan and its results were both successful and informative. All that was needed was the necessary stimulus. That was provided by the French foreign minister, Robert Schuman who, using the ideas of Jean Monnet, in May 1950 cut through all the objections and hesitations within the European debate to propose a pooling of coal and steel resources.

Schuman's proposal was that coal and steel resources in Western Europe should be pooled and jointly administered by the states and a supranational authority, and that all tariffs in these heavy industries should be gradually eliminated. There was nothing particularly novel about the proposal, since the notion of economic union was currently a popular topic for discussion; in addition, there was the working experiment of Benelux. The plan had been drafted secretly by Monnet before being launched, not as a governmental report, but at a press conference. The choice of industries and the scheme itself had been partly influenced by two recent publications emanating from the Strasbourg Assembly and the Economic Commission for Europe, an agency of the UN. In addition, France was worried by the future political, military and economic potential of West Germany. Since 1945 French policy had aimed at keeping Germany weak and subordinate, in part through strong Anglo-French collaboration. That strategy ended with the 1948 decision to establish a West German state. The subsequent alternative offering, the International Ruhr Authority, was not working properly, and French complaints about it tended to be rejected or ignored by the United States, Britain and the Federal Republic of Germany. Hence, the supranational principle embodied in the Schuman Plan was attractive to France because it offered a way of binding West Germany to French influence while it was still relatively weak. The German strategy lay at the heart of the Schuman Plan which opened with the direct statement that 'the French Government proposes that . . . Franco-German coal and steel production should be placed under a common High Authority within the framework of an organization open to the participation of the other countries of Europe'.

The Plan was therefore much more than a formula for resolving possibly short-term economic problems in a specific industry. For its supporters, it would be the first step in a broader programme which, economic sector by economic sector, would remove national economic barriers in Europe. From there it would be but a short step towards some form of political union. It is in that sense that the Schuman Plan can be regarded as the basis of future discussions on how European integration should be organised. It allowed for a transitional period of five years to deal with the problems and difficulties that would inevitably arise, and to permit the industries within each country to rationalise themselves and come to terms with a radically different situation.

In some ways the ECSC was the outcome of committed Europeans occupying positions of authority in several countries: in addition to Schuman and Monnet in France, it was supported by Konrad Adenauer in West Germany, Paul-Henri Spaak in Belgium, and Alcide de Gasperi in Italy. Britain refused an invitation to join the new organisation, being unwilling to accept beforehand the principle of a new and binding supranational authority. Only six states – France, West Germany, Italy, the Netherlands, Belgium and Luxembourg – were to sign in 1951 the treaty which in April 1952 formally established the ECSC. In some ways it was a Christian Democrat achievement: all six foreign ministers who signed the treaty were Christian Democrats. The foundation of the ECSC marks the first significant step towards European union that went beyond being merely consultative and intergovernmental in character: Jean Monnet hailed it as 'the first expression of the Europe that is being born'. It set the tone of a debate which in the coming decade was to divide Western Europe, at the same time as setting in motion a groundswell that eventually produced the European Communities.

CHAPTER 8

FROM COLD WAR TO THAW

The attack upon Korea makes it plain beyond all doubt that communism has passed beyond the use of subversion to conquer independent nations and will now use armed invasion and war.   (*Harry Truman, 1950*)

The possibility and necessity of peaceful coexistence.
(*Georgiy M. Malenkov, 1955*)

In 1948, Western European interests had been submerged in the concern and anxieties caused by the Cold War and the possibility of a global conflict in which the continent would be the first to be destroyed. By early 1950 the worries about Soviet expansionism seemed to have receded. The American commitment of support enshrined in the Truman Doctrine had been made more concrete with the establishment of NATO, while Berlin, Yugoslavia and Greece seemed to indicate that there were limits to Soviet power, which had been checked everywhere since Czechoslovakia. With a greater semblance of order in their own houses, the Western European states could spare time to consider the possibility of further economic advance and cooperation. This air of relative optimism was abruptly dispelled in June 1950 with the outbreak of war on the Korean peninsula.

THE KOREAN WAR

The wartime Allies had been unable to agree upon a satisfactory solution for Korea, which Japan had absorbed decades earlier. Instead, they opted for the compromise of partition, drawing an artificial boundary along the thirty-eighth parallel between a Communist-dominated state to the north and a Western-oriented one to the south. This boundary had been a constant irritant to both Korean regimes. This local factor was perhaps sufficient reason why North Korean forces crossed the parallel in 1950 to invade the south. While the Soviet Union may have been doubtful about the exercise, it is improbable that Stalin had not at least tacitly approved the assault in advance. He may have misinterpreted previous American statements about their limited degree of

interest in Korea. More likely, the Soviet Union may have hoped that possession of the whole peninsula would provide a counterbalance to the provision
in the current peace treaty negotiations between the United States and Japan
for American bases to be maintained in the latter.

The United States immediately invoked the Truman Doctrine and resolved
to aid South Korea. It sought approval from the UN, which endorsed the
establishment of a UN force in South Korea under American command. The
endorsement was possible only because the Soviet delegate on the Security
Council had recently walked out in protest against the retention of China's
permanent seat on the Council by Nationalist China: there was not, therefore,
a Soviet veto on the Korean proposal. Although some Western European and
Commonwealth states sent contingents to Korea under the UN banner, the
defence of South Korea was primarily the concern of the United States, which
supplied the vast bulk of money, supplies and troops.

The Korean War was not simply an isolated war in a remote part of Asia.
It was the first open conflict between Communist and Western forces; previously, as in Greece, Communist aggression had been waged through internal
insurrection, not by the invading armies of a foreign state. The Western fear
was that the Soviet Union had not renounced ambitions of further conquest,
that having been baulked in Europe, it had turned to the more fluid situation
in Asia where it had already achieved a major success with the victory of the
Communist guerrillas in Korea's giant neighbour, China, in 1949.

The immediate fear was that Korea would escalate into a global conflict, in
much the same way as the Spanish Civil War had been a prologue to the
Second World War. For Western European governments the dilemma was
whether to press for a speedy repulsion of the invaders or whether the consequent hardening of the bipolarity between West and East would provoke
further armed clashes elsewhere – particularly in Europe where the division
of Germany was analogous to that in Korea. The first reaction, however, was
an increase of confidence in the United States. Despite American pledges, the
Truman Doctrine and NATO, there remained a lingering suspicion that in the
last resort the United States might not be prepared to take a firm stand, retreating back to 'Fortress America'. The determined American response in Korea
allayed such fears, and increased confidence in NATO as a satisfactory deterrent against a possible Soviet advance against Western Europe.

Confidence and relief soon changed into fear when the Korean War entered
into a different and more dangerous stage. The preponderance of American
military strength was ultimately sufficient to force the invaders back across
the thirty-eighth parallel. The United States, however, did not stop there and,
in turn, invaded North Korea. In addition, it was an open secret that in some
official American circles there were those who were pressing for a full-scale
attack on the North Korean supply lines in Manchuria, now part of Communist
China. Almost inevitably, this provoked a Chinese intervention, a supply of
'volunteers' to help their North Korean comrades. In reality, the volunteers
were members of the regular Chinese army.

The Chinese intervention and the Soviet-Chinese mutuality of Communist interest caused another world crisis. The fears in Europe of a direct clash with Communism on the continent itself were reawakened. The Western European governments were reluctant to become further involved in the Asian conflict: they saw little need to aggravate Soviet hostility as a direct consequence of a war in which they were not directly implicated. The one exception to this general mood was possibly France, whose military and economic resources were already being strained beyond their capacity in a losing battle against Communist and nationalist forces in French Indo-China. As time went on, it became clear that a military victory in Korea for either side could be achieved only if a worldwide confrontation brought about the defeat of one or the other of the two super-powers. Ironically, the emergence of Communist China on to the world stage presaged the end of the straightforward bipolarity of the 1940s, introducing a new threat to American interests in Asia and a new contender for the leadership of the Communist world. The Korean imbroglio was to remain unresolved until 1953.

MILITARY CONSEQUENCES: WEST GERMAN REARMAMENT

It was inevitable that war in Asia would affect domestic politics in Western Europe, most obviously in the military sphere. Korea had not just intensified the Cold War; it also placed an extra burden on American financial resources. The United States, faced with an allocation problem, began to think in terms of military rather than economic aid. In addition, American assistance to Europe was made conditional upon the promises and actions of the governments to strengthen and enlarge their own forces. Korea had made the American concept of containment a global concept. In American eyes the Soviet quest to utilise the great power status it had achieved during the Second World War to reshape the world in its own image had become a global quest. The Soviet Union therefore had to be contained all around its perimeters. To counteract the Soviet superiority in conventional forces, American thinking led by 1954 to the notion of massive retaliation: a large-scale nuclear response against Soviet territory would be the consequence of any Soviet attempt, no matter how localised, to break out of its containment.

More than ever, the United States had become the world's policeman: its resources, vast though they were, were spread more thinly. Its review of its defence commitments led the United States to the conclusion that in the event of a military confrontation with the Soviet Union in Europe, the existing strength of the Atlantic alliance, expressed through NATO, was insufficient. Seeing no need why it alone should be expected to make up the deficit, the American argument went further to state that if the European members of NATO were unwilling or unable to strengthen NATO, then this could be achieved by permitting West Germany to rearm. With increasing persistence, the American government argued that West Germany should be brought into the Western defensive alliance with its own military forces.

Yet another of the decisions of the wartime Allies bowed to the force of postwar exigencies, although pressure for West German rearmament had, in fact, begun before the outbreak of war in Korea. Disarmament had already been flouted in the DDR with the raising of a 'people's police force' which, despite all protestations to the contrary, was seen as the nucleus of a projected East German army. In West Germany there were worries that this might be the prelude to an invasion of the Federal Republic by a 'liberation' movement to reunite Germany without direct Soviet involvement. These worries were reinforced by the comparisons made between Germany and Korea. Adenauer had already suggested that West Germany should be allowed the means of defending itself, and that the surest way of winning the population over to a massive commitment to democracy was to give it an equal stake in the responsibility of defending Western Europe. Otherwise, he argued, many Germans might be seduced by the lure of a neutral, but unified Germany which would, however, be essentially within the Soviet sphere of influence.

Although it was hardly disputable that a West German contribution to NATO would be invaluable, especially as the other countries did not wish to, or could not, meet the new levels of requirement set by the United States, this American demand still appeared to come as something of a surprise, particularly to France. After 1945, France's primary objective had been the prostration of Germany: it had continued to seek to absorb the Saar, and in many ways it would have been content with a divided Germany. The French claims to the Saar were strongly disputed by West Germany, and despite the commitment of both to the Schuman Plan, relations between the two states were not entirely cordial. A rearmed Germany merely served to arouse all the old fears about French security.

But to all West Germany's neighbours, the idea of a German military force only a few years after the defeat of Hitler's armies was still repugnant. On the other hand, it seemed obvious that the United States would not back down; and Western Europe was still heavily dependent upon the United States. An American economic and military withdrawal from Europe would leave it highly vulnerable. Although President Truman had admitted that it was in the American interest to participate in a European defensive alliance, many Europeans did not wish to provoke the United States into thinking about withdrawal. The European problem was not to oppose the American proposal adamantly, but to find some compromise that would both satisfy the United States and assuage the fears of a revived German militarism. The shackling of a German military contribution to NATO would have to be achieved by placing it under non-German control. Moreover, whatever the course adopted, it would have to receive the blessing of Germany's traditional enemy, France, for it to have any chance of success.

It was France which eventually offered a novel way out of the impasse. Taking ECSC as an example, it suggested a pooling of military resources, a European army (an idea, however, that had already been floated in the Council of Europe). In that way there would be no distinct German army under a separate German command. This idea was the basis of the proposed European Defence Community (EDC). Once again, because of the reluctance of Britain and the Scandinavian members of NATO to become too closely involved with any creation that hinted at the abrogation of sovereignty, it was taken up only by the six states which had formed the ECSC. All that remained was its ratification by the several national parliaments.

At first glance it seemed that the vision of Monnet and Schuman of European unity coming about gradually by the creation of a range of sectoral supranational bodies that bound the participants ever closer together was one important step nearer realisation. The EDC may have superficially followed this pattern, but its fundamental implications were different. ECSC consisted of six equal partners. EDC had been suggested and was designed as a means of preventing German military parity, in contrast to the implications of the original American suggestion of a West German military contribution to NATO. The plan was for the other five EDC members to allocate only a proportion of their armed forces to the European army: the West German contribution to EDC, by contrast, was to be almost the total sum of its military resources.

This limiting specification did not altogether allay the fears in Europe about Germany. There was still a strong anti-German sentiment in Western Europe. Even in West Germany itself, opinions were deeply divided. A strong anti-militarist streak had emerged in Germany after 1945. Furthermore, it was felt in many circles that the risks involved in rearmament were too great and might well make Germany the primary battlefield in any possible conflict. The opposition SPD was opposed to the whole idea, fearing that by tying West Germany closer to the Western ideological camp, it might jeopardise any opportunity for reunification. Adenauer and the CDU, however, were firmly in favour of EDC. Adenauer believed that the best way forward to reunification was for West Germany to be in a position of strength and superiority *vis-à-vis* the DDR, and that that could be achieved if the Federal Republic were to be accepted on equal terms by the Western world. For Adenauer, German participation in EDC, even though on unequal terms, was an important step in the right direction. Moreover, his government relied more heavily upon the United States than probably any other Western government. When the United States suggested German rearmament, Adenauer therefore also supported it because of the wish to maintain a close accord with his country's main protector, and to keep the United States engaged in Europe.

Adenauer's views on the choice between reunification or the Western alliance were also influenced by the actions of the Soviet Union, which had not given up hope of neutralising West Germany and which inevitably was hostile to the idea of an armed West Germany within the Atlantic alliance. In March 1952 it reopened the German question by suggesting that the wartime Allies should meet to consider a peace treaty with Germany and the consequent reunification of the country. The Soviet proposal was designed not so much to appeal to Western leaders as to West German public opinion. Two factors meant that the Soviet Union was bargaining from a relatively weak position. A treaty signed in 1950 between the new East German state and Poland had confirmed the Oder–Neisse line as a *de jure* boundary, something that was still vehemently rejected in West Germany, which insisted that the territories east of the Oder–Neisse line were only under temporary Polish administration.

Similarly, West Germany was upset by the deaf ear the Soviet Union consistently turned to all appeals for free elections in the DDR: a UN commission appointed to study electoral procedures in the two Germanies was denied permission to enter the Eastern state. Against this background, the Soviet intervention had the reverse effect of strengthening Adenauer's policies and West German support for the United States. Adenauer was equally firm in his rejection of a second Soviet offer on possible reunification in 1954.

The Western leaders themselves placed little credence in Soviet sincerity. In their reply to the 1952 proposal, the foreign ministers of the United States, Britain and France clearly indicated that they thought it was motivated entirely by a desire to prevent EDC. By implication, the reply also demonstrated that the West had shelved indefinitely any hope of a *rapprochement* with the Soviet Union, and hence also of German reunification. The American doctrine of containment, coupled with the obsessive fears of the numerical superiority of Soviet conventional forces, made the loss of one-third of the prewar German state less important than the desire to strengthen their own alliance. However, while EDC might enable German militarism to be supervised and contained, it could not remove completely the suspicions of Germany's neighbours: all it did was to create a new variant of the German problem.

Even if it had been put into force, the whole operation might well have run into such innumerable difficulties as to render it unworkable. But it never escaped from the drawing board. The French proposition, in fact, had not perhaps been intended to further the cause of integration. The logic behind it had been to prevent an independent German military force, even perhaps to delay indefinitely any West German rearmament. Taken aback somewhat by the rapidity with which the idea was embraced by the other proposed members and their willingness to ratify the treaty, French governments were extremely reluctant to submit it for ratification in France. The rearmament issue was highly controversial; nor was there much enthusiasm for EDC. The governments, even if not themselves doubtful of the project, knew that they were too fragile to force the treaty through an immobilist and fragmented National Assembly. From its inception until 1954, the EDC treaty was a sword of Damocles hanging over French politics, albeit only one of the many problems that afflicted government. The parties of the narrow centre sector, from which all governments had to be drawn, were agreed only on the fundamental issue of preserving the Republic: they had reserved their right to disagree on anything else. The consequence was inertia; no controversial issue could ever hope to be resolved satisfactorily, so governments, almost wholly preoccupied with survival, merely tended to forget about them or postpone them to some indeterminate future date. This may have ultimately led to the downfall of the EDC, but it did not provide an answer to German rearmament.

TOWARDS DÉTENTE AND BALANCE

In 1953 the climate of international affairs shifted considerably, and this necessarily affected political developments in Western Europe. The year saw a lessening of the acute tension which had marked the Cold War since its inauguration some six years earlier. For Western Europe the import of this thaw in American-Soviet relations was a belief that the threat of a direct military confrontation of the two super-powers on the continent had receded significantly. The four events which together made a major contribution to this climatic change were the ending of the Korean War, the American presidential election of 1952, the death of Stalin, and the acquisition by the Soviet Union of the hydrogen bomb.

The Korean War was as yet the only open sore on the globe in which the two super-powers were, in one way or another, directly involved and committed. But by 1952 it had become apparent that short of total war, there could not be a military settlement in Korea. The conflict had degenerated into an uneasy but absolute stalemate where neither side was willing to pour in its full resources: in particular, President Truman had vigorously vetoed pressure from some of his generals to use nuclear weapons. Even so, it seemed that a negotiated settlement could not come until there was a change in the American presidency; the Soviet Union refused to negotiate with President Truman and what it called his 'war-mongering' party.

The Republican Party, after twenty years in the political wilderness, thus had a golden opportunity to use the promise of peace in Korea, which most Americans wanted, in their 1952 election campaign. Coming on top of their good fortune in obtaining Dwight Eisenhower, the supreme Allied commander in the Second World War and later of NATO, and the country's most popular military figure, as their presidential candidate, this put the Republicans in an almost invincible position. After the expected victory duly occurred, President Eisenhower proceeded to honour his electoral promise of negotiating a peace in Korea, emphasised by a symbolic trip to the war-torn country. After nearly three years of conflict, the result was the not unexpected one of a return to the original partition boundary of the thirty-eighth parallel.

The Korean settlement was only one aspect of a changed emphasis in American foreign policy. The Republican Party had traditionally been less concerned about involvement overseas, being more closely identified with the 'isolationist impulse' which had a long and proud tradition in the United States. Although there was no question of a withdrawal from Europe – for example, the Republicans continued to press hard for German rearmament – there was a less intense concern with European affairs. Many European leaders welcomed this change in American foreign policy. For one thing, they felt that Eisenhower, who had twice been their military commander, could be trusted not to treat the European commitment too lightly. On the other hand, their improving economies were leading Western European states towards a feeling that they ought to have more political independence, that the continent should not cling so closely to American coat-tails. If the United States had maintained the same high degree of involvement in European affairs as in the 1940s, the mid-1950s might well have seen several clashes of will between the two sides of the Atlantic. As it was, such a disagreement was delayed until de Gaulle re-emerged in France as the champion of an old-fashioned pride in nationalism and anti-American resentment.

Correspondingly, the threat of the Soviet Union seemed to recede sharply with the announcement in Moscow of Stalin's death in 1953. In his last years, the Soviet dictator appeared to lose that shrewdness which had marked his long political career. In a state bordering on paranoia, his suspicions and ruthlessness increased greatly. His lieutenants were never certain of being able to avoid accusations of treachery or of anticipating what abrupt changes Stalin would decree in Soviet policy. Because of this aura of uncertainty, there had been, as it were, a built-in fuse which at any moment might ignite a major international conflict, notwithstanding the acknowledged nuclear lead of the United States.

Stalin's successors appeared to be more aware of the dangers to the Soviet Union of a nuclear war, and hence seemed more reluctant to pursue a policy of brinkmanship. The so-called thaw which in future years would ebb and flow regularly, in part according to the Soviet analysis of the current international situation, was not so much the outcome of a renunciation of the messianic aims of Communism; rather it was an indication that the new Soviet leaders felt that their interests and their competition with the West could be pursued by safer methods.

This did not mean that the Soviet Union was willing to relax its hegemonic grip upon Eastern Europe. In June 1953, demonstrations in East Berlin over the introduction of higher work norms turned into riots and a full-scale protest against the Communist regime. While the decree was rescinded, the protests continued to the point where the rebellion might successfully reject Soviet influence. Thereupon the Soviet Union, which at first had refrained from action, swiftly deployed military units to re-establish authority. Similarly, in Hungary in October 1956, demonstrations turned overnight into a revolt against the regime itself. Within a week the old hard-line leadership had gone, but the new leaders went too far in their stated intention to become a neutral state, albeit remaining Communist. The Soviet Union was not prepared to tolerate such a disruption to its security system: after an initial hesitation, it moved in to quell the revolt. These two abortive uprisings, following the pattern established during the Berlin blockade, again demonstrated that the Soviet Union was not willing to yield up any of its *de facto* control in Europe, its acceptance in 1955 of the end of four-power control in Austria notwithstanding. Similarly, the United States was not prepared to intervene east of the iron curtain as long as this involved the risk of world war.

Nevertheless, the new Soviet declaration of peaceful co-existence with the West did allow Western Europe to breathe more freely. Oddly enough, the knowledge that the Soviet Union possessed the hydrogen bomb produced a similar effect: the news was received calmly in Western Europe, unlike the situation in 1949 when the first Soviet atomic explosion was hysterically regarded almost as a declaration of war. As interpreted by many European observers, the essence of the new situation was that the Soviet technological advance, in reducing American nuclear superiority, brought with it stalemate. Neither side could ignore the risk of massive and instantaneous nuclear retaliation. Peace and accommodation thus became more imperative and, paradoxically, more probable.

The symbol of the new 'understanding' between East and West was the 1955 summit conference in Geneva, suggested by the West and accepted by the Soviet Union. The control of nuclear weapons and the German question were the main items on the agenda. A month earlier, Adenauer had visited Moscow, a visit which had established diplomatic and trade relations between the two countries. Geneva did not substantially add to this. The Soviet Union rejected West German rearmament, which the West argued was necessary to counter-act Soviet conventional superiority, and sought the removal of American bases from Europe. For its part, the United States was not prepared to go along with an unconditional ban on nuclear weapons without adequate provisions for inter-national inspection, a proviso the Soviet Union did not accept. Although the Soviet Union did relax its stance on some European issues – easing its pressure on Finland, accepting the restoration of Austrian sovereignty, and recognising the non-aligned status of Yugoslavia – no broad conclusions were reached at Geneva: only a supreme optimist would have expected otherwise. Yet the con-ference was significant. It was the first time since Potsdam, ten years earlier, that Soviet and American leaders had met face to face. The fact that the two sides could sit at the same table seemed to indicate an agreement that short of total war, an 'unstable peace' was the only way out of the nuclear stalemate.

Western European democracy, which had felt under the threat of war virtu-ally since 1945, readily adapted itself to rather better conditions. A new polit-ical vigour, boosted by economic growth and prosperity, conduced a more optimistic mood of self-confidence. On its feet at last, Western Europe felt for the first time that it was capable of holding its own in the changed postwar world, though for the remaining colonial powers, especially Britain and France, there would be a painful and somewhat delayed acceptance of their demotion as world powers. Consequently, both the United States and the Soviet Union were to find it more difficult to direct or influence the course of political affairs in Western Europe. Only of government circles in West Germany might it be said, sometimes unjustly, that there was an undue willingness to follow Amer-ican proposals: but West Germany's particular dilemma was unique in Western Europe. However, both major powers would continue to play an important role in Western Europe. The Soviet Union was still interested in prising it apart from the United States, while the latter, as long as it made the major input into Western defence, would have a voice that could not be entirely ignored.

MILITARY SOLUTIONS: EDC, WEU AND NATO

The purely military imperatives which had hitherto dominated Western foreign policy did not now seem to possess the same urgency. The thaw in the inter-national climate inevitably affected the fate of the proposed EDC, which still awaited ratification. The relaxation of tension permitted France, the original sponsor of EDC, a way out of the dilemma it had created for itself. It seemed that if the EDC treaty collapsed, the protests from France's allies, including the United States, might not be as vehement as they would have been one year earlier.

But there was another facet of the military problem. In American strategic circles, Truman's policy of containment had been expanded to incorporate the concept of roll-back, a more aggressive posture which implied that the United States was not prepared simply to sit back and only react to Soviet pressure. Truman's Democrat administration had believed that the ideological mission of Communism was as dangerous as its military threat, and had concentrated just as much on the political aspects of the Cold War: containment had essentially been a policy that operated simultaneously on political, ideological and military fronts.

The new Secretary of State, John Foster Dulles, who in many ways was more important than President Eisenhower as the architect of American foreign policy in the 1950s, was convinced that the military aspect overwhelmed everything else, that the Cold War as played by the Soviet Union was just a new variant of traditional power politics. He believed that the United States should avoid another Korea, but that where confrontation was unavoidable, then the venue should be picked by and be favourable to the United States. From this thinking, there developed the concept of massive retaliation.

The effects of American foreign policy were paradoxical. There was a tendency to prefer remaining more aloof from foreign contact, yet simultaneously seeking to project a more positive and aggressive image. This side of American policy was not calculated to appeal to Europeans. For EDC, to which the United States was committed, it tended to strengthen the opposition. In particular, in France, which held the key to EDC, no politician could take kindly to American pressure or interference in domestic politics on behalf of the treaty. Dulles' accusation in late 1953 of 'dilatory manoeuvres', and the later threat of an 'agonising reappraisal' by the United States of its foreign commitments, made it even more unlikely that a French government would be able to push the EDC treaty through the National Assembly.

The French premier who eventually unlocked the dilemma was Pierre Mendès-France. A member of the influential Radical Party and a man who commanded substantial personal loyalty, he had been a strong critic of previous governments. He wanted to inaugurate a programme of domestic economic reform and expansion. First, however, he had to remove from the agenda two pressing crises which had crippled French political life: the colonial war in Indo-China and the EDC issue. Mendès-France successfully negotiated a French withdrawal from Indo-China and then, one month later, in August 1954, he brought the EDC treaty to the National Assembly, assured of certain defeat. However, since the original military justification had almost disappeared, and because the compromise had never really been acceptable to France, Mendès-France did not even attempt to defend it. It was simply introduced as a hindrance that had to be disposed of before other business could be tackled: the vote, negative as expected, was not on the treaty itself but simply on whether it should be debated.

This procedural tactic was the burial ceremony of EDC. In addition to disrupting the plans for the Western defence system, it was a setback to the hopes and ambitions for a more united Europe. The United States had continued to base its conception of Western defence upon the increased resources which a West German contribution would provide. Some alternative to EDC had to be found. The search was remarkably brief. All else failing, Western Europe fell back, with British encouragement, upon the 1948 Treaty of Brussels, the defensive pact signed by Britain and four of the proposed members of EDC. Britain had refused anything but an association with EDC, but felt that a revamped version of the 1948 agreement would be sufficiently diluted of supranational overtones to permit it to participate as an equal partner.

Britain had originally objected to the EDC proposal for several reasons. Looking at the wider implications of an Atlantic community, it had felt that EDC would adversely affect a successful overall integration within NATO. Britain had also argued that the time lag that would elapse between proposal and implementation would not satisfy the immediate need for a West German contribution. Far more important were the British suspicions about being pushed into a federalist Europe and of being left to hold the burden of European defence because the United States was seeking to lighten its own responsibilities. At the time of the original proposal in 1950, the British Labour government had also been wary of participation in any structure that would be dominated by Christian Democrats. But the menacing shadow of Stalin had forced Britain to swallow several scruples and move closer to both Europe and American demands.

In 1955 it was the Conservative premier, Anthony Eden, who took the lead in salvaging something from the wreck of EDC. He took the opportunity to bring forward again the British view that West German rearmament could easily be achieved and supervised within NATO itself. Konrad Adenauer, who saw rearmament as an indispensable part of his own Western-oriented policy of strength, quickly fell into line behind Eden, and the others followed shortly thereafter. In order to soften any possible clash between France and West Germany, it was agreed that British participation in the new body, to be called Western European Union (WEU), would involve the stationing of British troops in West Germany unless a majority of the Brussels signatories, now expanded to include the Federal Republic and Italy, consented to their withdrawal.

An independent structure for the new organisation was out of the question. It was too weak to support one and, in any case, Britain would almost certainly refuse to commit itself to anything that smacked of supranationalism. Rather than leave it out on a limb, it was decided that its interests would best be served by direct incorporation within NATO, while national delegates to the Council of Europe would act as its Consultative Assembly. At last the United States had achieved its aim of levying a German military contribution, while Adenauer had moved another step forward in his ambition to have West Germany fully accepted as an equal partner of the other Western democracies. Ironically, the failure of EDC led to what France had most desired to avoid: the creation of a German army.

Apart from advancing German claims for equality, the WEU structure achieved no significant results. It was occasionally activated in the 1950s, but proposals on defence from its Consultative Assembly were invariably ignored by the member governments. Essentially a paper organisation, it remained moribund until the 1980s. France, which had left NATO in the 1960s and had previously suggested in the 1970s that WEU might provide a link between it and NATO, proposed its reactivation in 1981, again as a liaison body. After 1984, it presented an emerging European voice on defence issues distinct from a NATO position at a time when it seemed that the two super-powers might actually manage to reach an agreement on levels of nuclear armaments; by 1987 the Netherlands could suggest that WEU was an appropriate body which might, for the first time, seek a common European position on a non-European issue, the Iran–Iraq war and the deepening Persian Gulf crisis. The rehabilitation of WEU continued into the 1990s, stimulated by the ending of the Cold War and a consequent feeling that a more coherent European defence voice might be desirable given the prevailing uncertainty about what the future role of NATO might be after the disappearance of its defined foe, the Soviet Union. In addition, the Maastricht Treaty on European Union identified WEU as the potential defence and security arm of the new European Union, although that was a view that was not shared by all the EU member states.

It was the nuclear issue which in the 1950s had rendered WEU irrelevant. The development of Soviet nuclear capacity had very largely invalidated much of the strategic thinking on the defence of Western Europe: it was improbable that war in Europe could now be fought only with conventional ground troops. It had to be assumed that the temptation to play the nuclear card could well be overwhelming. In the later 1950s the United States and NATO had to reconsider the role and organisation of the latter. On the other hand, NATO had gone beyond its original geographical confines in 1952 when Greece and Turkey joined the organisation. With West German accession in 1955, the United States had maximised the territorial reach of NATO. Apart from the self-declared neutral states, only Spain remained outside, though American bases were set up there in 1953. Spain finally joined in 1982.

AN ILLUSION OF DÉTENTE?

The Geneva summit of 1955 symbolised the spirit of détente in the mid-1950s. Its major contribution was the indication that the two super-powers were willing to talk to each other, that they were beginning to grasp that, despite everything, they might have interests in common, and that they were willing to explore and expand that common ground. In the years that were to come, despite all the false hopes and reversals back to antagonism, the United States and the Soviet Union were willing to continue the dialogue begun at Geneva, though not always at the highest political level. While the United States might often consult with its European allies and report on results, Western Europe was essentially an observer of the dialogue. This was the other side of a less frenetic international atmosphere: a worry that the dialogue might present Western Europe with a *fait accompli* that, among other things, might expose it to greater Soviet influence as the result of a reduction of the American military presence in and commitment to Europe.

On the whole, this first exercise in summit diplomacy had no marked effect upon the European divide: indeed, Geneva was not concerned with changes to the postwar European reality. While the summit may have been preceded by Soviet concessions in Austria and Finland, the repression in Hungary one year later demonstrated the limits of Soviet tolerance in Europe. While the manoeuvrability of the Western powers was limited by their disputes over the Anglo-French Suez episode of a few months earlier, the lack of a positive Western response to Hungary nevertheless indicated that the West was not prepared to cross the iron curtain. Nor, however, was it prepared to risk giving up the strong defensive network it had constructed in the late 1940s. In short, the diplomatic initiatives that led to Geneva were not designed to unfreeze what the Cold War had produced in Europe, but rather for each super-power to persuade the other to accept the *status quo*. Future initiatives, such as the 1957 Rapacki Plan, named after the Polish foreign minister, for a demilitarised zone in Central Europe, stumbled on the same stony ground. However, beginning in 1958, Geneva became the home of an ongoing series of conferences which looked at ways of controlling nuclear tests and eliminating the possibility of surprise nuclear attacks: they bore fruit in 1963 with the signing of a test ban treaty.

If peaceful co-existence were to survive, it would be a more complex and difficult objective than that envisaged by the spirit of the mid-1950s. The United States still regarded itself as a world policeman and continued to pursue a policy of containment, albeit in different guises. For its part, the Soviet Union detested the ring which the United States sought to place around its borders, and strove for world influence. Both sides therefore continued to probe each other's weaknesses. The model for the future, if there was one, would be Korea, with each employing client states as surrogates – classically in the 1960s, Cuba for the Soviet Union and South Vietnam for the United States. In Europe, however, the battlelines were firmly drawn; only Berlin remained as an anomaly.

By the end of the decade, Soviet diplomacy had become more aggressive. In Europe the major target was Berlin. Twice, in 1958 and 1961, the new Soviet leader, Nikita Khrushchev, tested the West over the fate of the city. The second crisis produced the final confirmation of the complete division of Europe: the building of the Berlin Wall in August 1961. Emboldened by the limited Western response in Berlin, which in the end attacked the Wall only verbally, Khrushchev was encouraged to test his luck further afield, a venture which culminated in the Cuban missile crisis of 1962. The point is that a declaration by both sides that they believed in peaceful co-existence did not automatically produce a peacefully co-existing world. Instead, the two super-powers pulled the world towards a new possible war scenario. Soviet assertiveness may well have been encouraged by its launching into orbit, in October 1957, of the first 'Sputnik'. The Soviet satellite shook the American belief in the unassailability of its own technological superiority. It contributed to a massive increase in American arms expenditure under President Kennedy after 1960. Above all, Sputnik heralded the era of the ground-to-ground intercontinental missile. Once the two super-powers had acquired an arsenal of such weapons, the era of reciprocal deterrence had definitely arrived, ending the utility of massive retaliation. This would have implications not only for the style of American-Soviet relations, but also for the nature of the American relationship with Western Europe, where it produced doubts about the willingness of the United States to continue its European commitment in a nuclear situation where its own cities and homeland would be exposed to a nuclear attack.

CHAPTER 9

THE ROAD TO ROME

> Those who drew up the Rome Treaty . . . did not think of it as essentially
> economic; they thought of it as a stage on the way to political union. . . . If
> [it is] bound to happen, so much the better; but it is wiser to work steadily
> and urgently to make [it] happen.
>
> (*Paul-Henri Spaak, Council of Europe Consultative Assembly, 15th
> Ordinary Session (1964) Deb. iii, p. 596*)

The ECSC treaty was signed by representatives of the Netherlands, Belgium,
Luxembourg, France, Italy and West Germany in 1951. Ratification took a
further year to complete. One reason why ECSC succeeded relatively easily in
escaping from the drawing board was the strong Christian Democrat presence
in all six governments in the crucial 1950–52 period. However, the ECSC proposals were supported by most parties, though for different reasons: perhaps
only in the Netherlands can we speak of a party consensus on the reasons for
support. Opposition was most vocal in West Germany, where Schumacher's
SPD argued against it on nationalist grounds, and France, where de Gaulle's
description of it as a directionless 'mish-mash' was backed by the ideological
opposition of the Communists. The broad support it did receive was perhaps
possible because it was rather inchoate: the vague and ambiguous terms of the
treaty permitted it to be interpreted in different ways. In that sense, ECSC was
a child of a specific coalition of interests. As later events were to prove, there
was no guarantee that this constellation would persist over time or even continue to support moves towards integration.

THE SECTOR MODEL

The treaty schedule was for a five-year transitional period of two distinct
stages. ECSC would first have to demolish tariffs and other trade restrictions
before it could move on to establish a free common market. The programme
could only be achieved under the supervision of a supranational authority
with the necessary powers to determine what the policies of the member states
ought to be.

99

The overseeing institution was to be the nine-man High Authority, with not more than two representatives from any one member state. Their term of office of six years was staggered to provide continuity, with one-third retiring every two years. Its authority ranged from recommendations to binding decisions taken by a majority vote, positively by directing investment and controlling both prices and production, negatively by punishing those who ignored its decisions. Hence the significance of the High Authority was its ability to influence the national coal and steel industries without being countermanded by national governments. This was the fundamental supranational element in the ECSC.

Yet the High Authority was far from being a sovereign body. It was paralleled as an executive by the Special Council of Ministers, insisted upon by the Benelux countries as a means of defending the interests of the smaller participants. Its members came from the national governments and had the task of counterbalancing the High Authority's supranationalism. On the other hand, the governments were constrained somewhat because they did not directly finance ECSC. Funding was received by the High Authority, which levied a tax upon coal and steel production directly from the firms concerned.

A further constraint upon the High Authority, though less potent or practicable, was to be offered by a Common Assembly, the first international parliament with legally guaranteed powers, and designed to be the repository of ultimate control. This did not materialise. The Assembly was not a true legislative body. Its significance rested upon its ability to censure the High Authority and to demand its collective resignation, a blunt sanction that was never to be applied. Two further checks upon arbitrary High Authority action were offered by the avenues of law and public opinion. The Court of Justice of ECSC would rule on the legality of any High Authority action on the basis of complaints submitted by either national governments or private enterprises. At the outset, ECSC tended to move cautiously rather than jeopardise expansion of the European ideal by alienating public opinion. This was reinforced by the tendency of national governments not to handle unpopular decisions if they could be transferred to the High Authority. In the longer run, this practice strengthened the latter in its relationship with the member governments.

Caution and the ambiguity of the treaty made for some slow progress. In 1955, for instance, Belgian coal and Italian steel still enjoyed national protection, while even by the end of the transitional period French government discrimination and obstruction in its subsidisation policies meant that the French coal industry still remained to all intents and purposes outside the common ECSC structure. Despite such problems of national differences, the ECSC experiment was something of an economic success. By 1958 much trade discrimination had been eliminated, and both production and the volume of trade had greatly expanded. While it still struggled with the painful problem of modernisation in the coal industry, its economic statistics compared extremely favourably with those of other countries. However, it failed in its first real test, a crisis of overproduction and falling demand in the coal industry in 1959. The High Authority, which as a supranational body was intended to handle precisely that kind of crisis, could not prevent the member states from unilaterally introducing their own measures.

While the economic record was rather mixed, ECSC had not been intended just to be an economic body. For people like Schuman and Monnet, it was to be the first unit in an interlocking sectoral integration that would ultimately fulfil the dream of political unification. Superficially, not much seemed to have been achieved in this direction. ECSC had not conditioned the European public in favour of supranationalism, nor had it successfully established an unambiguous authority over national governments and parliaments. Nevertheless, it did create a European ambience, particularly through an alliance of High Authority and Assembly. Far from restraining the former, the Assembly constantly urged it to make even greater supranational efforts. And within the Assembly itself, political formations began to coalesce along party rather than national lines, a practice encouraged by the official recognition of, and payment of administrative expenses to, transnational party groupings.

In addition, ECSC stimulated other developments. Since 1945, pro-Europeans had tended to argue for a federal political system, which at some point would entail a single act of abrogation of national rights to a supranational authority, whose precedence over the former national units would be constitutionally defined. ECSC was not this type of institution. Its method of integration was to be more gradual, cultivating an atmosphere of mutual confidence through tackling a list of specific problems by specified deadlines. As the barriers fell, the institutions could move, with the consent of all participants, to a further list of commitments. In this, as well as in its structure, ECSC paved the way for the creation of the European Economic Community (EEC), with the same six members. Rationalisation came about in 1967 when the executive institutions of the three operating communities – ECSC, EEC, and Euratom – were merged into a single executive organ, creating overall the European Communities (EC).

FAILED COMMUNITIES

During the initial negotiations over ECSC, the international climate changed for the worse as conflict broke out in Korea. The subsequent reassessment by the United States of its global defensive and military commitments led, through its demand at a NATO meeting in 1950 for a West German military contribution, to the French proposal for a European Defence Community (EDC) as a way of precluding an independent West German army.

EDC was to be a military organisation, but for some it was also to be a further step along the road to European integration. Its structure was to be like that of the ECSC, though its supranational executive, a Board of Commissioners, would have considerably less leverage against the national representatives on the Council of Ministers. Unlike ECSC, it had been advanced as a body in which Britain might participate, which might partly account for the diluted supranational element. Again, unlike ECSC, it was not to be a partnership of equals. West Germany would be the poor relation, with its military units being placed under non-German command. Since it was expected that both the

United States and Britain would continue to station troops on the continent, not only as a token gesture against a possible Soviet invasion, but also as a guarantee against German militarism, EDC was as much an anti-German structure as an anti-Soviet one. Even if it had survived, it is a moot point how long this bias would have been tolerated by West Germany.

Notwithstanding these problems, there was reason to believe in late 1952 that the push towards integration had passed the critical threshold and so could only go forwards at a much faster pace. ECSC and EDC, it was believed, would finally consign the shibboleths of nationalism to a tardy grave. Having accepted that previous attempts to build a comprehensive Europe had failed through the effort to incorporate Britain into the design, it was believed that a multi-purpose unit could be built by the little Europe of the Six.

A principal source of the new enthusiasm was a problem raised by EDC itself, a dilemma summed up by Adenauer on his first visit to the United States in 1953, when he said that a European army would be somewhat illogical without a correspondingly unified European foreign policy. That would require an institutional framework and a more comprehensive political community. This was the reasoning which persuaded the foreign ministers of the Six to invite the ECSC Common Assembly to consider and report within six months on the feasibility and structure of a European Political Community (EPC).

EPC was not just to be a third community, but nothing less than the beginning of a full federation, to which ECSC and EDC would be subordinated. This, however, proved to be the high watermark of European union in the early 1950s. The pace and enthusiasm flagged considerably when attention had to switch from abstract designs to practical details. In the end, only ECSC seemed to have avoided the scrap-heap. A withdrawal from the frontier of full integration was noticeable in the further discussions of the six countries in the latter half of 1953, where the topic was debated only in very general terms.

However, the great argument of these years was not over EPC, but EDC; for EPC stood or fell with the ratification or rejection of EDC. The EDC treaty had not been ratified by anyone when the EPC treaty was published, though West Germany and the Low Countries did so early in 1954 – in the former only after a prolonged battle in which the SPD took its opposition all the way to the country's supreme court. In Italy, de Gasperi also faced formidable opposition, but was never obliged to put EDC to the test, preferring to defer the issue until French ratification. Thus the fate of the new Europe hinged upon France, the original proposer of EDC. France had never been enthusiastic about EDC, regarding it at a minimum merely as the lesser of two evils; moreover, since 1950 the more pro-European parties in France had lost support, and government survival at the best of times was problematical. The other interested states, notably Britain and the United States, were unsympathetic towards the domestic French ramifications of the treaty and, ultimately, it was allowed to sink without trace – and with it went EPC.

The EDC concept was perhaps too idealistic to have great hopes of concrete achievement. In its implications for European integration, EDC was something of a paradox. Ideally, the sensitive area of defence should be one of the last spheres for the renunciation of national sovereignty, needing behind it a solid background of integrative experience and mutual trust. Realistically, then, EDC should have come later in that chain of integrating communities envisaged by Schuman and Monnet. The damage done to the cause of integration was severe. Only ECSC survived, but even it did not entirely escape the shockwaves. Jean Monnet announced his decision not to seek re-election as President of the High Authority: he planned to pursue integrative schemes as a private citizen. Almost simultaneously, de Gasperi died. Schuman was no longer central to French politics. The forces of federation were in disarray, and at the time one conclusion drawn was that the whole momentum of European integration was grinding to a halt.

NEW DEPARTURES

Despite the mood of despondency that seemed to shroud the whole idea of European unity in 1954, there was nevertheless a wide array of international cooperative bodies in which the European democracies were involved: the Council of Europe, OEEC, WEU. Above these, as beacons for ardent federalists, there were the working examples of economic integration of Benelux and ECSC. Further afield there was the Scandinavian venture into closer cooperation, the Nordic Council, launched in 1952. Western Europe had come a long way since 1945, so the crucial question was not whether the integrative urge had foundered completely, but finding a context into which its energies could be channelled.

World events following the fall of EDC conspired to make Europeans more aware of Europe as an entity. The uprisings in East Germany and Hungary, and the abortive Suez expedition of 1956, were further rude reminders of the contraction of Europe's world role. A similar lesson was being drawn from the surge of nationalism in Africa and Asia, which precipitated the end of the colonial era and which geographically entailed a retreat back to Europe. Furthermore, for a while at least, peaceful co-existence seemed to permit a greater air of relaxation. Taken together, all these factors allowed more time for a consideration of Europe, especially since the democracies were enjoying an economic prosperity which tended to demote the urgency of specific national problems.

The question of whether integration could proceed beyond a limited sectoral level was answered three years later by the Treaty of Rome. Perhaps one prime motive for European unity in the first postwar decade had been the anxieties caused by the proximity and strength of the Soviet Union. As long as this fear persisted, national differences and prejudices were partially submerged under the protective cloak of defensive unity. When this feeling of pressure eased after the death of Stalin, these differences were forced out into the open, and integration could be discussed with a more honest and constructive estimation of its own intrinsic value. The advocacy of peaceful co-existence from the two super-powers and its own new economic confidence allowed Western Europe to examine more critically its relationship with the United States. Some suspicions had been aroused by Dulles' threat of an 'agonising reappraisal' during the EDC crisis. In 1956, further worries were awakened by the American reaction to the prolonged Suez episode, although few countries themselves were willing to endorse the Anglo-French attitude and subsequent invasion of Egypt. The American stance, plus the knowledge that long-range strike and retaliatory weapons were on the horizon, caused some concern about the level at which the United States would be prepared to maintain its overseas commitments. While a defence arrangement outside NATO was never on the agenda after EDC, such interpretations of world affairs helped Western Europe to consider more positive ways of cooperation without excessive reliance upon outside assistance.

Protagonists of unity may have been despondent about the loss of EDC and EPC, but were not routed. Benelux, with Paul-Henri Spaak at the forefront, took the lead in urging new departures. And even before the EDC reverberations had died down, the ECSC Common Assembly was pressing for the establishment of a committee to explore means of further integration – not the more ambitious political union of a EPC, but the more realistic economic integration of a common market. After leaving the ECSC, Monnet had formed an Action Committee for the United States of Europe in 1955. With Monnet's prestige behind it, this Committee enjoyed a considerable membership throughout the Europe of the Six and across the political spectrum. More specifically, it helped to remove the deep wedge which EDC had driven into the French Socialist Party, and was partly instrumental in the conversion of the West German SPD to integration.

The integration cause was also aided by the current pattern of international trade and the fact that the OEEC structure could not sponsor any forward movement without the consent of all its members. Hence there was a legitimate argument that could be used to spawn a common economic market, membership of which would be open to any willing OEEC signatory. The lines of division over political unity and economic integration versus association and cooperation had already been clarified and determined in the previous debates over the Council of Europe, ECSC and EDC. Thus it was not surprising that the initiative to take up again the idea of a common market, first raised by the Netherlands in 1952, was grasped only by the six countries of little Europe. In mid-1955 their foreign ministers met at Messina to launch 'a fresh advance towards the building of Europe', drafting a joint proposal for the pooling of information and work on the uses of atomic energy and for the establishment of a customs union that would lead to a common market. An intergovernmental committee headed by the tireless Spaak was formed to flesh out these schemes. Approval was given by the foreign ministers of the Six at subsequent meetings. Finally, the Spaak blueprint was revealed to public debate in March 1956 in a special session of the ECSC Common Assembly, where only one vote was registered against the proposal for a treaty establishing a customs union as a step towards a full economic community. The last preparatory act was governmental approval: meeting in Paris in February 1957, the six premiers reached agreement on the final points at dispute. The following month, two treaties, one establishing a European Economic Community and the other a European Atomic Energy Community, were duly signed by the Six in Rome and referred to the national parliaments for ratification. The most amazing point about the Rome treaty was the speed with which it was reached: only three years after the EDC reversal, European unity was set to take a giant leap forward.

The Six had reverted to Schuman's view that political union be achieved in the long run through a sustained effort at economic integration across a broad front. The sector-by-sector approach of the ECSC had proved too problematic: in the end it was still trying to integrate only one part of complex industrial economies, and could not possibly pursue its aims in isolation from other economic segments. The long-term perspective would also avoid a clash of economic interest with OEEC. Tariffs and trade restrictions were to be reduced only gradually, so allowing the Community to concur with the world agreement of GATT (General Agreement on Tariffs and Trade) to which the OEEC states belonged. Signatories of GATT could institute tariff changes which might discriminate against third parties only if done over a fairly long period of time, so giving those third parties the opportunity of adjusting to the change without severe economic disruption.

Hence the drive towards integration was caused by a conjunction of political and economic factors both inside and outside the Six. The EEC, while ambitious, was less revolutionary than EPC; it placed an economic cloak over the political goals, in a hope that it could accommodate as many interests and groups as possible. For some it might mean economic fulfilment, but the ultimate political goal was already implicit in the treaty's preamble with its desire 'to establish the foundations of an ever closer union among the European peoples'.

THE ECONOMIC COMMUNITY

After the fiasco of EDC, the French National Assembly was generally accepted as the place where the Treaty of Rome would stand or fall, particularly as the weak but long-lived Socialist government under Guy Mollet had departed and the Fourth Republic was entering its final prolonged crisis. In the event, the treaties easily overcame this baptism of fire, with the French parliament being the first to approve ratification. Finally, with ratification by the Dutch parliament in December 1957, the EEC and EURATOM were ready to operate.

The EEC began its existence with an Assembly meeting in Strasbourg in March 1958. Meeting in the home of the Council of Europe, it brought back memories of that body's inaugural session nearly ten years earlier; the same mood of excitement and sense of history was present. It called itself the European Parliamentary Assembly and symbolically arranged the seating of delegates by political orientation rather than nationality. The buoyancy of the moment led also to the rejection of the nominee of the six foreign ministers for the presidency of the Assembly; instead, they honoured one of the pioneers of integration by electing Robert Schuman to the post.

The provisions of the Treaty of Rome were inevitably complex, since the new organisation was to range over an extremely wide area of activity. Transformation into a common market was to be spread over a period of twelve to fifteen years, though there were disagreements over this timetable: France thought it too short, while others wanted to move faster. The treaty did not debar members from forming a smaller customs union, and this the Benelux states did in February 1958. But the treaty went beyond a simple customs union: the EEC was committed to the free movement of labour, capital, goods and services through the elimination of trade and other restrictions, a common investment policy, and the coordination and rationalisation of social welfare policy. However, several escape clauses permitted divergences in national policy on grounds of national security. Agriculture was designated as a special economic activity to be handled completely at the supranational level in a way that would be compatible both with EEC principles and the protection of national agricultural interests.

The institutions created to administer the work of the EEC were drawn from their ECSC predecessors. The supranational element was to be provided by the quasi-executive Commission of nine members appointed for renewable four-year terms by the member governments. West Germany, France and Italy were each entitled to two commissioners, the other states to one each. The Commission's primary responsibility would be to recommend and to administer the Treaty of Rome. Though in 1967 it also took over Euratom and ECSC, it was to have less scope than the ECSC High Authority to take decisions. The reason was that the latter had been given, once and for all, a large grant of power in a defined sector. The conception of Rome was different: it was a framework treaty covering a much wider area, where agreement by the drafting partners on everything would not have been possible. Nevertheless, the Commission was expected to be a dynamic element in the further moves towards European integration.

Paralleling the Commission was the Council of Ministers, the organ of the national governments, which was to carry the main burden of coordinating policies. A complex pattern of voting was drawn up for the Council, varying according to the nature and source of the proposal under discussion, and with the requirement ranging from simple majority, through qualified majority, to unanimity. It was, however, still possible for a member state to drag its heels and delay a programme. It was the ECSC experience which occasioned the change in the relationship between the supranational authority and the member governments. It had been learnt that progress could not be made if a member state objected to a particular part of a programme. The EEC structure was designed therefore to bring about a much closer collaboration between the Commission and Council. As in ECSC, the two executives were to be supported by a consultative committee made up of representatives of national interest groups.

The third major institution was the Parliamentary Assembly, which again enjoyed rights of consultation and recommendation. It had the ability, if there was a two-thirds vote of no confidence, to dismiss the Commission, but had no influence on the selection of a new one. Although it soon adopted the title of the European Parliament (EP), it possessed no real legislative authority, and a true parliament had still to come into existence. The final major institution was to be the Court of Justice, composed of seven judges appointed for re-newable six-year terms. The Court was given the responsibility for handling cases arising from the treaties or from disputes between members. In the last resort the interpretation of its verdicts would depend upon the national gov-ernments and the national court systems. It was not long, however, before the Court, against whose rulings there could be no appeal, would find against every government and against the Commission, quickly establishing itself as the guardian of the Community.

One problem raised by the creation of the EEC was the proliferation of institutions within Europe. A first rationalisation was achieved by making only one assembly serve ECSC, EEC and Euratom, though it was not until 1965 that the treaties were revised to provide for a single Commission and Council. The 1965 changes were the most significant constitutional development since 1957, bringing into being in 1967 the more integrated European Communities (EC).

The first test of the Treaty of Rome came in January 1959, when the prelim-inary stage of tariff reductions was due to go into operation. There was some apprehension not only because of the newness of the EEC, but also because of possible French recalcitrance. France, now governed by de Gaulle, but still preoccupied by a war in Algeria, did not, however, obstruct the deadline. Dur-ing the first few years of operation, progress was quite satisfactory. By 1961, internal tariff barriers had been substantially reduced and quota restrictions on industrial products had almost been eliminated. Trade within the EEC had increased at a rate double that of trade with non-members, and the new body had become the world's largest trading power. In effect, it seemed that notice had been served that the EEC was a successful operation. Other countries cer-tainly regarded it as such. In 1959, Greece and Turkey had already drawn this conclusion and had applied for some form of association with the EEC. And in 1961, Britain publicly changed its attitude towards the principles of the EEC.

In any event the EEC would not have been a viable proposition if it had run into serious trouble within a year or so of its launch. A hint of what might lie ahead could be gleaned from Benelux. The EEC was attempting to do within fifteen years what Benelux did in three, but it was only after that transitional period that Benelux had had to face up to serious difficulties. The wider scope of the EEC and its larger membership might well impose strains long before the end of the interim period. Yet paradoxically, this very scope demanded rapid resolution of such stresses, particularly as, by the end of the decade, it could be seen that a much greater momentum and will than that supplied solely by the Treaty of Rome would be required to push the Six firmly into full economic union and political unity.

BRITAIN IN THE WINGS

The great advance took place without British participation, since British accept-ance of the fundamental supranational element could not be given. In fact, in many ways Britain disapproved of the whole venture, though lending vocal encouragement to the idea of unity. The drive towards integration upset British conceptions about the relationship with Europe, no matter how outmoded the old concept of the balance of power might be. For those countries outside the Community club, Britain was the natural leader: many would be willing to follow the Six in their ventures if Britain were prepared to join. After the defeat of EDC, the British approach to Europe during the 1950s consisted of three phases: WEU, the 'Grand Design' and the European Free Trade Association (EFTA).

WEU, in many ways, was an irritant to Britain, placing upon it a burden as great as EDC membership might have done, with the pledge to maintain troops in Germany. In 1957, for example, when Britain decided to switch the basis of its defensive system from conventional to nuclear arms, it had to negotiate through WEU for it to reduce its troop levels on the continent. WEU was an anomaly: a defensive organisation designed to permit West German rearmament. Yet West Germany was soon an independent member of NATO. Once the original rearmament furore had subsided, WEU largely became a useless appendage. While it did establish an institutional structure, its meetings were sporadic and its commitments overlapped with those of NATO, the Council of Europe (which in 1960 took over the social and cultural functions it had inherited from the Treaty of Brussels) and OEEC. It might have served as a link between Britain and the Six, but it was not until after its first application to join the EEC had been rejected in 1963 that Britain suggested that WEU might be a vehicle for closer cooperation between the two sides. More generally, however, Britain, which had taken the initiative in founding WEU out of the wreckage of EDC, placed little credence in the structure. Britain was not prepared to allow WEU to intrude upon Anglo-American relations and placed it a poor second to NATO.

The gulf which separated Britain and the Six was simply too wide to be bridged by such a tenuous organisation. In integrative terms, WEU was an inferior substitute for EDC. But for Britain, it was perhaps satisfactory: it allowed for some association with the leaders of integration, if necessary, and might have permitted some form of British influence. This state of affairs changed abruptly with the Treaty of Rome and its implications. If Britain wished to retain some leadership in Europe or even to maintain what it regarded as its special position there *vis-à-vis* the United States, some new arrangement would have to be found: WEU was insufficient.

The speed of developments after the 1955 Messina meeting, to which Britain had declined an invitation, forced the reappraisal. The first clear sign of Britain's attitude towards the changing situation came at a NATO Council meeting in December 1956, when the foreign minister, Selwyn Lloyd, introduced proposals for what became known as the Grand Design. These were further elaborated in the Council of Europe the following year. The essence of the British suggestion was that the time had come to rationalise the proliferation of European institutions that had sprung up over the past decade, most specifically by introducing a single European assembly which, unrelated to any organisation, would serve them all. The second part of the British scheme was a comprehensive free trade area covering the whole of Western Europe, a counter-effort to the projected EEC. The proposals immediately aroused the suspicions of the pro-Europeans within the Six, for it seemed typical of previous British offers: so vague as to be meaningless or free to be interpreted in innumerable ways.

Suspicions were easily aroused, for almost simultaneously Britain had announced its desire to reduce the number of troops stationed in West Germany under the WEU agreement, as part of its switch to a nuclear-based defence. Nevertheless, the British proposals were discussed, and involved the whole of Western Europe since they ranged widely over both defence and economics. Countries adopted their traditional postwar stances: the debate was on an Atlantic or a European community. On the political and defence issue, the main argument actually took place over a more limited Italian amendment for a single assembly to serve only WEU, EEC and the Council of Europe: the reconciliation of the other bodies seemed to be impossible. The Italian scheme was preferred for discussion because the British design offered startling changes for the existing structures without any identifiable concrete improvements. Furthermore, for federalists, the British proposal once again seemed to seek to wipe out everything that had been created since 1950 and freeze Europe in the intergovernmental mould of the Council of Europe and OEEC. It ran into further objections from the neutral states, who wanted to avoid both close integration and military entanglements.

The Grand Design suggested that the broad free trade area should not cover agriculture. For all other economic spheres there would not be a common external tariff; instead, members would negotiate separate tariffs with non-members. It seemed clear to many that Britain was seeking to secure the best of two worlds: to take advantage of the market opportunities in Europe through decreasing tariffs while still retaining its special economic arrangements with the Commonwealth. Overall, therefore, the defenders of union felt that the entire British strategy was devoted to destroying what had been achieved by diluting it beyond recognition.

The opposition within the Six came from two distinct sources. There was the clear economic argument which believed that countries outside the projected EEC, particularly Britain with its preferential Commonwealth arrangements, would be in too advantageous a position. The second opposition grew stronger as the discussions dragged on: no matter how much the pro-Europeans desired British association with their ambitions, they saw a free trade area as a retrograde economic step and feared its adverse effect upon the ultimate goal of political union. If the economic benefits of a larger market could be accrued without the closely-knit EEC structure, then the whole drive towards integration might well falter or grind to a halt.

The key lay with France and, to a lesser extent, West Germany. If these two countries had agreed to the Grand Design, it might well have succeeded. However, in December 1958 the negotiations, which had been conducted under the auspices of OEEC, were abruptly terminated by France: the other five EEC members had to follow the French lead or risk the unravelling of the new body. Since President de Gaulle had met Adenauer only the previous month, it appeared likely that the West German Chancellor knew of and perhaps endorsed the French decision. The latest effort to prevent too wide a wedge being driven through the concept of Europe had failed.

The net result of the abortive free trade negotiations was a sharp deterioration in European relations. They had done nothing to diminish Britain's isolationalist attitude and simultaneously had confirmed a belief that any British proposal was a wolf in sheep's clothing. Moreover, Britain had failed to convince de Gaulle that it could be nothing but a rival to France for European leadership. De Gaulle's known views on reforming NATO and his desire for a greater prestige for France influenced his final decision; they were still influential in his rejection a few years later of the British application to enter the EEC.

Britain's next act was to go ahead with the formation of a European Free Trade Association, along with Austria, Denmark, Norway, Portugal, Sweden and Switzerland. Plans were approved in July 1959, leading to the signing of the Stockholm Convention by the 'Outer Seven'. The economic aim of EFTA was to work for tariff reductions among its members, with their final abolition and an industrial free trade area coming by 1970. But there EFTA's work would be ended. There would be no common external tariff and no economic union. Some doubts were raised over Britain's real motives for founding EFTA: economically, the smaller members would benefit far more. Quite possibly the ulterior motive was to convince the EEC states of the virtues of EFTA's low tariffs, with the end objective of persuading the EEC to return to the conference table to negotiate a multilateral trading agreement that would hold the two parts of Western Europe together.

This was the interpretation prevalent within the EEC, and one which was reinforced by the debate in the House of Commons upon the Stockholm Convention, in which the speakers concentrated more upon the relationship with the EEC than the organisation and aims of EFTA. A salutory note in the debate was provided by the Labour spokesman, Roy Jenkins (who was to become an EC Commissioner in the 1970s), who said: 'In negotiating the EFTA we have been too much concerned with showing the Six that what they rejected is a perfectly workable arrangement. I think that the EFTA will be perfectly workable, but I do not believe that in the last resort the Six rejected the Free Trade Area because they thought it would not work. They rejected it because, whether it worked or not, it was not what they wanted.' That is precisely the point.

As the 1950s came to a close, Western Europe was truly at sixes and sevens. It had taken ten years for the states definitely to decide where they stood on the question of integration or association. In 1960 the pattern which had emerged seemed likely to remain for some time, with the EEC countries preferring a maximum of integration and the remainder opting for a minimal level of intergovernmental association. This arrangement might have been satisfactory but for the rancour aroused in previous years. The EEC and EFTA went their separate ways and began to regard each other as rivals, not a partners.

Since most of the states were members of its Western alliance, this rift was a matter of grave concern to the United States. American policy disliked EFTA as an unnecessary complication, not for what it was, but because the aims of the EEC seemed to fit better with its own interests. The United States therefore stepped in to seek to preserve some semblance of economic unity. While wider economic considerations were also relevant, the European rift was one factor in the American proposal for a reconstruction of OEEC so as to allow non-European membership. It was transformed into OECD, the Organisation for Economic Cooperation and Development, charged with concentrating upon international problems of economic development. The establishment of OECD reinforced the lessons of the late 1950s that Britain was not necessarily something special. Through OECD, the EEC would have a direct link with Washington, with Britain in the wings.

CHAPTER 10

THE DEATH OF COLONIALISM

A wind of change is blowing through the continent.
(Harold Macmillan, 1960)

We prefer self-government with danger to servitude in tranquillity.
(Kwame Nkrumah, Autobiography, London, 1957, p. 94)

The late 1940s saw a reduction in the world influence of the European states; the 1950s witnessed a retreat back to Europe. The promise of independence to their colonial territories by the European powers had more or less been forced upon them immediately after the war, particularly in the Middle East and Asia where there was a strong tradition of vigorous nationalist movements: here, European control was already weak or precarious by 1940. During the 1950s the pace of independence accelerated so swiftly that few colonial areas remained by the end of the decade: most of these, in any case, had received a promise of imperial withdrawal, and by 1965 virtually the whole of Africa was independent. The stampede to give up their overseas possessions had considerable effects upon the internal deliberations and functioning of the colonial powers, irrespective of the plans they may have had for their colonies. The subsequent trek of the Western European states back to the old continent also influenced their domestic political life.

The Second World War itself was a major catalyst. The Arab world in the Middle East and North Africa, and South-East Asia had all been involved in the global conflict – often against the wishes of the indigenous political leaders and population. The two power blocs had pursued military strategies without considering either local opinion or the possible repercussions that might affect these areas. India, the largest colonial territory in the world, had been mobilised by Britain even though the recognised national leader, Mahatma Gandhi, had not been party to the decision. The crucial area of the Middle East was placed under military control to prevent its capture by the other side, while Britain and the Soviet Union occupied and partitioned Iran, in theory an independent state, to prevent its oilfields falling into enemy hands. The fate of the French colonies demonstrated the passive role of local populations. They were brought into the war only if the local French governors supported de Gaulle's Free French Movement; whereas if the local commander preferred the Vichy regime, the colony usually remained on the sidelines as a spectator.

The war defeated colonialism, for repeated military reversals in the early years of the war demonstrated imperial vulnerability. Not only were the European states driven out of many of their colonies; it also severely hurt their prestige. The fall of France in 1940 and the dilemma of choice which de Gaulle and Pétain presented to the French colonial garrisons underlined the inherent weaknesses of a French military authority which had hitherto been successfully concealed behind a glamorous reputation. Similarly, the Japanese advance through South-East Asia revealed the weaknesses in the British and Dutch colonial structures in the area. The damage to prestige and authority still remained at the war's end, something the more perceptive of the local nationalist leaders were swift to realise. There was no triumphant return of colonial military power in the Far East. Japanese forces were still occupying most of the former colonial territories when the first atomic bombs were dropped on their homeland, compelling Japan to surrender. Moreover, the most dominant liberating power was the United States, with its marked anti-colonialist bias.

EUROPEAN ATTITUDES AND POLICIES

Allied postwar decisions meant that Italy lost its colonial possessions, just as German colonies had disappeared in 1918. Only five major colonial powers remained: France, Britain, the Netherlands, Portugal and Belgium. Where these powers had been ousted in the early years of the war, they returned in an attempt to re-establish their former control. Their policies and plans varied greatly. Generally speaking, the two major powers, Britain and France, faced the problem of authority and prestige with more realism: at least they seemed prepared to make some concessions to local political movements. The three smaller states adopted a more intransigent attitude. But for all, the major problem to be faced after the war was whether they had the military capacity to sustain or reimpose their authority completely over colonies where even a minority of the population actively opposed their continued rule. At first, the European states were reluctant to admit their inadequacy to do so, but sooner or later the answer had to be negative in every instance.

The Netherlands was in the weakest position. The Dutch wished to re-establish the old pattern of colonial rule in their East Indies possessions, the produce of which was an important asset of the home economy. But the Japanese armies had not only retained full control throughout the war; they had also encouraged the development of nationalist organisations, and these took up arms against the returning Dutch. The struggle lasted for four years, but the result was never in doubt. The Netherlands simply did not possess the military capacity to quell insurrection, and in 1949 was obliged to concede independence to Indonesia.

Belgium and Portugal had been more fortunate. They had never encouraged the development and training of an educated native elite, and were able to continue this policy after 1945, partly because their large African colonies had been far from the war zones. It was only towards the end of the 1950s that they were faced with serious colonial rebellion. The largely undeveloped Portuguese territories would gain their independence only in the 1970s, one of the last acts of decolonialisation in Africa. Belgium, however, was forced to leave the Congo in 1960. By then, the Congo faced independent states across most of its borders, an inspiration to and a haven for dissidents. Although Belgium belatedly switched from a paternalist attitude to envisage a complete union between itself and the Congo, the time had passed for such gestures, especially as it was rejected by Congolese leaders. When armed conflict broke out in 1959, Belgium, incapable of mounting any serious military offensive, abandoned any pretence of gradualism and opted for immediate withdrawal within the year. The sprawling Congo with its multitude of tribes was one of the most poorly prepared areas for independence. The new state had hardly begun to breathe when it collapsed into bloody civil war: some sort of order was eventually re-established through the mediation of UN forces.

Portugal's scheme of things was to regard its colonies as an integral part of the home state. In theory, therefore, they were not colonies, and demands for independence could be regarded as 'treason'. On the other hand, Portugal pursued the same policy of debarring political activity in both Europe and Africa. It did mean a relative absence of racial conflict, strengthened by the influential role of the Catholic Church, despite the neighbouring state of South Africa and its rigid policy of apartheid. The net result was a relatively mild form of paternalism; but with a weakening dictatorial control at home, unrest among its own armed forces, and with almost all of Africa under native control, Portugal simply could not gainsay independence.

Britain and France did in part recognise the postwar urge for independence and they did seek ways of accommodating it within a framework that would guarantee the retention of close links with the mother country. On the whole, the more flexible approach was adopted by Britain. Before 1939, Britain had already created an international organisation which permitted it to retain a close association with the independent dominions of Canada, Australia, New Zealand and South Africa. It was only natural that this Commonwealth design should be considered appropriate for extension to the colonies. Opinion in Britain may have been divided – Churchill himself had declared that he did not intend to preside over the liquidation of empire – but the question was settled by the 1945 election. The Labour Party was committed to liberalisation as quickly as events would permit and immediately set in motion the process of winding up Britain's colonial suzerainty. By the time the Conservatives returned to power in 1951, the process was well under way. It could be slowed down, but not reversed or checked.

India, with its teeming millions, was the epitome of colonial rule, for its masses were equal to the total population of the rest of the colonial world. The Raj was the jewel in the crown, the symbol of the British Empire. Though the decision in 1946 to leave the Indian subcontinent was based on economic factors as well as a commitment to decolonialisation, the granting of independence to India in 1947, along with that of Indonesia in 1949, marked the beginning of the independence snowball. The remaining British possessions in Asia soon followed India. Independence for the British colonies in Africa and the Western hemisphere came shortly afterwards. However, where strategic factors were deemed crucial, as in Aden or Cyprus, British resistance to independence was determined and prolonged. Similarly, where a congenial climate had encouraged significant European settlement, as in Kenya and Rhodesia, white opposition to independence was bitter. The white settlers in Rhodesia defied British plans in 1965 and declared unilateral independence for themselves. Despite the application of sanctions, backed by the UN, the Rhodesian rebels were able for more than a decade to defy a series of hesitant British governments which were reluctant or unable to use force. External pressure and economic problems brought it back under British tutelage in 1979, a transitional phase before the independent state of Zimbabwe was declared in 1980. Rhodesia notwithstanding, the empire on which the sun never set had by the 1960s been reduced to a few scattered, small and mainly island outposts.

The Commonwealth idea was adopted as the best means of allowing Britain to retain economic and social ties with its ex-colonies. Commonwealth membership was to be open to all the ex-colonies. Most joined it after independence, though a few, like Burma, preferred to go their own way. The tone was set at a conference of Commonwealth leaders in London in 1949 to discuss a future arrangement with newly independent India. Out of this meeting a new definition of the Commonwealth emerged. By 1950 India had become a republic with its own head of state: the sole formal link remaining with Britain was the recognition of the British monarch as the symbolic head of the Commonwealth. The Commonwealth concept had been stretched to its limits: without any easily recognisable structure and institutions, it became little more than a 'concept of convenience', a cooperative association bound together by ties of historical memories within which members could collaborate if they felt so inclined.

France had historically settled upon a scheme of integration and assimilation, a civilising mission of cultural transformation, though application of the plan had never proceeded much beyond educating small local elites. The whole design rested upon its acceptance by the colonies. But while French aid, culture and educational facilities might be welcomed, assimilation was usually rejected. The wartime trauma of France, with the split between Vichy and the Resistance, meant that any re-establishment of assimilation would have to labour against heavy odds. To lure the colonies to his Free French Movement, de Gaulle had promised them a more democratic structure, an associative French Union, after the war. This was later introduced by the Fourth Republic, but in practice Paris continued to be the only constitutional decision-making centre in the French system. Even so, it had to cope not only with national liberation movements, but also with the fact that its weak governments were often obliged to condone acts of repression undertaken by local French colonial authorities on their own initiative which often challenged government policy and the whole concept of the Union. However, provisions had been made for the colonies to be represented in the French parliament. As the Fourth Republic drifted from one short-lived government to another, these representatives were nothing less than a relatively influential parliament- ary interest group pressing for independence, often in parallel with national- ist leaders engaged in direct action against French rule back in the colonies. France's struggle to maintain its empire may not have been the cause of the weakness of the Fourth Republic, but it contributed to its continuing problems and eventually to its downfall.

The immediate French problem was Indo-China, the only major colony which had retained an allegiance to Vichy. Japan itself only formally occupied the territory towards the end of the war. There were two French factions in Indo-China in 1945, hostile both to each other and to a nationalist movement under the Communist, Ho Chi Minh, which controlled substantial areas of what was to become Vietnam. Initially, the strength of nationalism persuaded the French government that negotiation about some form of self-government would be the sensible course of action. This was not popular in several polit- ical and military circles, and ultimately was torpedoed by the unilateral actions of local French representatives.

The Paris government was unable or unwilling to discipline such insubordi- nation. By the end of 1946 the Indo-China problem had escalated to a fully grown colonial war. The inability of French governments to control the army and colonial officials was a prominent feature of the Fourth Republic; the action which sparked off the Indo-China war was the first in a long chain of insubordination. It led to almost eight years of unremitting jungle warfare which France could never hope to win, especially after 1949 when the Com- munist victory in China created a readily accessible resource base for Ho Chi Minh's guerrillas just across the border. The war became ever more unpopular in France, a constant drain on the economy and military capacity. Only the professional army was deployed: no government dared send conscripts to Indo-China. This policy was welcomed by many army officers: only the repu- tation of the army would be involved, and for many it represented a search by the military to regain the pride it lost in 1940.

Some relief for France seemed to be in sight with the outbreak of war in Korea. It could now argue that the two wars were but two fronts of the same struggle against Communism. To some extent, this was a view shared by the United States, which hitherto had been unsympathetic towards French policy in Indo-China. It pumped supplies and money into the French effort, eventu- ally to cover some three-quarters of the cost of the war. But it still was not sufficient to turn the tide; and when war ended in Korea, this American assist- ance largely ceased. The outcome was inevitable. The symbol of French col- lapse was the fall of Dien Bien Phu, an isolated fortress near the Chinese border into which the French command had poured much of its military strength. Besieged for many months, the stronghold was eventually overrun in May 1954, and a substantial part of the French army passed into captivity. Its fall meant the fall of France in Indo-China, and its implications were enormous. The French government was forced to resign, highlighting again the weaknesses of the Fourth Republic and bringing the political parties into further disrepute. Moreover, it fostered within the army a smouldering resentment against the political system. Many officers, who had thought themselves engaged in a kind of *jihad*, felt betrayed by 'untrustworthy' politicians in Paris. This military discontent was to explode when France and its army were again involved in a losing battle in Algeria.

French colonial authority had also been challenged in Africa, but a ruthless military suppression of armed uprisings in Algeria in 1945 and Madagascar in 1947 effectively discouraged protest for some years. During the 1950s, France pursued two distinct policies in Africa: intransigence north of the Sahara; a greater willingness to concede nationalist demands and compromise further south. A framework law of 1956 gave these more southerly colonies representative government under French tutelage. The upheaval two years later which marked the end of the Fourth Republic gave a decisive push towards independence. The new Fifth Repulic offered a new French Community to replace the Union, along similar lines to the British Commonwealth, but with French predominance. The colonies were offered the choice of an autonomous status (with French aid) within the Community or complete independence without French assistance. Only Guinea opted for the latter course. However, the Community notion was illusory: it did not possess the elasticity of the Commonwealth structure, yet fell short of nationalist aspirations. Inevitably, the French colonies in black Africa soon progressed from Community status to full independence, and France did not seek to use the Community as a means of retaining primacy once it was evident that such a policy was unacceptable to the African leaders.

This rather smooth progress was in sharp contrast to the political events in France's Arab possessions in North Africa. The basic problem was again that of a substantial white minority; these areas were surpassed only by South Africa in the proportion of the population who were of European descent. Tunisia and Morocco were in a more advantageous position than Algeria. In theory, both were protectorates, not colonies, and so had retained indigenous rulers and institutions which possessed considerable legitimacy in the eyes of their peoples. In addition, the level of white settlement was negligible compared to that of Algeria. Both were able to achieve independence in the 1950s, though not without a high level of unrest and violence, especially in Morocco. Their independence was not just the result of French magnanimity. France could not hope to maintain even an uneasy peace in the two protectorates because its troops were required to sustain the French position in neighbouring Algeria.

Over 10 per cent of the Algerian population was white, and this large French settlement had in the past led governments to incorporate Algeria constitutionally into metropolitan France: it was seen as being no different from any other French province. Hence, in French eyes, there could be no legitimate demands for independence. The Algerian war started in late 1954, only four months after the weary French army had been ejected from Indo-China. France was in no mood to countenance a further retreat after the humiliation of Dien Bien

Phu, the army was eager to rescue its prestige and to apply the lessons of guerrilla warfare painfully acquired in Asia, and the white settlers rejected vehemently any form of dissociation from France. The war steadily became one of brutal acts of repression and torture by both sides. France had sufficient strength not to be defeated outright; on the other hand, even though most of the French army, including conscripts, was eventually deployed in Algeria, it was never sufficient to gain a decisive victory.

Political life in France became completely centred on the Algerian conflict: all events and policies were judged in the light of Algeria, which also sucked in more and more of France's monetary resources. The war was a colossal economic burden and eventually became identified with all that was wrong with France, with discontent rife among the population, within the army, and among the Algerian white settlers. It became more difficult not just to sustain, but even to form governments: few politicians wished to be burdened with the albatross of war. The Algerian conflict proved to be the final crisis of a fragile regime. In 1958 the Fourth Republic was toppled primarily because of its inability to find a way out of the morass, though Algeria itself had to wait for several years before independence could be gained.

THE EFFECT ON EUROPE

The passing of colonialism naturally left its mark on European politics, quite apart from the burdens of maintaining control over rebellious territories. It meant primarily a process of adjustment to changed and reduced circumstances. In economics and industry, it meant a rethinking and replanning of strategy and market outlets: the ex-colonial markets would no longer be closed to all but the departing imperial power. All the colonial powers sought to develop schemes, none entirely successful, to maintain what had been privileged and reasonably lucrative economic links: economics was central to designs such as those of the British Commonwealth and the French Community. In government and administration, it meant the end of a perceived role and dream. For colonial administrators and settlers, it meant the end of a profitable profession and invoked a painful choice: to remain as a minority in the new states or to be rehabilitated in the mother country. Either choice meant a much reduced status and income.

The political and economic effects of this withdrawal back to Europe were rather different. Many economists argued that decolonialisation was a blessing in disguise: that released from the burden of administration, the colonial powers would have a greater freedom and capacity to develop their own domestic economies. The control of vital natural resources, particularly oil, had perhaps been the strongest economic argument for continued European control and influence in colonies and ex-colonies; without this control, it had been argued, the Western world could be held to ransom at the whim of a few politicians and its industrial base put in jeopardy.

However, this economic line had gradually been discarded. It was pointed out that the new states needed the products of the West, and that therefore a bilateral and smooth trading arrangement would be in everyone's interest. As for political control of raw materials, Italy, a state without any political voice in oil-producing areas, was already successfully undercutting those powers which attempted to retain some political influence over the oilfields. Furthermore, the recent experiences of colonialism, particularly those of France, seemed to indicate that the retention of control had become a heavy drain on the home economy. By the late 1950s it was more conventional to accept that Western Europe would be better off without colonies. That economic belief, however, did not necessarily take into account the political adjustments that had to be made.

One major political effect of the winding-up process of decolonialisation was the strengthening of a nationalist and conservative mood in Western Europe. Most particularly, it injected the issue of race more strongly into domestic politics. The 1950s and early 1960s saw the European states seeking to recruit workers from their colonies and ex-colonies to meet the labour shortages occasioned by their rapidly expanding economies: many people from the Third World voluntarily migrated to Europe to seek a better life for themselves and their families. In the host countries they were met at best with indifference, at worst by an outright hostility. Although the worst outbreaks of racial violence were still far in the future, racial prejudice and tension were present more or less from the outset, and on occasions erupted into major incidents of violence.

To some extent, racial discrimination was fuelled by the European view of their old colonial worlds. Generations of Europeans had been brought up on the concept of empire, and many still dreamed of its glory and civilising mission among backward peoples. Consequently, there was bitter opposition to the course of postwar events in the colonies. Their cause and beliefs were strengthened by the sentiments of the colonial settlers, with whom they felt a special bond. The repatriation of many colonists from Asia and Africa, some coming to a Europe they had rarely or never seen, reinforced the conservative mood. Out of it grew a resentful feeling that Europe had been in retreat for too long – first before the Soviet Union and the United States, and now before the Third World nationalism of peoples for whom they had little respect – and a determined desire to demonstrate, even if only once, that Western Europe could not be hounded from pillar to post by newly independent states which were still seen by many as barely being civilised. The event which demonstrated that old-fashioned imperial action was no longer possible, that the colonial powers could not defy a united world opinion and resort to unilateral punitive action in Asia or Africa, was the Anglo-French Suez expedition of 1956.

Britain had renounced all treaty rights in Egypt in 1954 and had agreed to leave the Suez Canal zone. However, in 1956 the Egyptian leader, Gamel Nasser, decided to nationalise the canal itself in order to generate dues of passage which would finance public works programmes in Egypt. The money was needed because Britain and the United States had reversed their previous pledge to fund the programmes. The British prime minister, Anthony Eden, who had described Nasser as a potential Hitler, needed little persuasion that punitive measures should be taken against Egypt. France, which also had a major stake in the Middle East and North Africa, was willing to cooperate in any such action, not least because its opponents in the Algerian war were receiving considerable aid from Egypt.

However, Britain and France delayed too long. Nasser had taken over the canal in the summer, but the first Anglo-French military response did not come until the end of October. By then it was doomed to failure, as world opinion was swiftly arrayed against the venture. A summer assault upon the canal zone might well have succeeded, politically more than militarily, as the nationalisation had at first aroused tempers throughout the maritime world. By November, however, passions had subsided as the Egyptians demonstrated that the administration of the canal and the passage of ships through it were functioning as smoothly and efficiently as before. It became obvious that Britain and France had delayed their assault because of the involvement of a third party: Israel saw participation in the venture as an opportunity to punish Egypt for its persistent border harassments. Consequently, the first invasion of Egypt was by Israeli forces. Britain and France then had a second string to their bow: as the Israelis made rapid progress, they could justify their own intervention as being necessary to bring peace to the area.

World reaction, however, was swift, unanimous and negative. Third World states were furious. The Soviet Union threatened to intervene in the region. Even their West European neighbours were at best only lukewarm sympathisers. Most disappointingly for Britain and France, the United States refused any support whatsoever. The Americans, who all along had disapproved of any Western involvement, were further annoyed because the invasion occurred just before their presidential election: to the United States, it appeared as if the action had been deliberately arranged for a time when American attention would be focused almost exclusively upon domestic concerns. Faced with a complete lack of world support, an almost unanimous hostile vote in both the General Assembly and Security Council of the UN and, above all, an enraged and threatening United States, Britain and France had no alternative but to withdraw. It was Britain, where domestic opinion on the wisdom of the exercise was more divided, which first bowed to the inevitable. France seemed more willing to defy world opinion. Their forces in the canal zone were replaced by a UN command which proceeded to reinstate the Egyptian *status quo*.

The Suez expedition was the final fling of European colonialism. It was rather different from the delaying and rearguard actions that the colonial powers had been waging and were to wage for some time to come in their overseas possessions. Rather, it was an attempt to resurrect the gunboat diplomacy of the nineteenth century. Its lesson was invaluable, for it illustrated the irreversibility of the process of decolonialisation. In the wider sphere of international politics, it pointed to the growing numerical voice of the Third World in the UN. Above all, it emphasised the inability of Western European states to act individually and to use military force in a major world crisis without American support.

For Britain, it demonstrated that there were financial risks in undertaking a major military action on its own. Britain's gold and dollar reserves slumped, and there were rumours that sterling might have to be devalued. Eden later suggested that these financial consequences were a crucial factor in the British decision to accede to the UN resolution. The episode also had repercussions in France. It was another humiliation for the French army, and did little for the low prestige of the Fourth Republic. It may also have strengthened the view of de Gaulle that France should disengage itself from too close an involvement with the United States, since such an association had been, and might in the future be, at variance with France's basic interests. But above all, although much of the Third World still awaited independence, and although the colonial powers would continue to use military force to control their colonies for some time to come, the failure of the Suez expedition was the burial ceremony of traditional West European imperialism with its gunboat philosophy.

CHAPTER 11

THE GOLDEN ECONOMIC SUMMER

What distinguishes the postwar era from most other periods of economic history is not only its growth but the extent to which this growth was 'contrived': generated and sustained by governments and the public.
(*M.M. Postan*, An Economic History of Western Europe 1945–1964, *London, 1967, p. 25*)

The days of uncontrollable mass unemployment in advanced industrial countries are over. Other economic problems may threaten; this one, at least, has passed into history.
(*Michael Stewart*, Keynes and After, *London, 1967, p. 254*)

After the harsh austerity of the 1940s, economic prospects for the next decade were bright. Together, Marshall Aid and government controls seemed to have placed Western Europe on a reasonably sound fiscal basis, one which even the Korean War was unable to disturb more than minimally. The economies rode out its inflationary pressures with relative ease and, thereafter, entered a period of sustained growth in which more and more accoutrements of prosperity became available to most segments of society. The last vestiges of postwar rationing were soon to be swept aside; inflation and unemployment dropped to negligible levels; technological innovation accelerated, eventually to stimulate a radical reorientation of the traditional European industrial structure.

Paralleling the growth of individual prosperity was a vast expansion of state activity. The state was an active partner in, indeed in many ways a direct generator of, economic growth. It also supervised an explosion in the number and level of the services and financial benefits provided by the public sector for its citizenry. The 1950s and 1960s saw the concept of the welfare state largely brought to fruition.

All of this interacted with sweeping changes in the structure and attitude of European society, including a general mood of contentment, if not complacency. The extent and pace of socioeconomic change were substantial, something which inevitably helped to shape the political style of Western European government and the fortunes of various political movements. If there was a dominant belief that was prevalent among both leaders and masses, it was that the economic cake would continue to grow in size indefinitely, so providing more and more benefits and wealth for everyone. While storm clouds were gathering on the horizon – for example, a lessening of demand, a slowing of growth, and the challenge of cheap competition from overseas spearheaded by a vibrant Japan – their dangers, let alone their arrival, were perhaps not really appreciated until the 1970s. It was in that decade that the growth bubble burst. The symbolic date is 1973, when the whole foundation of European economic prosperity seemed to have been undermined by the dramatic rise in world oil prices imposed by the cartel of oil-producing states, the Organisation of Petroleum Exporting Countries (OPEC).

THE FOUNDATIONS OF THE ECONOMIC BOOM

Not many people had expected that the rapid economic expansion fuelled by Marshall Aid would persist for more than a few years. Yet economic growth continued to be substantial throughout the 1950s. It was interrupted only by the impact of the Korean War and again by a slight recession in 1957. The Korean War, while a boon to manufacturers of military material, generated sharp price rises and the threat of a new bout of inflation. Yet this did not halt an economic growth financed by Europe itself and spearheaded by a continued rise in exports. The recession of 1957 was caused by restrictive measures imposed by several countries to prevent their economies from overheating because of international pressure on their currencies and a worsening balance of payments. The measures were in any case meant to be temporary, and certainly did not seem to have any unduly distorting effects. These two hiccups to European growth by no means indicated a return to prewar problems. Through to the early 1970s, the Western European economies, perhaps with the partial exception of Britain, displayed none of the features of the boom–slump cycle that had typified earlier economic periods.

The reasons for this sustained period of growth seem to have been several. The international financial system was stable, and by 1958 the West had achieved the aims of the Bretton Woods agreement, with convertibility among fixed-rate currencies. If a single balance of payments problem did occur, then fixed convertibility would enable it to be overcome by slight deflationary measures imposed by the government concerned in conjunction with assistance from the IMF. In addition, there was a steady increase in foreign trade, which raised not only exports, but also domestic demand. To a considerable extent, this expansion was due to the relaxation of tariff restrictions, sponsored in part since 1947 by GATT. After the late 1950s the further removal of trade restrictions was a major objective of both the EEC and EFTA. The United States, too, continued to push for further liberalisation. In 1962 it initiated the Kennedy Round of tariff reductions within GATT to bring the United States and Europe closer together on the question of tariffs, and so permit an even broader expansion of trade. European growth was such that the era of undisputed American dollar superiority also came to an end in the 1960s. By 1963 the flow of private investment had been reversed, with more European investment in the United States than vice versa.

In addition to the international context, there were also specifically European factors which contributed to growth. The first of these was demographic in nature. Despite substantial emigration to other parts of the world, the population of Western Europe grew by some 25 per cent between 1945 and 1970. Population growth stemmed from two sources: a high postwar birthrate, and an influx of refugees and overseas immigrants. The postwar baby boom, coupled with the need for reconstruction, created pressures for infrastructural developments, most obviously in housing and educational facilities. The influx of immigrants was stimulated by the fact that in the 1950s there was, in much of Western Europe, a chronic shortage of labour. It was first apparent in West Germany, which received large numbers of German refugees from the East. When this source of labour supply dried up, most obviously after the building of the Berlin Wall, foreign workers were attracted to West Germany, as they were to other countries, from the undeveloped southern fringes of the continent: from Iberia, Italy, Yugoslavia and Turkey. Sweden, by contrast, proved attractive to many workers from Finland, lured by higher wages and better economic prospects. The colonial powers had a different labour reservoir: their colonies. From the 1950s onwards, Britain received a steady stream of immigrants from the West Indies, Africa and the Indian subcontinent; until 1962 there was no control upon the volume of entry into Britain. France retained an open door for immigrants much longer: the bulk of these came from its old North African territories. The level of immigration was substantial, and in the years to come was to create new problems for European governments. The absolute level of immigration was highest in Britain, France and West Germany. Proportionally, however, the immigrant labour force was greatest in Switzerland, peaking after 1964 at just under one-quarter of the total labour force.

Coal and iron had provided the motor force of European industrialisation. However, supplies were limited and increasingly more costly to extract. While production tended to remain at more or less the same level, by the 1960s Western Europe's total energy requirements had almost doubled. While coal was imported from other parts of the world, from the early 1950s onwards Western Europe switched more and more to oil and refined petroleum products, primarily drawn from the vast oil reservoirs of the Middle East. By the mid-1960s the bulk of energy demand was being met by oil. As a raw material, it was cheaper even than domestic coal and, because production was controlled not by the supplying countries but by an oligopoly of seven international oil companies (five of them American-based), the West was able to enjoy a long period of low oil prices.

The commodity was not without its potential problems. It had to be paid for in dollars, which could generate strains on the domestic economies if its cost ever rose sharply. Politically, its supply might easily be disrupted by hostile powers. It was, for example, concern about the future of oil supplies which in part persuaded Britain and France to embark upon the ill-fated Suez expedition.

Some of the worries seemed to be confirmed by the formation of OPEC in 1960. The oil-producing states set up the organisation in an attempt to counteract the dwindling returns they received on what for many was their only marketable commodity. OPEC's aim was to overturn the concessionary system of the international oil companies so as to gain for themselves control of production and prices, something they were able to achieve by 1970. It was the political factor which partly persuaded Western Europe first to seek to stockpile supplies and, secondly, to develop alternative sources of energy to meet an ever-increasing demand. Explorations off the European shoreline led first to the discovery of large wells of natural gas, primarily in sectors belonging to Britain and the Netherlands. By the end of the 1960s the North Sea was also to yield large oil reservoirs, and a decade later Britain and Norway were to become substantial oil producers in their own right.

A further potential energy source was nuclear power. Britain was the early leader in developing a nuclear energy programme, but many other states – especially France, Sweden and West Germany – also began to invest heavily in this new industry. It was not until the 1970s, when public fears arose about its safety, that nuclear power became a political problem and issue in many countries.

Economic growth and prosperity would not have been possible without an adequate communications network. In 1945 the railways provided the essential landlink, and shipping the overseas link. While both survived as important and necessary means of transportation, they had to face increasing competition from other means. The transport revolution took place in the air and on the roads, again aided by the easy accessibility, cheapness and price stability of petroleum. From small beginnings, the volume of air traffic increased tenfold within fifteen years. More significant for European economies was the expansion of the car industry. For those countries which had a domestic car industry it, rather than steel, became the flagship of a modern industrial economy. For the individual consumer the car became the status symbol of the new prosperous society. In 1948 there were only some five million cars on the roads of Europe: some twenty years later this total had exploded to 45 million.

THE ROLE OF GOVERNMENT

One reason why the flow of economic growth in the 1950s and early 1960s was not unduly disrupted by slumps was the more active role that government played in the economy. Under the influence of Keynesian thinking and as a reaction to the mass unemployment of the 1930s, governments had largely abandoned the notion of *laissez-faire* economics, and instead sought to direct their economies on an upward path through a manipulation of both taxation and expenditure in order to secure full employment, and so sustain both demand and the provision of goods. Inevitably, the expansion of state ownership of certain industries made governments an interested party in economic policy and development. Essentially, however, Western Europe remained capitalist, with a predominance of private ownership and private enterprise. What evolved, to confound those who had, on the experience of the interwar period, predicted the demise of capitalism, was a vigorous mutation based on a public–private collaboration in which the performance of private enterprise was monitored by government and sustained by government application of Keynesian prescriptions of borrowing and spending in such a way that it fitted with nationally accepted notions of social and economic justice. Neocapitalism was the word coined to describe this new form of economic activity and mixed economy.

The policy objectives of government were several: national economic growth, price stability, a balance of payments equilibrium, full employment, greater productivity, better social security, a more equitable distribution of income. All these goals were deemed possible because the 'discovery' of Keynesianism, it was believed, almost eliminated the intrusion of uncertainty into economic planning. The stress placed upon any one of these targets varied from country to country, not only in terms of ability to pay, but also according to the political complexion of governments and national historical memories. For example, memories of the 1930s made full employment a relatively more important concern in Britain, whereas in West Germany price control received rather more emphasis because of the horrendous runaway inflation of the 1920s.

Overall, the 1950s and 1960s was a period of neocapitalist growth, of the elaboration of a welfare state structure, and of a high political consensus on these goals. The European right, after initial reservations, accepted the principles of government activism and welfare egalitarianism, while Social Democrat parties and trade unions concentrated on the reformist and pragmatic goals of higher wages, more fringe benefits, price stability and shorter working hours, paying at most only lip-service to revolutionary dogma.

Keynes' writings may have offered governments a theory which they could interpret and seek to apply, but they still had themselves to pull the threads together into some comprehensive system of action. This led them to an interest in planning the economy and its future development. The notion of an economic plan was pioneered in the 1940s by France, though several other countries, the Netherlands and Norway for instance, also took up the theme in the same period. Enthusiasm for planning spread everywhere in the 1950s, to foster further growth and to correct those imbalances (for example, differential regional economic development) which that very growth had thrown up. To a greater or lesser extent, governments sought the participation of employers and trade unions in these ventures. Some smaller countries, most notably Sweden and Austria, established formal institutions of tripartite representation which had a key role in the deliberations on public policy. Britain was a late convert to the virtues of systematic planning, but its relatively poor rate of growth eventually persuaded the government to follow in European footsteps in 1961, though never with much success. Only West Germany seemed on the surface to reject the concept of economic planning, but in practice the West German economy was subject to government guidance in much the same way as those of its European partners, particularly after the late 1950s, when commitment to liberal market ideas began to wane.

Wage and price levels were important for planning. In the 1960s, when more worries were beginning to surface about the ability to maintain sustained growth, more interest began to be expressed in incomes policy as a further facet of government planning, as a strategy for determining what the broad outlines of the distribution of national income ought to be. A wages policy, in fact, had been recommended in the Beveridge Report, and such designs, based upon the formal collaboration and agreement to annual contracts of the major economic interest associations, had already been institutionalised in a few countries: Sweden, the Netherlands, Austria. In 1961 a working party of OECD reported on the Dutch system and recommended that its members introduce some form of wages policy, but few acted immediately.

The problem was that governments lacked the necessary techniques for establishing detailed and fair criteria of what each job was worth. The success of an incomes policy would depend in the first instance upon a high degree of national consensus on the justness of the criteria. This was more readily forthcoming in the more egalitarian society of Sweden or under the more rigorous elite control of a segmented society like the Netherlands than in the more complex and larger societies of Britain and France. But even here, success also depended upon economic growth to satisfy demands. As that tended to diminish towards the end of the 1960s, such policies became both problematic and desirable everywhere. Perhaps all that could be expected was that those responsible for prices and incomes should expect their decisions to be publicly scrutinised and be able to justify them.

Planning was both easier and more imperative because governments themselves had taken control of many important industries, though the style of management, policies and control of publicly owned enterprises varied considerably. Much of what government had taken into public ownership was capital-intensive and hence important as a means of control over investment within the national economy. This 'rationalisation' of state-owned enterprises was matched by a rationalisation of private industry through mergers and takeovers. In most European countries there emerged giant corporations whose turnover far surpassed that of companies of the past. Their size may have made planning easier for government; it also made it more imperative that their activities did not go against what government perceived to be the national interest. In the 1960s, Western Europe was confronted with a new phenomenon: the multinational corporation, whose decision-making headquarters lay abroad, most often in the United States. Multinational companies had existed for some time, but their increase in the 1960s had political and economic implications which helped governments to think perhaps even more closely about economic planning and direction.

There were significant national variations in economic growth. Throughout the 1950s and early 1960s, West Germany was the market leader, giving rise to the mystique of the German economic miracle. However, the growth rate of several other countries – Italy, Austria and Spain – was equally impressive through to 1963. By the end of the 1960s, West Germany had been overtaken in the growth stakes by several countries. Expansion in France, Portugal, the Netherlands and Switzerland was closer to the West European average, though in all there was an acceleration of growth towards the end of the 1960s. By contrast, gross domestic product tended to rise more slowly in Scandinavia, Belgium, Ireland and, especially, Britain. While the Belgian growth rate showed signs of life in the 1960s, that of Britain continued to display a stubborn sluggishness.

Though the British economy grew in the 1950s and 1960s, and though its performance was superior to that of the interwar years, the rate of growth lagged behind that of its major competitors. It was also punctuated by so many balance of payments crises that the latter were regarded as simply symptomatic. Several reasons have been advanced to explain the relative decline of the British economy: a greater reluctance by all governments to abandon *laissez-faire* principles and interfere in industrial affairs, high levels of direct taxation, too great a state share of national income, the costs of the welfare state. But none of these seemed to be specific to Britain. Some critics pointed to the level of war debts and sterling's role as an international currency; others to the poor investment record of Britain – a cut in investment was invariably the first government reaction to an economic crisis. Yet others pointed to the poor record of management–trade union relations and the reluctance of both to be too closely associated with government. What is true is that the level of collaboration was much lower than in many other countries, and the tendency for trade unions to strike on what seemed to be minor issues much greater. Another factor which may have contributed to British problems was the status of sterling as a reserve currency. The importance of London as an international financial centre may have had some adverse effects: sterling was exposed to international pressures which other European currencies were able to avoid. The 1950s and 1960s represented one long struggle to preserve sterling parity with the dollar as a major reserve currency, a struggle which was finally abandoned with devaluation in 1967. That also marked a change in domestic attitudes towards economic policy. Despite the problems, there had hitherto been a high degree of political consensus. That gradually came to an end as the Conservtive Party drifted right to embrace the notion of the free market, while the left also turned its face more staunchly against government, with the trade unions even more dogmatically rejecting any suggestion for an incomes policy or possible curbs on their independence.

One should not perhaps be too dogmatic about country comparisons, because of the different base points from which each state started. Several continental countries were faced with a much greater task of reconstruction and so had an opportunity to invest in more modern conceptions of economic infrastructures. Similarly, countries along the Mediterranean littoral were still heavily rural and agricultural in the 1940s, whereas Britain was almost unique in Europe in having no vast agricultural labour reservoir that could fuel and press for industrial expansion and occupations. Hence, while Greece and Spain registered high growth rates in the 1960s, they still lagged behind the northern countries, including Britain, in their level of economic performance. In other instances, the national rate of growth could be misleading as an indicator of national health. For example, the high levels of growth in Italy benefited only its richer northern half. Governments pumped vast sums of money into the undeveloped south after 1950, but to little avail: indeed, the economic gap between north and south continued to widen steadily.

The sluggish growth rate of Britain and its stop-go pattern of deflation and reflation notwithstanding, the most striking economic feature of Western Europe by the late 1960s was the same as in the 1940s: the gap between the more industrialised north and west on the one hand, and the more agricultural and undeveloped south on the other. Mediterranean Europe began to develop tourism as a major industry and currency-earner in the late 1950s. On the other hand, it had been relatively overpopulated. The possession of a 'surplus' population and the weaker economy combined to make the factories of northern Europe more attractive to many as sources of employment. In some instances, this harmed indigenous development, where professional people and skilled workers, as well as unskilled labourers and poor peasants, were lured northwards by the prospect of a higher standard of living. Emigration may have been a short-term benefit to underdeveloped regions, especially when the latter relied upon remittances sent back by the emigrant workers to their families that had remained behind, but when the rate of European growth slowed and stuttered, many emigrants were obliged to return home, to place even more pressure upon their native economies and social systems.

In the 1960s there were perhaps few who were prepared to speculate openly that the golden summer of economic growth might not continue indefinitely. In retrospect, several warning signs were registered during the early part of the decade. The Bretton Woods agreement, which had finally reached fixed-rate convertibility only in 1958, was disturbed by persistent problems with its two reserve currencies: sterling was more or less consistently under pressure, while in the 1960s the American balance of payments deteriorated rapidly. Though the United States did not want to abandon parity, it did have problems, with the number of dollars circulating abroad far exceeding its gold supply. The United States sought to bring more pressure to bear upon Western Europe to expand domestic demand so as to provide an outlet for American exports. This was one factor that pushed Western European governments more towards deficit spending, though they needed little encouragement to do so. Furthermore, the economic downturns of the 1960s were more severe and more frequent than in the previous decade. Italy and France, for example, went into recession in 1963 and 1964, while longstanding problems continued to afflict Britain. In 1966 a widespread slump affected much of Western Europe, including the mighty West German economy. Both inflation and unemployment began to creep upwards. Yet governments continued to accept higher real wages, income maintenance, wage indexation and the persistent expansion of welfare costs. Deficit spending became even more marked, and all major political actors – trade unions, employers and parties as well as governments – seemed happy to concede rather higher levels of inflation.

Changing circumstances gradually led governments and industry to concur that the record levels of the 1950s would not easily return. In some ways this was not surprising. After the war, Western Europe had a spare capacity that could be harnessed to growth. Once that capacity had been utilised and most trade restrictions removed, the rate of economic growth, except in the undeveloped peripheries, was perhaps likely to fall. However, it was still widely assumed that growth would continue, albeit more slowly, and that Keynesian techniques, by giving governments the tools for managing their economies, would allow continued deficit spending to be tolerated. Though economic consensus was fraying at the edges, even in consensus-oriented Sweden, Western Europe was simply not prepared for the high inflation and unemployment of the 1970s.

THE WELFARE STATE

Paralleling the unprecedented levels of growth was an equally impressive extension of government welfare provision. Governmental responsibility, mainly in social insurance, has a pedigree back to Bismarck and the German Empire. By 1914 most European countries possessed some welfare provisions; these were gradually extended and improved in the interwar period. However, if they did have a logic behind them, it remained closer to Victorian precepts of charity, of a minimal and selective safety net for the very poorest members of society. The reforms initiated after 1945 were in one sense just another extension and application of those already in existence. They were different, however, in terms of their systematic nature and their universality.

Post-1945 social policy was based upon two new imperatives. First, since the embracing of Keynes meant that the social goal of full employment was accepted as being paramount, social and economic policy were seen as being interrelated. Social spending, it was believed, would help secure the economic objectives of full employment, greater investment and productivity, and a stable currency. Social policy was therefore not seen as being an act of charity, something immune to economic laws. The other imperative was belief in equality of opportunity, in health, education and pensions. Social policy was therefore argued to be a collective good and not something aimed only at the poorer elements of society. Together, these two imperatives meant that the volume and range of postwar social policy were such that they had a cumulative effect upon the Western European state, profoundly changing its nature.

Each country had its own version of the welfare state. There were considerable variations in financial arrangements, breadth, structure, order of priorities, and extent of direct government management. But in all instances the social goals were to be achieved by a combination of the direct payment to individuals of cash benefits, indirect benefits granted through tax concessions and credits, and the direct provision of services by the state. The major restraint upon welfare state development was simply the level of economic development. The welfare provisions of poorer countries like Spain, Portugal, Greece and Ireland were substantially more limited in scope. Perhaps the most extensive welfare states were those constructed in Britain and Sweden, but each one tended to have a distinctive feature. Particularly generous pensions were available, for example, in West Germany and Belgium, while France was noted for the level of its family allowance and sickness benefits. However, the differences were only of degree, not of kind. No significant political opposition to the welfare state concept survived beyond the early 1950s. It was thereafter accepted that something permanent had been built.

The centrepiece, perhaps, of the welfare state was health provision. Medical care was not free everywhere, but where charges had to be met directly by the individual, they were kept to a minimum. A marked improvement in European health followed the spread of health services and advances in medical knowledge: infant mortality dropped sharply, and the average life expectancy steadily increased. In the 1950s, Western Europe was spending 400 per cent more on health care than in the 1930s. While there was little political dissension about the necessity of an adequate system of medical care for all, as time went on worries began to be expressed about its cost implications for the future. Invention was steadily pushing outwards the frontier of medical knowledge, making treatment available for diseases and ailments previously incurable. The new drugs, equipment and treatment were inevitably cost-intensive. In addition, greater life expectancy and universal pension provisions were producing a greater army of state dependents. When the postwar baby boom came to an end in the late 1950s, the implications for the future became more alarming.

The other major change within the welfare state concept was in educational opportunity. The length of school education was extended, and funded entirely by the state: in most countries, governments were also willing to provide at least the bulk of the funding of private church schools. More particularly, the welfare state offered a greater opportunity for entry into higher education, first by making the latter financially accessible to those coming from low-income backgrounds, and later in the 1960s by increasing considerably the number of places available. Throughout the first two postwar decades the proportion of the gross national product devoted to education tended to rise faster than national income.

The achievements in health and education were repeated across the whole range of social policy. But so were the costs which, almost without exception, exceeded the original estimates. The welfare state was a major cause of government deficits: its demands steadily grew faster than economic resources. The welfare state was in some ways a victim of its own success. As it inexorably grew, so did criticisms of it, of the way it tended to erode individualism and self-sufficiency, by making it so easy for everyone to depend upon the state. In particular, those who contributed more through the progressive taxation systems, the middle classes, were more likely to be greater beneficiaries, partly because they were more aware of what could be claimed, partly because in all welfare states there was an element of the insurance principle whereby benefits were related to contributions. On the other hand, even if such criticisms had gained some general credence, a reduction in the level of welfare would have been political suicide for any government that looked to that path as a solution to escalating costs. The welfare state had created its own vast clientele which had not just expectations of it, but increasing ones, and which also had acquired a greater ability to articulate these expectations. Demand simply outstripped supply. More importantly, its benefits came to be viewed in terms of relative gains and status. Each group compared its situation with, and sought to keep pace with, other groups. Competitive group demands eroded the social egalitarian imperative and, in so doing, allowed some weaker segments of society to fall further and further behind.

Hence, no matter how severe the financial problems or how inefficient the actual operation of the welfare state, it would have been a brave government which dared to raise questions of rationalisation or reduction in provision. The welfare state had been founded on economic growth: initially, that had given social policy a low political cost. Expansion and provision would be covered by the continuation of economic growth. Hence it was politically easier to meet the demands of those who felt that they had fallen behind in the competition for benefits and shelve possible problems to the future. After the initial pronouncements of intention, the element of logic tended to evaporate: the welfare state grew just like Topsy, lacking coherent system or shape. As long as economic growth could be sustained, perhaps the welfare state could continue to grow, with a continuing upward redefinition of what constituted the minima, and remain unbridled. A day of reckoning would have to come some time. As Western Europe moved, in the 1970s, from growth to stagnation and recession, the climate became more conducive for a re-evaluation of the welfare state and its priorities.

THE CHANGING NATURE OF EUROPEAN SOCIETY

Economic development and the welfare state both had a profound impact upon Western European society. Development radically changed the socio-economic structure of society and its attitudes in ways that had perhaps far-reaching political implications. The same is true of the welfare state, especially in how it changed people's views and expectations of, and the nature of the demands they placed upon, the state.

The 1950s and 1960s saw dramatic improvements in average incomes, standards of living and the possession of consumer goods across the whole of Western Europe. The new, more affluent society was, in its socioeconomic characteristics, very different from that which had typified prewar Europe. The first obvious change was the flight from the land. Before the war, all states bar Britain had a significant proportion of their population dependent upon agriculture; by the end of the 1960s the exodus from agriculture was more or less complete. It remained important mainly in the undeveloped periphery – in Iberia, Ireland and Greece. However, this movement had not been immediately reflected in a vast expansion of the industrial working class. The second major change was the growth of the tertiary sector, of public bureaucracies and service industries. By the late 1960s the size of the working population employed in the service sector had surpassed that in industry in Britain, France, Belgium, the Netherlands, Switzerland and Scandinavia; a few years later, West Germany and Italy had joined the list.

While Western Europe had become more industrialised and urbanised, its society was characterised by an explosion of white-collar occupations, which blurred what had earlier often been depicted, for example by Marxists, as a society inevitably polarised between a bourgeois ownership class and a labouring proletariat. Class distinctions, however, had not been based only on occupation and income. Education had been a decisive factor, and this remained everywhere as an important variable related to class differences. Nuances of speech could also be important, as in Britain. The class basis of Western European society did not disappear: income, education, housing and occupation were all important differentiating characteristics. As such, they would fashion sociopolitical attitudes and also perhaps the structure and style of politics. Their impact, however, became more blurred. Urbanisation in the more advanced areas of Western Europe gave way to suburbanisation, producing a mixed geographical distribution of social groups. The increase in disposable income and welfare provisions also helped to break down class distinctions, while the gap between income levels was to some extent restrained by the widespread and more or less rigorous application of progressive taxation.

There emerged among the large youth population a culture which tended to question and reject traditional class differences. The youth cult, which flowered most fully in the 1960s, was but one aspect of an erosion of the traditional social structure which affected the whole range of social mores. One area where the increasing questioning of traditional authority had political significance was religion. Church attendance collapsed all over Western Europe, most notably in the Protestant north and west. This had implications for Christian Democrat parties whose core electoral base was the church faithful. In fact, this problem of a declining electoral core was the same as that of those Socialist and Communist parties which had traditionally claimed the industrial working class as their electoral clientele.

The increase in individual disposable income – the amount available for consumption after the deduction of fixed items such as taxes and housing costs – had steadily risen. It enabled the bulk of society to enjoy a lifestyle which had traditionally been regarded as middle class. The growth of the white-collar sector and the greater spending power of the worker led towards the concept of the embourgeoisement of society, with its implication that classes as traditionally conceived would ultimately cease to exist. This was part of a thesis advanced in the 1960s that Western Europe was following the United States into a new form of social and industrial organisation: a post-industrial state dominated by technology and automation in the productive sectors, with the service sector providing the bulk of human employment. Skills were becoming more specialised and society more complex, fragmenting the old concept of monolithic classes. The specialised division of labour, it was argued, would destroy the old ideological basis of politics, mainly because embourgeoisement would weaken Marxist-inspired ideologies and movements. Instead, there would be a more pluralist society characterised by a host of specialised organisations that would impose a different pattern of political activity, where a continued corporatist collaboration between government and interest organisation would supplement, if not supersede, the old electoral pattern of party competition. Yet others argued that by the 1960s the material needs of much of Western Europe had been satisfied by the new levels of affluence: politics in the future, according to this view, would be post-materialist in nature. With a high level of economic contentment and a belief that economic needs would continue to be met easily, people would become more concerned with factors pertaining to the quality of life (for example, environmental protection) rather than having a commitment to a continued headlong pursuit of economic growth. Whatever the truth of these assertions, what is clear is that radical social and economic change was a dominant feature of the 1960s, the foundations of which were built upon the economic growth and prosperity which had begun in the previous decade.

CHAPTER 12

POLITICAL STABILITY AND CONSENSUS

You've never had it so good. (*Harold Macmillan, 1959*)

No experiments – Konrad Adenauer. (*West German CDU slogan, 1957*)

Paralleling, or perhaps because of economic growth, Western Europe also entered into a period of seeming political stability and consensus. By the 1960s it was argued that what had to be explained was not political change, but its apparent absence. Apart from the dictatorial regimes of Spain and Portugal, right-wing authoritarianism remained weak except in France, where it flourished as a potential danger in the 1950s because of its association with the charismatic figure of de Gaulle. At the other extreme, after the turmoil of the 1940s, Communism had sunk into insignificance except in France, Italy and Finland, but even these Communist parties had been more or less isolated as frustrated spectators on the sidelines. The early flush for radical reform had faded, and Western Europe in general became more conservative. Conservative parties returned to power in Britain and France, or consolidated their grip, as in West Germany. The persisting coalitions in the Low Countries were dominated by conservative-oriented parties. Christian Democrat parties almost everywhere jettisoned the remnants of their more radical postwar ideas and/ or were taken over by more conservative leaderships. In part, of course, all this was a reaction to the international turbulence of the late 1940s and worries about the external and internal threat posed by Communism. A more aggressive foreign policy, military preparedness and patriotic pride were slogans that were more closely identified with conservative-oriented parties: certainly, the left had a tinge of pacifism in its make-up.

However, Social Democrat parties also became more conservative, partly in an attempt to dissociate themselves from the radical left, in some instances even formally renouncing a Marxist ideological heritage. In Britain, the Labour Party was torn between left and right in the 1950s, beginning with the resignation of three left-wing ministers from Attlee's government in 1951 in protest against the new priority given to defence requirements over health services. Other party leaderships were more successful in stifling internal radical dissent:

after several warnings, the Norwegian Labour Party in 1957 eventually expelled a faction which since 1949 had consistently agitated against Norway's membership of NATO. And in France it was the Socialist Party of Guy Mollet which in the mid-1950s prosecuted the most vigorous government action against the nationalists in Algeria. The major exception to this rightward trend in the 1950s, at least for a while, was Italy, where Pietro Nenni, despite the secession of the moderate Social Democrats, preferred to hold his Socialist Party in close alliance with the Communists. It took the Soviet suppression of the 1956 Hungarian uprising to persuade Nenni to abandon a popular front which had been disastrous for his party.

The electoral strength and success of parties was determined to some extent by the credit each could claim for creating the positive economic climate. This tended to benefit less those which had begun the reconstruction of economy and society after the war than those which happened to occupy government when the economic boom took off. In countries like Britain and West Germany, this worked to the advantage of conservative parties; in Norway and Sweden the beneficiaries were the Social Democrat parties. By 1960 the election slogans of the parties in power – 'You've never had it so good', 'no experiments', 'growth and prosperity' – stressed this relationship. By the end of the decade, too, satisfaction seemed to be symbolised by the portrayal of successful leaders as the personification of prosperity, as benign father figures who symbolised admired national values and traits. Britain had Harold Macmillan, and West Germany Konrad Adenauer. In the Social Democrat bastions, Norway had its Einar Gerhardsen and Sweden its Tage Erlander. In 1956, too, Urho Kekkonen of the agrarian Centre Party began his quarter-century occupancy of the presidency of Finland. While this paternalist symbolism was, apart from Kekkonen, fading from the scene in most countries in the early 1960s, it emerged even more powerfully in France after 1958 with the dominating presence of de Gaulle.

Elections may have been just as fiercely contested, but opposition parties found it difficult to argue for change in such a healthy aura of optimism; and indeed, up to the mid-1960s, elections did not seem to produce much in the way of dramatic change. It was a competition that was contained within a broad political consensus in which most parties chose to abandon or not to stress their ideological distinctiveness. In Britain the word 'Butskellism' (an amalgam derived from the Conservative Rab Butler and the Labour leader, Hugh Gaitskell) was coined to indicate the minimal differences that were perceived to exist between the two parties. It conveys well the sense of this consensus, as did the persistence in Austria of the Grand Coalition of its two dominant parties, which together regularly garnered well over 90 per cent of the vote. Even Italy, with its chronic problem of rapid government turnover, was described as a system of unstable stability. Only France, still engaged in a seemingly perpetual search for political stability, appeared to be the odd man out, at least until de Gaulle emerged from retirement for the second time to offer France salvation on his own terms.

Governmental change increased in the 1960s. Labour returned to power in

Britain in 1964; the SPD joined the CDU in a West German grand coalition in 1966 – the same year that the Austrian Grand Coalition eventually broke up; the Norwegian Labour Party lost its overall majority in 1961. Yet such events did not at the time seem to detract from or invalidate the notion of a contented consensus, for that was based upon beliefs about future economic growth, the validity and vitality of the welfare state, and the appropriateness of Keynesianism for government socioeconomic management. Although the consensus was being eroded throughout the 1960s, the politics of the decade can still be regarded as the dying continuation of the spirit of the 1950s. If any one date can be taken as a symbol of the end of consensus, it is 1968, a year of revolutionary protest.

CONSERVATIVE STABILITY

The most stable picture in the 1950s was presented by West Germany, Norway, Sweden and Britain. In the first, Adenauer led the CDU through constant electoral victories and along fairly consistent policy lines: in 1957 it became the first, and to date the only, German party ever to win an absolute majority in an election. Nevertheless, Adenauer preferred to rule in coalition with any willing non-Socialist partners. By persuading these small parties to enter a CDU coalition, he hoped to pre-empt the whole centre-right of the political spectrum and swallow up his partners. The strategy mainly succeeded: by 1961, only the Free Democrats remained to prevent a monopoly by the two big parties.

Adenauer and the CDU benefited enormously from the West German economic miracle, largely attributed to Ludwig Erhard, the Minister of Economics, who had defied the Allies by launching the quasi-liberal economic policy at the height of Germany's economic problems in 1948, and from the popular endorsement of the government's foreign policy. Given the divided nature of Germany, foreign policy was ever a serious issue. Its centrepiece was the Hallstein Doctrine, which essentially denied the existence of the DDR and committed the Federal Republic to refraining from usual diplomatic relationships with states, with the exception of the Soviet Union, which recognised the other Germany. Although in tying West Germany more closely to the Atlantic alliance, Adenauer made the likelihood of German reunification more remote, his pro-Western policy was largely instrumental in raising West Germany's international status from that of a defeated power to that of an accepted and equal partner. In any case, despite criticism from the SPD, which leaned more towards neutrality as a means of achieving reunification, it is probable first, that the path pursued by Adenauer was the only one possible in the atmosphere of the times and, secondly, that it helped to provide a basis for the *rapprochement* with the East which occurred in the 1970s.

Adenauer's supremacy in foreign affairs was equalled by his domestic pre-eminence. The 1949 Basic Law had provided for a number of checks and balances designed to prevent a repetition of the closing years of the Weimar Republic. The copestone of the new constitutional structure was the chancellorship.

With CDU dominance, and without any serious challengers from within his own party, Adenauer took the strong constitutional authority and combined it with his own indomitable personality to carve such a powerful niche for himself that critics of the regime coined the phrase 'Chancellor Democracy'.

There were increasing worries about the negative impact of too great a reliance upon one man, especially one with such an autocratic nature as Adenauer. His ascendancy also increasingly proved a thorn in the side of his own party. Rumblings of dissent began in 1959. While Adenauer privately indicated after the 1961 election that he would step down before the next election in 1965, he was uprooted from his entrenched position in 1963. The major turning point, perhaps, was the *Der Spiegel* affair of 1962. The arrest, on the direct orders of Franz-Josef Strauss, the defence minister, of several editorial staff of the major weekly, *Der Spiegel*, for publishing 'classified' military material raised questions about both his and, by implication, the CDU's commitment to democracy. While the CDU was to continue in government until 1969, it suffered from a lack of coherent leadership. Adenauer had developed a personal style of leadership within a decentralised regional party structure. To some extent the party remained one where regional 'barons' enjoyed great influence, but also with a weak central authority which provided no straightforward means of leadership selection other than an assumed or proven ability to win elections. Adenauer's CDU successors lacked both panache and charisma. The party, in a sense, succeeded despite itself. In 1966 it was obliged to invite the SPD into government, with a consequent change in policy emphasis, and in 1969 it passed into an opposition that was to last for thirteen years. Chancellor Democracy, despite similar degrees of supremacy enjoyed later by Helmut Schmidt and Helmut Kohl, did not survive the demise of Adenauer.

The issue of an old and tired leadership gained the limelight in Britain around 1962. During the 1950s the Conservatives had governed under three premiers: Churchill, Eden and Macmillan. During this period the party had largely accepted the innovations of the postwar Labour government, taking pride in its ability to improve the organisation and efficiency of the new welfare state. The Conservatives benefited from an identification with economic prosperity and, despite the frequent balance of payments crises, there were as yet few in Britain who expressed concern about the country's relatively poor growth rate.

Much of Britain's attention was focused upon its perceived world and colonial role, and it was out of this that the major crisis of the 1950s occurred. The 1956 Suez expedition completely divided domestic public opinion, and created unrest within the Conservative Party. An ill Eden was soon forced to resign as prime minister. The succession went to Harold Macmillan, whose first task was to restore external relations, especially with the United States, damaged by the Suez episode, and internally to re-establish Conservative credibility and unity. With shrewdness and panache, he swiftly rallied the party and led it to a third electoral victory in 1959. Macmillan seemed to dominate his party and politics to the same extent as Adenauer and de Gaulle. Yet within a few years his ascendancy began to disintegrate, and with it went Conservative confidence.

The crisis probably began with the Profumo affair which, with the association of a government minister with people implicated in an espionage and prostitution scandal, shook the party's imperturbability to its foundations. Conservative malaise was heightened by accusations from a revitalised Labour Party about its unwillingness or inability to handle what was now seen as relative economic decline. The final push came with a weakened and more lacklustre Macmillan's attempt to determine his own successor. In a sense, however, the stability and prosperity of previous years had persuaded the Conservatives to rest upon their laurels. People may never have had it so good, but the party sank into a complacency which was to hinder efforts to pull it out of the rut into which it had fallen. After two electoral victories in 1964 and 1966, the new Labour premier, Harold Wilson, could signal the end of Conservative dominance by claiming that his was the natural party of government.

SOCIAL DEMOCRAT STABILITY

Norway and Sweden lay at the opposite end of the spectrum from Britain and West Germany, with Social Democrat supremacy. The Norwegian Labour Party held an absolute majority through to 1961, and was able to reshape society in a way which the other parties largely had to accept. Opposition to it was divided among four parties of more or less equal size, but separated by the possession of distinctive electoral clienteles and historical antagonisms. The Labour Party could often be guaranteed support from one of the four on any specific issue: most importantly, the Agrarian/Centre Party was happy as long as its agricultural interests were protected. The major worry for Labour was not electoral defeat, but internal opposition to its NATO policy. This opposition, expelled from the party in 1957, formed the Socialist People's Party which won two seats in the 1961 election. This deprived Labour of an absolute majority which it was never able to regain. Labour chose to continue as a minority government, but was defeated over a vote of no confidence in 1963 over a mining disaster in Spitzbergen. The four non-Socialist parties replaced Labour in government, but without a majority lasted only four weeks. Nevertheless, the experience gave them a taste of power and they were later able to overcome their historical antipathies to form a durable coalition government after the 1965 election.

Despite lacking an absolute majority on occasions, the Swedish Social Democrats did not face the same problems as their Norwegian counterparts. Foreign policy was not a political issue, and the party had been able to foster a widespread consensus on the welfare state and its egalitarian goals. Under Tage Erlander it had sought to achieve broad agreement from most other parties and important interest associations on its proposals, often simply abandoning them if that agreement was not forthcoming. As in Norway and Finland, the party had looked to the Agrarians for additional support when that proved necessary. The red–green coalition was finally disrupted in 1957 when the Agrarians refused to accept the government's proposed pensions reforms. This forced the Social Democrats to look to their left, to the Communists, for support. In the 1960s, Swedish politics became more clearly a left–right competition between two blocs of parties.

In that sense, Norway and Sweden resembled each other. In both, the dominant left party had been faced by several parties which slowly strove throughout the 1950s to reach a *modus vivendi*. In some ways the key lay with the Agrarians. In both countries (and in Finland) the Agrarian Party, worried by the decline of agriculture and therefore also of its historic electoral clientele, changed its name to Centre Party, symbolising a strategy of securing broader support. This strategy both placed the Agrarians in more direct competition with Liberals and Conservatives within the same electoral market, and paradoxically also had the effect of pushing them closer to these other parties, so making a non-Socialist coalition more possible. In Norway the four non-Socialist parties had such a coalition thrust upon them in the government crisis of 1963, and in 1965 were able to form a majority coalition. The Swedish parties found it more difficult to form a satisfactory and consistent working relationship, and electorally were not able to achieve a majority position until the 1970s. But in both countries the 1960s saw a gradual erosion of Social Democrat hegemony.

COALITION STABILITY

Most of the smaller European democracies were governed by coalitions, usually of several parties. In many instances the coalitions incorporated both left and right parties, and straddled the religious divide. The net result was frequently grand coalitions – not necessarily of the Austrian variety, but in the sense of being significantly larger than the minimum necessary for a working majority. Consociational democracy was the phrase coined to describe the operation of coalition governments in the Netherlands, Belgium, Switzerland and Austria. It was meant to convey the securing of stability in situations where the opposite outcome of instability might be expected, because of a multitude of parties and/or deep political cleavages based on highly distinctive and ghetto-like social subcultures. Stability, it was argued, was achieved not by political competition, but by an overarching elite cooperation which ensured that all significant political forces were represented in government, or at least were consulted on all proposals that might affect the interests of members of their own subculture.

In practice, the dominant dividing lines between the organised subcultures were mainly based on historical religious differences, either between different churches or between the faithful and secular/anticlerical groups. Class divisions were present only in the secular segment of society. For example, the Netherlands and Belgium both had a middle-class Liberal and a working-class Socialist party facing parties based upon religion which successfully mobilised support from all social classes. In practice, too, the method of grand coalition effectively meant the abrogation of simple majority rule. To preserve the coalition, the elites had to ensure that no subculture or its political party felt a persistent sense of discrimination. One consequence was a tendency to use subcultural structures and organisations as the medium for distributing state resources. Another was the acceptance that each group had the right to veto legislative proposals; in short, action was taken only where there was unanimity.

It follows that elections did not necessarily decide government composition, most clearly so in Switzerland and Austria. That, and by implication government policy, was consequent upon post-electoral bargaining by the parties. The Netherlands has always had a plethora of parties, but the key to government was the Catholic People's Party, the lynchpin of all coalitions through to the mid-1960s. The Netherlands seemed to be the epitome of consociational government – highly stable and consensual despite its many parties. Yet in the mid-1960s that system seemed to disintegrate. The most immediate cause was the collapse of the Catholic Party. In Belgium, too, politics and government were dominated by the Christian Social Party. It had been the largest formation for almost all the twentieth century. However, all Belgian issues tended to be affected by the linguistic division of the country between Flemings and Walloons; and that included party support. The Catholic Party was much stronger in Flanders, the Socialists in Wallonia. The two provinces had taken different stands on the royal issue after the war, and in the 1950s over the long-standing issue of the Church's rights in education. This issue was eventually settled by the Schools Pact of 1958, signed by all parties, which formally recognised the Church's claims. Thereafter it was the different economic development of the two provinces which exacerbated differences between the linguistic communities. It gave rise to new linguistic parties and by the early 1960s it seemed to be heralding the end of consociational practice: the parties found it much more difficult to handle the interplay between economics and language, and in 1965 and 1968 language disputes brought about the fall of governments. In Austria the conservative People's Party won an absolute majority in 1966, the first since the 1945 election, and decided to rule alone. Conservative euphoria was short-lived: in 1970 they lost power, and were not to return to government for another sixteen years. Nevertheless, the end of the Grand Coalition did not mean a revolution in political practice: its pattern of party consultation and intensive cooperation with major interest groups, especially on wages and prices, was maintained after 1966. On the surface, therefore, greater competition and/or uncertainty seemed in the 1960s to be replacing the previous stability of the consociational democracies – except in Switzerland where the same four-party coalition continued as it had for several decades.

Whereas in the so-called consociational democracies, coalition government had generally been centre–right in complexion, in Denmark and Finland it was mainly centre–left. No party in Finland was anywhere near the majority point, but stability was acquired first by the influential constitutional position of the presidency and, second, by the general willingness of the Agrarians and Social Democrats to cooperate. The Conservative Party was relatively small and kept apart from the others by historical antipathy and the disapproval of the Soviet Union, which kept a watching brief on Finnish affairs. The Agrarians' prestige was heightened by the election of their candidate, Urho Kekkonen, to the presidency in 1956. But in the 1960s their place as Finland's key party was weakened by internal dissension which led to the formation of a rival agrarian party. In turn, this made red–green collaboration more problematic and, in part, opened the way for the entry of the powerful Communist Party into government in 1966, something which ultimately weakened coalition cohesion.

After 1947, Danish governments were led by the Social Democrats, except between 1950 and 1953. Its two major opponents, Conservative and Liberal, while willing to collaborate with each other, could not command the regular loyalty of Denmark's fourth party, the Radicals, which often preferred to support the Social Democrats. The weaker position of the latter and the fact that they usually presided over minority governments meant that they moved more slowly towards a welfare state than their Nordic *confrères*; and they experienced opposition in the 1960s when they attempted to speed up the process. Nevertheless, the Social Democrats pursued a moderate line, and the major opposition parties were generally supportive of the broad principles that lay behind government policy. However, as in Norway, there was a vocal left wing whose major concern was NATO membership. In the late 1950s this issue produced a split and a new left-wing Socialist People's Party. The split simultaneously weakened the Social Democrats, forced them to consider adopting a more radical profile to combat the new challenge on their flanks, and made government stability more problematic.

THE SEARCH FOR STABILITY

On the surface, Italy appeared to be in a similar position to Britain and West Germany in the 1950s: the Christian Democrats (DC) persisted as the premier government party. However, the cost to Italy of this supremacy was that government formation and survival were largely determined by factionalism within the party. The DC was essentially a broad coalition of interests ranging from the moderate left to the far right. Whatever coherence existed was primarily due to the party's link with the Catholic Church. After the death of de Gasperi, the DC lacked a dominating personality who could rule unquestioningly and hold a rather inchoate coalition together behind a consistent policy line. The fissiparous nature of the DC made government fragile, and created possibilities for the other parties to seek state patronage for distribution to their own clienteles.

Consequently, a basic instability was a feature of Italian Christian Democracy as well as of the system as a whole. The DC refused to associate with the Communists and Socialists who maintained their popular front alliance until 1956. At the same time, the party's left wing was strong enough to hinder any close relationship with the radical right (Monarchists and Neo-Fascists), which had gained strength in the 1950s. The problem was ever the same. The largest party was supreme, but far from the majority point. It had to find partners from the remainder of the narrow centre segment of the political system, or rule as a minority. Either way, its problems increased because of the divisions between its own factions and their constant jostling for influence within the party and the state bureaucracy.

The decisive battles, then, occurred within the DC. Because of the shifting factional contests within the party, its leadership changed frequently, with six premiers between 1953 and 1960. Since political decision-making took place within the DC, with little healthy competition between parties to force the ruling group to maintain a sense of proportion, real issues and problems were rarely broached. Governments found it difficult to indulge in long-term planning with any certainty. Italy tended to drift along without much direction and with too much clientelist patronage. One result was a mood of complacency among many politicians, and a general apathy and cynicism among an electorate who felt that public life was corrupt and indifferent to social problems.

During the 1950s the more conservative elements within the DC gained greater ascendancy, and for a while even seemed willing to dispense with the small centre parties in order to rule as a minority with the support of the far right. At best, such a strategy could be justified only by arguing that it might neutralise the revolutionary tendencies of the extreme right, though even that was a dubious proposition. Public discontent finally erupted in 1960, partly because of the unpopularity of a minority DC government backed by the Neo-Fascist Social Movement. The government collapsed overnight, and the DC attempted to close ranks by reforming as a government that included no fewer than three ex-premiers. But that could only be a short-term expedient that would do little to resolve the quandary of the party. Despite its severe factionalism, only two courses of action were open to the DC if it wished to secure a greater regime stability. In its hesitating drift to the right it had explored one of the paths, but it was one that proved to be widely unacceptable. The only other avenue was to look to the left, to an alliance with the Socialists.

Despite the fact that the Communist Party (PCI) had gradually moved away from a strict adherence to the Moscow line, condemning for example the Soviet invasion of Hungary, the popular front came to an end in 1956. The alliance had been a disaster for the Socialists: they had increasingly become the junior partner. The PCI vote had risen at every election and, indeed, was to continue to do so right through to 1976. The PCI was too powerful to be ignored completely. While its support might be very necessary for some government legislation to be passed, there could never be any question of allowing it any formal influence or recognition. Admitting the Socialists to government, especially after their break with the PCI when they began to express an interest in collaborating with the DC, was a different matter. The 'opening to the left' was strongly supported by Aldo Moro and other left-wing Christian Democrats, who argued that the party must push for further social reform if it wished to remain in power and neutralise the growing PCI appeal. The unrest of 1960 placed the centre–left option in the limelight. While the ensuing discussions between the two parties represented a significant breach in the dyke of mutual suspicion, several years were to elapse before they were able formally to agree to join in coalition. In Italy too, therefore, the early 1960s hinted at a possible change in political mood and style.

THE CONSERVATIVE REVOLUTION

The troubles and problems facing Italy perhaps pale into insignificance when compared to those facing France. The Fourth Republic had been born badly deformed, with a lack of strong popular support, and had never operated in the manner originally conceived. While it was continually beset by domestic problems, its final death throes, undetected at the time, began with the fall of Dien Bien Phu, the last in a long line of crises arising from the colonial war in Indo-China. The final *coup de grâce* was delivered by yet another colonial crisis in Algeria. Between 1954 and 1958 the Fourth Republic made a last vain attempt to change and strengthen itself.

After the collapse of tripartism in 1947, with the powerful Communist movement in uncompromising opposition, stability depended upon the ability of the MRP and Socialists to collaborate. Yet while they shared many common socioeconomic perceptions, they were more often kept apart by historic hostility over religious issues: moreover, both tended to lose electoral support as more conservative groups came to prominence. The problem was that the latter tended to lack any coherent hierarchical organisation. This internal anarchy prevented them from being a positive force for government, while their numerical strength effectively gave them substantial influence over the composition and direction of government. More serious was the problem of de Gaulle. In 1947 he had emerged from retirement to form the Rally of the French People (RPF), which soon made sweeping gains in local elections and which, in 1951, became France's largest party. By then, however, de Gaulle had become even more disillusioned with the Fourth Republic and with party politics. In 1953 he abandoned the RPF to a fate of disintegration. While he released his followers from any pledge of allegiance to himself, back in retirement he remained the symbol of a clear alternative to the struggling Fourth Republic.

The reforming government of Mendès-France that emerged after Dien Bien Phu proved to be too vigorous for the taste of many deputies and was soon brought down after it had disposed of the problems of Indo-China and EDC. The 1956 election produced a Socialist government under Guy Mollet, which relied for continuity primarily upon Radical support. It also confirmed the great negative force of the cautious and bureaucratic Communist Party, as well as throwing up a brief-lived and extremely disruptive movement of the far right led by the populist Pierre Poujade. Effectively, there was no room for governments to manoeuvre on domestic issues. In any case, Algeria occupied more and more attention. Mollet's government became more ruthless in its colonial policy, but the strain of government and lack of victory in Algeria led to its collapse in 1957, in the longer run contributing to the discrediting and disintegration of the Socialist Party itself.

There was no obvious successor to Mollet: Algeria would be a millstone around the neck of any prospective prime minister. France drifted from crisis to crisis, from one short-lived government to another, with the white settlers and the army both hostile to the Republic. In May 1958, settler groups rose up in rebellion, with the acquiescence of army units. Amidst rumours of a military coup in France itself, the Republic turned in desperation to the one clear alternative – de Gaulle, whose name still carried a mystique and who still had a dedicated following that sought his return to politics. Though the army commander in Algeria had proclaimed de Gaulle head of state even before Paris had come to any decision, his investiture had not necessarily been the aim of the revolutionaries or the army, but they themselves had no other acceptable alternative to offer. The Fourth Republic might have been able to ride out the storm of either the settlers or the army if the other and de Gaulle had not been present. But the juxtaposition of all three factors in 1958 proved too overwhelming.

The crisis provided de Gaulle with the opportunity to create the kind of government he had always wanted, and the constitutional structure of the new Fifth Republic was tailor-made for him. The power of the legislature was greatly reduced, and while prime ministerial government was retained, the new regime was presidential in nature. The reforms of 1962 enhanced further the powers of the presidency. In those areas of policy-making designated to the presidential sector, especially defence and foreign policy, de Gaulle brooked no interference from anyone. Thus the problem of Algeria became his alone. By 1960 he had effectively demonstrated his control over the Algerian situation, accepting the inevitability of independence. A further attempt at military intervention by the army in that year failed: neither the army nor the settlers could dictate terms to Paris. Backed by a massive parliamentary majority for a new, hastily constructed Gaullist party, the Union for the New Republic, de Gaulle was effectively in control of France, though his great popularity had begun to decline by 1964.

In the early 1960s, France had more the appearance of patriarchal benevolence and constitutional monarchy than a republic. The other parties had been electorally weakened and were in disarray: the Socialists eventually disintegrated, the MRP was formally to dissolve itself, while the Communist Party became even more introspective. His own party was totally passive and ignored by de Gaulle. His presidency was to have a great impact not just on France, but also on Western Europe. As long before as 1946, de Gaulle had declared his belief in a national arbiter standing above party politics who would act in the interests of the whole people and advance the destiny of France. Accordingly, his foreign policy was designed to restore internal pride and confidence and to emphasise France's international status. Thus he sought to elevate the role of France within the Western alliance, protesting against American dominance in Europe and the 'special' Anglo-American relationship. Militarily, he made France the world's fourth nuclear power in 1960. He turned to forge a *rapprochement* with Adenauer and West Germany, and the understanding reached between the two men survived the retirement of both to rank as one of the more significant events of the late twentieth century. In some ways France in the 1960s decried modernity with its emphasis upon destiny and national grandeur. It would create problems for the Atlantic alliance, for European integration and for democratic party politics within France itself.

THE DECLINE AND RISE OF SOCIAL DEMOCRACY

The de Gaulle revolution was the greatest single symbol of conservative predominance in Europe around 1960. In contrast, the Socialist parties, except for Scandinavia and Austria, seemed largely to be out in the cold. Throughout much of Western Europe the left was forced to ask what had gone wrong, for the paradox was that those parties which were dedicated to social change and welfare policies were largely out of office when the pace of change was noticeably quicker than ever before.

The conventional wisdom of the early 1960s suggested that while originally Social Democracy may have been adversely affected by the international crises of the 1940s and its identification with austerity and rationing, essentially it had failed to move with the times. Conservative parties had proved more flexible in adjusting their appeal to the emerging consumer society, while at the same time successfully presenting themselves as better and firmer supporters of social security. There appeared to be a great deal of spontaneous improvisation about the actions of non-Socialist parties which in some areas paid rather large dividends. In addition, common interpretations of the time stressed a more widespread popular aversion to dogmatic politics and issues. Very popular in the 1960s was the notion of the end of ideology, an idea which was related to the concept of the post-industrial society that had led to the erosion, even destruction, of the traditional class structure of European society. A new social structure and prosperity had, in other words, revitalised capitalism and made redundant Marxist-inspired ideology.

Socialist parties tended to be depicted as still being locked into a Marxist class-based perception of the world which was increasingly irrelevant, typically shackled by an archaic party organisation which emphasised routine, rewarded length of service rather than ability and merit, and clinging to a belief in a preordained salvation that could come about only through a class struggle. Organisation did appear to be a major difference between left and right. Non-Socialist parties gave the impression of having leaders who led and controlled the organisation; on the left, the image was of parties whose leaders were subservient to stultifying and machine-like organisations. It is perhaps not insignificant that the two most successful Social Democrat parties of the 1950s, those of Norway and Sweden, presented a pragmatic face to the world, attracted significant support beyond the industrial working class, and were headed by strong personalities who were respected far beyond their own party confines for their qualities of leadership and statesmanship.

At the same time, it was obvious that Socialist parties were the only possible focal point of left-wing political opinion. Non-Socialist alternatives were virtually non-existent, and attempts to establish them had failed to secure any mass base. Similarly, Communist parties were weak and/or isolated. So one had to return to Social Democracy to discover how it could break out of its electoral straitjacket. The solution, proposed by Socialist and non-Socialist alike, was that it had to undertake a radical re-evaluation of its fundamental ideological assumptions.

Broadly speaking, two general alternatives presented themselves. The first, more widely accepted, was a more or less complete abandonment of original Socialist dogma. The most dramatic moves were made in Austria in 1957 and West Germany in 1959 where the Social Democrat parties totally rejected Marxism as a doctrinal base. The Socialist Party in Switzerland went down the same road, while in the Netherlands a revised Labour Party programme argued for constructive policies within the existing socioeconomic framework. In West Germany the change from a workers' party towards an electorally oriented national party was symbolised by the selection of Willy Brandt, the young and popular mayor of West Berlin, as the SPD candidate for the chancellorship in 1961. Towards the end of the decade the Austrian Socialists had found a similarly attractive and strong personality in Bruno Kreisky. The Austrian Socialists won a majority in 1970, thereafter remaining the largest party: Kreisky remained as chancellor until 1983. In West Germany the SPD grew in stature, prestige and size in the 1960s, first entering a grand coalition with the CDU in 1966, which gave it an opportunity to demonstrate its capability for government, and then in 1969 being able to head a government in collaboration with the small Free Democrats. The SPD was to remain in government until 1982.

A similar attempt in Britain after a third electoral defeat in 1959, and perhaps also in the Netherlands after 1958, were not so successful. The proposal by the British leader, Hugh Gaitskell, to abandon the hallowed Clause Four of the party constitution – the collective ownership of the means of production, distribution and exchange – was vehemently and successfully resisted. After his election as leader, Harold Wilson chose basically to ignore this ideological issue and presented Labour as the modern party which was best equipped to steer sluggish Britain towards the new technological society. Here, too, Labour was to become the dominant party of the 1960s and 1970s. Similar efforts of transformation were perhaps less necessary in some of the smaller countries with their complex multiparty systems. The tradition of Social Democrat participation in coalition and electoral alliances, of necessity, had demanded a greater flexibility in policy and dogma, while paradoxically also making it less urgent and practical for them to seek electoral expansion beyond their core clientele. Even so, some changes were undertaken in Switzerland and the Netherlands.

This greater pragmatism, which had been a hallmark of Scandinavian Social Democracy, was opposed by a more militant argument which clung to varying interpretations of Marxist ideology. In most parties this militancy was confined to a minority which found a perpetual source of ammunition in foreign policy, the changing strategy of NATO, too close an involvement with the United States, and the nuclear arms race. Only in Italy perhaps, in what had traditionally been the most left-wing European Socialist party, did this line of thinking enjoy substantial popularity. But even here the party slowly and tortuously moved back to the centre after its breach with the PCI. A centre–left coalition with the DC became reality in 1963, and because the PCI could not be considered as a possible government partner, this combination remained the basis of possible government stability until the whole Italian political world was turned upside down by political and financial scandals in the 1990s.

On the whole, then, the Socialist left became more pragmatic in the 1960s, though its more radical elements continued to act as gadflies of the parties' historical conscience. While the dominant strategy was to become broad electoral alliances – and the most successful Social Democrat parties represented more than narrow class interests – there was no end of ideology. Instead, it was rejuvenated by the dialectic within each party between left and right. It gave the parties a sharpness which fitted more the mood of the 1960s as the complacency of the previous decade began to fade with the gradual decrease in economic growth and the perceptible accretion of economic problems. Socialist thinking, in short, was not jettisoned, but it tended to be retained not primarily because of its economic tenets, but more because it was a symbol of the moral change in social values that was desired. Even in France, where by the mid-1960s the Socialist Party had seemed to sink without trace under the weight of Gaullist supremacy, a rejuvenated party eventually emerged in 1971 under the leadership of François Mitterrand. It was soon to take over the mantle of left-wing credibility from the ossified Communists and, in 1981, the presidency and government of France.

By the end of the 1960s the shifting nature of super-power bipolarity and worries about the tenor and direction of American foreign policy, especially in Vietnam, and much greater domestic pressure about policy priorities gave Social Democrat parties a more radical stance. That was also due to a concern for protecting their flanks not just from parties to their left, but also from a new radical ideology, rooted in youth protest, that seemingly scorned all forms of party and parliamentary politics. That extra-parliamentary protest erupted in 1968, though some manifestations had occurred much earlier. It was most prominent in West Germany and France, at one point seemingly poised to topple de Gaulle and his Fifth Republic. The 1950s and 1960s had seen conservative complacency, satisfaction and dominance changed to a more vigorous competition. But on the whole it was a competition that was still largely contained within the established party systems and the institutional framework of national parliamentary government. From the mid-1960s onwards, the *status quo* was to be challenged by alienation and protest, not just from left-wing and youth-based extra-parliamentary radicalism, but also from new parties and new types of parties espousing different causes, some of which had the objective of changing and even dismantling the state itself.

CHAPTER 13

A SEESAW OF DÉTENTE AND TENSION

When internal and external forces that are hostile to socialism try to turn the development of some socialist country towards the restoration of a capitalist regime, where socialism in that country and the socialist community as a whole are threatened, it becomes . . . a common problem and concern of all socialist countries. . . . Military assistance to a fraternal country designed to arrest the threat to the social system is an extraordinary step, dictated by necessity.   (*Leonid Brezhnev, 1968*)

After a period of confrontation, we are entering into an era of negotiations.
(*Richard Nixon, 1969*)

The early 1960s did not appear to be auspicious for the Western alliance. Since Truman's decisive actions more than a decade earlier, it seemed that only rarely had the West seized the initiative in what had become a more silent struggle for world supremacy. While the situation may not have been as critical as in 1947–48, there was still perhaps grave cause for concern. The United States had drifted towards stagnation and less involvement during the closing years of President Eisenhower's administration. Despite continuing super-power conversations, the aura of goodwill that had surrounded the Geneva summit had gradually dissipated. It was torn apart in 1960 after the U–2 incident, in which an American reconnaissance plane was shot down over Soviet territory. Such flights had been routine practice for some years and, although the American response to the incident was inept, it is hard to believe that they had occurred unbeknown to Moscow. At any rate, the Soviet Union ostentiously chose to cancel a summit meeting planned for Paris later in the year which, it had been hoped, would build upon the several lower-level discussions of previous years between the super-powers. One reason, other than seizing the opportunity to embarrass the United States, may have been division on the desirability of détente within the Kremlin. Another may have been the refusal by China, still effectively ignored by the West, to accept any agreement on disarmament to which it was not party: Soviet relations with China had become more tense, as the two began to vie more openly for Communist leadership.

Within Western Europe too, there was a certain amount of dissension. Soviet hints and threats on a solution to Berlin interested Britain, but were strongly resisted by France and West Germany. The latter still felt torn between its commitment to the Western alliance and a reliance upon American protection on the one hand, and the dream of German reunification on the other. Yet the uncompromising stance of its Hallstein Doctrine, which refused recognition of the German Democratic Republic (DDR), was becoming more untenable. More serious perhaps was a growing tension between Britain and France. President de Gaulle, ever sensitive about French prestige and still resentful of his treatment during the war by Roosevelt and Churchill, was deeply suspicious of American influence in Europe and of the Anglo-American relationship.

Overall, the Soviet Union and its leader, Nikita Khrushchev, were the stars of the world stage, their brilliance symbolised by their exploits in space. After 1956 it was the Soviet Union which seemed to have the initiative everywhere – not just in space, but in suggestions for new actions and new directions. Soviet policy, while always positive, veered sharply between conciliation and bellicosity. The West found it difficult to respond to the Soviet fireworks, in part because the United States was still concerned to present a united Western front. The need to consult its allies made for slow responses, given the divergency of foreign policy interests in Western Europe. Often, by the time a common reply had been formulated, the Soviet initiative had been abandoned or replaced by a new idea. In addition, since the death of Stalin there had arisen across Western Europe a body of opinion that scorned the notion of Soviet imperialism and agitated for nuclear disarmament, particularly after NATO adopted nuclear weaponry as a major line of defence. All of this inhibited Western responsiveness or, indeed, the ability to take the initiative. However, since the Soviet Union was highly unlikely to yield any ground in Europe, it may well be that nothing was lost by the West, though that did not seem to be the impression at the time.

The 1960s also saw world attention switch more often away from Europe: to Cuba, South-East Asia, Israel and the Middle East, the Indian sub-continent, and Africa. The spotlight moved to Europe only occasionally – inevitably on Berlin, and on Czechoslovakia in 1968. While the United States and the Soviet Union continued to spar with each other over Europe, their major concerns seemed to lie elsewhere. This gave Western Europe more breathing space, consolidating not just a détente that began in the 1950s, but one that confirmed the inviolability of the postwar division of the continent. The spread of super-power competition across the world led both, in their European connections, towards introspection and concern about the solidarity of their own defensive alliances, while continuing to participate in an ongoing series of bilateral and multilateral consultations designed both to accommodate each other's interests and to ease the pressure on each within the existing *status quo*. At the beginning of the 1960s the U–2 episode seemed to symbolise an American lethargy. By the early 1970s the United States appeared to have sunk back into inertia as it endeavoured to understand and recover from the trauma of its involvement in Vietnam. Within the continuing and changing bipolar relationship, two issues were of particular importance for Western Europe:

the German question and the fate of Berlin, and the ongoing debate over the nature and role of a Western defensive alliance.

AMERICAN AND SOVIET POLICIES AND PROBLEMS

The two super-powers were still locked into a contest for world leadership. The new American administration of John Kennedy, stung by the string of Soviet successes in space, pledged itself to a massive increase in space expenditure in order to place a man on the moon by the end of the decade. With the obvious military connotations of space rocketry, the arms race between the two powers, now based on the deadlock of intercontinental ballistic missiles (ICBMs), continued apace, but with increasing sophistication. The super-powers and the world were entering an era of mutually assured destruction.

One of the most significant episodes in the super-power relationship, which almost brought the world to the brink of war, was the Cuban missile crisis of 1961 and 1962. At first, the overthrow in Cuba of a corrupt but pro-American dictatorship by Fidel Castro and his left-wing guerrillas seemed to be another setback for the United States. The subsequent abortive attempt, in the Bay of Pigs fiasco, by American-backed exiles to regain Cuba served to discredit American foreign policy even further. It reinforced Castro's anti-Americanism and pushed him closer to the Soviet Union. The world hovered at the brink of a nuclear war when, shortly afterwards, the United States produced photographic evidence of secret Soviet missile bases on the island. President Kennedy promptly delivered an ultimatum to the Soviet Union to dismantle the bases or risk a direct military confrontation. His bluff called, Khrushchev had no option but to withdraw since, contrary to Western fears at the time, which were based upon an assessment of their own weaknesses, Soviet military capacity was still inferior to that of the United States, especially in the western hemisphere.

While the Cuban missile crisis persuaded the Soviet Union to be more circumspect in the future, it also made the Kremlin even more determined to rectify the Soviet disadvantage. For all its strength, the Soviet Union was still very much a Euro-Asian power: elsewhere in the world, it had to rely upon indirect influence through remote proxies. It continued throughout the 1960s to expand its conventional forces and nuclear strength, achieving ICBM parity with the United States by 1969. More significantly, it laid the groundwork which led in the near future to its emergence as a global naval power. It was naval power as much as nuclear strength which spread super-power rivalry across the world. Equally, Khrushchev's challenges over Cuba and Berlin prompted the huge American military expenditure of the Kennedy administration.

Despite the escalating arms race, Cuba was the high point of tension. The two states continued to talk to each other, and in 1963 agreed to a treaty limiting nuclear testing to underground sites. Cuba brought home to the superpowers the need to have dialogue in order to reduce tension and stabilise their relationship. What was significant after the Cuban crisis was the nature of the ensuing dialogue between Kennedy and Khrushchev, which sought to extricate both from the crisis without damaging the interests, prestige and dignity of either. Castro and Cuba were not consulted. Bipolarity meant that in essence problems could be resolved only by bilateral negotiations and agreements. In the last resort, other countries were more or less irrelevant to this dialogue.

However, as the two powers spread, or sought to spread, their tentacles across all parts of the world, it steadily became more evident that both were finding it more difficult to keep their erstwhile allies or client states under firm control. In a sense, the confrontation of the two over Cuba heralded the end of a phase in their relationship which had begun with the Cold War in Europe. While it is true that Cuba emphasised that a satisfactory solution to many of the world's problems that arose from the spheres of interest of the two military giants could, in the last resort, be achieved only by direct consultation, the 1960s also illustrated the obverse. The super-powers were not entirely success-ful puppet masters. The first major example occurred in the Middle East in the conflict between the Arab states and Israel, backed respectively by the Soviet Union and the United States. The determination of both super-powers not to be outflanked in a region which they both regarded as strategically important resulted, especially after the Six-Day War of 1967 (in which Israel emerged triumphant with its conquest of Jordanian, Syrian and Egyptian territory as well as Jerusalem), in a heightened arms race between their clients, which both seemed obliged to encourage, sometimes even against their own inclinations.

The fear of being pushed into a military confrontation against their will in a context which they could not control was one reason why the United States and the Soviet Union were able to sustain a certain communion of interest. Both worried that extrication might be more difficult and hazardous than in-volvement. The construction of a direct telephone link, the so-called 'hot line' between the White House and the Kremlin, indicated a recognition that the two sides might have a common concern in reducing the possibility of military confrontation arising by accident, the accelerated arms race notwithstanding, particularly where there was no apparent direct clash of interests.

Several collaborative initiatives were first launched in the 1960s. A partial Nuclear Test Ban Treaty in 1963 was followed by a concern that neither outer space nor the lunar surface should be used for military and nuclear purposes. The two also attempted to limit the spread of nuclear arsenals to other coun-tries, initiating the Nuclear Non-Proliferation Treaty of 1969; its success, how-ever, would always be dependent upon its ratification by other countries – an agreement still not entirely forthcoming from several states with aspirations of achieving nuclear status. The next stage in this long conversation was the establishment in 1969 of the Strategic Arms Limitation Talks (SALT), an insti-tutionalised debate and discussion which, despite several reversals of willing-ness, completed a first agreement (SALT I) in 1972 and persisted for more than a decade thereafter. This long-running dialogue sits strangely with the 1969 declaration of the newly elected President Nixon of the advent of an 'era of negotiations'.

Apart from Berlin, which seemed to be removed from the political agenda after the erection of the Wall in 1961, Europe did not appear to be a primary concern of the super-powers. However, the world was forcibly reminded of the importance of Europe to the Soviet Union by the ending of the ill-fated 'Prague Spring' in 1968. Leonid Brezhnev, who had ousted Khrushchev as Soviet leader in 1964, invoked his eponymous doctrine – that the Soviet Union had a right to intervene in Czechoslovakia or in any other Socialist state to preserve Socialism against both internal and external threats – to remove the new liberalising regime in Prague. There was nothing new about the Brezhnev Doctrine. It simply reiterated the central tenets of Soviet policy in Eastern Europe, reminding its associates that there were limits beyond which the Soviet Union would not allow them to go. Czechoslovakia in 1968 merely reinforced the freezing of Europe between East and West. What perhaps worried the United States more were the wider implications of the Brezhnev Doctrine, which seemed to hint that the Soviet Union was also entitled to lend military support to its friends in the non-Communist world. It may have reinforced American determination to prop up regimes in the Third World which were facing pressure from guerrilla armies or hostile neighbours. It certainly made the United States more determined to quarantine Cuba within the Americas, while simultaneously making an American disentanglement from the morass of Vietnam more difficult.

Soviet policy essentially displayed no change from Khrushchev to Brezhnev: its objectives were to explore détente in order to avoid dangerous situations and to boost its own economy through the injection of Western capital and technology, while simultaneously striving for military parity with the United States and seizing any opportunity that might arise to exploit differences of opinion within the Western bloc. One reason why the Soviet Union was interested in détente was the challenge it faced from a second front. Relations with China had been deteriorating for some time. The rift became final and public in 1963, and made the two competitors for influence in Asia and Africa and for the leadership of the Communist world. China was resentful of Soviet conceptions of tutelage and of the reluctance with which Moscow volunteered economic aid and assistance for its own nuclear development. While the argument was couched in ideological phraseology, with China objecting to Khrushchev's famous denunciation of Stalin in 1956 and arguing that it, rather than the Soviet Union, was pursuing Leninist orthodoxy, the rift was also about national interests. China was simply too big to be contained as a client state in the manner of the Eastern European countries.

Soviet worries over China increased markedly in the 1960s. The nuclear development of China from first test explosion in 1964 to thermonuclear status in 1967; their long and sparsely populated common border; the historical Chinese claim to some Soviet border regions; China's ideological rejection of Soviet claims to world Communist leadership – all forced the Soviet Union to pay more attention to its eastern borders and to desire quiet on its western front. The Sino-Soviet conflict was lightened only because China still chose to isolate itself from much of world life, becoming even more introspective during the convulsions of the 'cultural revolution' (1965–68) launched by Mao Zedong.

The Chinese problem was one factor which led to the Soviet suggestion of 1966 for a general European security conference, which would prepare a series of guarantees based upon the existing territorial arrangements, where a new security system, endorsed by all the European states and the two super-powers, would replace NATO and its eastern equivalent, the Warsaw Pact. It was a scheme that was not particularly attractive to the United States and several of its partners, for while the Warsaw Pact might be dissolved, the same would not be true of the bilateral agreements which the Soviet Union had with each of its clients. These would have permitted Soviet forces to remain on the West's doorstep, while the abrogation of NATO would necessitate the end of an American military presence in Europe. Even so, there was some interest in Western Europe for pursuing the idea as a basis of discussion. Explorations, however, were broken off with the 1967 Six-Day War in the Middle East and because of Czechoslovakia. The security conference idea was nevertheless important to the Soviet Union: it would return to the theme in the following decade.

The Sino-Soviet rift contributed to an erosion of Communist solidarity, as Communist parties throughout the world identified with one or the other. The term 'polycentrism', first used by the veteran Italian Communist leader, Palmiro Togliatti, in 1956 to define his conception of the Communist world and the Italian party's right not to follow slavishly the Moscow line, was adopted to describe the new Communist system. Not surprisingly, the East European states adhered to the Soviet position in the dispute: only tiny Albania, separated from the Soviet bloc by Yugoslavia (which, as it were, had adopted its own version of polycentrism in 1948), opted to support China. It was perhaps the new elasticity of the Communist world which led the liberalising regime in Czecho-slovakia to believe that its proposed reforms – 'socialism with a human face' – would be tolerated by the Soviet Union. The fate of the Prague Spring contrasted markedly with the position adopted by Romania, which elected to follow a semi-independent foreign policy line, which included maintaining a friendly relationship with China. Unlike Czechoslovakia, however, Romania had no intention of loosening the rigid internal control of the Communist Party and so escaped the wrath of the Soviet Union, which did not regard the Romanian stand as endangering its collective security system in Eastern Europe. For the Western Communist parties, however, Czechoslovakia was decisive in a way that the Sino-Soviet rift was not. Few had previously been so outspoken as the Italian party, but most were highly critical of the reasser-tion of Soviet control in Czechoslovakia: their internal unity and relationship with Moscow would never be the same again.

After the Berlin crisis of 1961, the United States also found its attention increasingly diverted away from Europe. Hard on the heels of Cuba came the mire of the war in South–East Asia, which by the end of the decade embraced Laos and Cambodia as well as Vietnam. The roots of the problem lay in the way the French colonial war had been resolved in 1955: Vietnam, to which the war had largely been confined, had been partitioned between a Communist north and a non-Communist south. Partition was never accepted by Ho Chi

Minh and his Communist forces, which had dominated the struggle against the French. The two states of Vietnam went to war almost as soon as their independence was declared. Within a few years, it was a war which seemed to be going North Vietnam's way.

The United States, still concerned with the containment of Communism and fearing that the small countries of the region might fall one by one like dominoes, was drawn to aid South Vietnam. Assistance began with President Kennedy's decision to provide military advisers. American involvement escalated sharply to a huge military commitment under his successor, Lyndon Johnson, who had believed that 'overkill' would bring the war to a speedy end within two years. Johnson miscalculated the situation totally: by 1968 not only was North Vietnam still standing, but its forces were waging major counter-offensives in the south. The tail, in fact, soon appeared to be wagging the dog. The United States seemed to be controlled by its client state of South Vietnam and, certainly under Johnson, trapped in a quagmire from which it could not escape without severe loss of prestige.

The Vietnam War had several important consequences for the United States. The preoccupation of the government and military circles with the war meant that their attention elsewhere was distracted. Domestically, as both the costs and the death roll of American servicemen increased, the war became more and more unpopular, and set the country on an inflationary path. The government attempted to gloss over some of the adverse effects of the conflict, sometimes by deliberate deception. Johnson himself accepted that, with a deeply polarised nation, he should not seek re-election in 1968. Above all, the war became a symbol of youth protest, not just in the United States, but throughout the Western world. Eventually, opposition to the war in Congress was able to force a policy of disengagement upon the new administration, and in 1969 President Nixon announced plans for 'Vietnamisation', a gradual withdrawal of American troops from the front line.

Vietnam had two major consequences for Western Europe. First, unlike the earlier conflict in Korea, very few parallels were drawn with Europe and Germany. The war was very unpopular in Europe, and NATO countries made it very clear to the United States that neither material nor moral support could be expected. In government circles, comment ranged from a more or less diplomatic silence to outspoken criticism from Sweden. One effect was that Western Europe began to question whether its and America's defence interests were compatible. Secondly, the cost of Vietnam and the subsequent groundswell of American opinion against the military establishment and its political influence produced a questioning of the necessity of maintaining high troop concentrations overseas. This included Europe, where NATO members were accused yet again of not fully meeting their obligations under the terms of the pact. Both Johnson and Nixon came under strong pressure to reduce the level of military manpower in Europe.

Western Europe had already expressed some concern in 1966 over the Soviet proposals for a European security conference, seeing it as a ploy for removing American nuclear weapons and troop contingents from the continent. A few years later, it was faced with similar views from across the Atlantic. All of this persuaded Western European countries to search for a more distinctive foreign and defence policy. The outstanding alternative was that already propounded in de Gaulle's conception of a Europe stretching from the Atlantic to the Urals, a notion somewhat reminiscent of what some Eastern European leaders had suggested would be the rewards of a successful security conference. But before any moves could be made towards such a conception, something had to be done about the problem of the Germanies and the status of Berlin.

Just as the Sino-Soviet rift marked the end of the Communist monolith constructed by Stalin, so the 1960s, first because of the policies of de Gaulle and then because of Vietnam, marked a loosening of the Western alliance, at least in the sense of the quality of determined American leadership as exhibited earlier by Truman and Dulles. Moreover, the rectitude and reliability of American foreign policy were questioned more openly by its European allies.

Vietnam hurt the United States deeply; it was to take at least a decade before it could work through an introspective self-analysis of how and why it had become involved in the quagmire. Nixon had achieved respect for his decision first to withdraw gradually and then to cut the losses and terminate the American commitment. His historic visit to Beijing in 1972 heralded a positive Sino-American relationship. He was able also to point to other foreign policy successes, all conceived by him and his roving Secretary of State, Henry Kissinger, as part of a long-term strategy where one traded with the Soviet Union rather than believing it could be defeated or persuaded to abandon its 'old ways'. Ten years after Cuba, Brezhnev's and Nixon's efforts at détente reached a pinnacle in 1972 with the signing in Moscow of SALT I, with its concept of equal security. The following year, the two super-powers signed agreements on preventing nuclear war, which implied that they might even consider joint action against other countries which might endanger the nuclear peace and balance. They also began talks on mutual, balanced force reductions in Europe, and planned for a European security conference in Helsinki. Détente, therefore, had not necessarily been harmed by America's involvement in, and subsequent brooding on, Vietnam. However, détente and American-European relations were shaken by a domestic scandal when a bungled burglary escalated into the Watergate affair, which implicated President Nixon and many of his senior advisers in illegal wiretapping of perceived political opponents, corrupt practices and deception. When Nixon resigned his office rather than run the risk of impeachment, it was not just the reputation of the man or the presidency which suffered. It was also, in foreign eyes, a further demotion of American moral integrity, reliability and responsibility. It is in this sense that Vietnam and Watergate indicated a change in the nature of Western collaboration.

FROM BERLIN WALL TO OSTPOLITIK

The Cuban solution quite clearly could not be applied to a similar scenario in Europe: it was inconceivable that the Soviet leaders would concede so gracefully on their home ground. An undeclared struggle by proxy could take place in Africa, and limited wars occur in South–East Asia; there, the situation was more fluid. As the bipolar competition spread across the world, it created a series of no man's lands where the rules of the game were not well-defined. In Europe, however, the iron curtain remained very much a reality, even if not as impenetrable as before. The invasion of Czechoslovakia in 1968 emphasised that while the Soviet Union might be willing to pursue the question of a European détente, this would be acceptable only within the existing patterns of military blocs and what it conceived its own strategic interests to be.

Within this frozen world, the outstanding problem was Germany. For the West this raised several important questions: recognition of the western boundaries of Poland at the Oder–Neisse line; reunification or the *de jure* recognition of the East German state; the problem of Berlin. Perhaps the two Germanies might more readily have been able to compromise their differences if West Berlin had not occupied such an anomalous position as an enclave deep within the DDR. The Federal Republic resented the East German designation of East Berlin as its political capital, since the West regarded the whole city as still being under four-power military jurisdiction. The DDR resented the existence of West Berlin and the West German inclination to treat it as part of the Federal Republic. Hence the city remained the flashpoint of East–West tension in Europe, although the major powers continued to respect the unwritten rules of behaviour which had emerged in 1948.

West Berlin was an exposed nerve upon which the Soviet Union could press as an essential part of its policy. It was also a beacon for East Germans, and throughout the 1950s was a gateway to the West through which there passed countless East Germans, many with skills the state could ill-afford to lose. It was a haemorrhage which the DDR, struggling to build up its economy and present itself as a viable alternative to its Western twin, had to staunch. In 1958, Khrushchev began a series of alarums and excursions on Berlin, threatening to hand over Soviet functions in the city to the DDR unless the West agreed to a general German peace treaty and the demilitarisation of West Berlin. Soviet preoccupation with China in 1959 may have distracted Khrushchev from carrying out his threat. But in 1961 the constant Berlin problem did become yet another Berlin crisis.

In August a wall was erected, to divide completely the two halves of the city. The flow of refugees became only a sporadic trickle of people who by luck managed to surmount the barrier of concrete, barbed wire and mines. Berliners found it impossible to cross the few border points even on a legitimate basis. The United States immediately rushed in a token reinforcement of its West Berlin garrison, and President Kennedy paid an emotional visit to the city. While the Western Allies continued their military patrols through East Berlin to emphasise the occupied status of the whole city, the wall had created a totally new situation. Short of openly challenging the Soviet Union to dismantle the wall and thus run the risk of direct military confrontation, the West had no alternative but to accept the new *status quo*.

The Soviet Union itself seemed to be reluctant to push much harder: a steady undermining of the Western position in the city by incremental actions might more easily achieve gains without risks. Certainly, the sealing of the gateway gave the DDR regime a much needed boost of confidence. It was able to concentrate upon economic development without its programmes and policies being sapped by a constant drain of manpower. The growing economic strength of the DDR, the seeming durability of the regime, and the undeviating support given it by the Soviet Union all forced the Western states, particularly the Federal Republic, to reassess their relationship with the DDR.

West German policy had been determined a decade earlier by Adenauer. It was a policy of strength by which West Germany, an integral part of the Western alliance, would demonstrate its superiority over, and to, the East German model. Integral to this strategy was a refusal to compromise on the Oder–Neisse line and non-recognition of the DDR, as if the refusal to recognise the existence of the latter would somehow cause it to disappear. The Hallstein Doctrine of 1955 also stated that diplomatic recognition of the DDR by other states would be regarded as an unfriendly act towards the Federal Republic. It meant that West Germany had no diplomatic links in Eastern Europe, except with the Soviet Union which, since Adenauer's visit to Moscow in 1955, had been accepted as a necessary exception to the rule.

In the 1950s the United States and its allies had gone along with Adenauer's strategy, but with détente the Hallstein Doctrine had become an anachronism, and irritating to many. The CDU government attempted to soften it around the edges with a so-called policy of movement, which essentially endeavoured to open cultural and economic ties with Eastern Europe while keeping the DDR isolated, a strategy that had little hope of success. It was clear that any satisfactory developments must involve the abandonment of the Hallstein Doctrine.

A further impetus for change came from within West Germany itself. Central and Eastern Europe had been traditional German markets, but the Doctrine effectively debarred West German trade with the Eastern bloc. The heightened search for new markets led West German manufacturers to see these countries as a logical, close and profitable outlet for their goods. In addition, the new SPD leader, Willy Brandt, was convinced of the need to reach, and the value of reaching, a *modus vivendi* with the DDR. During the 1960s, therefore, there gradually emerged within West Germany a broader acceptance of the insufficiency of the Hallstein Doctrine, which was steadily ignored rather than officially dropped. Even though Adenauer had departed in 1963, he had saddled the CDU with a legacy which it found very difficult to jettison. Though some useful initiatives were launched by Brandt as foreign minister in the 1966 grand coalition, the decisive opportunity for change had to wait until the CDU defeat in 1969 and the formation, under Brandt's leadership, of an SPD government in coalition with the Free Democrats.

In 1970, Brandt negotiated draft treaties with both the Soviet Union and Poland, the latter one recognising the Oder–Neisse line as Poland's western boundary, as well as providing for the repatriation to the Federal Republic of the German community that remained in Poland. Ratification of the treaties was delayed because of strenuous opposition from the CDU and from within the Free Democrats. The improved SPD performance in the 1972 election, however, which was fought almost solely on the issue, indicated popular support for Brandt's *Ostpolitik*, and the treaties were ratified soon afterwards. Similarly, the 1973 treaty normalising Bonn's relations with Czechoslovakia was ratified in 1974.

At the same time, the two Germanies began to speak directly with each other. In 1972 they concluded a 'Basic Treaty', which accepted the exchange of representatives, though not full diplomatic recognition. Despite domestic criticism of *Ostpolitik*, the Federal Republic was simply accepting the facts of life. It conceded nothing that had not already been lost because of military defeat in 1945 and its consequences. Rather, it gained something that had been denied since the war: improved access to traditional markets, a more flexible foreign policy and a more positive political status. In a sense, *Ostpolitik* was West Germany's coming of age. By accepting the DDR as a separate entity, Brandt hoped that non-political ties between the two Germanies would be preserved and improved: his strategy was summed up by his belief that there were two German states but only one German nation.

The Federal Republic persisted with its *Ostpolitik* after the early 1970s, and concluded additional treaties with Poland and the DDR in 1976. West German public opinion paralleled these policy changes. Throughout the first postwar decades, a positive endorsement of reunification was almost a gut reaction: it persistently was ranked as the most important issue. By the 1970s, less than 20 per cent opposed acceptance of the postwar division, and reunification by 1976 was no longer seen as an overriding issue. Internationally, the permanency of partition in practice was symbolised in 1973 by the entry of the two Germanies as distinct sovereign states into the UN.

The success of Brandt's *Ostpolitik* was also dependent upon some reciprocity over Berlin. In many ways a Berlin settlement was the *sine qua non* for normalisation between East and West: yet it would be the most difficult to achieve. West Berliners worried that they might be abandoned by the West, even by West Germany, because in the last resort the alternative of nuclear war would be too horrendous to contemplate. Thus in its search for some kind of answer on Berlin, the West had found it necessary to bolster the morale of its citizens. Two issues were important for West Berlin: restoration of movement between the two halves of the city, which had more or less ended with the erection of the Wall in 1961, and a guaranteed land link to the city from West Germany that would be free from harassment and obstruction by the East German authorities.

In the new climate of *Ostpolitik*, yet another series of four-power talks on Berlin began in 1970. Perhaps because the Western allies indicated that the Soviet Union's favoured project of a European security conference would be contingent upon some progress over Berlin, the talks were partially successful. They resulted in the Quadripartite Agreement of 1971, which essentially granted to West Berlin a permanent form of occupation by the four powers while recognising that it had special links with the Federal Republic. West Germans and West Berliners were also to be permitted to travel to the DDR, while the promise of access to the city was guaranteed. However, the shadow of the Cold War could not be dispersed so easily. Travel proved to be only one way: generally, with the exception of pensioners, East Germans were still not able to visit the West while West Berlin was excluded from formally joining the Federal Republic. In addition, unless Berlin were to be connected to West Germany by a land corridor under Western jurisdiction, any agreement or guarantee on surface access to the city could be infringed quite easily: such an option would never be acceptable to the DDR, as it would involve the renunciation of some of its territory. Above all, the Berlin Wall remained as an effective and symbolic barrier. It was not until 1987, during the historic visit of Erich Honecker, the East German leader, to the Federal Republic that any hint was made that the Wall might become more permeable.

The Berlin problem, then, was only partially resolved in the early 1970s. West Berlin survived as a capitalist enclave within a Communist state, but its economic problems, especially an unfavourable demographic structure and lack of a natural hinterland, constantly created doubts about its continued viability, despite massive injections of aid from the Federal Republic. Despite the agreements of the early 1970s, the basis for a confrontation over the city remained as it did because of the presence of two German states. For the DDR the basic strategy was to try to close the German problem. By contrast, West Germany would try to keep it open, for *Ostpolitik* was conceived as an essential tool for maintaining links within a single German nation. Nevertheless, the four-power agreement and the extended communications between the two Germanies marked a decisive change in the postwar political map of Europe.

PROBLEMS OF DEFENCE

The Berlin crisis of 1961 shook West German faith in the American protective umbrella. Berlin, however, was only partly responsible for West German unease. The main cause, perhaps, was the debatable position of West Germany within the Atlantic alliance. However much the shadow of President de Gaulle seemed to envelop European defence arguments, it was West Germany which was the most vulnerable NATO state, the front line of defence and, as such, a key to Western European harmony.

Superficially, the main anxieties facing the Western alliance appeared to be de Gaulle's well-publicised criticisms of European and Atlantic defence, which culminated in 1966 in his decision to withdraw France from the operational structure of NATO. De Gaulle's action was the logical conclusion of his pronouncements and policies since 1958. The unilateral withdrawal was the result of a conviction that European defensive arrangements were unduly dominated by the United States, and of his fears that this domination had spread to politics and economics. Thus his criticisms of defence and his motives for leaving NATO were primarily political.

Two aims seem to have been paramount in de Gaulle's mind. He saw his action as furthering the chances of a European settlement, and also enabling

France to establish an independent base for French leadership and influence in Europe. His view of Europe suggested that the United States was not part of the continent, whereas the Soviet Union was: thus it was sensible for other European countries to come to terms with the Soviet Union. An implicit aspect of this thinking seemed to be that the Soviet Union would regard and treat Western Europe, especially France, as an equal. The defence connection with the United States was regarded as an obstacle to this accommodation. In order to pursue this policy and to reassert French influence, he clearly felt obliged to free France from American domination, and NATO was seen as the clearest symbol of American supremacy.

His action also emphasised the corollary view that France was the equal of the United States and Britain, and that it should be treated as such. His resentment at a special Anglo-American relationship extended back to the war years, and had been growing since 1958 when, shortly after his accession to power, he had suggested privately to Eisenhower and Macmillan that future military and defence strategy in Europe should be formulated and directed by a 'troika' of the three countries. The suggestion had been rejected by the United States and ignored by Britain. His interpretation of the Anglo-American link seemed to be confirmed in 1962 when the United States abandoned work on the Skybolt air-ground missile. Skybolt had already been promised to Britain, which was struggling to remain an independent nuclear power. Under the Nassau Agreement of 1962, Britain was offered the Polaris missile as a replacement. De Gaulle believed that Britain had signed away its independence. Polaris was also offered to France, albeit belatedly, but this de Gaulle rejected, preferring to develop his own independent nuclear arsenal.

Quite clearly, NATO was weakened by the French withdrawal. In addition, the organisation's integrity was being strained by several other factors: American attention was being diverted to Vietnam; Britain's economic problems were hindering it from playing a more positive role; pacifism and unilateral nuclear disarmament were becoming respectable on the European left, which itself was staging an electoral revival; several members wanted to reduce their troop commitments further, preferring to boost expenditure on welfare services; West Germany was becoming restive under the existing restrictions on its role. While adjustments were carried out quite rapidly through a series of multilateral and bilateral negotiations, the functioning and efficiency of NATO were still in dispute.

The main significance of de Gaulle's action perhaps was that it went beyond the mere military confines of NATO, being indicative of a mood that was by no means confined to France. The major issue was the great debate over the distribution and control of nuclear weapons within NATO and, more specifically, the role and powers of West Germany. American governments, under strong domestic pressure and because of their own analyses of the conditions for world peace, had been very reluctant to share nuclear control with their partners. Washington conceived its alliance network as a circle, with all nuclear authority resting firmly at the centre in the person of the American president and Congress. It feared that if other countries had an independent nuclear capacity or participated in nuclear decision-making, its dialogue wth the Soviet Union would be hindered on the one hand, and that on the other it would inhibit a rapid response to any Soviet threat. This was the kind of reasoning which contributed also to the Non-Proliferation Treaty.

There were voices in Western Europe which argued that the continent's risks in the event of a nuclear war were at least as great and that therefore it should have a commensurate share of the responsibility. This view was linked to European concerns about the American doctrine of flexible response, first elaborated in 1962. Because the earlier concept of massive retaliation had been nullified by the advent of ICBM warfare, flexible response suggested that in the event of an attack, the West would respond with a level of force appropriate for meeting the particular challenge, escalating upwards if necessary to the ultimate of a nuclear strike. While Western Europe was worried about the restriction of nuclear control to the United States, it was equally worried that flexible response might lead to an American nuclear withdrawal from Europe, so making a conventional war more possible. And Western Europe was, as ever, loath to spend its resources on the provision of an adequate conventional defence. This, too, increased the European determination to seek a greater voice. It was only in 1967, after much argument, that NATO was persuaded to accept flexible response.

Out of these attitudes, but not entirely because of them, there arose an increase in anti-American sentiment. De Gaulle's break from NATO was only a symbol of this resentment. Many Europeans, while not endorsing de Gaulle's decision, nevertheless approved of his proposals for a 'third force', an American-European partnership in which the two would be co-equal, but which also seemed to imply a return to a polycentric structure of independent national armies. But for de Gaulle, it would seem that a European nuclear force ultimately meant no more than France's *force de frappe*, control of which would be solely the prerogative of France: in other words, his views were very similar to those of the United States. And if pushed, most European governments would probably have acknowledged their greater trust in an American than a French nuclear umbrella.

Criticisms of the existing defensive structure and its aims became more common after the French withdrawal. Views which had once been dismissed as nonsensical or heretical were heard with increasing frequency. The growing unease was, in a sense, inevitable, for it arose out of the continuing search for détente and the seeming desire of the two super-powers to find a working arrangement in Europe based upon the existing *status quo*. Notwithstanding the continued Soviet military build-up, fears about the likelihood of a European war diminished somewhat, and Western Europe was less inclined to be simply a pawn in a power game played by the two giants. Thus it was inevitable that Western Europe should reassess its relationship with the United States, particularly as Washington was enmeshed in a war far removed from Europe, a war moreover about which most Europeans were unconcerned or disapproved. While the Soviet invasion of Czechoslovakia in 1968 generated some re-evaluation of the situation, it did not necessarily produce any greater cohesion. Western Europe ignored President Nixon's 1969 reiteration of self-help, that while the American commitment would be honoured, the United States expected any state under threat 'to assume the primary responsibility for providing the manpower for its defense'. NATO continued to be accepted as necessary, but many of its European members appeared to do so only half-heartedly, adopting a more minimal interpretation of their commitments and responsibilities. After 1969, only one year's notice of intended withdrawal from the organisation was required.

The American fear of escalation was one reason why the United States was keen for European integration: it might greatly reduce the number of actors to be taken into consideration. On occasions there were hints that nuclear responsibility would be Western Europe's reward for getting itself organised, unlikely as the promise might seem. One particular problem was the American fear, shared by many countries, including the Soviet Union, that West Germany might flex its renovated muscles by seeking to be a nuclear power, a position from which it might be tempted to cut through the Gordian knot of reunification by force. West German discontent grew in the 1960s, not so much against the denial of nuclear weapons as against what it felt was the latent refusal of other states to treat West Germany as an equal, especially since it believed that it bore more than a fair share of NATO's conventional defence. In addition, West Germany was always concerned that the United States might arrive at a European settlement over its head. After the Berlin Wall, its relations with the United States became more strained. While Adenauer reiterated both his determination to remain in the Western camp and the policy of non-recognition of the East, at the same time he turned towards de Gaulle and France for extra reassurance.

Tacit German support for France's independent views on defence and European union seem to have been the French price for continued recognition of West Germany's intransigent attitude towards the East. But by 1963 de Gaulle's policies were becoming less acceptable to West Germany, while Adenauer's own domestic power was being undermined. By 1965 a change of government and a shift in the balance of power within the ruling CDU, the French attempt to negotiate directly with the Soviet Union, and de Gaulle's apparent rejection of European political integration, all pushed the two countries further apart. Nevertheless, the understanding struck between de Gaulle and Adenauer survived these *contretemps*. It laid the groundwork for an axis of stability in the centre of Western Europe that would reach maturity after the mid-1970s.

Short of national ageements on union, the United States sought an alternative which might satisfy its European critics. In 1961 it first advanced the idea of a multilateral force (MLF). Briefly, the proposal was that servicemen of various nationalities should be brought together in military units. If the MLF had been put into practice, it might have linked the two sides of the Atlantic more closely, but it was too similar in its conception to the ill-fated EDC for it to have been accepted unreservedly. The similarities between the MLF and EDC were striking. Both were plans which in a sense utilised defensive and military arrangements for political purposes; and consequently the projected military efficacy of both was doubtful. It also proved easier to mobilise forces opposed, for diverse reasons, to the schemes than a coherent body of opinion in favour. While some Europeans did regard the MLF as a possible way of developing a new partnership with the United States, it was not popular with most governments, especially those of Britain and France. Consequently, the United States quietly dropped the plan at the end of 1964 without, however, formally abandoning it.

The failure of the MLF proposal and France's withdrawal from NATO threw European defence arrangements into some disarray. A discerning observer at the time might have detected that even during the several discussions the United States had remained adamant in its opposition to the dispensing at will of nuclear knowledge and capacity to its allies. On the other hand, it was apparent in 1964 that France was having little success in persuading West Germany to loosen its ties with the United States and that, consequently, the Gaullist conception of European defence was also doomed to failure. The problem was that while the original justification for NATO seemed to have diminished, it possessed no unambiguous goal. At times its purpose seemed to be a protective alliance against the Soviet Union; on occasions the containment of and reassurance against a possible German resurgence seemed to be uppermost.

However, despite the unwillingness of the United States to continue to expend so many resources on European defence without a concomitant increase in expenditure by its European allies, and despite the minimalised interpretation of NATO by some European countries, there was never any question of an American withdrawal or an end to the American strategic deterrent. There seemed to be little justification for scrapping NATO and little possibility of finding an adequate alternative. American participation was still vital. Without the United States, NATO would be nothing, while without NATO the United States could not hope to play so important a role in Europe and so prevent the possible emergence of a strategic vacuum on the continent. What seemed to be necessary was a more flexible arrangement that would reflect the changed world circumstances, encourage both a distinctive European contribution and more consultation, and reduce the role of the United States in the decision-making process. These would be questions which would continue to concern the organisation: although the collapse of the Communist bloc after 1989 may have created a very different environment, the issues facing NATO remained unchanged.

CHAPTER 14

WHAT KIND OF EUROPE?

To yesteryear belongs the political concept of national sovereignty, the idea that the national unit, relying on itself, its own strength and skills, should be the final and only yardstick of the historical process.

(*Walter Hallstein, 1964*)

However big the glass which is proffered from outside, we prefer to drink from our own glass, while at the same time clinking glasses with those around us. (*Charles de Gaulle, 1965*)

The tensions between the EEC and EFTA abated in the early 1960s, and by 1962 it seemed that the avenue to a wider, more closely integrated Europe was direct and without any concealed obstacles. Applications for membership of the EEC had been received from Britain and some other EFTA states, and their negotiations with the Six seemed to be progressing satisfactorily. The EEC, in anticipation of its enlargement, was also considering how it could accommodate countries like Sweden or Austria, whose self-avowed or imposed neutral status would prevent them from opting for full membership of the Community because of its implications of political union.

Within the EEC itself, the goals of the first transition stage had been achieved and its protagonists were looking forward with confidence to shortening the planned duration of the second phase. Negotiations on the establishment of a customs union were ahead of schedule and the Commission was forecasting that the union could come into effect by 1967, three years earlier than originally planned. The EEC had also taken the basic decisions to found a common agricultural policy. The Commission was recommending that attention now be turned to the much more complicated task of establishing a genuine economic union. Since, in 1963 and 1964, some members, like France and Italy, were registering larger trade deficits while West Germany's embarrassingly large trade surplus continued to grow, governments had become more interested in the idea of an economic union with coordinated monetary and budgetary policies.

Yet within the space of only a few years, this optimism, not for the first time, was in tatters. De Gaulle's veto on British membership had effectively blocked any geographical expansion of the EEC. At the same time, internal dissension among the Six called into question not just the desirability and possibility of the ultimate goal of political union, but also the current shape of the Community.

ENLARGEMENT: A DECADE OF PERSEVERANCE

In 1961 the Macmillan government had destroyed traditional British policy in one stroke when it announced its intention of applying for admission into the EEC, only two years after its own brainchild, EFTA, had begun to operate. Four factors had contributed towards the revision of Conservative thinking on Europe. First, while EFTA may have been living up to its limited expectations, it had done little to counteract the growing importance of the EEC. Some of its members, Austria and Switzerland as well as Britain itself, were still trading more with the EEC than with their EFTA associates. The problem was that EFTA had the appearance of a temporary organisation. Geographically disparate, it lacked any strong rationale. In particular, its members held different attitudes towards the EEC. While Switzerland, for example, preferred to remain aloof, Denmark was keen to come to terms with the EEC; only the importance of the British export market for its agricultural economy held it back. The weakness of EFTA was emphasised in 1964 when the new Labour government in Britain unilaterally imposed a 15 per cent surcharge on EFTA imports. It meant that the EFTA states enjoyed no preferential treatment in the British market: they were, in fact, worse off, for example in terms of prior notice, than the United States.

The second factor was the continuing reassessment by the British government of its world role. As the Commonwealth expanded in numbers, it had become clearer that Britain, while still dominating trade with most of its ex-colonies, could not retain the same exclusive trading advantages as before. Projections of the future suggested that trade with the Commonwealth would steadily decline as a percentage of Britain's total trade. Equally, it had become more painfully obvious since the Suez episode that the United States either interpreted the 'special relationship' very differently or preferred to deny its existence. The reorganisation of OEEC into OECD in 1960 emphasised this point, as did the election of John Kennedy to the American presidency in the same year. Kennedy's vision of the relationship between the United States and Western Europe envisaged interdependency, most particularly with a successful and enlarged EEC. Britain would have no special favours if it persisted in remaining outside the Community by choice.

A further motive which pushed the Conservatives towards membership was worries about Britain's economic performance. While there was cause for concern about the level of industrial productivity, Macmillan did not want the changes that would be necessary to raise that performance to become a party political issue. Entry into the EEC was seen as a way of possibly changing the agenda without destroying consensus. It would be competition from the

EEC which would administer the cold shower of reducing problems such as overmanning.

The final factor was the development of the EEC itself. In 1960 the Six had declared an intention to speed up the programme of movement towards a common market. A few months later, de Gaulle asserted that the Six should now be considering ways of introducing political union. In 1961 the EEC set up a committee to consider this possibility, and to draft a political treaty that would embody more concretely the various political ideas expressed in the earlier treaties. While disagreements among the Six prevented this committee from completing its task, its establishment did serve notice not only that the EEC was proceeding towards becoming a viable and integrated unit, but also that it was serious and confident about its ability to establish a political unit. In other words, if its future plans were successful, Britain's influence on both world and European developments would be reduced if it stayed outside the EEC. The later that Britain took the plunge in reaching a decision about wishing to join, the more difficult it would be to obtain satisfactory terms, and the harder the problems of adjustment to membership would be. Macmillan not only put the economic case as to why Britain should join the EEC; he also stressed that while it did not mean abandoning the Commonwealth for Europe, the move was nevertheless necessary 'to preserve the power and strength of Britain in the world'.

Shortly after Britain announced its intention to seek EEC membership, Denmark, Ireland and Norway declared an interest in following the British lead. It appeared as if the dream of a comprehensive European community in both size and function had received its greatest impetus since the Treaty of Rome. The British application was warmly welcomed by the smaller EEC members, who saw British participation as a counterbalance to the Franco-German axis. Yet there were still suspicions that British policy on the desirability of European union had not fundamentally changed, suspicions that were later to be succinctly expressed by de Gaulle. Doubts as to Britain's real intentions were probably not lessened by the tone of the British application. Britain wanted a guarantee of safeguards for what it defined as its special interests, for example agriculture and its links with the Commonwealth, and it also wanted some guarantees for the remaining EFTA states that would not or could not join the EEC. It gave the impression of being a potential benefactor rather than a supplicant. The outline presented by Britain's chief negotiator in 1961, Edward Heath, if it had been accepted, would have involved a radical change in the operation of the EEC, even perhaps its submergence in a diffuse Atlantic-*cum*-Commonwealth system.

The main theme of the negotiations between Britain and the Six, however, was a gradual but steady retreat by Britain from its starting position, and some considerable progress had been made by the end of 1962. However, the negotiations came to an abrupt end when de Gaulle, in a press conference in January 1963, announced what amounted to a veto on British entry. De Gaulle's statement, which summed up almost twenty years of difference between Britain and Europe, is worth quoting at some length:

England is, in effect, insular, maritime, linked through its trade, markets and food supply to very diverse and often very distant countries.... The nature, structure and economic context of England differ profoundly from those of the other States of the Continent.... The question is to know if Great Britain can at present place itself with the Continent and like it, within a tariff that is truly common, give up all preference with regard to the Commonwealth, cease to claim that its agriculture be privileged and even more, consider as null and void the commitments it has made with the countries that are part of its free trade area. That question is the one at issue. One cannot say that it has now been resolved. Will it be so one day? Obviously Britain alone can answer that.

Thus the French argument was based upon its interpretation of the Treaty of Rome and on doubts about the sincerity of Britain's intentions. However, two further factors were probably important in influencing de Gaulle's views. The first was the fear that British participation might mean a challenge to the strength of French influence inside the EEC and de Gaulle's own bid for European leadership, which he saw as depending primarily upon a Franco-German axis. The second was de Gaulle's interpretation and dislike of the American role in Europe. He was strenuously opposed to the concept of Atlantic partnership outlined by President Kennedy and saw Britain's entry as being that of an American Trojan horse. His resentment at the nuclear exclusiveness of the two countries had been smouldering since their dismissal of his 'troika' proposal in 1958. The agreement reached between Kennedy and Macmillan at Nassau, only one month before he gave his historic press conference, which had provided Britain with a quasi-independent deterrent in the shape of the Polaris missile, served him as both pretext and further confirmation.

One further point should be borne in mind. De Gaulle's 1960 proposal that the Six should consider ways of reaching political union had been explored by a committee which, in 1961, produced the Fouchet Plan. De Gaulle regarded this development as being more important than Britain's entry. The Plan deviated strongly from the principles of Rome and was opposed by the smaller EEC members, which also were reluctant to discuss it further until the matter of Britain's application had been resolved. And if Britain did enter, de Gaulle was convinced that his brainchild would never see the light of day, and that only the 'perfidious' United States would benefit. In the same 1963 press conference, he went on to state:

It must be agreed that the entry first of Great Britain and then that of those other States will completely change the series of adjustments, agreements, compensations and regulations already established between the Six.... We would then have to envisage the construction of another Common Market which would, without any doubt, hardly resemble the one the Six have built. Moreover, the Community, growing in that way, would be confronted with all the economic problems of its economic relations with a crowd of other States, and first of all with the United States. It is foreseeable that the cohesion of all its members, who would be very numerous and very diverse, would not hold for long and that in the end there would appear a colossal Atlantic Community under American dependence and leadership which would soon swallow up the European Community. This is an assumption that can be perfectly justified in the eyes of some, but it is not at all what France wanted to do and what France is doing, which is a strictly European construction.

France had a perfect right to exercise a veto on any prospective member: entry into the Community had to be by the common consent of all its members. Despite the anger of the other five over both the French verdict and the format in which de Gaulle had chosen to deliver it, the veto had to hold. It seemed that for several years at least a united Europe would continue to be restricted to the Six, for although the veto did not apply to the other three applicants, they were not prepared to pursue the matter without Britain. The general gloom seemed to be confirmed by the election of a Labour government in Britain in 1964, since the Labour Party had been violently opposed to Macmillan's decision to seek membership. On the other hand, the EEC displayed a resilience after the failure of the British application. Although the veto helped to plunge the Six into a crisis which lasted for several years, the EEC was not torn apart. The commitment to the Community concept remained as high as ever among the Six: it demonstrated how much the bonds had grown since the first steps in 1950.

With British entry into the EEC blocked, EFTA experienced something of a rejuvenation. In Lisbon in 1963 its members agreed upon a new schedule for further tariff reductions. While these were beneficial for trade, they did little to tackle the problem posed by the EEC and its much greater market. As the EEC proceeded with its own programme of tariff elimination, the economic division within Europe remained as broad as ever. Almost inevitably, perhaps, Britain returned to Europe in 1967, this second application being lodged by a hitherto hostile Labour government. Once again, Norway, Ireland and Denmark announced that they too would wish to consider EEC membership.

While most of the party's rank and file still evinced strong anti-European attitudes, the British Labour leaders were converted, like the Conservatives before them, by the actualities and problems of government. It was even clearer that more Commonwealth states were actively diversifying their trading patterns. Britain's trade with the Commonwealth had continued to decline, while after 1964 trade with the EEC had stagnated. The political limitations of the Commonwealth and Britain's military weaknesses had also been underlined by the unilateral declaration of independence in 1965 by the white minority regime in Rhodesia; despite the application of voluntary, and later UN-backed sanctions, Britain failed in its attempts to force the Rhodesians from their adamant position. The American attempt to introduce the MLF emphasised anew Britain's relative loss of power. Traditional Labour suspicions of the American relationship were in any case reinforced by the American involvement in Vietnam, a war which the party found repugnant. Britain's EFTA partners were disillusioned and bitter about the imposition of a surcharge, while the domestic economic situation, plagued by continued slow rates of growth, a large balance of payments deficit and a large borrowing requirement, contrasted sharply with the healthier economies of the Six.

Between 1965 and 1967, pronouncements by Labour spokesmen on the need to come to some kind of arrangement with the EEC were strongly reminiscent of those issued by Conservatives between the failure of their free trade area proposals at the end of 1958 and their decision in 1961 to seek EEC entry. The prime minister, Harold Wilson, continuing the technological theme of his 1964 and 1966 election campaigns, pointed to American predominance in such high-technology fields as space research and computers, and backed his application by arguing for the broadest possible European cooperation in technological development, and also that British membership could enhance the EEC in these fields of the future.

Superficially, prospects looked bright. The possibility of a second application had been discussed in meetings of WEU (where Britain sat alongside the Six) in 1966: French spokesmen indicated that France was not 'doctrinally' opposed to British membership. However, despite radical changes in the conception and operation of the EEC since Britain's first application, nothing had occurred that would persuade the French president to revise his opinions. This time the negotiations had hardly got off the ground when, five months later, de Gaulle, likening the application to the 'fifth act of a play during which England has taken up very different and apparently inconsistent attitudes' towards the EEC, explicitly confirmed, again in his favourite forum of a press conference, 'the impossibility of bringing the Great Britain of today into the Common Market as it stands'. While the British application was not withdrawn, remaining deposited, so to speak, on the doorstep of the Six, the second veto confirmed that as long as de Gaulle remained at the helm of French politics, British entry was impossible. De Gaulle recognised that he was perhaps the sole barrier: commenting upon criticisms of his first press conference veto in 1963, he said that 'Britain will enter the Common Market one day [but] no doubt I shall no longer be here'. As before, the other three states which had expressed their interest in membership chose not to pursue the matter further.

Advocates of British entry within both European government circles and private associations, such as Jean Monnet's Action Committee, worked hard to keep open channels of communication between the two sides. Immediately upon de Gaulle's resignation from the French presidency in 1969, the Action Committee, which by then included representatives from all three British parties, launched a new campaign for British entry. The way forward was cleared at a summit meeting of the Six at The Hague later that year. However, it was not until after de Gaulle's death and the formation of a new Conservative government that the British application re-entered the stage of negotiations. While the new French president, Georges Pompidou, was more sympathetic, France still had to be satisfied about the seriousness of Britain's intent, and it was indicative of the actual power relationships within the European Communities (EC) that the way towards establishing terms of entry was opened only after a personal meeting in Paris between Pompidou and the new British premier, Edward Heath. France also now regarded British membership as important to counter-balance the growing weight of West Germany, particularly fearing that Willy Brandt's *Ostpolitik*, a *rapprochement* with the East, might destabilise the security situation in Central Europe and damage the EC.

The terms would have to be ratified by the Six, but after Paris it was the first time since 1961 that the choice lay with Britain. Given the past record, if this application had been turned down, it might have been the last one. Alternatively, if the terms had been rejected by Britain, it might well have drawn the final curtain on the search for ways to make Britain politically and economically part of Europe. In the event, the British parliament ratified the terms, despite the decision of the Labour Party to revert to opposition to entry. The Treaty of Accession was signed in Brussels in January 1972 by Britain, along with Ireland, Denmark and Norway, and one year later Britain formally became a member of the EC after a decade of perseverance. It was, however, to be a Europe of only nine states, not ten.

The other three applicants had more or less pursued the same path as Britain. Despite not being a member of NATO, Ireland did not allow worries about a possible compromising of its neutrality overcome the reality of its very close and dependent economic linkage with its giant neighbour. Indeed, one of Ireland's hopes was that, with both itself and Britain inside the EC, it might be able to develop a more diversified trading pattern and economic structure. The Irish negotiations proceeded smoothly, with all-party support, and the proposal received an overwhelming endorsement in a 1972 referendum, held in order to ratify amendments to the constitution that were necessary to permit EC membership.

Denmark and Norway did not experience such a smooth transition. For both, their economic links with Britain meant that economically they would be advised to go where Britain went. On the other hand, they were more suspicious about European involvement, having remained aloof from all but a minimal participation in all developments since 1948. Moreover, they had to reconcile the move with their identification with the cultural concept of a Scandinavian community, which since 1952 had been sponsored by the Nordic Council.

Inspired partly by the Council of Europe, and by the failure of the 1948 attempt by Sweden to construct a Nordic defensive alliance, the Nordic Council had come into being as an intergovernmental consultative body which *inter alia* had a brief to seek Nordic cooperation across a broad front. While it had no statutes, permanent headquarters or the ability to force governments to act upon its recommendations, the Council had achieved a great deal in the harmonisation and coordination of social, labour and cultural policies. The one area where progress had been virtually non-existent was in economic cooperation. The idea of a Nordic customs union had been discussed in 1954, and a draft treaty prepared in 1957. Events, however, overtook the treaty, and it was abandoned with the establishment of EFTA. The question of a Nordic alternative to EEC membership did not really surface during the first two bids to Brussels, though a convention on cooperation was signed in 1962, and there was widespread agreement that the negotiations on entry should also involve terms that would be acceptable to all the EFTA states as well as to Finland.

Sweden was the state that was most keen on a Nordic alternative. In 1961 it had been sharply critical of what it regarded as Denmark's hasty declaration of an intention to follow Britain. The Nordic alternative emerged more visibly after de Gaulle's second veto. Meetings began in 1968, and by 1970 a draft treaty for a Nordic economic union (NORDEK) had been prepared, with a view to launching the institutional framework at the beginning of 1971. However, the structure was still to be essentially intergovernmental. NORDEK would not be a facsimile of the EC: there were too many differences of interest for that. Sweden supported the idea of a common external tariff, but this was opposed by Denmark and Norway. Denmark, with its important agricultural sector, wanted a common agricultural policy, but Norway feared that this would have severe consequences for its own rather uneconomic farm sector. Finland had several worries about NORDEK, not least of which was the possible effect upon the country's delicate relationship with the Soviet Union, yet feared being left outside it.

The act which killed NORDEK was not the renewal by Denmark and Norway of their interest in the EC, but the 1970 statement by President Kekkonen that Finland wished to establish a trade agreement with the EC provided that it could be achieved without compromising its neutrality. But this simply confirmed the lack of Nordic agreement on virtually every point and that, with the departure of de Gaulle, success would likely attend a renewed British application to the EC. In 1971 the NORDEK project was simply abandoned.

Opposition to a further approach to the EC in Denmark was primarily restricted to the left: the new far left Socialist parties and factions within the leading Social Democrat Party. But this opposition failed to generate much mass support. The debate was primarily upon the economic virtues, or otherwise, of membership, with pro-EC groups stressing the value of membership for Denmark's balance of payments and its agriculture. The 1971 Treaty of Accession easily passed through the Danish parliament. However, because the vote fell just short of the five-sixths majority required by the constitution for permitting the delegation of sovereignty to international bodies, a referendum had to be held. Here, too, the treaty gained considerable popular approval.

Norway was not so fortunate. There had been opposition to EC entry in both 1962 and 1967, but this had been relatively muted: on both occasions, the issue had not acquired a very high political profile, mainly because discussions had still been at a very preliminary stage by the time of the French vetoes. The opposite was true in 1969. The issue of EC membership aroused such deep feelings that it almost ripped the country's fabric apart. Between 1969 and 1973 the European issue generated the rise of a huge popular movement which, despite its lack of any coherent organisation and the strong pro-Europe stance of virtually all the country's political and economic elites, captured the agrarian sector of society and, in its crusade against entry, effectively hijacked the symbols of independence in a rhetoric of chauvinistic nationalism. It caused the fall of a coalition government in 1971, ostensibly over a leakage by the prime minister of the contents of a confidential document relating to the accession negotiations to a leader of the anti-EC movement. It deeply divided the dominant Labour Party, caused a permanent and fatal split in the Liberal

Party, and helped to stimulate two new political formations on the far left and the far right.

The minority Labour government which took over in 1971, while willing to sign the Treaty of Accession, had decided to hold a consultative referendum. Given the vocal opposition and his own minority position, the prime minister, Trygve Bratteli, stated that, even though it was only consultative, his government would treat the referendum result as binding, and that if the vote went against membership, the government would resign. The campaign was very bitter, and a narrow majority of 53 per cent voted against Europe. The government immediately fulfilled its promises: it halted all discussions with Europe and resigned. The imbroglio left a deep scar on Norwegian politics, which would remain for at least a decade. It effectively meant the deliberate elimination of European membership from the Norwegian political agenda: no political party wished a repeat performance of the early 1970s. It was not until the late 1980s that it became possible openly to discuss anew the relationship of Norway with the EC.

The Norwegian referendum result shocked Europe. It was the first time that the EC had been rejected by anyone, and Sicco Mansholt, the Dutch President of the Commission, admitted that it was 'a step back for Europe'. However, the Norwegian decision neither politically nor constitutionally annulled the application of the Accession Treaty to the other three entrants. Hence only Ireland and Denmark joined Britain in 1973 as full members of the EC. It was, however, a rather different kind of organisation from that which they had first attempted to join a decade earlier.

CRISIS IN THE COMMUNITIES

The tendency in the 1950s to regard the European debate as being simply between Britain and the continent blurred several divergences of opinion within the Six about the nature of integration and the way it should develop. The coming of de Gaulle did not cause these divergences: it merely served to crystallise them. The crisis which racked the EC in the 1960s for several years began with de Gaulle's veto of Britain in 1963. One immediate consequence was that it shook the confidence of the smaller members, especially as it occurred in the same month that a Franco-German Treaty of Friendship was announced. The relative passivity with which West Germany accepted the veto gave rise to suspicions that Adenauer's silent endorsement was part of the bargain with France. However, it was not just the veto which caused a crisis of confidence: every member had the right to blackball an applicant. Rather, it was the manner and forum in which de Gaulle had announced his verdict, without formally discussing it with the other members.

The crisis hardened two years later in clashes over a range of issues, which led to a French boycott of meetings of the Council of Ministers. It was in many ways a logical consequence of de Gaulle's seeking to put into practice his vision of the future Europe, which contrasted sharply with that of committed integrationists of the school of Schuman, Monnet and Spaak. It is perhaps ironical that while the British applications implied a tacit acceptance of the ultimate inevitability of the supranational principle, the Gaullist design for Europe, the *Europe des Patries*, harked back to the traditional scheme, so popular with British politicians, of an alliance sustained primarily by frequent conversations between national governments. Such a blueprint could not help but leave to an indefinite future important questions facing the integrative bodies already in existence. In its wider aspects, it was an indication that nationalism was far from dead in Western Europe.

It was in any case only to be expected that a serious move by the EEC to advance further through a reduction of national sovereignty would generate a stronger nationalist opposition. The key to further integration lay with France, which ever since the days of Schuman and Monnet had been the acknow-ledged leader of the Six. Pro-Europeans had, in fact, feared in 1958 that given the well-known views of the new French president, de Gaulle might well choose to sabotage the EEC. However, France honoured the first statutory ob-ligations of the EEC and until 1965 continued to accept without much demur the principles of the Treaty of Rome. In 1960, indeed, de Gaulle had sug-gested that the Six should seriously consider accelerated movement towards political union. While 1963 gave a strong indication that de Gaulle's interpre-tation of the treaty might be very different, the Six on the whole tended to work in reasonable harmony. The understanding reached between de Gaulle and Adenauer undoubtedly helped to facilitate this mood of cooperation.

The internal crisis that hit the EEC in the mid-1960s was a complex nexus of proposed policies affecting the Commission and national governments alike. Four separate issues were involved. The European Parliament (EP), supported by the Netherlands, wished to acquire more substantial powers for itself and so become a genuine legislature. Secondly, there was a proposal that the EEC should have an independent source of revenue out of which it could finance its own activities. This was advocated by the Commission, which sought con-trol of the revenue from tariffs imposed on imports from third countries. Both these proposals would have increased the supranational characteristics of the EEC, enhancing the powers of both the Commission and the Parliament. It was for these reasons that France was hostile to both proposals: de Gaulle had earlier suggested that the Commission already had too much power. A third proposal before the EEC involved the finalisation of the financial regulations concerning the adjustment of the several national agricultures. A common agricultural policy had been on the agenda ever since Sicco Mansholt, the Dutch politician whose brainchild it was, had put forward an early version of the scheme to the Council of Europe in 1950. The Treaty of Rome obliged the EEC to adopt a Common Agricultural Policy (CAP), and France was its most strenuous protagonist. The long-term aim of a CAP in theory was to ensure an adequate food supply, a reasonable standard of living for farmers, and a pain-less reduction in the number of small inefficient farmers. Finally, the EEC was approaching the date by which the Rome Treaty had stipulated an increase in the use of qualified majority voting in the Council of Ministers.

Until this point the EEC had worked fairly smoothly because all, or most, major socioeconomic groups and the six governments had believed that its benefits for their own interests outweighed its disadvantages. Agriculture was perhaps an area where there always would have been a clash of interest between supranationalism and national concerns. In 1965 the clash was more marked because it was the first serious attempt by the EEC to inaugurate a common policy. Now it was West Germany which dragged its heels, worried that a common policy would alienate its farmers; and the ruling CDU did not wish to offend one of its most important electoral customers just before the impending 1965 general election.

The Commission sought a way out of the conflicting demands by attempting to bring the proposals into one package deal. If France wanted an agricultural settlement, it would have to accept an increase in the supranational characteristics of the EEC. This the French government was not prepared to accept. When it became clear that the EEC would not be able to concur on the financial regulations of the CAP by the stipulated deadline, France simply refused to attend further meetings of the Council of Ministers. The point was that France was protesting not so much about incorporating the agricultural policy into a package deal, but more about the political or supranational elements of the package. This was not surprising in view of the well-known Gaullist attitude that the Commission was already too powerful. The French view was reiterated in a press conference given by de Gaulle where he stated: 'But we know – and heaven knows how well we know it – that there is a different conception of a European federation in which, according to the dreams of those who have conceived it, the member countries would lose their national identities, and which . . . would be ruled by some sort of technocratic body of elders, stateless and irresonsible'. Behind the French attitude, of course, was the additional worry over the scheduled plans for an extension of the principle of majority voting in Council decisions, which would further contract national independence.

De Gaulle's statement was a direct attack on the Community's methods of operation, and it stressed that France was not willing to resume participation until fundamental features of the Treaty of Rome were modified or dropped. It brought into the open the argument about the kind of Europe which was sought, an argument which had simmered beneath the surface since 1958, but which until now, partly deliberately and partly unconsciously, had been successfully avoided. The other five members, however, also refused to alter their stance, resenting what they regarded as a violation of EEC rules. In particular, Adenauer no longer headed the West German government, and his successors were noticeably cooler in their attitudes towards France.

Although the French boycott lasted for seven months, the EEC did not disintegrate under the conflicting pressures. In fact, the French withdrawal had not perhaps been a serious danger to the day-to-day operations of the EEC as the summer months had always been a quiet period in the daily management of affairs. However, by the end of the year the stalemate could not have been permitted to continue without the risk of endangering the EEC. New decisions and directives were needed. Either the five had to be willing to take these alone, or they had to yield somewhat to encourage France to return. Similarly, France had to relax its position or risk seeing the five go ahead by themselves. The result was a compromise settlement under which the dispute would continue in a more disguised form. The French government would continue its efforts to reduce the power of the Commission and to prevent more majority voting in the Council of Ministers. The five, on the other hand, would continue to oppose the French view of Europe.

The crises of 1963 and 1965 were basically about the same theme: the nature of the Europe that the Six were trying to construct. In both instances, France believed that its basic national interests were being threatened, in 1963 by Britain and the United States, and in 1965 by the EEC itself. The effects of the disputes were far-reaching. France very largely lost its undisputed leadership of the European movement which it had held since 1950, though its influence remained exceptionally strong. On the other hand, there was no heir apparent to occupy the throne: West Germany, the only possible contender, understandably showed a marked reluctance to do so. The EEC moved more towards a communal, balanced leadership. In addition, while de Gaulle failed to bring the other five to their knees, his aims of reducing the supranational element in the EEC and of preventing a more widespread use of majority voting largely succeeded: the five may have remained united, but the 'victory' largely went to France. The crisis was resolved by negotiation and discussions between national governments. The Luxembourg Compromise of 1966 permitted a member state to exercise a veto on discussion of matters which it believed might adversely affect its own national interests. The timetable of the Treaty of Rome was derailed, and the powers of national governments increased considerably *vis-à-vis* the authority of the Commission. The EEC and its methods of operation after 1965 were rather different from the future that had been painted in the early 1960s.

THE COMMUNITIES AFTER THE CRISIS

Despite the turmoil of the mid-1960s, there was throughout the EEC a widespread acceptance of its aims, and important national groups and associations increasingly tended to define their interests and values and to plot their actions with reference to the EEC. The economies were slowly becoming more interlocked, and European trade, not least because of the EEC, had been freed from the previously high levels of national state control. This the British Labour govenment discovered in 1964 when it was strongly criticised for imposing a surcharge on EFTA imports: during the party's last spell in office before 1951, such controls had been accepted as normal, but by the 1960s they were frowned upon by convention.

Despite the climacterics of 1963 and 1965, the governments of the Six illustrated through their actions a basic acceptance of the value of the EEC. In the face of French opposition, the other five realised that the alternative of destroying the EEC over the question of British membership was more unacceptable to them than it was for France. On the other hand, France accepted the need to pursue at least some parts of the EEC timetable: despite its boycott and the worries of its associates, France did cut internal tariffs at the end of 1965 according to schedule. There was, in short, a realisation of the fundamental importance and vitality of the EEC. Integration had become, at the governmental level, a positive political concept, albeit one with many different interpretations.

The decade saw the steady increase in the world influence of the organisation. The EEC countries had begun to act as a bloc in trade negotiations with external bodies, despite the considerable obstacles that were raised internally against arriving at such a common position. The size of their combined economies and the more persistent singularity of their voice was giving them considerable influence and bargaining power, as for instance in the discussions on the Kennedy Round of tariff cuts between 1964 and 1967. The EEC had also spread its trade tentacles to most of France's ex-colonies. The 1963 Yaoundé Convention between the EEC and eighteen African states was a symbol of the desire to offer preferential treatment to developing countries on most ranges of imported industrial goods. Through to the early 1970s, a series of agreements on association status was negotiated with several Mediterranean countries: Greece in 1962 and Turkey in 1964, and eventually Malta in 1971 and Cyprus in 1973.

Internally, progress was perhaps not so dramatic, though the 1965 decision to rationalise the executive structure of the three Communities was implemented in 1967 with a single Commission and Council of Ministers serving the European Communities. The new start in integration ran into problems, with slower progress towards economic integration and none at all on political union. Yet that would be to underrate the foundations which the EC were building for the future. An industrial customs union was established, and the principle of the free movement of labour introduced in 1968. By 1970 the EC had begun to switch the basis of funding from direct contributions by the member states to one based on their own resources: the Commission was to be able, building up over a transitional period of seven years, to generate its own funding from levies on agricultural imports and external tariffs on industrial goods. Two major innovations, which were to create much debate in the 1970s and 1980s, were the common agricultural policy and monetary integration.

Agriculture had been an important economic activity in the Europe of the 1950s. After the war all governments had encouraged a massive growth in agricultural output. While this policy generated inflationary pressures, the high costs that accompanied the greater yields were political rather than economic. Each state was determined, through subsidies and discrimination, to protect its own agricultural economy and reduce dependence upon external food supplies. Almost from the beginnings of the Six, a common agricultural policy, first advocated by Sicco Mansholt, was on the political agenda. Discussions resulted in 1960 in the enunciation of three principles that were meant to be the guiding light of a CAP: the agricultural population must be guaranteed a reasonable standard of living; markets must be stabilised; consumers must be guaranteed fair food prices. However, the structural reform element soon disappeared as the incompatibility between producer and consumer interests reasserted itself. The strength of national farm lobbies and their perceived electoral strength firmly kept the CAP in the tradition of protectionism. The CAP was to provide a single market for agricultural products with common prices and free movement of goods throughout the EC. Within the EC, its own farm produce would receive preference through variable levies collected on external products entering the EC, and the whole structure would be buttressed by a system of guaranteed prices to farmers through intervention buying by the EC of surplus produce either when supply exceeded demand or if prices dropped below a defined threshold.

The CAP was more or less in place by 1968, but by then world prices had fallen, leaving EC prices stranded at a much higher level. The CAP became what it has remained ever since: ironically, in an organisation committed to the liberalisation of trade, it was essentially an instrument of European protectionism. Though under strain virtually from its birth, it soon became something of a sacred cow, not least perhaps because it was almost the only common policy to which the EC could point. Its viability and rationality were to be continually questioned in the expanded EC of the 1970s and 1980s, especially by Britain.

The greater economic fluctuations, especially in exchange rates, that emerged in the late 1960s and the effect they were having on agricultural policy lent greater urgency to the declared intention of establishing a common monetary policy. At the Hague summit meeting of 1969, the six government leaders and their foreign ministers agreed to inaugurate an economic and monetary union, and also to consider yet again means of creating a political union. However, the only hard decision taken on a monetary policy was to reduce, but at first only on an experimental basis, the margins between their currencies and the American dollar. The devaluation of the French franc in 1969 and the subsequent revaluation of the West German mark emphasised both the dangers and difficulties that currency coordination entailed. The struggle to obtain a monetary policy went on throughout 1970, but with little real success. The problems were re-emphasised by the prolonged currency crisis of 1971, when West Germany, followed by the Netherlands, Switzerland and Austria, decided to let its currency float to find its true value against the dollar, despite the protestations of France against such a course. But even though a successful monetary policy had not been arrived at by the time of the enlargement of the EC, the previous years had nevertheless created a framework of commitment, like that of the CAP, into which the applicant states had to fit.

However, they would be joining something which was still far from a political union, where the supranational element was different, and perhaps weaker than that envisaged by the architects of the Treaty of Rome. The treaty had created a dual executive, with the Commission being constitutionally somewhat weaker than the Council of Ministers. Nevertheless, the first years of the EEC saw a dynamic and aggressive Commission, under the presidency of Walter Hallstein, that proposed and pushed for initiatives to such an extent that it was widely seen as the motor force of integration. All that changed in the aftermath of 1965. The true implication of the Luxembourg Compromise was a significant increase in the importance and influence of the Council of Ministers, particularly of COREPER, the Council's Committee of Permanent Representatives. The crisis had, in fact, been resolved not by the Commission, but by consultations and bargaining between the national governments.

The Commission would still retain the power of policy initiation and the ability to place proposals before the Council, but more and more, major proposals and initiatives emanated from the national governments, with differences between them being resolved within COREPER. In particular, the link between West Germany and France was to become of decisive importance. What this meant was first, that the Commission could not so easily make a decisive move without the groundwork already having been prepared by one or more of the six national governments, and secondly, that the key to decision-making would lie with the national premiers. The Commission, therefore, became less a policy formulator and more a broker, whose primary tasks were to strike a balance and compromise between national viewpoints and to construct packages that were acceptable to all six capitals. But it would also remain the supranational element within the institutional framework, and one which could still wield significant influence, even though decision-making was more clearly in the hands of the Council of Ministers. The 1969 Hague summit was a recognition of the role that national premiers would have to play if the declared goals of the EC were to be achieved. Because the broad economic and political goals were reaffirmed at The Hague, the style and framework of the arguments within the EC after enlargement in 1973, despite the turmoil and fracas of the mid-1960s and the changed internal power relationships, were not to be radically different from those set down in 1957.

CHAPTER 15

ALIENATION AND PROTEST

Among the possible sources of alienation in western democracies . . . is the new democratic Leviathan itself . . . welfare-oriented, centralized, bureaucratic, tamed and controlled by competition among highly organized elites, and, in the perspectives of the ordinary citizen, somewhat remote, distant, and impersonal.
(Robert A. Dahl (ed.), Political Oppositions in Western Democracies, *New Haven, 1966, p. 399)*

After 1945 an accumulation of political, military and economic problems had posed a severe challenge to parliamentary democracy in Western Europe. That threat had been successfully countered, and by the 1960s Western Europe was depicted as being on the threshold of post-industrialism, a coming society where economic growth and technological advance would reduce much of the drudgery of labour and satisfy the material needs of the population. Socioeconomic change, it was believed, had, through increasing affluence, launched a process of societal embourgeoisement. The net political outcome would be the end of ideological conflict: Keynesian-inspired neo-capitalism had defeated revolutionary Marxism. Competition would be more stylised, more concerned with the allocation of plentiful material goods and services than with principles. Guarding and directing this sanitised picture of material satisfaction was the welfare state, the paternalist benign government that had the economic base and techniques to ensure an effective distribution of goods and services among all segments of the population.

Within the space of a few years, such prognostications about the future – the belief in the durability of consensus and stability, economic growth, the satisfaction of material needs, the virtues of the welfare state – were shaken to the core. But long before the oil crisis of 1973 brought Western Europe face to face with a new world of economic stagnation and decline, it was confronted with an escalation of direct action which, with its ideological rejection of the political precepts of two decades of economic and political construction, rocked the continent's complacency. The new groups and movements which sprang up after the late 1960s may have had specific policy objectives, but taken together they implied a desire for a reorganisation of the status and power relationships within society, a territorial reorganisation of the state system, and a return to principles and values which they felt had been jettisoned by governments and parties in a quest for economic growth that had turned into an auction where elites sought to outbid each other for popular support. The 1970s would be a decade of protest and alienation, of new movements, mostly organisation-ally inchoate, that expressed new principles, and involved a search for and demanded new forms of participation. The first major wave of rejection was a mobilisation of the young, especially students. If there was a catalyst of this rejection by youth, it was the Vietnam War, not just as an expression of super-power politics, but also as a symbol of an economic and cultural imperialism that threatened to swamp Europe.

1968 AND STUDENT PROTEST

The youth generation of the 1960s had been shaped by the stable and more prosperous postwar conditions: the harsh 1930s, Hitler and even Stalin were entries in history books. There was almost a veneration of a youth culture that itself was more articulate, possessed substantial spending power, and tended towards a rejection of traditional social morals and standards. Rejection was at the heart of the 'hippie' culture, which chose to opt out of the economic race, emphasising instead egalitarianism and communal self-sufficiency: the Netherlands, and Amsterdam in particular, had by the mid-1960s become the acknowledged European capital of this alternative culture. However, it was essentially apolitical. It was not until 1968, when a tide of student action swept over Western Europe, that youth seemed to pose a political challenge to the established order of things. While a politicised student movement appeared everywhere, its impact was peripheral in most countries. The major exceptions were France, Italy and West Germany. Most notably, a student demonstration in France in May 1968 was the starting point of widespread social unrest which for a while seemed likely to topple the Gaullist regime.

Some warning signs had already appeared. Governments had welcomed and encouraged a massive expansion of higher education. However, in several countries, most notably Italy, France and West Germany, infrastructural provi-sion had not kept pace with expansion of numbers. Students were confronted with archaic authority structures in the universities, insufficient teachers and inadequate curricula, and overcrowding so gross that they found it simply impossible to get into classrooms, even buildings. It was in this milieu that radical student groups took root. Their members, primarily middle class in origin, rejected not just the consumer society, but also established authority of all kinds. The difference with the past was their rejection of classical Marx-ism and of the notion of the working class as the motor of change: for them, the workers had been bought off by the lures of the welfare state and neo-capitalist materialism. The impetus for change could only come from the young, relatively uncorrupted and therefore redeemable. The new radicals had a new pantheon of heroes – Che Guevara and Fidel Castro, Mao Zedong, Ho Chi

Minh, Leon Trotsky – all of whom symbolised the virtues of revolution as the necessary path for cleansing society of all its perceived evils.

The most surprising outburst came in France, where de Gaulle's star still seemed to be in the ascendant, and where students, despite grievances over the educational structure, had hitherto been rather quiescent. Protests erupted in Paris late in 1967 over a proposed government university reform, which did not plan to take student views into account. University reform merged with hostility against the Vietnam War, American imperialism and the autocratic nature of the Gaullist regime. The conflict became symbolised in the person of the man who emerged as the leader of the revolutionary student left, Daniel Cohn-Bendit. The attempt to expel him from his university was a catalyst that generalised the situation. Students took to the streets of Paris in ever-increasing numbers in a massive confrontation with the police, where violence was met with violence.

The turn of events took the authorities by surprise, even though the atmosphere of 1968 was perhaps more tense than usual since the Gaullists were due to celebrate the tenth anniversary of the Fifth Republic. The contagion spread rapidly from Paris throughout the country: what began as a demand for educational reform grew into wide-reaching demands for social and political change that threatened to overthrow the regime. Without trade union or party leadership or approval, workers embarked upon a series of strikes and factory occupations: within a few days, ten million were on strike. Even middle-class groups joined in the protests. It was, in short, a huge demonstration against an autocratic centralisation of authority; it seemed as if all the dissatisfaction held back by the dam of de Gaulle had finally spilled over.

Both the government and the parties faltered in their response to what amounted to national paralysis. It had taken everyone unawares: both de Gaulle and his premier were abroad on state visits. The workers' action was endorsed only belatedly by the left parties, though the powerful Communist Party was reluctant to back wholeheartedly an action which it had not initiated and did not control. The president possessed the constitutional authority to restore law and order, but an invocation of emergency powers would need both popular and military support. De Gaulle disappeared mysteriously from the capital. Upon his return it was clear that he had secretly obtained a pledge of the army's allegiance. With this he could then ask the country to choose between two stark alternatives: Gaullism and order, or Communism and anarchy. The outcome was a wave of even greater demonstrations in favour of the government. The protests disappeared almost overnight, and the ultra-radical student groups were banned as a newly confident government displayed its muscle. The following month, de Gaulle received a massive landslide victory in a general election.

The major consequence of May 1968 was upon de Gaulle and Gaullism. The party began to make more conscious efforts to secure an existence independent of that of its leader. For de Gaulle, it meant that he could not continue to ignore, lecture and chastise the electorate as in the past. Whether or not de Gaulle had become disillusioned with France, his role after the events of 1968 was more muted, and one year later he staked his continuation in office upon a positive result from a referendum on three relatively unimportant issues, treating it, as usual, as a vote of confidence in himself. When an adverse result was announced, he promptly resigned. An era of French and European politics had come to an end.

Student political activity in Italy and Spain had been rife in the mid-1960s, but it did not escalate into the widespread challenge of its French counterpart, nor did it have the ideological weight of the German movement. However, Spanish students did contribute to the weakening of the Franco regime, while the Italian movement provided the seed-bed of the terrorist activities that wracked the state in the 1970s and 1980s. The Red Brigades came out of the radicalised middle-class students of the 1960s, and continued to find sustenance and assistance from that environment.

Two events specific to West Germany buttressed its version of student protest. The first was the brief rise and fall of a new extreme right party, the National Democrats (NPD), which sharpened the critique of complicity in Hitler's regime that the radical youth levelled against their elders, as well as giving rise to fears of a neo-Nazi resurgence. The second was the decision of the two big parties, CDU and SPD, in 1966 to form a grand coalition. The tiny Free Democrats, the only other party in the parliament, were regarded as too small and too conservative to provide an effective opposition to this massive coalition. That, it was argued, could be furnished only outside the institutional structure, by an Extra-Parliamentary Opposition (APO). Passions were further inflamed by the government's decision in 1967 to introduce an Emergency Law that would enable it to act effectively in a crisis situation.

The APO was a sprawling movement without much coherence. However, an organisational core was provided by the Socialist German Student Alliance (SDS), and it benefited from its interface with the situation in the universities. The SDS had formerly been the student wing of the SPD. Strongly opposed to the party's earlier rejection of its Marxist heritage, the SDS had finally been disinherited by the SPD in 1961. The SDS vanguard was highly visible in the mass demonstration in West Berlin in 1967 against a visit by the Shah of Iran; during the confrontation with the police, a student was killed, to be instantly elevated to martyrdom. The Berlin episode occasioned even more protest, which had an immediate target in the right-wing press magnate, Axel Springer, and his chain of newspapers, which were highly critical of the student movement. It buttressed the belief of the SDS leader, Rudi Dutschke, that violence to protect oneself against police provocation and an oppressive state was justified. The German movement was by far the most ideological in its rejection of neo-capitalism, an objective confirmed at a massive national conference in which Dutschke called for 'permanent revolution in the universities' to destroy bourgeois ascendancy and the materialist bureaucratic state. Activity peaked and culminated with massive street demonstrations and battles in 1968 after an assassination attempt on Dutschke. Badly wounded, he went abroad to convalesce, and disappeared as a driving force.

The movement rapidly degenerated into factional disputes, and the SDS formally dissolved itself in 1970. Instead of permanent revolution, the future was to be secured by a 'long march through the institutions', a steady infiltration of radicals into positions of responsibility within the establishment. Those who clung more rigidly to the belief in violence were the source of the radicalism that plagued West Germany in the 1970s – anarchic terrorism. Other reasons contributed to the disintegration of the APO. Many students were involved only on an *ad hoc* basis, concerned really only with the theory, not the practice, of political revolution. The bulk of student unrest dissipated when the educational authorities introduced reforms for university structures and government. Moreover, the SDS and its allies had failed to find support outside the universities. The working classes had remained unmoved and the trade unions had been as stern in their rejection of the APO as any conservative. By 1969 the Emergency Law, with some modifications, had been enacted, giving the government more teeth with which to tackle unrest. The SPD government under Willy Brandt that came to power in 1969 was as rigorous as its grand coalition predecessor. In 1972 it went one step further with the *Radikalenerlass* (radicals' decree), a kind of loyalty test for all public employees: an affirmation and proof of support for the 'free democratic order' of the constitution became a necessary condition of public employment. This was in part a response to, and a strategy to prevent, the radical left's threat of a long march through the institutions.

TERRORISM

The student movement faded almost as quickly as it had erupted. With little coherent ideology and organisation, with no clear aims other than university reform, inconvenient rather than dangerous, it overestimated its own political strength and the resilience of the political system. The same conclusions might be drawn about another form of guerrilla warfare which took shape in the 1970s. Terrorist groups could be found on both the extreme left and the extreme right. However, the most dramatic effects were achieved by, and the continent's headlines dominated by, those on the left. They sought through violence to destabilise the system, to invite repressive state retaliation which would eventually alienate the population, which in turn would become more receptive to the terrorists' own political perceptions. A similar strategy was pursued by those nationalist groups like the Irish Republican Army (IRA) and the Basque ETA organisation which sought to destroy British and Spanish rule in their respective provinces.

Left-wing terrorists claimed an existence in most countries – Britain, for example, had its Angry Brigade – but it was West Germany and Italy which bore the brunt of the onslaught. In West Germany, terrorism arose out of the more anarchic segments of the APO of the 1960s. Eventually calling itself the Red Army Faction (RAF), it was popularly and generically known as the Baader–Meinhof group after two of the early leaders, Andreas Baader and Ulrike Meinhof. Typically coming from affluent liberal middle-class families, the group rejected the precepts of the West German state, setting out with the intention of 'shocking the people', making them aware of state and capitalist oppression.

Their reign of terror was brief but frantic. In 1970 and 1971 the Baader–Meinhof group embarked upon a series of daring bank robberies and bombings. More deliberately, they targeted leading public figures for kidnapping and death. While they enjoyed some underground support from fragments of the 1968 generation, the general public response was one of revulsion. Most of the original leaders, including Baader and Meinhof, were captured and jailed for life by 1972, but this did not stop the spate of terrorism. However, there was a steady disintegration, partly because of more effective government counter-measures, of whatever unity that had existed; after 1975 the RAF operated mainly as a series of isolated units which had little contact between each other.

The turning point, perhaps, was the hijacking in 1977 of a German airliner, which was diverted to Somalia. A special police squad was despatched there, where, with the permission of the authorities, it successfully liberated the passengers. A few days later, Baader and two of his associates were found dead in their prison cells; Meinhof had already committed suicide in prison the previous year. The day after Baader's death was announced, the body of a prominent German industrialist, Hans Martin Schleyer, kidnapped several weeks earlier, was found in an abandoned car in France. The events of 1977 marked a final divorce between the public and the terrorists. Counter-measures effectively brought the terrorist era to an end, though RAF activity continued sporadically. Baader and Meinhof may have begun their careers with the sociopolitical objective of an 'ideal' world built out of the destruction of the present, but very rapidly West German terrorism assumed the guise of destructive nihilism, without any idea about, or concern for, what it could or would do if the system actually did collapse.

The same was perhaps also true of Italian terrorism. Although some outrages were committed by shadowy extreme right-wing groups, the focus was more on the Red Brigades (BR), a generic term covering several different groups which were also an offshoot of youth protest: their founder, Renato Curcio, had been prominent in the student demonstrations of 1968 and 1969. Their campaign of robberies, kidnappings and assassinations began in 1970, intensifying after 1974. Again, there was no clear perception of political aims except for platitudinous references to the need for a 'just' and 'incorruptible' system. All too easily, the BR seemed to drift into nihilism for its own sake; terror became an end, not a means. Although Curcio was captured in 1976, the Italian authorities found it difficult to come to grips with the decentralised nature of the BR. The climax was the kidnapping and eventual assassination in 1978 of Aldo Moro, a prominent Christian Democrat Party (DC) leader and a former premier. The government refused to negotiate: a politician's life could be treated no differently from that of other people exposed to similar risks. The discovery two months later of Moro's body in the boot of an abandoned car in Rome produced a feeling of national revulsion. Curcio in prison might hail it as an act of revolutionary justice and 'the highest act of humanity possible in this class-ridden society', but the BR hopes were dashed by the consequent popular support given to the state.

After 1978 the Italian police became more adept at countering terrorist operations, although the scale of outrage did not decline for some time: in 1980, for example, there were still 122 murders and assassinations. However, special anti-terrorist units were gaining muscle, and in 1983 they gained an impressive victory when they successfully foiled an attempt by the BR to revive flagging fortunes with a repetition of the Moro episode, a kidnapping of an American general. By then most of the BR leaders, particularly those with organisational ability, had been captured or killed. Shortly after the abortive kidnapping attempt of 1983, a statement of surrender was announced by the jailed leaders of the BR, who admitted that 'the cycles of revolutionary struggles . . . based on the wave of workers' and radical student movements have substantially ended'. It marked the death knell of the youth focus of 1968, the end of a rebellion that became a rebellion without a cause.

The deaths of the major RAF figures and the self-dissolution of the BR did not mean the end of terrorism in Western Europe. Radical right and left groups persisted for some time in Italy. Between 1979 and 1989 the left-wing *Action Direct* waged a bombing and assassination campaign in France. There were suspicions that the murder of the premier of Sweden, Olof Palme, was a terrorist act. Regionalist militants such as the IRA and ETA continued to resist governmental attempts to eradicate them. Nevertheless, the successful resistance of West Germany and Italy reaffirmed the general stability of Western Europe and its commitment to liberal democracy: in particular, two states about which there had been doubts about the depth of their stability had passed a severe test with flying colours. In the 1980s and 1990s the terrorism in Europe that hit the headlines was of a different variety. The continent became a recipient of state terrorism imported from outside, especially the Middle East, which sought to extend its political ideology and to eliminate dissidents and refugees who had been given asylum in Europe.

THE ANTI-NUCLEAR THEME

In the 1970s the radical left found a new cause for which there was potentially much more widespread support. The European economic boom had been fuelled by cheap energy, but the quadrupling of oil prices by OPEC in 1973 and the embargo which the Arab producers levied against some states such as the Netherlands drew attention to the political vulnerability of Western Europe in terms of what had become its primary energy source. In the aftermath of 1973 there was a renewed interest in coal, but its extraction was costly as well as creating pollution in a new political climate where environmental issues were being taken more seriously.

Almost inevitably perhaps, governments began to consider with rather more urgency the question of nuclear power as an alternative and cost-effective energy source. Britain already had a long-standing programme, and France,

Sweden and West Germany also had well-developed plans for a large-scale nuclear industry. The construction of nuclear plants awakened or reinforced all the old fears about the safety of nuclear power and the degree to which safeguards against a possible accident or sabotage could be guaranteed. These fears were fuelled by a major accident at an American nuclear plant at Three Mile Island in 1979. The nuclear debate continued through to the 1990s as some states pressed ahead with nuclear development. Nuclear power, if it could be harnessed properly, could be cost-effective, but doubts about its safety and how to dispose of its radioactive waste could not be erased. The consequences of a nuclear accident were brought home by a massive radiation leakage from a nuclear reactor at Chernobyl in the Soviet Union in 1986. The radiation cloud extended as far as Western Europe, having severe consequences in several areas, especially northern Scandinavia.

The debate was one which was not readily amenable to dispassionate discussion. Positions were adopted for moral, emotional and ideological reasons, permitting little common ground where the two sides could meet. Protest demonstrations against the siting and construction of nuclear plants occurred throughout Western Europe: they were most impressive in West Germany. Occasionally, the anti-nuclear lobby saw its cause adopted by a political party, but of these only the Swedish Centre Party experienced a rise in support, but by the 1980s even that proved to be ephemeral. In Norway the fading Liberals adopted a strong green and anti-nuclear profile in the 1980s, a stance which, it was widely agreed, contributed greatly to the party's elimination from parliament in 1985.

What counted for a party was not the issue, but its own strength. The nuclear issue was only one of many, and it was more important for it to be taken up by a major party that could reasonably hope to control government, as with the British Labour Party or the West German SPD in the 1980s. Only in Sweden, however, with the return of the Social Democrats to power in 1982, did a major party have an opportunity to implement the anti-nuclear cause. The party, which in any case was bound by a painful referendum campaign of 1980 which had voted against nuclear energy, announced the dismantling of Sweden's well-advanced nuclear network. Popular pressure led to a similar referendum in Austria, which effectively ended nuclear construction there. The anti-nuclear movement failed more singularly to achieve similar objectives in Britain, France and Italy, though a 1987 referendum in the latter gave the politicians pause for thought. By the 1990s, however, the belief in nuclear power was in retreat almost everywhere, although cost rather than moral or environmental considerations was what had swayed governments.

The vitality of the anti-nuclear theme was not due primarily to its backing by a political party, but more because it spotlighted an issue that worried a great number of people and because it provided a new outlet for many activists schooled in the left-wing protest movements of previous years. The latter had acquired considerable experience in mass campaigning and direct action. What counted was the extent to which their arguments against nuclear energy overlapped with other issues. There were two: the consequences of a nuclear accident could be disastrous for the environment, hence there was a mutuality of interest with 'green' groups concerned about the deleterious effects of the industrial consumer society upon the environment and the delicate ecological balance; the second important link was with the peace movements.

Peace movements of one kind or another were as old as the Cold War. Leftist in inclination, they objected to military strategy based upon the nuclear deterrent, particularly to the nuclear arsenal possessed by NATO. The adoption by NATO of a nuclear strategy in the 1950s had increased the appeal of unilateral nuclear disarmament; in Norway, Denmark and the Netherlands it had helped the appearance of parties to the left of the Social Democrats which urged withdrawal from NATO. Broad and ostensibly non-party anti-nuclear peace movements were comparatively rare: the major example, the British Campaign for Nuclear Disarmament (CND), was formed in 1958 as a consequence of Britain's opting for a nuclear-based defence policy.

Initially, CND enjoyed considerable mass support through demonstrations and marches. By the mid-1960s, however, it had become a staid and quiescent organisation on the fringes of British politics. It was rejuvenated in the 1980s, at the same time finding allies in similar movements throughout the continent; in 1983 the national groups attempted to come together as European Nuclear Disarmament (END). The catalyst for the new lease of life was the 1979 NATO twin-track decision to install intermediate-range nuclear missiles in Western Europe as a counter to the presence of similar Soviet missiles in the Warsaw Pact countries. For a few years the peace movements and their opposition to the NATO strategy, strongly backed by the Soviet Union, seemed to dominate the media because of their ability to guarantee a huge turnout for demonstrations. In West Germany the movement claimed to have obtained by 1982 almost three million signatures for its anti-nuclear Krefeld Appeal. Defence bases, especially those harbouring nuclear devices, were 'besieged' by protesters, who occasionally were able to breach perimeter defences.

Perhaps the major import of the peace movement was its success in persuading some Social Democrat parties to embrace its cause. Unilateralism became a prominent element of the party programme in Britain, the Netherlands and West Germany. The Scandinavian parties took up with renewed vigour the idea of a Nordic nuclear-free zone. The results were mixed. Unilateralism was attributed as a major reason for the poor electoral performance of the left in Britain and West Germany in the 1980s. In some countries, France and perhaps also Italy, the movements failed to establish themselves as an effective force. END soon became little more than a façade. Long before the United States and the Soviet Union moved in 1987 towards a treaty that would eliminate intermediate nuclear weapons from Europe, the peace movements were in decline. While they would claim some credit for bringing the superpowers to the conference table, it is more likely that it was NATO's firm stand, and the potentially adverse effects of a renewed arms race upon its own inefficient and straining economy, that persuaded a new Soviet leadership to accept what had become known as the Double Zero Option.

In the longer run it was probably the ecology or green movement that was more significant as a new bearer of radicalism. At the local level, activists were able to find common cause with citizens concerned with a local issue – river pollution, industrial discharges, dying trees. Out of these local issues there arose a greater awareness of an ecological fragility across a whole range of areas which constituted a national and perhaps international problem that demanded an organisational response. Local protests, petitions and marches were supplemented by broader organisations such as the 1972 West German Federal Association of Environmental Citizens' Initiatives.

If anything, it was the nuclear issue that provided the ecology movement with cohesion and politicised it. Nevertheless, the divergence of interests within it gave it a package of demands which were unlikely to be accepted *in toto* by political parties, though gradually its protests contributed to the scope and rigour of government policies regulating the environment and its utilisation. By the 1980s, there was a broad recognition of the damage that was being done to the environment and of the need for government action. Political parties, however, often found it impossible to accept the basic logic of the green movement that what was necessary was a rejection of the growth-oriented consumer society and instead a commitment to zero, even negative growth. To parties and governments – even those on the left, whose trade-union associates were pressing hard for more economic investment and growth – wrestling with problems of unemployment and economic decline, this was an unwelcome call.

In the last resort, therefore, if the green cause wanted to leave the streets to conquer the citadels of power, it would have to be through its own political organisations. Ecology or green parties had emerged in most countries by the late 1970s; the only dramatic impact, however, was in West Germany. There the various action groups had formed an alliance in 1979 to contest the first direct elections to the European Parliament. While it had only a modest success, the alliance was the basis of the Green Party formed the following year. From a small beginning, the Greens grew steadily, and in 1983 gained a substantial parliamentary representation. The rise of the Greens, with their preference for alternative and extreme democratic forms and practices, created potential complications for coalition government in West Germany. Standing to the left of the SPD, the Greens could argue that they were the true left in German politics. If the SPD did not respond to their challenge, it might well be undermined by the Greens, who appealed especially to the young. If, on the other hand, the SPD tried to protect its left flank, it ran the risk of forfeiting that broad middle ground of public opinion whose support was necessary if the party wished to remain a major contender for government. By the 1990s the German Greens had matured somewhat. They had abandoned some of their more extreme demands, and had become more accepted as a mainstream left-wing party. The drama of the West German Greens was not repeated elsewhere. Although by the late 1980s ecology parties were represented in a few national parliaments, they possessed little more than a toehold. The extent to which they would be able to expand or even survive was something which still in the 1990s remained to be tested.

FEMINISM

Associated with the extra-parliamentary left, at least in much of the popular mind, were the movements that sought equal rights for women, some of which sought to root their campaigns in a feminist world view or ideology. Spreading from the United States, where women activists had been politicised in the student protests of the 1960s, these movements had an impact of some sort upon the whole of Western Europe. Equal rights and equal opportunities was something that all governments could accept, at least in theory. However, in terms of creating conditions for an effective socioeconomic and political promotion of women, let alone equal representation, governments inevitably moved more slowly than feminist activists desired, especially in a period of economic retrenchment. The 1970s saw new women's movements mushroom everywhere, in various areas of social activity and espousing a multitude of causes, both practical and impractical. Like other inheritors of the new left of the 1960s, these new movements were characterised initially by a rejection of organisation and hierarchy, and a preference for spontaneity and direct action.

Several reasons have been advanced for this politicisation of women after the 1960s: there were more educated women, and more women in paid employment outside the home; divorce was more common; new and more effective contraception techniques were widely available. The women members of the extra-parliamentary left found that it tended to give a low priority to their own gender-based concerns; equally, however, they regarded the established political system as something which prevented full emancipation and equal rights for women. Although perhaps it was only a small section of the feminist movement that eschewed the formal political arena, stressing distinctiveness and attempting to construct an almost millenarian ideology of feminism, their ideas infected traditional women's organisations, which took up the same themes with equal vigour: equal pay and equal rights at work, the promotion of women to positions of responsibility in both the public and private sectors, legalisation of abortion, more and better pre-school nursery facilities, effective measures against violence against women, especially rape.

By the end of the 1970s, these demands, if not the original feminist movements, were highly visible everywhere, and governments, parties and trade unions were having to take account of them. The impact and strength of feminism varied considerably. It was most immediate perhaps in Scandinavia, where practices of sex equality were introduced over a much broader spectrum of social life. The market leaders were generally regarded as being Denmark and Iceland. Progress was much slower in southern Europe and Ireland. On the other hand, strength and size of movement did not necessarily guarantee success. Iceland, for example, had a woman president after 1980: yet one might wonder whether the decision to form a Women's Alliance Party in 1983 was an acknowledgement of success or an admission of frustration over the lack of progress. The Women's Alliance was one of only three such parties to be formed in Europe, and the only one to achieve a modicum of parliamentary success.

Women's movements were also strong in Britain and the Netherlands. In Britain, however, the progress of women up the promotional ladder, especially in politics, was at first relatively slow, despite the fact that in 1975 Margaret Thatcher became the first Western woman party leader and the first Western woman premier in 1979. By contrast, while the mass feminist base in France was relatively small, the Socialist Party was won over to the cause; upon election to government in 1981, it established a Ministry of Women's Rights with a wide brief for action. The success of the Ministry was mixed, and it was abolished by an incoming Gaullist government in 1986. A different pattern was evinced in West Germany where, despite the prominence of women in left-wing activities in the 1960s and 1970s, an effective women's movement failed to develop. In part, the feminist push was subsumed by the Green Party: women were prominent within the party, which had adopted parity of representation as one of its tenets.

By the 1980s much of the ideological heat had gone out of the movement; the subsequent years were more a period of consolidation and frustration. The strength and weakness of the feminist upsurge had been its spontaneity and eschewal of hierarchical organisation. But that alone proved insufficient to create a revolution in the institutions of state and society. While there was a widespread acceptance by all parties and major socioeconomic organisations that equality of opportunity was essential, and that the advancement and promotion of women was both necessary and desirable, few were willing to go so far as to adopt a policy of positive discrimination in favour of women. When the Labour Party in Norway returned to power as a minority government in 1986, the fact that Gro Harlem Brundtland (the second woman premier in Europe) constructed a cabinet with women as one half of the membership raised not a few eyebrows. The number of women nominated for and elected to parliament varied considerably from country to country, being substantially better in Scandinavia and the Netherlands than elsewhere. But the overall level of participation at the higher levels of politics was still low, and the prospects for further advancement perhaps not overly optimistic. Similar conclusions were not quite so relevant for the world of work, but even so there was by the 1990s a seeming withdrawal by more women from some of the precepts on equality and advancement advocated by feminists.

The dilemma facing the women's movements in the 1990s was the same as that confronting the ecologists and that which had confounded the left-wing protesters of the 1960s and 1970s. The early vitality had been spawned by a sense of spontaneity and a more or less deliberate decision to spurn hierarchical organisation, to bring decision-making back to ordinary people. But to affect the political system, and to be efficient, the feminists had to sell their ideas and already fragmented ideology to that system, to enable women to gain access to and advance within the channels of political and socioeconomic influence. By the 1990s, some of the policy priorities may have been accepted by governments, women may have entered the policy-making areas in greater numbers, but to many the overall goal at times seemed as remote as ever. The system proved resilient to conquest from the outside, therefore feminism had to enter the system. That raised the central dilemmas of whether ideology served any purpose and of how to accommodate to established practices while still retaining a commitment to and belief in the virtues of a decentralised and spontaneous movement. The march through the institutions could be very long indeed.

RACIALISM AND THE EXTREME RIGHT

The memories of the Third Reich effectively discredited the extreme right for some time after 1945. Only in Italy, in the shape of the Social Movement, did it continue to enjoy a certain vogue and support, mainly in the more backward south of the country. As memories of the war and Nazi atrocities began to fade, right-wing protest began to make itself heard again, first gathering some momentum in the 1960s, partly as a reaction to the growth of extra-parliamentary activity on the left. Again, it was often the materialism and Americanisation of European society which came under fire. However, the desire on the right was not to create a brave new world, but more usually to secure the restoration and survival of what were conceived to be traditional national values. These were sentiments that were shared by elements of conservative parties, which gave the far right a patina of respectability; but, on the whole, conservative parties sought to distance themselves from organisations such as the National Front in Britain or the several paramilitary 'black' brigades that sprang up in Italy, which were willing to indulge in direct and violent confrontation with all they deemed their 'enemies'.

Violence, however, was studiously avoided by the potentially most dangerous new movement of the 1960s, the West German National Democrat Party. Viewing itself (though never specifically admitting it) as the inheritor of the Nazi tradition and certainly seen as such by others, the rise of the NPD after 1966 sent shock waves throughout the Federal Republic and Europe. Its star, however, was to be short-lived. It narrowly failed in its bid to gain parliamentary representation in 1969, and soon afterwards disintegrated into several weak and mutually hostile factions. It was not as if the West German system had done anything to hasten its demise: the major parties had been unsure how to tackle the NPD. In the end, indecision proved to be the best policy: the NPD failed of its own accord.

In the 1970s, the far right found new material on which to feed: the colossus of the bureaucratic state and the growing burden of taxation required to nourish it. It was a theme that was later to be taken up with increasing insistence by conservative parties in most countries. But it was also the issue which led to the creation of anti-tax Progress parties in Denmark in 1972 and Norway in 1973. However, if there was one issue that was identified with the far right, it was the racial question, the increase through immigration of the non-white population of Europe and its consequences. Some of these immigrants had come voluntarily to Europe to seek a better economic future for themselves and their families: others had been 'recruited' by a Western Europe faced at the height of its economic boom with a labour shortage, especially in low-paid unskilled jobs. By the early 1970s the number of 'guest' workers without European citizenship had reached ten million.

Britain was the recipient of large-scale migration from the Commonwealth. In France, immigration was mainly from its previous North African possessions. Other states had encouraged and welcomed guest workers, first from southern Europe – from Italy, Spain, Portugal and Yugoslavia – and then from further afield, most importantly from Turkey and Pakistan. In the 1970s and 1980s, this influx was swelled by refugees from countries as far apart as Chile and Vietnam, while after 1989 there were widespread fears, especially in Germany, that the ending of the Cold War would lead to large number of economic migrants from Eastern Europe seeking to settle in the West. In absolute terms, the numbers were greatest in the large states of Britain, France and West Germany, though still a tiny minority of the total population. Economically, however, their significance could be much greater: by 1974, for example, while guest workers and immigrants constituted only some 4 per cent of the West German population, they made up almost 20 per cent of the manual workforce. In Switzerland, incomers formed some 20 per cent of the population.

The guest workers were not granted citizenship as of right; they were meant to be a supplementary workforce which could be reduced in the event of an economic downturn or labour surplus, which is precisely what Western European governments anticipated doing after 1973. There were, however, two drawbacks. In many occupations, the guest workers remained indispensable for the provision of services which the native population refused to do. In addition, many had been allowed to bring their families to Europe and did not wish to return to their homeland. Refugees, obviously, could not return. For ex-colonial powers like Britain and France, repatriation or dismissal was not an option. As part of the winding up of empire, the right of citizenship had been offered to the peoples of their colonies. Unless some redefinition of citizenship was adopted, as in Britain in 1981, the flood of entrants would continue.

The newcomers formed the bottom stratum of European society. They congregated in the large urban areas, especially in the declining inner-city areas where cheap accommodation was more readily available. Whole sections of European cities became ghettos. British cities had their black and Asian quarters. In France, cities like Paris and Marseilles had clearly identifiable Arab neighbourhoods, while West Berlin and other German cities had their Turkish areas. Racialism and racial prejudice was something the new groups had to face, for example in securing accommodation and in violent harassment, right from their day of arrival, and bodies like the National Front in Britain thrived on it. The situation took a marked turn for the worse in the 1970s as the economic climate worsened. The newcomers could be treated as convenient scapegoats for a country's economic ills; even trade unions saw them as an inconvenient problem. On the other hand, unemployment bit more deeply and widely among the immigrant populations.

Several Western European states had become multi-racial, and at least those which had received substantial numbers of immigrants were having to face up to problems of assimilation and prejudice. The far right, already racialist itself, attempted to use the race question to boost its own support and influence upon government, including a resort to direct action. But while anti-racial legislation might be given a low priority, no government was prepared to follow the path of the far right. Perhaps the most significant move against guest workers was made in Switzerland under the country's liberal rules for popular initiatives and referenda. In 1970 the country's two extreme right-wing parties were able to force a referendum on a savage reduction in numbers and eventual repatriation of all foreign workers (who were overwhelmingly European). The proposal was not carried, though a worryingly large minority endorsed it. More typically, governments introduced a virtually total ban on further immigration. To reduce the level of those already *in situ*, France and West Germany offered to pay the costs of repatriation of those immigrants who were willing to return to their homeland, an offer for which there were few takers. The situation threatened, from a government perspective, to get out of hand again in the 1980s as Western Europe, especially West Germany, was swamped by a flood of refugees from the Third World. Many states were obliged to introduce strict limitations on the entry of refugees, most severely in Denmark, where the flow almost dried up completely after new legislation in 1986. In the 1990s the barriers were extended to hinder easy access from Eastern Europe – a softer, but no less visible, 'iron curtain'.

By the 1980s the immigrants were beginning to react against the physical attacks upon them, the institutional practices that discriminated against them, their greater relative deprivation, and the much higher levels of unemployment they had to endure. New organisations appeared to press their arguments in the political arena. Immigrant groups clashed in the streets with both white groups and the police and, occasionally, there were riots against the system. Such violent confrontation was not new: riots, for example, had occurred in London in 1957. But in the 1980s, first in 1981 and again in 1985, London and other British cities were the scene of violent destruction and looting as blacks rioted in, and burnt down, the streets. Similar race riots, though on a much less destructive scale, appeared throughout Western Europe, even in countries like Norway which had experienced relatively little immigration.

The authorities took immediate measures to quell the riots, and for the long term were jolted into planning actions for integrating the newcomers more thoroughly in an equitable manner. Bodies such as Britain's Commission for Racial Equality were charged with the duty of monitoring and combating racial prejudice and discrimination. To some extent, the problem of integration was made more difficult by monitoring decisions which served to annoy the white population further, and by the doubts that were sometimes raised as to whether immigrant groups wanted assimilation or separate but equal development.

The acute level of racial tension experienced by Britain in the 1980s was due not only to the high levels of immigration, but also because most of the newcomers were also citizens of the state. In France, white hostility was directed more towards non-citizens, especially Arabs: unlike the British case, many North Africans who came to France after 1963 refused to seek citizenship. But at any rate, by the late 1970s there was throughout the continent a new generation for whom Europe was home and yet who felt that opportunities for employment and personal improvement were worsening relative to those for the rest of the population. As the second and third immigrant generations emerged elsewhere in Europe, similar violent expressions of discontent began to appear everywhere. In many countries, the immigrants were not citizens and were denied citizenship. Sweden was the first state to permit non-citizens a limited political participation: in 1978 it gave resident foreigners the right to vote in local elections, but not at the national level. By the 1990s very few states had followed the Swedish example.

With forced repatriation impossible and voluntary repatriation unlikely to succeed, Western Europe was left with the problem of integration. It remained undecided, however, which route to follow: equality and assimilation, the historical path; or equality and 'segregation', which is what some immigrant groups seemed to want. The former strategy was in line with traditional precepts of liberal democracy; the latter, while granting immigrant communities some specific rights – for example, by public authorities providing information in languages other than the official state language, or by granting special concessions in religious education – may well have fitted with the concept of the multicultural society, but it equally ran the risk of sponsoring a form of cultural apartheid.

On the other hand, the higher level of racial tension in the 1980s and 1990s did not generate a powerful political backlash from the extreme right. The latter almost disappeared as an active and organised force in Britain, while in Switzerland, despite the earlier referendum, the issue did not electorally benefit the far right parties. The few exceptions to this relatively quiescent political scene included France, Austria and, after 1990, a reunited Germany. In France the 1980s saw the rise of the National Front, under the vigorous leadership of Jean-Marie Le Pen, to a position of some political influence, with substantial electoral support after 1984. Le Pen's unashamed beating of the racialist drum, especially in Marseilles with its large Arab population, alarmed the other parties, which found it difficult to muster a rational defence against his emotional appeals, though in certain localities the Communists for a while, and not entirely surreptitiously, attempted to outbid him on the race issue. Le Pen articulated fears, no matter how irrational, held by many French citizens and for electoral reasons the mainstream French right felt obliged to take on board at least some of the Front's concerns. A new hard-line government policy became evident after the victory of the Gaullist Jacques Chirac in the 1995 presidential election, and incidents like the indiscriminate bombing campaign in Paris in 1995, widely ascribed to Algerian Islamic fundamentalists, helped to keep the general issue alive.

Austria, by contrast, was the first country where a mainstream political party, the small Freedom Party, seemed to embrace ideas of the radical right. This shift was evident after the election of the populist Jörg Haider to the party leadership in 1986. Haider, already well-known for his nationalist views, subsequently argued for the end of all immigration and the repatriation of all non-Austrians. His further favourable allusions to some aspects of the Third Reich may have outraged politicians in Vienna and abroad, but did not seem to damage his popular appeal: in 1994 he led the Freedom Party to its best ever election result and a position where it could challenge to become the country's second largest party.

Undoubtedly, the country where any form of racialist politics would generate considerable international concern was Germany. While prejudice in the Federal Republic, especially against the large Turkish immigrant community, was regarded as endemic, extreme right-wing political forces remained insignificant and fragmented after the splintering of the NPD. For a short while this seemed to change after reunification in 1990. There was, especially among youth in the former DDR, a heightened interest in the Nazi past and Nazi memorabilia. There were after 1992 several incidents of racial violence, especially arson attacks, against immigrant families. However, these were not reflected in strong electoral performances by right-wing forces. Nevertheless, pressures of integration and fears of immigration, along with such incidents, were instrumental in the decision to implement restrictive amendments to the hitherto liberal right of asylum in Germany. While nowhere did racial politics dominate a country, the issues of assimilation and immigration could well continue to offer potential solace and profit to the extreme right, and racial problems will likely persist as something that governments will have to tackle for some time to come.

MINORITY NATIONALISM

If we regard a state as a territorial as well as a legal entity, then perhaps potentially the most serious challenge to Western European states in recent decades has been that of regional protest, since its demands implied both a reduction of the legal powers of state centres and a redrawing of state boundaries. Discontent with government was especially marked in regions that were geographically distant from the decision-making centres. While such resentment and feelings of remoteness were widespread, they received additional force where they could focus around some cultural quality, for example a different language, distinctive to the region. It was another reaction against the growing impersonality of the state, persuading people to search for roots and identity nearer home.

Around 1960 the violence and irredentism that could be found among the German-speaking population of the Alto Adige (South Tyrol) in Italy was more usually regarded as an atavistic intrusion into the politics of Western Europe, conventionally accepted as the home of the nation-state where such issues had long been resolved. If there was a norm, it was considered to be that of the Swedish-speaking population of Finland. The Swedish Finns may have had their own political party, but that was part of the mainstream, regularly serving in government coalitions; the group accepted not just the rules of the game, but also the territorial shape and legitimacy of the state in which it found itself. Regionally based groups which aspired to devolution, autonomy or separation were more likely to be dismissed as criminal terrorists, as in Spain, or ridiculed, the fate, for example, of nationalist activity in Scotland and Wales.

Over the next few decades the picture changed completely. There was a growth in electoral support for ethnic regional parties in Britain and Belgium, persisting ethnic activity in Italy, Spain and Switzerland, and an attempt by several historic areas, most notably Brittany, Corsica and Occitania in France, to reaffirm or resurrect a communal identity. Paralleling these ethnic movements were similar expressions of anti-central sentiment: equally striking examples were the political alliance engendered by the 1972 EC referendum in Norway and the 'state of revolt' in 1970–71 by the south Italian town of Reggio di Calabria against the government in Rome.

In retrospect, most of these regional parties have been relatively small within their own perceived region and ethnic group. Apart from longer established parties, such as those representing the Swedish and German populations in Finland and Italy respectively, the major exceptions to this generalisation were to be found in Britain, Spain and Belgium. In Britain the Scottish National Party (SNP) established itself as a meaningful regional force after 1970. Northern Ireland was almost *sui generis*: always peripheral to the British mainstream, it moved even further away after 1969 as Catholic resentment over partition and the refusal by the Protestant majority to concede civil rights erupted into street fighting and riots. The polarisation between Protestant and Catholic communities hardened and escalated into guerrilla warfare which even the presence of British army units was unable to quell entirely. In Spain, decades of repression under the Franco dictatorship had failed to eradicate Basque and Catalan identity and resentment. As the question of Franco's mortality grew larger in the late 1960s, those grievances became more open, to emerge after the dictator's death in 1975 as major political forces in the two regions. In Belgium regional parties emerged in Flanders, Wallonia and Brussels, and by the 1970s their pressure had caused the major parties to fragment into completely separate linguistic/regional organisations.

What separated these movements out from the European mass was the nature of their claim upon the state, a claim which involved a diminution of the power held by the state centre, up to and including full independence. It challenged both the legitimacy and the territorial integrity not just of the regime which held power at any one time, but of the state itself. Because of this, states will always be willing to pay a high price in concessions or resistance to maintain both their integrity and their legitimacy. After a hesitant start, Western European governments accepted the need to consider the accommodation of regional demands, even in centralised France where provision was made in the 1970s, for the first time, for the teaching of the minority languages in schools. In 1981 the Socialist government promised extensive reform, but in the event that was limited to Corsica and never fully implemented. Two general strategies were available to governments: they could adopt some form of territorial autonomy for the region in question; alternatively, where the region was inhabited and claimed by two mutually antagonistic groups, they might consider some proportional system of sharing power between them. The latter was applied by Italy in 1969 in the Alto Adige, where a 'proportional package' provided a power-sharing arrangement between Italians and Germans, especially in public employment. In Switzerland the grievances of the Catholic population of the Jura region of the Protestant canton of Berne were resolved by the establishment of a new canton of Jura, though as a result of referenda on the issue it was confined to the French communes: the German Catholics preferred to stay with Berne.

In Belgium, the cleavage between Walloons and Flemings and the associated dispute over the status of Brussels had produced not only linguistic parties, but also the split of established parties along linguistic lines. One outcome was a reduction in government longevity: after the late 1970s the average life span of a government was less than one year. On the other hand, the state attempted to respond positively to the regional question. The process of constitutional reform began in 1971, with a comprehensive document produced in 1980. The proposals offered substantial autonomy to the language communities and to the provinces of Flanders and Wallonia. Broad agreement on these led to *de facto* decentralisation pending consensus on other outstanding issues, most notably the status of bilingual Brussels. These remaining questions were resolved in further constitutional agreements in 1991, and in 1994 Belgium formally became a federal state.

Spain, too, had considerable success in defusing the regional issue. Widespread devolution was included in the constitutional reforms that accompanied democratisation after Franco. In particular, the new regime immediately offered extensive autonomy to Catalonia and the Basque provinces, promises that were incorporated into the 1978 constitution and formalised the following year in a statute of autonomy. These reforms seemed largely to satisfy Catalan aspirations. In the Basque country, however, they were rejected by the more militant elements associated with the terrorist organisation, ETA (*Euskadi Ta Askatasuna*, Basque Homeland and Liberty), which pledged to continue an armed struggle for full independence.

British governments were less fortunate in Northern Ireland. After the province degenerated into a battlefield after 1969, British troops were sent in to keep the warring communities apart, and the province's territorial autonomy, granted in 1922, was abrogated in 1972 with the establishment of direct rule from London. British parties essentially pursued a bi-partisan policy on Northern Ireland, but the prospects for peace never looked bright until the mid-1990s. From the Sunningdale Agreement of 1973–74 through the 1985 Hillsborough Agreement to the 1993 Downing Street Declaration, all government efforts, which steadily also involved the government of Ireland, centred upon finding some way in which the two communities could share power, to end Catholic feelings of alienation while still persuading Protestants that such concessions did not represent their abandonment by Britain. Violence by the IRA and Protestant paramilitary groups never ceased until late in 1994 when, in the wake of the Downing Street Declaration, they announced a cease-fire;

this, however, was abruptly ended by the IRA in February 1996. By contrast to that in Northern Ireland, nationalist sentiment seemed to fade in Scotland and Wales after the Labour government's proposals for regional assemblies failed to receive sufficient support in referenda in 1979. However, the SNP experienced a resurgence of support after the mid-1980s, partly occasioned by a collapse of Scottish Conservatism, and in much of the country it could lay claim to being the major alternative to Labour. In the 1990s the latter also returned to the nationalist theme, promising, in conjunction with the Liberal Democrats, to introduce a devolved Scottish assembly.

In general, the nationalist wave seemed to have subsided or to have had its demands accommodated by the 1980s. It had never been as strong in active mass support as was popularly believed at the time. However, it was a reminder of the different cultural identities that existed in virtually all Western European states. As long as these identities survived, they could pose a potential source of mobilisation against, and intractable problems for, the state. The IRA and ETA were reminders of the complexity of the problem and the passions that could be aroused. While the wave of minority nationalism seemed by the 1990s to have become more circumscribed, there was no guarantee that it would not re-emerge in the future should conditions be ripe. On the other hand, the flowering of nationalist sentiment in Eastern Europe after the collapse of the Communist regimes, which led, *inter alia*, to the disintegration of the Soviet Union, Yugoslavia and Czechoslovakia, proved not to be contagious: Western minority nationalism seemed not to draw inspiration or example from the East.

DIRECT ACTION AND THE DEMAND-RIDDEN SOCIETY

Despite their differing ideologies and demands, all the various movments that mushroomed in Western Europe after the late 1960s had something in common: a greater preference for direct action based on a relative scorn for the established channels of political participation, a belief in alternative forms of democratic expression, a critique of the state as an impersonal and dictatorial colossus, and a conviction that their demands were entitled to be heard and implemented. Direct action has a long tradition in Europe, in both industry and countryside. In France and Italy the strike has often been used as a political weapon, and this tradition continued in both countries. Political strikes, both official and unofficial, were the hallmark in particular of British industrial relations in the 1970s. They began in 1970, objecting to Labour proposals to bring the unions more firmly inside the framework of the law. A similar attempt by the 1970 Conservative government led to nationwide paralysis, and a three-day working week to preserve essential services in 1973–74. The inability to control the unions was a major factor in the Conservative defeat of 1974. The next Labour government was equally hamstrung. The wave of strikes culminated in 1978 in the so-called 'winter of discontent' and a belated anti-union backlash that swept Mrs Thatcher and the Conservatives into power. By the 1980s strike action was also affecting corporatist Scandinavia. Direct action was common in the countryside: French farmers, in particular, were adept at ostentious actions such as barricading roads, hijacking foreign lorries and ceremoniously destroying produce. Even in more consensual Norway, the decision in 1979 to begin a new hydroelectric scheme in a remote and beautiful Arctic valley – a project which, it was argued, would damage the ecology and the livelihood of the local Lapp population – led to mass confrontations between protesters and police in the far north and a hunger strike by Lapps outside the parliament building in Oslo.

Alienation and protest, in all their versions, were fuelled, at least in part, by reaction to the changing nature of Western society: its materialism, its increasing complexity and division of labour; a growing concentration of power in the state; the extension of state regulation and its bureaucratisation. The pace of demands made upon the state, and of scientific and technological development, was outstripping the construction of adequate social and political mechanisms for administering and allocating its resources and curbing its adverse effects. Paralleling the extension of government, there had been a rapid growth in the involvement of major economic organisations with government, forming a vast array of consultative bodies. At times, this huge corporatist network, bureaucratic, faceless and elitist, seemed to be the essential determinant of policy, effectively demoting popular participation and the electoral process. This generated reaction from those excluded from the network, while those within it seemed at times to be claiming the right to set policy even against the government and electoral will. It was this perception that the state was becoming an unwieldy and remote Leviathan which helped spark off the waves of protest and alienation that swept the continent after the late 1960s, moulding an interest in new forms of participation and new kinds of demands. While protest and direct action would persist through to the 1990s, in general their ability to disrupt became more circumscribed. Not only were governments prepared to be more selective in what they extracted from the plethora of demands before them; their ability to satisfy demands contracted with the deflation after the early 1970s of the economic bubble.

CHAPTER 16

FROM DÉTENTE TO NEW COLD WAR

Détente does not in the slightest abolish, nor can it alter, the laws of the class struggle. . . . We make no secret of the fact that we see détente as the way to create more favourable conditions for peaceful socialist and communist construction.   (*Leonid Brezhnev, 1976*)

The Soviet Union can choose either confrontation or cooperation. The United States is adequately prepared to meet either choice.
(*Jimmy Carter, 1978*)

The incidence of localised conflicts upon which both super-powers were more or less forced to take a position continued to increase in the 1970s. It indicated the growing complexities of world politics and reflected the assertion of interests which, in themselves, had little connection with global strategic concerns. Indeed, for a while, it seemed as if the East–West dichotomy might well be superseded in importance by a growing economic and cultural divergence between the developed and non-developed worlds. Using the UN as their major forum, Third World countries were demanding a more prominent place in world affairs and a greater respect for their needs, opinions and independence, and on occasions they could inhibit the common wishes of both super-powers. Above all, the new north–south debate focused upon the economic gulf between the developed West and the non-developed world which, despite massive injections of aid from the former, continued to widen. The numerical preponderance of the Third World in the UN General Assembly ensured the proclamation in 1974 of a New International Economic Order. The intention was to establish a new way of organising the international economic system by improving the terms of trade for Third World countries. With OPEC as an example of how economic muscle could be used, many non-developed countries saw the UN declaration as a panacea for their problems. But however laudible the objective, it almost immediately foundered in the morass of national self-interest. The West, especially the larger states, was not prepared to allow a potential new order to disturb its strategic interests or to worsen its own economic problems. In any case, the Third World was itself divided. There were huge differences between those countries, such as South Korea,

201

which had already embarked upon a crash course of rapid industrialisation, or oil-rich states, and the many very poor African countries with scarcely any major resources.

But this mosaic of states inhabited one world, and north–south differences of opinion had perforce to fit with the military power and strategic interests of, and continuing competition between, the super-powers. Détente remained a keyword throughout the 1970s; indeed, the decade marked the peak of that détente which had been the objective of previous years. But by the end of the 1970s, détente and disarmament had undergone a qualitative change, to such an extent that the common interpretation was that détente had been destroyed and replaced by a new Cold War. The pinnacle of détente was the Moscow summit meeting of 1972 between Leonid Brezhnev and Richard Nixon. In retrospect, it symbolised the hopes for a new era, not just in what it achieved, but also in the several subsequent agreements that were directly inspired by it. What Moscow set out to do was to arrive at a joint declaration of principles by which détente and peaceful co-existence could be achieved and sustained. The two giants agreed to respect each other's sovereignty, equality and right to non-interference in internal affairs by the other, not to seek advantages, to avoid military confrontation, and to adhere to the 'renunciation of the use or threat of force'.

The strategy embarked upon by Nixon and his secretary of state, Henry Kissinger, was in tune with the mood of America in the 1970s. The trauma of involvement in, and withdrawal from, an unpopular and, to many, pointless war in Vietnam, together with the consequences of the Watergate scandal, which eventually forced Nixon to resign from the presidency, produced within the United States a deep mood of scepticism and a lack of confidence in politicians, a distrust of an overly active and 'imperial' presidency. While it was the revelation during the Watergate episode that Nixon had for a year secretly ordered the bombing of Cambodia during the closing phases of the Vietnam War which was the catalyst that led to Congress passing the War Powers Act, which drastically inhibited the ability of the president to act on his own initiative in overseas ventures, the Act was more a reaction against the general presidential style of the past decade.

The United States did not abrogate any of its alliance commitments. However, its postwar role as world policeman and defender of Western Europe had been predicated upon geopolitical strategic considerations, and upon its possession of an edge in nuclear and military potential. By 1980, there were powerful voices which argued that the pendulum had swung too far, that the United States had yielded the geopolitical high ground, and that the Soviet Union had achieved not just parity, but even the initiative, in nuclear weapons. What came to alarm the United States was evidence of a continued Soviet military build-up and a series of episodes from around the world which indicated a continued Soviet effort at expansion of influence. The Soviet navy had, by the late 1970s, a worldwide reach, while in Europe the USSR had begun to install intermediate or theatre nuclear weapons which had Western Europe as their target. In addition, from 1975 onwards, the Soviet Union had embarked upon a series of adventures, never directly, but with surrogate Cuban or East German military advisers and troops, designed to extend its area of influence: Angola in 1975, Somalia and then Ethiopia in 1977 and 1978, South Yemen in 1978. Taken together, they suggested to worried Western observers that the Soviet military had acquired a more decisive voice in policy-making and that, as a consequence, Soviet foreign policy was becoming militarised. The final proof, as it were, was the Soviet invasion of Afghanistan in 1979.

All this seemed to go against the grain of the keen Soviet interest in détente in the early 1970s. That interest had, in its own terms, been entirely genuine. It had hoped that détente would endorse and strengthen the *status quo*, especially in Europe, and had more or less willingly gone into several economic and cultural agreements with the West. It even backed Nixon in the face of Watergate, fearing that a new president might reject the accord reached between him and Brezhnev. However, for the Soviet Union, détente and peaceful co-existence had quite visible boundaries and specific aims. They did not, in particular, preclude the continuation of an ideological competition, or what Brezhnev called the 'laws of the class struggle', whereas the United States regarded détente as something that would underwrite peace and security, primarily through the preservation of the *status quo*.

Europe was not exempted from the tensions that arose from the different interpretations of détente. While the Soviet Union had no intention of weakening the Warsaw Pact structure, its dialectic view of détente saw nothing wrong in seeking any opportunity that might weaken the American presence and influence in Western Europe. Similarly, it continued to agitate against the extension of European integration, while simultaneously seeking to strengthen COMECON (Council for Mutual Economic Assistance), its cooperative economic body in Eastern Europe. Western Europe, which had applauded the earlier efforts at détente and had a vested interest in its survival, nevertheless became more concerned as the decade progressed about American competence and Soviet strength. Governments were driven both to think again about forms of accommodation with the Soviet Union, and to consider new ways of strengthening the Western defence and of increasing the American commitment to that defence.

THE WORLD OF DÉTENTE

The earlier crisis over Cuba had marked the beginning of a new phase in the super-power relationship, emphasising that in the last resort direct consultation between the two was a necessary prerequisite for any solution to many of the world's problems in which both had a strong interest. Neither one could completely control world politics (and, by inference, perhaps also its own destiny), even where the two seemed to be in agreement. For example, both endorsed the sanctions imposed upon the rebellious British colony of Rhodesia and its white minority government, yet these sanctions were perhaps breached more often than observed by many states. The same was true of the American attempt in 1980 to enforce at least Western sanctions upon the new revolutionary regime in Iran. Sanctions rarely worked since many states ranked their own economic interests higher than the application of any 'moral' condemnation, at least in the short run.

Nowhere in the 1970s was the fluidity and complexity of world politics so pronounced as in Africa and the Middle East. Partly perhaps because of its colonial heritage, Soviet influence in Africa increased markedly. But as the Soviet Union discovered in Somalia in 1977, aid did not mean alignment or the abandonment of intra-African disagreements. Somalia, one of the first African states to welcome a strong Soviet presence, claimed sovereignty over the Ogaden region of neighbouring Ethiopia. After a left-wing revolution in Ethiopia, the Soviet Union found, like the United States before it, that it was almost impossible to ride two horses at once. Given the hostility between the two states, the Soviet Union found that by committing itself to the Ethiopian regime, it forfeited its previous influence in Somalia. The Middle East was even more complex. The 1967 war between Israel and its Arab neighbours resolved nothing, and led ultimately to a military re-run in the Yom Kippur War of 1973. But the Arab and Islamic worlds were not united, except on the issue of Palestine. Egypt, the most important Soviet client in the region, chose to compromise its stand on Israel, and in the process revoked its treaty of friendship with the Soviet Union in 1976. The Islamic revolution in Iran, the subsequent Iran–Iraq War, and the Soviet invasion of Afghanistan all highlighted, through reactions to these events, the internal diversity of the region, as well as the inability of the super-powers to suppress or compartmentalise that diversity whenever their efforts at control went against national self-interest.

Nevertheless, the United States and the Soviet Union continued to have a communion of interest in their fear of being pushed into a direct military conflict against their will. That communion remained a major factor in the interest in détente, and was an important concern of Nixon and Brezhnev in their deliberations. Though the communion of interest would survive, its force was weakened after 1975 as the two states moved towards greater hostility. But if it was a new Cold War that was on the horizon, it was one that was very different from that of the 1940s. It was global in nature, with a greater stress not just on nuclear war, but also upon naval power and indirect political and military influence, than upon direct confrontation in Europe. It was complicated by the greater international assertiveness of China, and it was characterised by a widening of the chinks in the two European blocs that had been constructed after the war.

China began to emerge from its self-imposed isolation after 1971, especially in seeking a more normal relationship with the United States. The process began with the Shanghai Communiqué of 1972 and President Nixon's historic trip to Beijing. China's coming in from the cold was formalised when it replaced Taiwan in both the General Assembly and Security Council of the UN. China also reached an accommodation with Japan, signing a treaty in 1978 which formally ended the state of war between the two, and by 1980 was even considering an association with the IMF and the World Bank, two institutions consistently rejected by the Soviet Union as lackeys of capitalism. The new political strategy and economic modernisation were accelerated after the death of Mao Zedong in 1976, though this did not mean an end to strict internal control or China's territorial claims. China's new international outlook might have been gratifying to the United States, but it added a further complicating factor to world politics, especially in the Pacific and South-East Asia where economic and political factors made the area a high profile one for the United States. While Sino-American relations would not be entirely smooth, for the Soviet Union, China's development was perhaps more alarming. The American accord raised the spectre of containment. The Soviet Union began to express a greater interest in South-East Asia, and with the invasion of Afghanistan in 1979, it could almost be said to be pursuing its own policy of containment against China.

The coming out of China was important for Western Europe in two ways. Economically, it offered a further outlet for European goods and skills, all the more so as China did not wish to become totally dependent for its modernisation upon the United States, Japan or any single state. Politically, it emphasised that, for the super-powers, it might be more difficult to keep Europe and Asia as two separate policy areas. While this meant that Western Europe might not feel so squeezed as in the past, paradoxically it also raised the possibility that the Soviet Union might have less to lose from pursuing a more aggressive policy in the West.

Both super-powers continued to have problems with their European partners. While the Soviet Union's difficulties were to be more pronounced in the 1980s, some of the seeds of those problems were sown by the détente process. The issue of human rights had been, at least for the West, an integral part of that détente. It stimulated further activity by dissident groups in Eastern Europe (and even in the Soviet Union itself), which sought some loosening of the rigorous political control over individual behaviour. While these groups were allowed a looser rein in Poland and Hungary than elsewhere, where a more systematic and ruthless oppression was maintained, the Soviet Union and the Communist regimes were obliged to be rather more wary than in the past to maintain the goodwill of and aid from the West. The one event which perhaps gave most concern to the Soviet Union was the election of a Polish cardinal as Pope in 1978.

More difficult for the Soviet Union to handle, perhaps, were some of the economic problems of détente. Khrushchev had once promised that affluence and economic superiority over the West would be acquired by 1970. The year came and went with, in fact, the reverse being true. For the Soviet bloc, one of the major benefits that might flow from détente was better access to Western technology. A greater volume of East–West trade did result, but without necessarily having the desired effects. The West may have welcomed raw materials from the East, but not manufactured products, many of which were shoddily finished and unreliable. By contrast, the Eastern European economies were opened up to Western goods to some extent, but because of the non-convertible nature of COMECON currencies, trade had to be semi-barter. The danger for the Soviet Union was an increasingly restive Eastern Europe.

The American problem throughout the 1970s was a general malaise and a European disgruntlement with the United States. Despite its concern for détente, or perhaps because of it, the United States continued to be irritated by what it regarded as a general European refusal to provide adequate funding for its own defence. For the first time, serious threats were raised in Congress to reduce severely the American troop and financial commitments. For its part, Western Europe was annoyed with what it regarded as a condescending American attitude. The tone was perhaps set when Kissinger declared 1973 to be the 'Year of Europe'. Kissinger's comment, after the EC adopted a common position on the Middle East crisis of 1973, that 'Europe's unity must not be at the expense of the Atlantic Community', seemed to confirm that the United States did not wish to see an independent European policy line. Simultaneously, Western Europe felt that American trade and monetary policy since 1971 had not paid particular regard to the possible negative impact upon its allies and trading partners. The American-Soviet 1973 Agreement on the Prevention of Nuclear War, whose aims Western Europe applauded, paradoxically illustrated the rather schizophrenic European attitude to its American relationship. For Western European governments, it symbolised their exclusion from the essence of world policy and placed a question mark against the credibility of the American nuclear guarantee. Ironically, given de Gaulle's actions of the previous decade, it was France that was most forthright in expressing these worries about the consequences of American policy.

Relationships did not improve much in the latter half of the decade. After 1976, Western European hackles were raised by the tendency of President Jimmy Carter to make the application of détente and disarmament contingent upon Soviet concessions on human rights. While Western European governments were equally committed to human rights, they were less inclined to treat them as a moral absolute if that impeded the possibility of real progress in the normalisation of political and economic relationships with the East. On the other hand, this irritation was compounded by a concern over the continued Soviet military build-up in Europe. Towards the end of the decade, the alarm intensified because Soviet conventional superiority had been supplemented by the deployment of intermediate-range nuclear missiles which had Western Europe as their target. This raised the spectre of a limited nuclear war. Led by the West German chancellor, Helmut Schmidt, Western European governments began to argue that an American response was vital, that similar American missiles should be stationed in Europe. In short, as American–Soviet relations deteriorated, Western Europe in a sense rediscovered the virtues of the Atlantic alliance. At the same time, however, that rediscovery was mitigated by the feeling that the United States had lost its way, that it refused to recognise what the major problems of the international economy were, and that its policy course was inconsistent. Most particularly, confidence in Carter and his advisers plummeted almost to zero. To European minds, the president's inconsistency was typified by the neutron bomb episode. Carter successfully persuaded European leaders, despite their reservations, to accept the idea of the neutron bomb, a nuclear device that would kill people but not destroy buildings and other material objects. Within a short period of time, Carter abruptly abandoned the idea, embarrassing those European leaders, like Schmidt, who had been persuaded to endorse the scheme, even though doing so had damaged their domestic political credibility: the damage remained, but they had gained nothing to show for it.

In the early 1970s, Western Europe had been equally interested in limiting the intercontinental nuclear arsenal which the two super-powers had been accumulating for some time. This was the theme of the Strategic Arms Limitation Talks (SALT), which had begun in 1969. A first round of agreement was reached with SALT I in 1972. While this met the Soviet desire to restrict the development of defensive antiballistic missile systems, it did not include offensive weapons. Nor did it deal with intermediate-range missiles or conventional forces. In that sense, SALT I was limited. It did not fundamentally affect the deployment systems of either power. All it could hope to be was a first step in the process of seeking a strategic balance, in order to reduce the fear, even paranoia, of each nuclear giant that the other might somehow gain the upper hand and be able to launch an effective pre-emptive first strike.

But both sides indicated a willingness to build on SALT I. The talks were only one element of a package of discussions after 1971. In 1973, the two states began to discuss mutual and balanced force reductions (MBFR) to secure a limitation on the number of land-based troops. They were unable to decide whether reductions should be equal on both sides, or proportional to take account of the alleged Soviet conventional superiority: with no agreement after sixteen years of talks, the MBFR idea was finally abandoned in early 1989. A further round of SALT talks sought to reduce the level of military stockpiling in Europe. After much wrangling, a SALT II treaty was signed in Vienna in 1979 by Brezhnev and Carter. It did not, however, advance things very far, being in fact less extensive than SALT I. Its value was perhaps mainly symbolic of whatever survived of the desire to preserve the Moscow détente in a steadily worsening atmosphere, and it was one of the first victims of the deteriorating climate of 1979 and 1980. It was perhaps simply inevitable that if the Soviet Union did not abandon its invasion of Afghanistan, the American Senate, with the approval of Carter, would refuse to ratify SALT II. Vienna was to be the last summit for six years.

The notion of a broad détente in Europe was a central element of the super-power discussions. It was something which Nixon and Brezhnev, for different reasons, desired. For the Soviet Union, it might lead to a reduction of the American presence in Western Europe. For Nixon, it was part of his belief that the world was moving towards a pentagonal division of power: the two super-powers would be joined by China, Japan and Western Europe. His notion of bloc diplomacy was designed to prevent these emerging centres becoming autonomous actors and to subordinate them to the American line. The apparent success of the *Ostpolitik* agreements had removed the stumbling block which the German problem had laid in the path of the Soviet desire, forcefully expressed since 1966, for a general European security conference; it also helped that the Soviet Union had abandoned its original position that the United States should not participate in such as meeting.

The Conference on Security and Cooperation in Europe (CSCE), attended by all European countries bar Albania, as well as by America and Canada, convened in Helsinki in 1973. What it produced in the 1975 Helsinki Final Act was nominal agreement on three themes: economic, scientific and technological cooperation; closer contacts between different peoples and the respecting of human rights; and a lessening of tension through the exchange of military information. It was, perhaps, more a statement of intent and so susceptible to varying interpretations: hence, each side could claim Helsinki to be a success. Yet from a security perspective, the fruits of the conference were something of an anticlimax. It essentially did little more than confirm the territorial *status quo* in Europe, and what the West had already accepted. On the other hand, the Soviet Union did seem to offer concessions in the field of human rights.

If both sides could claim Helsinki to be a success, the same could not be said of the follow-up CSCE sessions in Belgrade two years later, when the West tried to press home some of the concessions which it thought the Soviet Union had ceded in Helsinki. But in 1977, international storm clouds were beginning to gather. The SALT talks were in difficulties. The United States was beginning to climb out of the slough of Vietnam and Watergate to convince itself that it had conceded too much in political and military matters. For its part, the Soviet Union was increasingly irritated and frustrated by the Western emphasis upon human rights within its own borders. The fate of prominent Russian critics of the Soviet regime, such as Alexander Solzhenitsyn and Andrei Sakarov, along with the general refusal of the Soviet authorities to allow the emigration of Russian Jews to Israel, aroused strong passions in the West.

Helsinki had only been partially concerned with the human rights issue; nevertheless, it emerged in the popular mind as perhaps the basic theme. While the Soviet Union may have made concessions on human rights at the CSCE in order to gain Western acquiescence on its own proposals on détente in security structures, the subsequent Belgrade meeting demonstrated the true gulf between East and West. Fundamentally, the Soviet Union was not interested in the Western concern for the free movement of people and ideas. Instead, it had wanted to focus on the principle of non-intervention, the immutability of the postwar European borders, and the improvement of economic relationships between East and West. To achieve these ends, it might have seemed willing to compromise in Helsinki, but ultimately it regarded the human rights campaign as blatant and unwarranted interference with its sovereignty and its hegemony over Eastern Europe. From 1976 onwards, it began to stamp down hard upon its own dissident groups, and expected its European allies to do likewise; for those dissidents who hoped for liberalisation, Helsinki was a false dawn. By contrast, Carter had taken respect of human rights as the essential indicator of a Soviet commitment to détente. Carter's stand was simply part of his general policy of making any regime's attitude towards human rights an important determinant of the American relationship with it. However, he had often been obliged to moderate his stand with regimes which were militarily allied with the United States, a discrepancy which naturally irked the Soviet Union.

Attempts at détente in the 1970s, therefore, were not entirely successful. The decisive turning point came in 1979, with the American refusal to ratify SALT II. Campaigning had already begun for the 1980 presidential election, with Ronald Reagan emerging as the probable Republican opponent of Carter. One of Reagan's main themes was American weakness and the need to correct it. However, the Carter administration itself had come to the view that SALT II would mean the United States losing whatever edge it still possessed, and had already begun to react to Soviet 'gains' in the Third World. American revisionism was reinforced by two important events of 1978–79. The first was the fall of the pro-Western Shah of Iran, whom Carter, perhaps because of his distaste for the Shah's record on human rights, was not willing to support unreservedly. The new revolutionary regime proved to be violently anti-American. When the exiled Shah was later allowed to enter the United States for medical treatment, the Iranian regime responded by sacking the American embassy in Teheran and seizing hostages, demanding the return of the Shah as ransom. Carter was placed in a no-win situation. All negotiations failed, as did an ill-planned military rescue attempt in 1980. The second event was the Soviet invasion of Afghanistan. The United States feared it might mark the first phase of a Soviet attempt to expand southwards to the oil-rich Persian Gulf and the strategically important Indian Ocean. The move also seemed to mark an extension of the Brezhnev Doctrine. The Soviet justification that it was redeeming its 'internationalist duty' in defending a Socialist revolution was remarkably similar to the notion of 'socialist internationalism' which had accompanied the earlier repression in Czechoslovakia. Carter reversed American policy, barring American participation in the 1980 Moscow Olympic Games and placing an embargo on American grain and technology exports to the Soviet Union. While this about-turn was not perhaps too late for the United States, it was too late for Carter. Elected in the wake of the reaction against the imperial presidency, he became tarred with the brush of vacillation and indecisiveness. His later assertiveness was not able to convince a more anxious electorate, and in 1980 he went down to defeat at the hands of Ronald Reagan.

The Soviet Union was also becoming more disillusioned with the results of détente. By the time of the Afghanistan invasion, it had probably accepted that it had nothing to lose from the action. From its perspective, the fact that Carter had already increased the American defence budget, ordered new intercontinental missiles, and accepted that theatre nuclear weapons should be placed in Western Europe, all indicated that détente was dying and could perhaps be written off.

What went wrong with détente was due ultimately to the different perceptions of its meaning to the two sides. For the United States, the essence of détente was the idea that neither state would strive for unilateral advantage at the expense of the other. The deal had been presented to the American public as one that would limit the arms race and halt Soviet expansion. On the other hand, détente for the Soviet Union meant peaceful *and* competitive co-existence. For it, there was nothing incompatible between a nuclear arms limitation and adventurist policies in the Third World. The essential problem of détente, therefore, was its ambiguity, and because of this there was no necessary tight linkage between a general principle and the technical specifics of many of the agreements that were concluded. The basic dilemma was perhaps best summarised by James Schlesinger, the American secretary of defense in 1976, who stated, 'If détente means everything, it means virtually nothing'.

It might be argued that the various discussions and conferences of the 1970s had only a marginal effect upon the political and military constructs of Western Europe. Yet the continent remained central to defence and arms limitation. Western Europe both welcomed détente, because of the more relaxed atmosphere it would generate and the economic benefits it might bring, and feared it, because it might lead to a reduced American guarantee. At first, welcome was perhaps more prominent than fear. But while Western Europe remained interested in, even committed to, détente, the shifting balance of military power over the decade forced it to reconsider the parameters of defence. By 1979, many Western leaders had become deeply concerned about the frailty of the Western alliance, and were urging the United States to do something about it. Defence and NATO again became matters of great concern.

A REDISCOVERY OF NATO

With the failure of the MLF proposals and France's withdrawal from the military wing of NATO, European defence arrangements had been thrown into some disarray in the late 1960s. The matter was still unresolved when the heightened fashion for détente in a sense left NATO high and dry in a cul-de-sac. The lessening of tension encouraged those who wished to dampen down NATO's role to become more vocal. The façade of a united body under firm and accepted American leadership began to peel during the decade. In the NATO north, the United States was sporadically faced with the threat of being asked to vacate its crucial base on Iceland, which guarded the northern approaches to the Atlantic and which had become even more important with the rise of Soviet naval power, whose main bases lay in the Arctic. The northern flank was already weak because of the neutrality of Sweden and Finland, and because of Norway's refusal to permit the stationing of nuclear weapons and foreign troops on its soil. As the decade progressed, it was Denmark which was to give rise to concern. Danish governmental stability had been shaken in 1972 by a fragmentation of the party system. A major newcomer was the populist anti-tax Progress Party of Mogens Glistrup, which saw savage cuts in defence expenditure as one way of achieving its aims. While the party never got its way, Denmark, more than other members, steadily evinced a reluctance to keep its defence commitments in line with the rest of NATO. At times, several other states queried its value to the organisation. Denmark became the foremost protagonist of the 'footnote', that is, it regularly refused to join in collective NATO statements, preferring to make its own position clear in an appended footnote.

More immediately serious for NATO was the threatened disintegration of the whole southern flank. Turkey and Greece, never the best of friends and already in dispute over the ownership of the Aegean continental shelf, moved towards open hostility in 1974 with Turkey's successful invasion and partitioning of Cyprus, a move designed to protect the island's Turkish minority and forestall a clumsy attempt by Greece's military dictatorship to incorporate the island into Greece. For NATO, the consequences were serious. Greece withdrew from its military command while Turkey, in retaliation against the American attempt to force it to leave Cyprus through the imposition of an arms embargo, requested the United States to vacate its several bases and 'listening posts' within Turkey. While American-Turkish relationships were eventually normalised, and while Greece returned to NATO in 1980, the dispute would remain a running sore, for Cyprus remained partitioned.

The Greece–Turkey dispute was serious enough, but at the same time there arose the possibility of Communist participation in government along much of the Mediterranean. In France, the Communists had joined with a revivified Socialist Party in a left-wing electoral alliance that could reasonably hope for electoral success, while in 1975 and 1976 the omens seemed ripe for the PCI to emerge as the largest party in Italy: under the declaration of a 'historic compromise', the PCI had indicated a willingness to collaborate with the DC, and so were claiming a stake to power. More or less simultaneously, 1974 and 1975 marked the end of the long-established authoritarian regimes in Iberia. In both Spain and, especially, Portugal, the Communists seemed to be major contenders for power. In the event, worries over Communist advances were ill-founded. It was only in France that the Communist Party entered government, but only in 1981 and only as the very junior partner in a Socialist government that asserted a staunchly pro-Western security policy.

All of this reflected a much broader disillusionment with the United States and a growing mass reaction against nuclear weapons and militarism. The line of thought, begun by de Gaulle, that argued for less Western European political and economic dependence on the United States seemingly gained extra ammunition from the years of the Carter administration. Peace movements experienced a regeneration in the 1970s, while protest and rejection of 'conventional politics' and of the materialist society were rife. This was the general backdrop against which internal dissension and the illusion of a satisfactory détente combined with the decline of firm American leadership eventually to produce the most serious crisis about the readiness and capacity of NATO since its formation some thirty years earlier; for while Western Europe may have welcomed, as a change, a non-imperial American presidency and its concern for arms control, it did not necessarily accept the implication that this might lead to a reduced American guarantee to Europe.

A major objective of American policy after 1945 had been to counter the massive Soviet conventional strength by ensuring nuclear supremacy. But the United States had also been interested in limiting the arms race. Beginning with unilateral decisions on limitation in the 1960s through to those of the late 1970s not to proceed with developing new types of weapons such as the neutron bomb, the United States insisted on believing in the sufficiency of its existing nuclear arsenal. However, while American expenditure on defence as a percentage of budget expenditure had been cut between 1968 and 1976 by almost one-half, Soviet military expenditure had increased remorselessly and annually. It was this which caused American and Western European concern. What set the alarm bells ringing in Western European government circles was the installation, after the mid-1970s, of intermediate Soviet SS-20 missiles targeted upon Western Europe.

It had long been accepted that the Soviet Union had the edge in conventional forces and strategic parity with the United States. The new intermediate-range weapons seemed to confirm that the overall balance had shifted in favour of the Soviet Union; they provided evidence for a different version of a possible war in Europe, by offering the Soviet Union theatre supremacy and the ability of a nuclear strike capacity that would not necessarily endanger American territory. This new scenario exercised Western European governments greatly, for if the American resolve was weak and preferred to avoid the alternative of total nuclear war, it might tempt the Soviet Union to seek, by invasion or threat, the subjugation of Western Europe.

Speculation or not, NATO was perhaps weaker in comparison to the Warsaw Pact than at any time in the past. However, particularly in the midst of the economic slowdown after 1973, to argue for increased defence expenditure would not have been a popular electoral ploy for any party. Western Europe had for too long relied primarily upon the American nuclear umbrella. Moreover, even though Western Europe might have been concerned about its, and the American, defence capacity, it wished to retain its vested interest in détente, especially in preserving its economic ties with Eastern Europe. While the United States was reverting to the view that economic ties did not necessarily bring about desired political progress, Western Europe still hoped that a stronger NATO would not distort what in its view was the better East–West relationship that had been achieved through trading links.

Only France still seemed to insist that an adequate defence was the essential criterion of security and independence, but France was not part of NATO. Even so, Western Europe could not completely ignore not just the military build-up to its east, but also what appeared to be a growing Soviet adventurism throughout the world and its possible consequences for Europe. West Germany was the state which, through Ostpolitik, had the most invested in a successful détente, yet simultaneously was the one that was most worried about the imbalance in conventional forces and most acutely aware of a possible Soviet threat. Despite being increasingly at odds with his own party, the SPD chancellor, Helmut Schmidt, was the European leader who was most prominent in seeking to renew and refurbish NATO, arguing that the Soviet lead in theatre nuclear weapons created a great gap between NATO's conventional forces stationed on the continent and the strategic stockpile across the Atlantic. In 1978 the NATO governments accepted the realities of Soviet military preponderance, looked at NATO as a whole, and reaffirmed that defence needed a strong American commitment.

This was the background to the decision to modernise NATO, though it would be a decade or so before a new generation of weapons would be in place. In the interim, the gap would be plugged by the placement in Western Europe of American missiles, capable of striking targets in the Soviet Union, to counteract those already installed on the other side of the iron curtain. NATO adopted what came to be known as the twin-track decision: the theatre weapons would be installed and made operational by 1983 unless the Soviet Union entered negotiations and withdrew its own theatre missiles. The NATO decision was not just taken on military grounds. It was meant to be a symbolic reaffirmation to an uneasy Western Europe, and a message to the wider world, of a continued American commitment to the continent.

Even though they had agitated for such a reaffirmation, Western European governments were to find that the instalment aspect of the twin-track decision was not entirely popular in their own countries. Most importantly, it made defence a party political issue in a way it never had been before, as many Social Democrat parties turned towards rejection. In 1983 the SPD opposed the NATO missile deployment, completing the isolation of Schmidt within his own party. The Norwegian Labour Party had taken a similar decision the previous year. And after its electoral defeat in 1979, the British Labour Party moved towards unilateral nuclear disarmament.

The geographic distribution of the missiles was to be limited, as Denmark and Norway, while welcoming the 1979 decision, refused them a home on the grounds of their traditional policy of not allowing nuclear weapons on their territory. The new British Conservative government of Margaret Thatcher endorsed the programme and wholeheartedly offered a home, despite powerful opposition from Labour and CND. By contrast, Italy housed its missile allotment without too much argument, and West Germany also accepted the missiles. However, in Belgium and the Netherlands installation was delayed for a number of years because of an absence of political consensus. The debate over the twin-track decision was to be one of the prominent themes of the early 1980s.

Even allowing for the fact that the twin-track decision was the most important factor that made defence a hot party political issue, also stimulating the resurrection or establishment of peace movements throughout Western Europe, including the umbrella END organisation, by 1980 NATO had, at the governmental level, shown a renewed will and commitment to positive defence. While Western Europe reserved its right to disagree with American policies and actions elsewhere, for example over Iran and Afghanistan, and stressed its continued concern for détente, multilateral disarmament and the preservation of its links with Eastern Europe, it was in one sense more at one than at any time since the early days of the Cold War. The minimalist interpretation of NATO might linger on, especially in some of the smaller countries, but new Conservative governments in Britain and West Germany were to give the organisation more vigour in the 1980s. France, too, continued to close the gap to NATO and to urge it to adopt a higher profile.

The old problems might remain. The United States would continue to complain about the costs of defending Europe and the reluctance of its allies to bear a commensurate financial share of the burden. Western Europe, in accommodating itself to the change from the hesitant Carter presidency to the more hawkish one of Reagan, would still remain undecided as to whether it preferred a passive or active United States. But as détente shifted to a new ice age towards the end of 1979, Western Europe in a sense rediscovered why NATO had been created in the first place, and the United States moved away perhaps from a narrower military interpretation of the Soviet problem, to return to the wider view of the Truman era. The new mood was perhaps summed up by a leading American authority on security and foreign policy who said in 1980 that 'the Kremlin leaders do not want war, they want the world'. While the 1980s were immediately to be characterised as inaugurating a new Cold War, the search would immediately begin for a new version of détente, but for the Western allies it would have to be a détente that was more firmly based on what they considered to be a necessary redressing of the imbalance of military power between the two blocs.

CHAPTER 17

ECONOMIC DILEMMAS AND PROBLEMS

We used to think that you could just spend your way out of a recession, and increase employment, by cutting taxes and boosting government spending. I tell you in all candour that that option no longer exists, and in so far as it ever did exist, it worked by injecting inflation into the economy. And each time that happened, the average level of unemployment has risen. Higher inflation, followed by higher unemployment. That is the history of the last twenty years.   (*James Callaghan, 1976*)

By 1970, Western Europe had come a long way from the economic self-doubts of the immediate postwar years. It was a vital and large element of a market economic system led by the United States. A freer flow of trade within the market had been aided by the activities of GATT. The Western European states collaborated on a host of matters with the United States and other industrialised democracies within OECD to foster further economic interconnections and growth. A stabilising monetary framework, it was believed, would be provided by the Bretton Woods agreement and fixed exchange rates, a system which, after numerous delays, was more or less finally in place by the early 1960s. On the domestic front, the conventional wisdom accepted that Keynesian demand management techniques had provided, and would continue to provide, governments with the essential tools for preventing unemployment and inflation. The continuation of economic growth would ensure the continuous expansion of public services to a grateful public through a benign welfare state.

Within the space of a few years, this whole edifice of assumptions and practices seemed to have crumbled into disarray. A new mood of pessimism and doubt enveloped the continent. Economic expansion might still be a desired goal, but it was one to which lip service was paid without any necessary and deep belief in its possibility or probability. Inflation was to be a persisting problem of the coming decades. High levels of unemployment and deindustrialisation were to be accepted as more or less unalterable facts of life. Retrenchment meant a more critical eye being cast at the costs, efficiency and merits of the welfare state. The unquestioning faith in Keynesianism went. Economic issues and problems were a major preoccupation of European governments from the 1970s onwards.

THE FLOATING AWAY OF BRETTON WOODS

The essence of Bretton Woods had eventually been reached by 1958, with convertibility across fixed-rate currencies. No sooner, however, was the edifice in place than doubts began to be raised about its viability. The immediate cause for concern was the long-standing American payments deficit. Western Europe feared that the United States might seek a solution either by reducing its defence expenditure, which would upset European security arrangements, or by devaluing the dollar, which would increase what Europe already re-garded as an 'unfair' competitive edge enjoyed by American exports. The United States seemed to be less concerned, only slowly shifting ground to accept that while the deficit may have been essential for the financing of world trade (which had been backed by dollars rather than gold), it nevertheless posed a possible threat to long-term monetary stability and a possible barrier to further economic growth.

A solution was sought through the International Monetary Fund (IMF): the United States suggested that members be permitted additional drawing rights without incurring extra payments, a kind of advance borrowing. This, it argued, would be a better mechanism for securing continued growth in trade than the more radical options of returning to the gold standard or abandoning the fixed exchange rate system. The new strategy had only short-term effects. It could aid the resolution of each problem as it arose, but could not prevent another one appearing. By the late 1960s, the international monetary system was much more unstable, with considerable fraying around the edges, and the pressures obliged some countries to devalue their currency. The problem was still the ever-growing American deficit and the problem of an even more dire situation in the future. Lying behind the problem was the central flaw, long recognised, of the Bretton Woods system. The fixed-rate system obliged all participants but the United States to discipline their currency. While all other currencies were pegged to the dollar, the latter was linked to gold. Sustaining dollar parity was the duty of the country concerned; the dollar itself had no responsibility. This basic weakness of the system had occasioned frequent soul-searching in many states, especially in Britain where the dilemma led eventually in 1967 to the decision to devalue sterling.

It was West Germany which first directly challenged the fixed exchange rate system, deciding to 'float' the mark in 1970. By itself, this was insufficient to correct the growing strains within Bretton Woods. A revaluation of all the major currencies might have provided a solution, but politically that was an impossible dream. It was the United States which held the answer, and even-tually that answer was that the Bretton Woods system was no longer viable. This was the implication of President Nixon's unilateral decision in 1970 tem-porarily to suspend the convertibility of the dollar against gold, as well as imposing an import surcharge in order to avoid devaluation. The United States persisted in seeing responsibility lying with others. While stability required a restructuring of exchange rates, the American view attached more blame on its associates, especially the protectionism of the EC and Japan. It argued that other countries should revalue their currencies, liberalise their trading regulations and accept a more equitable share of the burden of Western defence. As a package, it was not acceptable to America's allies.

A compromise was attempted with the Smithsonian Agreement of 1971. The dollar was divorced from gold and slightly devalued. In return, the fixed rates of exchange were loosened, with wider margins of permissible fluctuation around a mean. The Smithsonian accord was short-lived. It failed to cope with further financial and dollar crises in 1972 and 1973; on each occasion, it persuaded more countries, beginning with Britain in 1972, to allow their currencies to float. After 1969, the Western European states had found it increasingly difficult to maintain fixed exchange rates among themselves. One solution had been advocated at the 1969 Hague summit of the EC: to go for Economic and Monetary Union (EMU), with fully fixed rates leading eventually to a single currency. The EC, which then set 1980 as the completion date for EMU, regarded the Smithsonian parameters as too liberal, and devised a modified European system to operate within them. This European structure became known as the 'snake' that would wriggle within the broader Smithsonian 'tunnel'. The snake never succeeded: many countries left it within a short space of time, leaving it as a small truncated group dominated by West Germany. The unstable and uncertain economic picture meant that for Western Europe as a whole, the desire for some stability in the international monetary system was offset by the concern to retain some national financial autonomy. The flexibility inherent in floating one's currency, of allowing it freedom to find its 'natural' level, seemed to offer such a possibility.

The reasons why countries looked towards floating varied: to some extent, they depended upon the 'hardness' of a country's currency. West Germany had the strongest currency in Europe, and it became the centre of a hard currency group containing some of its smaller neighbours whose currencies floated alongside the mark. West Germany favoured floating as the way forward towards ensuring domestic price stability: the conditioning of the memories of the past made prevention of inflation the essential priority. Floating allowed West Germany to control its domestic monetary and exchange rate policy, and to handle more easily the relationship between domestic demand and the huge trade surplus it had steadily accumulated. By contrast, the other major countries of Western Europe had problems in maintaining the value of their currencies. Floating seemed to offer an opportunity to aim for economic growth without being fettered by the need to maintain a fixed exchange rate. In Britain, the Conservative government allowed sterling to float in 1972 as a means of helping it to achieve its own policy of achieving rapid domestic expansion and boosting consumer demand through monetary expansion. A similar strategy was pursued in Italy, with the lira being floated in 1973. Both states were launching themselves towards an inflationary boom. France had been heading in the same direction since devaluation in 1969, a trend accentuated in 1972.

One result of floating was that international coordination was made that much more difficult. In Europe it divided countries into hard and soft currency camps. Yet, ironically, the end of Bretton Woods had not removed the dollar from pride of place; indeed, with gold out of the running, the world had in effect accepted a dollar standard, and in the future the Western world would still be obliged, no matter how reluctantly, to dance to the tune of the vagaries of the dollar.

The new monetary system was forced to change its priorities consequent upon the quadrupling of oil prices in 1973. This led to a massive flow of wealth to the oil-exporting countries. Since floating protected countries from the kinds of problems that had afflicted them in the late 1960s, they were able to construct ways of recycling the accumulated wealth of the OPEC states, both to other developing countries and to those Western states whose balance of payments situation had been seriously disturbed. Despite the growing economic presence of West Germany and Japan, the oil crisis confirmed the supremacy of the dollar as the world currency, if for no other reason than that oil transactions were priced in dollars. That supremacy was reconfirmed at a meeting in France in 1975, where the leaders of the United States, France, West Germany, Britain, Japan and Italy met to review international financial relations. It was perhaps a more explicit recognition of the fact of economic interdependence, and which was to be the first of a regular sequence of summit meetings, popularly known (with the later inclusion of Canada) as the Group of Seven (G–7), which steadily extended their brief to a whole range of economic questions and problems.

While floating may have given a national government more flexibility in financial policy and a greater ability to decide upon its own domestic economic priorities, a country could not be shielded entirely from the international climate. This was partly why in 1979 the EC set up the European Monetary System (EMS). Until 1979, the dollar linkage did not seem to be so threatening. Debtor countries were helped by the recycling of petrodollars as investment loans. The American government allowed the dollar to float downwards. An American reaction began with the second oil crisis of 1979; it was reaffirmed after 1981 by the policies pursued by President Reagan. Influenced by a renewed belief in sound money, a different economic emphasis emerged in the United States. After 1982 the American economy experienced its greatest upsurge since the days of the Korean War, partly inspired by military investment and spending. The value of the dollar rose steadily against other currencies, at the same time as the domestic boom led to an American trade balance deficit with all its major trading partners.

The rapid rise in the value of the dollar in the 1980s, after only a decade of floating, generated a new interest in seeking a more effective management of exchange rates, though a return to Bretton Woods was hardly likely. One important watershed in seeking to induce more effective macroeconomic co-operation was a meeting in New York in 1985 of the finance ministers from the United States, Britain, West Germany, France and Japan, which reached agreement on coordinated exchange market intervention. Regular G–7 meetings in subsequent years pursued the same theme. The extent to which exchange rate and economic policy coordination was desirable or possible remained a matter of some dispute, but not for the majority of the EC states which throughout the 1980s were moving steadily to the view that the EMS should be transformed as quickly as possible into an instrument for EMU.

1973: RECESSION

In 1973, as a response to the Yom Kippur War between Israel and the Arab states, OPEC, which was dominated by the oil producers of the Middle East, especially Saudi Arabia, quadrupled the price of its product. In addition, a complete embargo was imposed upon the export of OPEC oil to those countries which the Arabs regarded as having given unequivocal support to Israel: the United States and the Netherlands were the major victims. The immediate result was chaos in the Western world. There was panic in the oil market as each country scrambled to preserve its own economic interests, seeking to strike some accommodation with the oil producers; not too much thought was given to the problems of other states, even the embargoed Netherlands. Domestically, attempts were made to hoard supplies. The combination of price rises, production cutbacks, embargo and hoarding produced an acute shortage of petroleum products, especially, as far as the consumer was concerned, petrol. Most countries hastily made preparations for rationing along wartime models; some introduced restrictions on the use of cars, while others allowed the market to determine rationing on a 'first come, first served' basis.

A coordinated Western European response was not forthcoming; even within the EC, each member state tended to emphasise its own problems and needs, and sought an appropriate national strategy. An attempt at coordination was made by the United States, one of the major sufferers, which in 1974 invited other Western countries to join it in an International Energy Authority (IEA), which would not only serve in the longer term as a forum for consultation on national energy programmes, energy conservation and how to reduce dependence upon imported energy, but would also develop contingency plans for oil sharing should similar emergencies re-occur. Most of Western Europe accepted the invitation, though Britain and Norway, on the verge of becoming major producers of North Sea oil, reserved their right to take independent decisions. France initially refused to join the IEA, arguing that it would aggravate relations with OPEC and reduce the possibility of a satisfactory agreement between producers and consumers. More generally, there were European hesitations because of the suspicion that the United States, the colossus among oil consumers, wanted to use the IEA merely to protect its own economy.

Most of the measures advocated by the IEA were in place by the early 1980s, but whether this was due to the IEA, which had become an autonomous agency within the OECD, was a matter of debate. Even so, few lessons seem to have been learnt from 1973. After the successful Islamic revolution that deposed the Shah, Iran halted its oil exports at the end of 1978. OPEC raised its prices again, this time doubling them. A second wave of hysteria swept the Western world, even though since 1973 states had adopted a policy of stockpiling oil reserves to meet such an emergency. There was, in fact, no shortage in 1979; the situation was one of overproduction and insufficient demand. Those OPEC members who had argued that, despite the surplus, the West could and would pay more for oil seemed to have been proved correct, as there followed a scramble to buy more, irrespective of price, but in the longer run this proved the high point of OPEC influence. No similar mass panic emerged after the Iraqi occupation of Kuwait in 1990 and the subsequent Gulf War.

What is clear is that, after 1973, Western Europe moved into a new economic climate. Previous conventional wisdom had believed in a trade-off between inflation and unemployment: as one rose, so the other fell. A new word, stagflation, was coined to describe the unhappy combination of escalating inflation, rising unemployment and decline in economic growth, a combination that hitherto had been regarded as highly unlikely, if not impossible, given the belief that had grown up about the ability of governments to manipulate and regulate their economies through Keynesian techniques. In the 1960s the average annual growth rate within the OECD countries had been 4.8 per cent; in the 1970s it sank to 3.4 per cent, and rarely again did it reach the earlier levels. Politically more important, perhaps, between 1974 and 1976, growth fell to almost zero. A limited recovery did not begin until after 1977, but in the decades to come a variety of additional factors fed into the problems of the 1970s to ensure that the old optimism and confidence did not return.

Unemployment rose inexorably after 1973; by 1984, it was quadruple what it had been a decade earlier. This vast increase concealed some marked national variations. The highest figures were registered most notably in Spain, but also in Britain, Belgium and the Netherlands; by contrast, unemployment was exceptionally low in Switzerland, Sweden and Norway. As with unemployment, so with inflation. In the OECD as a whole, prices had risen annually by an average of 3.7 per cent between 1961 and 1971. In 1973 the average rise was 7.7 per cent, and in 1974 13.2 per cent. The averages again concealed huge national variations. West Germany stood out at one extreme, cushioned to some extent by its powerful economy and large trade surpluses; in addition, memories of the havoc wrought by the hyperinflation of the 1920s created a unanimous view that containment of inflation had to be a categorical imperative. Excluding economically peripheral countries like Iceland, which had learnt to live with hyperinflation, the other extreme was represented by Britain where inflation had soared to a massive 25 per cent by 1975. With the pound in collapse and unemployment also rising, the Labour government, faced with an economic breakdown, was obliged to call upon the IMF for extensive financial assistance. Inevitably, the IMF attached strict conditions for aid, demanding much more rigorous measures by government.

At the time, it was commonplace to blame OPEC for the general misery. In order to combat the rise in prices consequent upon the 1973 crisis, governments adopted deflationary measures. The combination of deflation and shrinking energy demand headed Western Europe into a recession, the downward spiral of which was halted only in 1975. What placed governments in a dilemma was the persistence of inflation. If they persisted with deflation, one consequence would be greater unemployment; if, on the other hand, governments attempted to combat unemployment through expansionary measures, this simply fuelled the inflationary spiral. In various guises and with different levels of severity, this dilemma remained a conundrum for Western Europe through to the 1980s. Gradually, a consensus emerged that employment goals had to be sacrificed on the altar of reduced inflation. The latter was achieved in the 1980s and a modicum of growth acquired. But the cost was levels of unemployment which only a decade earlier would have been thought unimaginable, intolerable and highly dangerous for political stability. The emphasis upon combatting inflation persisted into the 1990s when Western Europe entered a new and more prolonged period of recession, with a further growth in unemployment levels, most extensively in countries which, like the Federal Republic and Sweden, had once been held up as models of economic propriety.

However, the OPEC action of 1973 was more a catalyst which merely brought to the surface and exacerbated trends which were already present. Western Europe had already begun to experience a fundamental industrial revolution, especially in 'flagship' industries – steel, shipbuilding, engineering, textiles and cars – where problems of overproduction and poor productivity were compounded by, and placed them in a poor situation *vis-à-vis*, competition from industrialising nations outside Europe, headed by Japan. All were having to compete in a market showing signs of decline where there was a growing number of suppliers. At the same time they had to face up to the prospects of an expanding labour force, the result of both high birthrates of previous years and an increasing number of women seeking employment. Across OECD Europe, the cyclical economic downturns around 1970 were already displaying markedly deeper dips than those of earlier years. To some extent, these were aggravated by the confusion in the international monetary system that surrounded the final disintegration of the Bretton Woods structure and the move towards floating currencies.

Governments had first responded to the economic downturn with the usual methods of reflation, of expanding the economy by boosting demand. Since the problem was endemic, all pursued a similar policy at the same time. Inevitably, the quest for more demand simply turned the screws more tightly on commodity prices: in 1972, both the costs of raw materials and inflation were escalating sharply. Even before the oil shock, therefore, there were signs that Western European economies were threatening to run out of control. As the Keynesian demand management techniques of fine tuning the economy faltered in halting the upward creep of inflation, reflation turned to deflation.

However, government efforts to pursue a stricter policy through, for example, wage restraints often met with strong resistance. The problem was most acute in countries like Britain, France and Italy where labour relations were more adversarial. The labour force had been socialised through decades of economic growth into a belief in rising expectations. Trade unions reacted strongly to suggestions for wage restraint, let alone the shedding of labour; in any case, in many instances recent legislation restricted industry's ability to reduce its labour force. During the long economic summer, companies had found it more convenient simply to accept wage increases and pass the costs on to the consumer. In the public sector, governments had done the same through tax increases. In the new climate, this would simply fuel inflation. On the other hand, many employers were not prepared to face up to, or could not afford, militant union action. Confronted with the unions' insistence that inflation should not mean a reduction in their members' living standards, employers were caught in a cleft stick. With declining productivity, strikes could not be afforded. But since wage increases could not be balanced against increases in production and reduced costs, the net outcome was either contributing to the growth of inflation or accepting a drastic cut in corporate profits, which in real terms reduced possibilities for investment. Either way, industry became exposed to market competition from low-cost countries. The European investment rate fell from 4 per cent in 1970 to 2 per cent by the early 1980s.

In short, the Western world was already in a downward spiral that was not responding at all well to the postwar tradition of demand management. The oil shock merely exacerbated the downward slide. Fearful for their electoral survival and still accepting the Keynesian priority of full employment, many governments preferred not to admit that unemployment was unavoidable or tolerable, and clung to consumer-led expansionism in the hope that the recession would only be temporary. But the international trading system could not come to the rescue of any one domestic economy. The oil price increases had produced a gigantic flow of revenue to the OPEC states: OPEC's current account surplus soared from one billion dollars in 1973 to 61 billion only one year later. These states, however, lacked the ability and the population to consume in the same way as, and at the level of, Western societies. They could not, in short, generate or rescue demand.

After 1976, Western Europe began to come to grips with the new situation, though any future growth would take place in a world of higher inflation and unemployment. To a limited extent, international cooperation helped growth. The OECD launched a strategy whereby the most powerful economies, West Germany and Japan, would take the lead in expansion, so pulling along behind them the weaker states, but success was only partial: West Germany, for example, still regarded inflation as the major enemy. The OECD plan paralleled the efforts to recycle the OPEC revenues through the banks to both industrialised and undeveloped countries. Some OPEC members, especially Saudi Arabia, also contributed by accepting that continued rises in the price of oil could irrevocably damage the Western economy, which in the long run would not be beneficial to OPEC.

By the turn of the decade, therefore, Western Europe had to some extent adjusted to the new situation. On the whole, however, it had not entirely discarded the economic thinking that had dominated the postwar decades. All governments suspected high unemployment to be an electoral liability. Consequently, though with considerable national differences, all preferred, if possible, to operate large public sector deficits to prop up demand and employment. It was perhaps the second oil crisis of 1979 which forced governments to think again about their priorities. The level of economic activity was already substantially lower than that of 1973, and some of the options that had been advocated earlier were no longer attractive. The idea of some countries acting as 'benefactor motors' for the Western economy had not been wholeheartedly accepted, especially as it simply seemed to lead to a massive increase in imports from Japan. In addition, the recycling measures for OPEC funds had failed in its long-term objective. The easy availability of money had led many Third World countries to borrow far in excess of their ability to repay, and several could scarcely meet the interest repayments, let alone the original capital: a Third World debt crisis was to be a feature of the 1980s. If governments had believed in 1973 that they could reassert control over the economic situation, that belief was considerably dashed after 1979. If there had been a model of the ideal government–economy linkage after 1945, it was the so-called 'Swedish model'. Central to the model was a system of centralised wage bargaining – the Saltsjöbaden Agreement – which geared pay increases to what the economy could afford. After the late 1970s, Sweden found it more difficult to hold all to the spirit of the agreement, which finally was abandoned in 1984: it was but one of several indicators that the world had turned.

KEYNESIANISM, MONETARISM AND THE MARKET

The problems facing Western Europe in the 1980s remained unchanged from those confronting it in 1973. There were, however, several differences: room to manoeuvre was substantially less; there was a greater acceptance that traditional government responses were no longer adequate or appropriate; the emergence of the view that governments should only minimally seek to regulate, direct and own the economy. The dilemma was that if governments wished to bring unemployment back down to the minimal levels of the 1950s and 1960s, then it was doubtful whether this could be achieved by the earlier practices of boosting demand and spending public money. The net effect in the 1970s had been to intensify inflationary pressures. For political reasons, governments might have been prepared to live with that side effect, if the goal of 'full employment' had been achieved. In the 1980s, however, that goal was as remote as ever. Unemployment persisted – indeed, it continued to rise – at the same time as inflation remained a threat to industrial competitiveness and investment in new technology. In addition, deindustrialisation had begun to affect several non-profitable sectors, while new technology and computerisation offered both new opportunities and a severe reduction in labour costs. Further costs were arising from demographic change. Higher birthrates of past years had produced a bulge of young people entering the labour market precisely at the time when the number of jobs was declining. At the other end of the demographic scale, the greater longevity of life was producing an ageing Western population that would generate strains on public requirements in the health and pensions sectors.

What was needed was a mechanism by which public spending could be fixed at a level that would enable governments to tackle economic and social problems without shackling the competitiveness and productivity of industry. By 1980, there was a growing acceptance within OECD that this dilemma could not be resolved unless inflation was tamed. The German perspective on inflation became a major policy objective of government: a firmer monetary policy and control of public expenditure, even if that meant exacerbating structural and regional unemployment levels. At the extreme, as in Britain, some governments opted for drastic surgery rather than fine tuning. The switch of emphasis meant the end of an unquestioning belief in the efficacy of Keynesian demand management.

In the new climate it became increasingly difficult for any Western country, locked into an intermeshing world economic nexus, to buck the dominant trend. Small countries, which had a lesser impact upon the world economy, might be able to pursue significant national deviations. But if any doubt remained about the notion of 'one economic world', about the difficulty, especially for a major economic unit, of pursuing one's own route, in a kind of 'siege economy' (as, for example, favoured in the early 1980s by the British Labour Party), or about the inflationary effects of large public expenditure and wage increases, the lesson of France in the early 1980s was perhaps salutory. Upon his election as president and that of a Socialist–Communist coalition government in 1981, François Mitterrand revised the economic policies of his predecessor and declared a rush for growth led by large injections of public expenditure and a consumer boom. The loosening of monetary policy and high wage increases that followed led inevitably to domestic inflation, a flight of capital, balance of payments problems and it increased the costs of exports in a contracted world market. Within a year, France was forced to abandon the strategy, to fall broadly into line with that of its competitors.

In their search for an economic formula that would help them understand the modern world and offer a prescription for bringing it back into equilibrium, politicians 'rediscovered' monetarism, a doctrine with a long history. Monetarism assumed that in the modern complex world it was still possible to define and measure what is meant by money. On this basic foundation rested the core of the doctrine: that it is change in the amount of money in the economy which essentially determines all other economic movements, especially changes in national income. The latter, which equals the value of all incomes in an economy, may increase because more is being earned or because prices have risen. Monetarism tended to equate changes in the money supply with rising prices. It followed that, for monetarists, the money supply was the key to inflation: to tame inflation, one had to control the money supply. Monetarists argued that such control was still possible in a modern economy: all that was required was the necessary political will.

Monetarist ideas had lingered on after 1945, most notably in the United States, where traditions of responsible monetary policy and balanced budgets perhaps had deeper roots: even after the strong Keynesian slant of the Kennedy and Johnson administrations, it was still regarded as something of note that in 1971 President Nixon could declare 'I am now a Keynesian'. And in Britain, similar ideas governed much of the policy of the Conservative governments in the early 1950s, re-emerging again to flavour Labour government policy in the late 1960s. To say that the 1980s saw the triumph of a new doctrine of monetarism over a disillusioned and demoralised Keynesianism would be an oversimplification. Monetarism was not new, and it had perhaps always had some influence on policy, despite Keynesian predominance. What happened in each country was a mix of the ideas advocated by the two broad theoretical approaches; what counted was the particular recipe favoured by any one government.

Several countries had employed a judicious mix of monetary and non-monetary controls since the early 1970s. After the IMF crisis, Britain embarked upon a more stringent monetary regime. While monetarist ideas, even if not publicly admitted as such, were to be more important elements of government policy in much of Western Europe after 1980, as for example in Denmark under the minority non-Socialist coalition that took office in 1982, it was perhaps only in Britain, in the new Conservative leadership around Mrs Thatcher, that monetarism became embedded, as it were, as the official economic philosophy of the state. Across the Atlantic, monetarists could also claim a victory after President Reagan's assumption of office and the application of 'supply-side' theory and 'Reaganomics'.

In 1979 the Conservative government presented its prescription for curing Britain's chronic economic ills: monetarism, strict public expenditure control, trade union reform, deregulation and privatisation were to be the order of the day. The Conservatives had accepted, with not too much difficulty, the arguments that British unemployment and inflation were aggravated by excessive trade union power, and that without strict control, even reduction, of the public sector, the burden of appropriate policy would fall disproportionately on the private sector – which for the Conservatives was to be the flagship of economic revival.

Despite popular mythology, the rule of monetarism in the Thatcher government was brief and imperfect. There was no single philosophy; several different versions of monetarism were on display, and their views were not necessarily consistent. Government policy was also inconsistent, not just because of the advice it was receiving, but also because of some of the promises and pledges it had inherited. Between 1979 and 1982 the Conservative attempt to pursue a monetarist line manifestly failed. While the government had been aware, indeed had insisted, that the economic prescription would not be without pain, it had not been able to estimate the true extent of the havoc that might arise. By the end of 1981 the imperfect experiment was in disarray, with inflation back up in double figures, unemployment rising steeply, and whole areas of British industry decimated. The time had come for a halt. In 1982 the Conservatives retreated, despite attempting to gloss over the *volte-face*, back towards pragmatism, though still insisting that control of inflation was the necessary prerequisite for economic health. In 1985, Mrs Thatcher could tersely dismiss monetarism as something 'to which I've never subscribed'. At more or less the same time, monetarism as a driving dogma for government was spluttering out in the United States. It is true that by the end of the 1980s British industry and the British economy were in much better shape than they had been for decades, but perhaps deregulation, privatisation, deindustrialisation and the limiting of trade union power were more important explanatory factors than the application of monetarist theory.

In many ways, the monetarist experiment, like the Keynesian era before it, was modified by political pragmatism and expediency. It did make a lasting impression, however: an acceptance of the fact that monetary policy does matter. That had been a view expressed by several European parties before the monetarist era; afterwards, it was accepted by almost all. But quite apart from its imperfect application, monetarism did not come to grips with the exchange rate and the pressure that change in the latter could place upon domestic economic policy. The era of floating exchange rates was not without crisis. Currencies did not stay in equilibrium; there were frequent and large flows of capital from one country to another. This reflected what was to be a continuous upward curve in the influence of international financial markets, markets, moreover, which were more likely to distrust governments and assume that they were apt to make an economic mess of things. It also partially explains, perhaps, why in the late 1970s the EC returned to the question of currency stabilisation with the creation in 1979 of the European Monetary System (EMS) with its important Exchange Rate Mechanism (ERM) component.

What is clear is that by the mid-1980s European inflation had been drastically reduced and, in so far as it was possible, perhaps even controlled. In the 1990s it even tended to hover at levels rather lower than those predicted by the markets. It was significant, for example, that the crisis in the ERM in 1992, created by market speculation against currencies which were deemed to be overvalued within the ERM and which led to currency devaluation or depreciation in several countries – Britain, Sweden, Finland, Italy and Spain – confounded the expert view that the latter would mean a surge in inflation that would wipe out any competitive trading edge gained by the countries. Inflation did not rise, the countries retained their competitiveness, and their exports grew. However, the major fall in inflation occurred in the early 1980s. In the OECD countries, it fell from 13 per cent in 1980 to under 4 per cent in 1986. The British fall was the most dramatic, from 22 per cent to around 3 per cent. The extent to which monetarism can claim the credit for this collapse is an issue which has been hotly disputed. It is more probable that it was only part, and perhaps a small part, of a nexus of factors. There was in the first instance a slide in oil prices after 1980 as demand fell dramatically, fragmenting OPEC pricing unity and lowering the relative cost of energy. More important were unemployment and a government withdrawal from economic involvement.

Among OECD countries, the average unemployment rate rose from 5 to 12 per cent between 1979 and 1986. The range varied considerably: unemployment was minimal in Switzerland, Austria, Sweden and Norway; high elsewhere, especially in Spain. In the 1980s, the climb of unemployment to unprecedented postwar levels had widely been regarded as an intolerable trend that was politically dangerous. Certainly, trade unions had been in the vanguard of actions demanding drastic measures to cut unemployment; in that respect, predictions about possible unrest were perhaps correct, and many governments and employers had bent with the wind. What was surprising was that the even greater levels of unemployment of the 1980s – more unemployment, more male unemployment, more youth unemployment, more long-term unemployment – did not generate similar agitation. By 1992 the British Conservatives had won a fourth successive electoral victory. The CDU continued to be confirmed in office in Germany. Generally, the 1980s saw a marked continuity in office in most countries, but where governments fell, in the 1980s or the 1990s, the unemployment issue did not seem to be the prime factor.

One key to understanding this sea-change in political wisdom lies with a revolution in popular attitudes. Whether one calls it resignation, realism or cynicism, there was a greater acceptance, even among the unemployed, that high levels of unemployment had arrived to stay, that there were no instant solutions, and that parties which claimed otherwise lacked credibility. On the other hand, the welfare state and security provisions had cushioned some of the more severe hardships and desperation that had accompanied the depression of the 1930s. There had, in addition, been continued economic growth, so that those in employment may have had cause to be materially satisfied with government performance and policies. More importantly, however, by the 1990s the popular mood was more one of economic uncertainty and insecurity. As a revolution continued to sweep the international economy, it was not the level of joblessness, but the threat that many of those still in employment might at any time be made redundant that characterised Western European societies. The notion that the standard of living would rise every year was no longer taken for granted.

The extent to which governments in the early 1980s were prepared to tackle unemployment depended first upon their political complexion and, secondly, upon the domestic relationship between the state, capital and labour. The two extremes were represented by Britain and Sweden. In the former, anti-inflation objectives became paramount for the Conservative government: the greater political divide in Britain and its traditional adversarial structure of industrial relations also militated against a strong commitment on unemployment. By contrast, Sweden attempted to remain committed to both full employment and anti-inflation measures. However, during the 1980s the more consensual Swedish model began to break up further as, here too, full employment was demoted down the agenda. The Swedish experience of the late 1980s confirmed the earlier evidence from France and West Germany that having a left-wing government was no guarantee that unemployment would be reduced.

Governments, by the 1990s, had also come to the conclusion, albeit with varying degrees of commitment, that their involvement in – and certainly their direction of – the economy could not guarantee economic success. While the deindustrialisation of sectors of the British economy after 1979 may have been directly stimulated by Conservative government policy, the same process spread inexorably across the continent as old faltering and overmanned industries failed to compete with low-cost challengers from other parts of the world. Equally importantly, the Thatcher governments' belief that the market, not a government, was the speediest way to a healthy economy, with its emphasis on refusing to allow the public purse to bail out lame ducks, deregulation and the privatisation of public sector services and activities, was also something that came to be accepted, sometimes, enthusiastically, sometimes reluctantly, almost everywhere. By the mid-1990s the process of privatisation had still gone furthest in Britain, with, for example, the public utilities, telecommunications and the railways passing out of government hands, but in every country the degree of government involvement in, and control of, economic activities was severely reduced from the level of the 1970s.

It was the market which had filled the vacuum. Competitive markets had, as it were, generated a snowball effect in which prices were not manipulated by government or rose regardless, but simply responded to pressures of supply and demand. Competition meant that increases in costs were not passed on automatically to consumers; instead, the pressure was on enterprises to reduce costs, most obviously by shedding labour. There were several further reasons why markets rose to the ascendant. Technological advances, especially in computers and micro-technology, had accelerated since the early 1980s at a bewildering speed. They had completely revolutionarised many areas of economic activity, particularly in previously labour-intensive service sectors such as banking, leading to a reduced need for labour. That pace of change was a further factor inducing a general public sense of economic anxiety about the future of employment. The world economy, furthermore, had become even more international. Globalisation was a term used to describe a changed world system where diversified production processes scattered across the globe effectively undermined the position of local monopolies, whether they were publicly or privately owned. In this new globalised world, high-cost producers were likely to be destroyed, and the survivors were under persistent pressure to keep their costs, and hence their labour force, under control. The last bastions to fall before the advance of the markets were in the public sector, but privatisation meant that there, too, the removal of state ownership exposed both management and workers to market pressures. In many areas of activity, further pressure was placed upon governments by the EC which, in terms of creating a level playing field across the member states to meet the objectives of its competition policy, was pushing strongly for governments to expose shielded and subsidised enterprises to open competition. One final ironical supplement to government withdrawal came as a result of the ending of the Cold War. The so-called 'peace dividend', which at one time people had believed would mean the transfer of resources from military to more socially useful projects, did not materialise. Instead, governments looked to a reduction of military spending as a way of reducing costs; the reduction of orders for equipment, of the amount of material deployed, and in the size of the armed forces all simply reinforced the prevailing economic picture.

In a sense, the victory of the markets was something that Western governments themselves had endorsed in their decades-long search for a more open international trading system. In 1963 the members of GATT had agreed to adopt a broader approach and a new set of principles that would go beyond manufactured products. These principles served as guidelines for subsequent GATT sessions – the Kennedy Round (1964–67), Tokyo Round (1973–79), and Uruguay Round (1986–94) – which were progressively more difficult to resolve. The Uruguay Round focused upon fifteen different trade areas, including agriculture, intellectual copyright, services and textiles. Its intention was to make the most significant advance yet to a truly globalised trading system, and to emphasise that point it was accepted that success depended upon agreement on the Round as a whole. Not surprisingly, perhaps, the talks did not end on schedule at the end of 1990, as countries fought to defend their own nationally privileged interests. They were interminably extended and hovered on the brink of collapse on several occasions. The Round was eventually concluded by the end of 1994, with GATT transformed into a new World Trade Organisation (WTO). Within Western Europe, developments in the EC pushed in the same direction. In 1985 the EC took up again the quest for a common market. This, along with the broader European Economic Area (EEA) which linked the EC with EFTA, was to be launched at the end of 1992. While the launch was less than perfect, to a large extent the objectives of the Treaty of Rome – the free movement of capital, labour, goods and services – were in place, reducing further the prerogatives of government.

Governments might respond to these conflicting pressures by establishing special aid and training schemes, but by the mid-1990s it was widely accepted that these were, at best, minimal in alleviating unemployment. The markets, and governments were left joined with increasing vigour in the hunt for foreign investment. It is ironical that in the 1960s the multinational company, mainly American in origin, was frequently seen in Western Europe as a danger to national economic control and labour markets. By the 1990s, the multinational world was much larger and truly multinational in character, and it was strenuously courted by all governments seeking investment in new factories and jobs. While all might live in hope, it nevertheless seemed that, despite the expression after 1995 that the EC should be more positive in responding to the problem, there was an acceptance that there could be no return to the all but universal full employment of the first postwar decades. That was the product of a conjunction of circumstances that was unlikely to re-occur. There was, however, no guarantee that unemployment would remain at the bottom of the political agenda.

CRISIS OF THE WELFARE STATE

Between 1950 and the mid-1970s the Western European welfare state and spending upon it had burgeoned. The average national expenditure on social security, defined broadly, had more than doubled, from 9 to 19 per cent of gross domestic product. The average rate of growth, moreover, had also accelerated, from 0.9 per cent to 3.4 per cent. Most of the expansion had occurred in pension and health expenditure, but other areas, such as education, especially higher education, had also benefited. If one takes a very broad definition of social expenditure, the European welfare state had expanded everywhere to swallow between one-quarter and one-third of gross national product. The biggest spenders on social policy were Sweden, Denmark, Belgium and the Netherlands. Of the advanced industrial states, only Switzerland stood out for its relatively low level of provision.

The plunge into economic difficulties that occurred after 1973 had severe implications for the welfare state concept, in terms of both the quality and quantity of provision it offered to its clientele, and the level of employment it offered. There was a question-mark about the amount of revenue that could be made available for welfare services, as well as an additional load on the system because of rising unemployment. However, the difficulties facing the welfare state were not just the consequence of specific events. They had been building up for some time, as a result of an accelerated expansion over the previous decade and because of demographic effects – the high birthrate of the late 1950s and early 1960s, the extension through medical advances of life expectancy and successful treatment of previous incurable diseases and disabilities.

In the 1970s, the welfare state was affected by the changing nature and decline of consensus in Western European societies. It faced not just loss of finance, but also a loss of consent. There emerged a greater ambivalence about its virtues. On the one hand, people had been socialised into accepting the state as the great provider of a whole range of services in education, health and pensions. Public provision of services had divorced, at the popular level, cost from provision. Groups jostled with each other in competition for resources which were not, contrary to popular belief, unlimited. Inevitably, some promises could not be fulfilled. On the other hand, employment in the public sector continued to boom. Taken together, these developments generated a critical reaction to a 'runaway' public sector, particularly its bureaucratisation, impersonality and denial of freedom of choice. The welfare state provided employment for around 20 per cent of the workforce in most countries; it was among the remainder that such negative attitudes appeared, perhaps also as a reaction to the growing unionisation of the public sector and the consequent willingness to use the strike weapon to achieve its objectives.

The new thinking about the welfare state was not divorced from the financial problems. Welfare systems had been on an upward escalator for so long that in a sense they had acquired a momentum of their own. But growth in revenue was declining even before 1973, meaning that funding would have to come from tax increases if services and jobs were not to be cut. In the private sector, pressures for greater productivity were to lead to the shedding of labour in substantial numbers and to a rapid growth in unemployment. The drive for greater efficiency, economy and productivity was a factor that helped to produce the change in the climate of public opinion that was to accept greater efficiency in the public sector as well, even though the welfare state was vital in cushioning the effects of unemployment.

One visible expression of changing popular attitudes, of a 'welfare backlash', was criticism of high tax levels. Protest was most pronounced in Denmark where, under the leadership of a tax lawyer, Mogens Glistrup, a new anti-tax Progress Party was formed in 1972. For a while it threatened to disrupt the system: though shunned by all other parties, it rapidly became Denmark's second largest party. Only in Norway, however, did a similar party, also called Progress, emerge; but it soon tried to present a distinctive profile across a range of issues once its founder, an admirer of Glistrup, died two years after its formation. In Denmark the Progress Party waned rapidly in the 1980s to minority status; Glistrup himself was jailed for tax evasion in 1983 and eventually expelled from the party in 1991.

That kind of tax protest as an anti-welfare state expression was an ephemeral phenomenon. More enduring were tax evasion and the black economy. The latter is difficult to estimate, but it was deemed to be important throughout Western Europe. In Italy, some estimates suggested it could be as high as one-quarter of the official gross domestic product; and even in law-abiding West Germany, official reports put it at 10 per cent of gross domestic product. The black economy was regarded as an important indicator that the limits of taxation had been reached, that each further increase in taxes would generate more evasion and avoidance. In short, the welfare state came to be seen as a great and inefficient consumer. By the late 1970s the notion that the welfare state must be restrained began to gain greater credence, with growing criticism about its costs and bureaucracy. The theme of restraining costs was taken up with greater frequency by conservative parties across the continent, as part of a broader reaction against the growth of government: the privatisation of public services, cost-effectiveness and the restoration of personal responsibility became political slogans.

Irrespective of the format of each welfare state, and the relative strengths and weaknesses of each, by the late 1980s these criticisms and attitudes had coalesced into acceptance of the view that costs were too high and benefits too generous, that what was needed was a restructuring away from universal provision towards targeting those groups most in need. As with unemployment, governments were not unduly penalised electorally. It proved, in fact, relatively easy to trim the welfare system around the edges: reducing and restricting the indexation of benefits or wage increases to public employees; redefining and tightening the rules of welfare eligibility in terms of contributions paid; introducing and raising charges for certain welfare services. Despite all this, the welfare state continued to grow: even in Britain where the Conservative government was the market leader in demanding more efficiency savings and more value for money, expenditure on welfare policies in real terms continued to rise. Among the European members of OECD, only in education did expenditure fall as a proportion of total social spending. In the other major areas of the welfare state – health, pensions and social security – the share of expenditure continued to grow. It was not perhaps until the 1990s that virtually all politicians accepted that the problem would not go away, indeed that future changes, most notably medical advances and an ageing population, and a declining active workforce, represented a time bomb for the early part of the next century.

In the 1970s, discussions on the crisis of the welfare state had raised the question of whether it would survive. Two decades later, the question had been answered: it would survive. It was the kind of welfare state, its structure, objectives and the extent of its obligations that were in dispute. What was not in dispute, however, was the belief that the heady days of expansion of the 1960s would not return. Nor was there much dissent with the belief that the welfare state needed to be 'rationalised', that resourcing could never and should not match demand. The basis of debate had broadened from what the welfare state had done for people to include both what it had done to people and what people could do for themselves. The welfare state may have grown to its maximum possible limits, but what should be done within those confines was an issue that would remain a matter of political contention between parties and among voters, particularly as the growing army of old people, those most dependent upon the welfare state, might in the future, as they had already sought to do in the Netherlands and Luxembourg, turn to wield their not inconsiderable mass in the arena of electoral politics.

CHAPTER 18

THE EXTENSION OF DEMOCRACY IN SOUTHERN EUROPE

Against those who make a practice of intolerance, who are contemptuous of co-existence and who have no respect for our institutions, I proclaim my faith in democracy.   (*King Juan Carlos of Spain, 1981*)

At the request of the armed forces, you have submitted your resignation. . . . You will follow further developments on the television.
                    (*Communiqué received by the Greek Prime Minister, 1973*)

Throughout the postwar period, three countries remained on the periphery of, even outside, the mainstream of Western European politics. The Western Europe that slowly emerged from the ashes of war was a state system that professed a deep commitment to the principles of liberal democracy and that was slowly learning new forms of international cooperation. The two Iberian states of Portugal and Spain and, to a lesser extent, Greece all seemed to stand apart from these developments. Admittedly, Portugal was a founder member of NATO and of EFTA, and Greece, in part inspired by the Truman Doctrine, joined NATO in 1952 and became associated with the EEC in 1962. Given the Communist pressure on it in the 1940s, Greece may have been regarded as being in the frontline of Western defence, but this value receded after Yugoslavia's rejection of Soviet hegemony, and was persistently weakened by Greece's disputes with Turkey over Cyprus and the Aegean. Turkey was even more frontline than Greece, with its border to the Soviet Union, and was generally regarded by the United States as a more valuable NATO member. Spain, by contrast, was not formally linked with any European or military developments, though it did allow American air and naval bases in 1953 in return for financial and economic aid: it did, however, join OECD and GATT in 1960.

While all three were therefore linked in some way to the rest of Western Europe, these ties were insufficient to deny their peripherality. All were dominated by conservative groups which were hostile to both the free market notions of capitalism and the collectivist notions of social democracy; all possessed extensive clientelist systems of government-sponsored patronage; and all were heavily impregnated by powerful and conservative religious traditions. In Spain and Portugal, authoritarian dictatorships were of long-standing. In Portugal, António Salazar had been in virtually complete control of the country since 1926, while Spain had been something of an international and European pariah since Generalísimo Francisco Franco's victory in the Civil War, its limited international participation, which began with joining the UN in 1955, notwithstanding. But Iberia's sense of remoteness from the rest of Western Europe, of being of Europe but not with it, tended to have deeper historical roots.

Greece was in a rather different situation. Until 1967 its political system was at least semi-democratic. However, political competition historically tended to revolve much more around personalities than durable parties, organisations and programmes, a pattern typical of prewar Balkan politics. Moreover, its constitutional regime was continually under stress between left and right, between republican and royalist. Its Balkan location and heritage made it somewhat suspicious of Western influences, which traditionalists feared would weaken the Orthodox fabric of Greek society. In 1967 the frail democratic system finally collapsed with a military coup. For the next seven years, a military junta pursued a particularly brutal form of repression.

Yet, remarkably, within months of each other, these three authoritarian regimes disintegrated in the mid-1970s. The first regime change occurred in Portugal with the revolution of April 1974. Three months later, the military regime in Greece collapsed almost without a whimper. Finally, Franco's death in November 1975 effectively brought to an end a long frozen period of modern Spanish history. The new regimes were to be democratic. Though there was severe right-wing opposition, especially in Spain, and an interim period of revolutionary instability in Portugal, it was not too long before the three had acquired the trappings of liberal democracy. Their rehabilitation was, in a sense, completed when Greece, in 1981, and Spain and Portugal, in 1986, became full members of the EC.

REVOLUTION AND DEMOCRACY IN PORTUGAL

Between 1926, when he emerged to the fore as the result of a military coup, and 1932, António Salazar gradually drew all the reins of power into his hands. His new state (*Estado Novo*) was essentially backward-looking and isolationist, seeking to recreate an idealised nineteenth-century state resting upon traditions of nationalism and Catholicism. Political influence and participation were restricted to a very small elite, with all decisions essentially being taken by Salazar himself. Portugal remained, as it were, in a state of suspended animation until 1968, when illness forced Salazar to resign. His successor, attempting to maintain the regime, promised some reforms, but soon abandoned all efforts to liberalise the system and overcome its inertia.

The catalyst for dramatic change was the increasing burden of the regime's pledge to retain its vast empire in Africa. Portugal had been facing nationalist guerrillas in Angola, Mozambique and Guinea since 1961. Its commitment, perhaps, may have been influenced by the indignity of losing its small enclave of Goa in 1961, which had simply been annexed by India in a bloodless takeover. At any rate, the strain on a poor country with limited resources was considerable. By the 1970s the wars were consuming about one-half of an expanding defence budget and recruiting one in four of all men of military age, with inevitable repercussions throughout an already weak and inefficient economy. It became increasingly obvious that the regime was incapable of resolving Portugal's problems. Change could come from only one source – the army, especially the junior professional officers, which had come to accept that it was no longer possible to hang on to the colonies.

The regime, in fact, simply faded away overnight in the face of a military coup in April 1974. The 'Carnation Revolution', named for the flower worn by the revolutionaries, was immediately greeted with great mass enthusiasm in Portugal itself. However, almost fifty years of paternalist authoritarian rule had deprived Portugal of any tradition of political participation and pluralist politics, and of the opportunity of experiencing and developing effective democratic institutions. The two years following the coup were a period of extreme political turmoil and confusion. Something in the order of fifty factions calling themselves parties emerged to contest for power; but none bar the Communists possessed any kind of effective organisation. In addition, the army was also divided, with several factions vying against each other and against civilian groups for political influence. The consolidation of a liberal democratic regime was by no means assured.

The national government formed after the coup was headed by General António de Spínola, who only recently had been dismissed as Deputy Chief of Staff for his criticisms of the old regime. But he headed a coalition which very quickly was dominated by two radical groups, the Communist Party and the Armed Forces Movement (MFA), a left-wing group of military officers who had engineered the coup. Spínola was too conservative for their taste and, after a bungled coup by his supporters early in 1975, he was forced to flee to Spain. His junta of national salvation was replaced by a revolutionary council, which claimed the right to initiate policy and to veto cabinet decisions. The Communists, in particular, made a serious bid for power by seeking to penetrate and control the major governmental and economic agencies. By endorsing and fostering the expropriation of land, particularly successfully in the southern half of the country, they also became an effective force within the labour movement.

Between the 1974 coup and the establishment of a constitution in 1976, Portugal experienced no fewer than six provisional governments. The fall of each reflected the shifting balance between the several, mainly radical, factions which were jostling for power. In general, however, there was a gradual movement away from the extreme left, as mass support slowly coalesced around more centrist parties and as more moderate military leaders reasserted control over or isolated the more radical elements within the army. Radicalisation peaked in mid-1975 with the MFA and the Revolutionary Council pushing hard for a policy of nationalisation and redistribution of wealth. At the same time, the Communist Party had successfully inserted itself at many crucial interstices of society and seemed to be poised on the verge of a naked bid for power. Opposing it were a host of political groupings, most using the word 'Socialist' in their title, of which the most important was the Socialist Party of Mário Soares, which was receiving substantial aid from European Social Democrat parties. External influence from the West increased in the latter part of the year: Western governments made it clear that any aid for the extremely precarious Portuguese economy was conditional upon its political house being put in order. This Western pressure helped to remove the Communist-backed government in November. Seeing the promised land slipping away from them, pro-Communist military units launched a further coup attempt. The uprising, however, was effectively quelled by a moderate army leadership led by General Ramalho Eanes. The failure of the 1975 coup marked the collapse of Communist influence, the fragmentation of the MFA and the effective removal of the radical left to the political periphery.

The revolutionary road was the only one open to the Communists, who had limited electoral strength. The 1975 elections for a Constituent Assembly had demonstrated broad support for Soares' Socialists and other moderate parties. The path was open, with the Socialist Party as the key, for the establishment of a constitution. The 1976 document retained the goals of 1974 and a defence of the gains made since then; it also acknowledged the existence of the Revolutionary Council, which was to retain an advisory role. The Council was finally disbanded by amendment in 1982. But the tone of the constitution was liberal democratic, and it provided an instrument by which a democratic mould could be imprinted on the country.

Once the constitution had been promulgated, elections were held for the new parliament and for the presidency of the republic. The results showed how far Portugal had moved since the turmoil of the previous year. While not gaining a majority, the Socialists strengthened their position as the leading party and were easily able to construct a centre–left coalition government. Furthermore, Eanes ran for the presidency with the support of all the major parties bar the Communists, and was elected by an overwhelming majority. Though there were nine coalition governments through to 1983, all were essentially centrist in complexion, and all accepted the rules of the constitution. Above them, continuity was provided by Eanes, who exercised his office firmly but constitutionally (though retaining his army position as Chief of Staff until 1981). By the end of the 1970s, Portugal was well on course towards establishing a working liberal democracy. Further proof of stabilisation came in the 1980s. In 1982, the constitution was revised to reduce the powers of the presidency, moving the country away from a quasi-presidential system which perhaps had been a more suitable format for an awkward transition period. And in 1986 Eanes stepped down at the end of his second term of office, to be replaced in a calm electoral atmosphere by the Socialist leader, Soares.

THE RESTORATION OF DEMOCRACY IN GREECE

The civil wars of the 1940s left a bitter legacy in Greece. The left was alienated from, and repressed by, a rightist regime that saw the world in simple terms of black and white, and which elevated anti-Communism to an official state ideology. The political right had powerful allies in the monarchy and the armed forces. Despite outward appearances, Greece was essentially only a semi-parliamentary regime where both the monarchy and the military enjoyed significant political authority and autonomy. One further issue complicated Greek politics: the historical conflict with Turkey, which had a major focus in the fate of the Greek and Turkish communities on Cyprus.

Greece was ruled by governments of the right until 1963; after 1955 these were dominated by the rather more moderate figure of Konstantinos Karamanlis. In 1963, however, the right lost the general election. Despite the rigidity of the political system, there had been significant socioeconomic change, with a growing middle class looking for greater political influence. The 1963 victor was the left-wing Progressive Centre Union, which had to rely for a majority upon Communist support. In 1965, the Union gained an absolute majority. The problem was that any reforms attempted by the Union would inevitably affect the institutional props of the regime. The right and the army were extremely hostile to the government, accusing it of Communist tendencies. An attempted government investigation of a secret organisation within the army split the Union and led to violence on the streets. There was also increasing agitation over Cyprus, where the UN had installed a peacekeeping force in 1964. Eventually, the king, quite unconstitutionally, dismissed the government, replacing it with a caretaker administration.

New elections were scheduled for 1967. The Centre Union, now more radical, stepped up its popular campaign, demanding both that the military must be brought firmly under civilian control and that there should be a reduction in military expenditure. Fearing a purge of the military, a group of army officers pre-empted the elections with a coup in April 1967. Party politicians were removed from office and were arrested or fled abroad. The king, whom many on the left suspected of complicity in the coup, tried for a while to put a brake on the new military leaders. However, after his involvement in a bungled counter-coup, he also was forced into exile, and Greece fell fully under the rule of the colonels. The collapse of the monarchy was important, for its exile was to prove permanent. The pillars of the anti-Communist state had splintered. In the eyes of the military, both the political right and the monarchy had been found wanting: it alone would uphold the ascendancy of the state but now, with full autonomy, it would stand or fall by its own efforts.

During the rule of the military junta, Greek politics went into abeyance. The regime was noteworthy for the severity of its rule and the numerous accusations of brutality and torture levelled against it. Its otherwise undistinguished career came to an abrupt and somewhat surprising end in June 1974. While some chinks in its armour were apparent, with disputes between moderates and hardliners, the catalyst of crisis was once again Cyprus.

Union with Greece had been a popular slogan among the majority Greek Cypriot population during the island's anti-colonial struggle against Britain in the 1950s. It was a sentiment that also had strong roots in Greece itself, though obviously one that was adamantly rejected by both the minority Turkish population on the island and by Turkey. The junta took up the theme of union with an ill-thought-out plan of incorporation through a coup against the constitutional Greek Cypriot government. Its immediate consequence was to precipitate a Turkish invasion of Cyprus which was quickly able to secure a *de facto* and enduring partition of the island. Given that Cyprus is more or less an offshore island of Turkey, the logistics of any Greek invasion or defence of the island would be very difficult at the best of times. But the Turkish action exposed the hollow military shell of the Greek junta. It clearly had no contingency plans to counteract Turkish activities, other than the issuing of long-range verbal threats. Its order for a general mobilisation backfired. It brought into the open a political and military fissure between hardliners and more moderate officers; simultaneously, it led to a more open expression of popular anti-regime sentiment. The military leaders made an amazing *volte-face* only one day after the declaration of mobilisation, admitting that the armed forces were not ready for war and that therefore a political solution would have to be sought. This was the death knell of a regime which had failed to consolidate and legitimise itself. It simply evaporated.

A small group of mostly conservative politicians were invited to participate with the junta in exploring how a transition back to civilian rule might be achieved with the minimum dislocation. The army wanted to retain as much as possible of its influence, including continuing to play a role in government, but it had forfeited its hand over the Cyprus fiasco. Its scenario was strongly rejected by the majority of the politicians involved in the discussions. Their aim was nothing less than a return to 'normal' competitive politics.

Towards the end of the month, the most prominent conservative politician of the postwar period, Karamanlis, returned from a self-imposed exile in France to become prime minister. Reconstituting his pre-coup movement as New Democracy, he received a substantial electoral victory. One of the first acts of the new government was to honour Karamanlis' earlier pledge to hold a referendum on the question of the monarchy: the result was a resounding rejection of any royal return. Karamanlis led New Democracy to a further, though less convincing, electoral victory in 1977, before resigning to become president of the republic in 1980. In 1981, New Democracy was heavily defeated at the polls by the left-wing Panhellenic Socialist Movement (PASOK), which had been formed in 1974. Compared to the agitation which had accompanied the rise of the left in the 1960s, the transfer of power occurred smoothly and in a calm atmosphere, heralding perhaps the acceptance in Greece of the rules of the game of liberal democracy.

One reason why the new system had perhaps a better chance of putting down firm roots was the removal of three issues which had bedevilled politics. The monarchy had been discredited by its initial condoning of the military regime: the decisive referendum verdict against its restoration removed it from the political agenda. Similarly, the events of 1974 effectively reduced the political importance of the military, while in practice, although agitation in foreign policy would continue, there was little that Greece could do about Cyprus.

Given the nature of the military regime, the circumstances of its downfall and the demotion of the pillars of the old anti-Communist state, one might have expected the popular mood to swing sharply to the left. That this did not happen was to a considerable extent due to the personality, reputation and strategy of Karamanlis. He had retired from politics in 1963 and later went into voluntary exile in Paris. Hence he was not tainted by association with the junta. Identified as being part of the moderate right, he was acceptable to a broad spectrum of political opinion. His strategy was to supervise a transition to an effective democracy: first, by isolating the far right and depoliticising the military and, secondly, by offering the left a stake in the system, including the Communist Party. New Democracy was constructed as a broad-based movement of the centre–right. The transition might not have been so easy if the threat of a conflict with Turkey had not loomed so large. Nevertheless, as a sop to Greek pride, Karamanlis withdrew Greece from the military wing of NATO. It was, however, only after his electoral victory and the successful quelling of a military conspiracy early in 1975 that the government felt strong enough to bring the junta leaders and others accused of crimes to trial. In 1975 the government submitted a formal application to join the EC, a move which Karamanlis hoped would help consolidate the new republican constitution and overcome to some extent Greece's geographical and psychological isolation from Western Europe. And, in 1980, Greece returned to NATO.

The 1981 election marked a further decisive step in the development of democratic stability. Mainly perhaps because of its poor economic record, New Democracy saw its support crumble. In the previous years it had had to compete with the rising star of the charismatic PASOK leader, Andreas Papandreou, who pursued an aggressive form of Socialist populism coupled with an emphasis upon national independence which was strongly anti-American and opposed to EC entry. Though there were worries that further turmoil would follow this election, Karamanlis as president accepted a PASOK government without demur. While Greece continued to face economic and political problems, the 1974–81 period of consolidation augured well for a more stable democratic system, and by the 1990s there were indications that, unlike in the past, durable party organisations had emerged that would outlast the personality of a leader.

SPAIN: THE END OF ISOLATION

From being historically a major imperial power, Spain had sunk into relative obscurity. Since the mid-nineteenth century it had suffered from periodic bouts of political unrest and violence. The final sequence in the chain of events was the catastrophic Civil War of the 1930s, which ended with the victory of General Franco in 1939. While Franco pursued a relatively cautious authoritarian line, all domestic political activity was outlawed, bar that of the 'official' National Movement (Falange). However, Franco's support rested primarily upon a small conservative elite and the army: the Falange, when it was favoured by Franco, was used as an instrument of bureaucratic control rather than one of mass mobilisation.

The Civil War left a bitter legacy in Spain. The left had been deeply divided between Communists and Anarchists, and at times their mutual hostility seemed to be more important than opposition to Franco's forces. The moderate centre had also suffered from internal dissension. The picture was further complicated because the core of Spanish industrialism lay in two regions, Catalonia and the Basque provinces, which had preserved and developed distinctive national and ethnic identities, and which had agitated for at least some form of autonomy. The left and the regions were vigorously suppressed by Franco's regime, hardening the introspective nature of a country still trying to come to terms with the extreme violence and brutality of the war.

The Civil War had been a prologue to the later world conflict, with Franco being actively backed by the Axis powers, while his opponents had at least the moral support of the Western democracies. Although pursuing an increasingly prudent policy of cautious neutrality during the Second World War, Franco was still *persona non grata* to the West in 1945. The Nordic states, in particular, argued passionately for an economic boycott of Spain, while the new French Fourth Republic closed its borders with its southern neighbour between 1946 and 1948. In 1946, too, many states accepted a UN resolution and withdrew their recognition of the regime. Spain's international isolation seemed to be complete.

Franco, however, was to govern Spain for a further thirty years. International rehabilitation came slowly and haltingly, mainly because of the Cold War and American strategic interests. In 1953 the United States agreed to provide aid in return for the lease of air and naval bases. Diplomatic recognition was slowly restored in the following years. Spain was admitted to the UN in 1955, OECD in 1959, and GATT in 1960. On the other hand, it was still politically ostracised by the rest of Western Europe; its applications in 1962 and again in 1964 for negotiations on EEC membership were rejected. The EC eventually signed a preferential trade agreement with Spain in 1970.

Internal political change was non-existent. Political parties were banned, those on the left and in the regions clinging on to a clandestine existence. The state was in a kind of political limbo which became exposed to chinks of light only in the 1960s. To some extent, this was a consequence of the socioeconomic changes of the previous decade. The regime had fairly successfully pursued a policy of rapid economic development, which ironically served to dilute its internal cohesion. In the 1960s, too, opposition to the nature of the regime emerged for the first time within two of its basic props, the Catholic Church and the army, and Franco was forced to accept some limited reforms. However, similar opposition from opponents of the regime was still met with stern, even violent, repression. Working-class agitation increased, while Basque and Catalan nationalism responded to the greater pressures upon them by a greater readiness to embrace political violence.

Perhaps a further reason for the unrest of the 1960s might have been the question-mark hanging over the political succession. Franco's government was very much a personal one. The Falange had been kept at arm's length since 1946, and Franco's strategy had been to play his supporters off against each other. As he aged, the question of Franco's mortality loomed even larger, reaching crisis proportions in the 1970s as his health declined. Two events which had a particular impact were the assassination by ETA in 1973 of his confidant and recent hand-picked successor, Admiral Carrero Blanco, and the collapse in 1974 of the sister authoritarian regime in Portugal. The assassination marked a final turning point for the regime: it was left without any clear line of succession, and Blanco's death stimulated the further momentum of several oppositions.

In 1947, Franco had proclaimed Spain to be a kingdom, but one without a king; under the law of succession, he had had himself defined as both head of state and regent. The law also gave him the right to designate his monarchical successor as either king or regent. He agreed to allow Juan Carlos, the grandson of Alfonso XIII, the last Spanish king, who had abdicated in 1931, to reside in Spain and attend military academy and university. However, it was not until 1969 that Franco designated Prince Juan Carlos as his successor. His strategy by the 1970s seems to have been for a successor government under Blanco; the monarchy, trained by Franco, would provide a symbol of the legitimacy and continuity of the authoritarian state. While this strategy was in tatters after Blanco's assassination, it is dubious whether its chances of success had ever been great.

Spain had changed enormously by the 1970s and pressures upon the regime and its pillars had increased correspondingly. Economic development and industrialisation had produced a greater working class which, chafing under political and legal restrictions, had since the 1960s turned more readily to strike action. This class was a profitable recruiting ground for the clandestine Communist and Socialist parties, which had also stepped up their activities. Increased student unrest also indicated a growing disillusionment with the regime among those social groups which had traditionally sympathised with it. Similarly, partly under Vatican pressure, there was a marked cooling in the attitude of the Catholic Church, which began to preach the virtues of a pluralist political system. Finally, there were the regions. Basque nationalism in particular had not just asserted itself politically, but also in urban guerrilla warfare. In 1968 the government was obliged to place the provinces under a state of emergency for several months.

All of this boded ill for Spain when Franco eventually died in 1975. There was no logical successor, and Juan Carlos was an unknown quantity. The conditions were even more explosive than in Portugal. However, the transition was to be surprisingly smooth, though it was a year before the move towards democratic restoration was begun, after the new government accepted that the initial attempt to forge a kind of 'restricted democracy' was doomed to failure. Two men must take most of the credit for the successful change: Juan Carlos and Adolfo Suárez. Juan Carlos, proclaimed king in 1975, proved to be a determined and skilful advocate of democracy; and because the post-Franco government seemed to lack the necessary will or capacity either effectively to continue the old regime or rapidly to move towards liberalisation, he had considerable freedom to manoeuvre.

The situation was, in effect, taken out of the government's hands, with an explosion of political activity. A host of political parties, all technically still illegal, surfaced and strikes and demonstrations, also illegal, increased in number. The King responded in mid-1976 by replacing the prime minister with his own nominee, Suárez. The appointment was greeted with some alarm by reformers, for Juan Carlos was still operating through the institutional structure of the old regime, while Suárez himself had served that regime in a number of important political posts. However, it soon became apparent that the two combined in a formidable team dedicated to realising the King's determination peacefully to achieve parliamentary democracy and a national consensus. By the end of the 1970s, even the Spanish left came to accept the King as a bulwark of democracy.

Suárez, in fact, was typical of the later generations that had risen to positions of influence under the Franco regime: a pragmatic technocrat without any ideological commitment to an authoritarian state, yet still essentially conservative and wary of radical change. He was able to outflank the unreconstructed supporters of the old regime, especially as the King could expect to be regarded as legitimate in the eyes of many conservatives. In their different capacities, the two men combined to utilise the institutions of the Francoist state in order to bring about its demise. The old regime, in other words, was dismantled from within rather than through the activities of opposition political forces. There was a plethora of these jostling for a place in the sun, but they were divided over current issues, views on the future political system, personal antipathies and historical memories of the 1930s.

Several reforms were pushed through the parliament which had been appointed by Franco, which then proceeded to vote itself out of existence. Suárez obtained massive popular support for his proposed constitutional reforms in a referendum at the end of 1976. Parties were legalised and arrangements made for the election of an assembly which would draft a new constitution. Putting himself at the head of a hastily constructed party, the Union of the Democratic Centre (UCD), Suárez arranged for a general election in mid-1977. It was a personal triumph for him. With the UCD easily the largest party, he was able to remain in charge of government and guide the new structure. The constitutional document was rather ambiguous in many of its details, but this perhaps was a reflection of the widespread desire to maintain a consensus: even the Communist Party pursued a consensual line, often being more conciliatory than the larger Socialists. The constitution was accepted by the parliament in 1978 and subsequently endorsed by a referendum. It was a landmark in that, in contrast to the past, it was backed by all the significant national parties, and because of its pledge for widespread devolution: indeed, substantial autonomy was immediately ceded to the two problem areas of Catalonia and the Basque provinces.

In its willingness to consider and grant regional autonomy, the new regime went some way towards defusing one dangerous challenge to its integrity. However, while Catalonia was largely satisfied with what it gained, tensions and violence would remain in the Basque lands, where the extremist organisation,

ETA, remained actively committed to securing an independent Basque state by violent means. The other potential danger was the army, where acceptance of the regime shift was far from total. On two occasions, disaffected officers attempted to use economic problems, the persistence of Basque terrorist activity and an increase in crime as an excuse for military intervention. The second attempt, which saw a small army group occupy the parliament building and hold the deputies hostage, was fraught with danger, albeit not without an element of farce. It crumbled in the face of forthright condemnation by Juan Carlos, widely respected in military circles, and further condemnation from all political groups, including the very conservative Popular Alliance, whose leader and policies were widely identified with the old regime. While this abortive coup did persuade the government to tone down some of its democratising and modernising policies, the young Spanish democracy survived a first serious test of its viability and vitality.

A second test came with the election of 1982. Suárez and his party had been confirmed in office in 1979 in the first election to be held under the new constitution. It was obvious, however, that the party still lacked organisational coherence: it was never much more than a loose alliance of diverse interests. This created problems for it in the next few years, especially in economic policy. Government difficulties, in fact, may have been one factor that persuaded dissident military elements that they had an opportunity to turn the clock back. The UCD gradually moved to the right to try to assuage military worries, as well as those of the Church over pressures to legalise divorce and abortion, and to limit the appeal of the conservative Popular Alliance. In the event, it was no surprise that the party disintegrated in the 1982 election. It perhaps had never been anything other than a vehicle for Suárez and his strategy of cultivating a national consensus during the awkward transition phase. When he resigned the premiership and withdrew from politics in 1981, it was left adrift without coherence and purpose. Perhaps it could never have been more than a temporary phenomenon; but it could be said to have more than served its purpose.

The failure of the UCD left a vacuum on the centre–right. The Popular Alliance still lacked sufficient credence with much of the electorate to be successful, and it was left to the Socialist Party to occupy the high ground, with a comfortable parliamentary majority. Under the leadership of Felipe González, the party had abandoned its initial dogmatism of the immediate post-Franco years and, with a revitalised organisation, had successfully outflanked the Communist Party, which fell back towards insignificance in 1982. It had also rejected Marxism as the basis and justification of its existence. This served to calm possible fears among potential voters, not least within the army, about its intentions; on the other hand, the adoption of a more moderate line by the party was, in a sense, highly political because of the still-important factor of the military. In that sense, the army presence may have contributed to the consensus and stability of the new regime and the changeover to a Socialist government in 1982. That change was the second litmus test of the regime: it was accompanied by none of the turmoil and hatreds which had surrounded previous left-wing victories (or even just the possibility of one) in Spain. In 1986 the country's new departure was confirmed by its entry into the EC.

Although there were significant differences between Spain, Portugal and Greece in the details of how they moved from dictatorship to democracy, the parallels between the three are perhaps more striking. Relatively forceful and talented political figures played a decisive steering role in all three. In Greece and Spain, at least, political leaders of most persuasions seemed to prize some form of consensus during the first post-dictatorship years more highly than an adversarial pattern of party competition. Most significantly, perhaps, once they had settled down to a new mode of operation, all three survived the test of a change in government without undue strain. What was important was that this change entailed the coming to power of the left: this was a powerful affirmation that the principle of pluralist competition had taken root, and that conservative groups were no longer determined to retain power at all costs and by any means.

CHAPTER 19

THE POLITICAL MOSAIC: A POLITICS OF UNCERTAINTY?

A week is a long time in politics.   (*Harold Wilson*)

The lady's not for turning.   (*Margaret Thatcher, 1980*)

The 1950s and 1960s had been decades of great political optimism in Western Europe. Rapid and extensive economic growth and the erection of the welfare state had dramatically changed both the structure of, and the expectations held by, society. Politically, these changes had helped to generate an apparent political consensus where, in most countries, the general principles of sociopolitical organisation and the direction of the future were not widely questioned. Conservative parties had, to a greater or lesser extent, accepted the notion of the Social Democratic state, some indeed taking pride in arguing that they, rather than the left, were the better managers and custodians of the welfare state. For their part, Social Democrat parties seemed to be abandoning whatever vestiges of dogma that remained from their ideological past. Apart from Italy, the extreme right had no significant following: most importantly, the challenge of the NPD in West Germany, with its evocation of the Nazi past, faded as abruptly as it had begun after only a few years in the limelight. At the other extreme, Communist parties were significant only in Finland, France, Iceland and Italy. However, in France the party was firmly excluded from power, ossified in a Stalinist mould, and seemingly weakened further after the coming to power of de Gaulle. In Iceland and Italy the Communist parties had striven to achieve a more distinctive national position, somewhat independent of any dictates that might come from Moscow. The Finnish Communists were brought into government in 1966, partly because of pressure from the Soviet neighbour. At any rate, by the mid-1960s the assumption of a political consensus could lead to claims that ideology was dead – at the extreme, that no real choices faced the electorate, that politics was between Tweedledum and Tweedledee.

If such a consensual mood existed, it was shattered by the wave of protest that began in the late 1960s, a wave for which 1968 became a symbol. If, indeed, political ideology had ever disappeared from the agenda, these protests, and the subsequent series of direct action, ensured its reinstatement. The

245

economic crisis of 1973 simply confirmed that, whatever the consensus that might have existed in the past, it could not be regained, for its implications challenged the whole conception of the Social Democratic welfare state. On the left, the threats of inflation and unemployment led to an intensification of the faith in the managed economy. On the right, they raised questions about the limits to government, about the need to curb public expenditure and costs. There may still have been a consensus on the welfare state, but there was to be a new debate about its nature, extent and objectives.

After 1973, economics was firmly rooted at the head of the political agenda. Only rarely did economic questions and problems not dominate the headlines. Despite concern about the deterioration of super-power relationships and, after 1989, the future of Europe and its defence, terrorism, environmental worries or fleeting episodes like Britain's 1982 war with Argentina over the Falklands, politics were to be about economics: inflation and unemployment, investment, taxation, the ability of the state to pay and deliver. Moreover, apart from a brief interregnum in the late 1980s, the atmosphere was decidedly pessimistic. The gloom at times spread from a concern about the survival of economic prosperity to embrace the future viability and possible bankruptcy of democracy itself. Typical of this mood was the remark attributed in 1975 to Willy Brandt that democracy in Western Europe could not survive for more than another two or three decades.

In retrospect, the intensity of the pessimism might seem rather surprising. While inflation and unemployment did creep upwards inexorably, there was no real comparison with the problematic situation of the 1930s or with that which prevailed after the end of the Second World War. The Western European economies may have over-extended themselves, but they were still consumer societies offering a high standard of living to their populations. And for a great number of people that standard of living continued to improve. No country had degenerated to a state of political anarchy or revolution. By the 1980s, the waves of protest had largely dissolved and terrorism seemingly curbed.

Several reasons have been offered for the rather abrupt climatic change. Perhaps the most basic explanations related to the changing nature of society and the expectations which people held of government. By the 1970s, structural and technological change had made society more complex, and had fragmented the old, and perhaps too simplistic, notions of class divisions. It was not that class and status differences disappeared; they merely became more complicated. Economic growth had spawned a consumer-oriented society and mentality in which individuals wished to spend money on items of their choice, and they expected the desired goods to be immediately available. It was, perhaps, a mentality that was less prepared to accept self-sacrifice and restraint. Improved educational and health provision had also helped to produce a more articulate and demanding electorate which, in the halcyon days of the boom, had been inculcated, often with government encouragement, into the belief that governments would and could provide an unlimited panoply of public services. A myriad of groups placed a variety of competing demands upon government, without having to pay much regard to their cost.

One further inheritance of 1968 was an increased impatience with traditional methods of arguing one's cause and, hence, a greater willingness to seek to force the issue through direct action and confrontation. The new concern with environmental protection and pollution led to demands that governments place more emphasis upon improving the quality of life, even if this meant a reduction in materialist consumerism. Even in the best of economic circumstances, governments would have found it difficult to meet and satisfy all the demands. Economic uncertainty simply heightened the dilemmas and pressures: governments could not respond satisfactorily across the board.

By the 1970s some of the old moral uncertainties had also gone. The 1960s had been a decade of change in moral values and their associated behaviour patterns. Issues such as homosexuality, divorce, abortion and contraception were discussed more openly, and within two decades laws governing behaviour in these areas had been liberalised almost everywhere. Even in Italy, the Catholic Church, which had put its prestige on the line in defending the illegality of divorce, was heavily defeated on the issue in a bruising referendum in 1974. Throughout Western Europe the changing nature of values reflected an acceleration of secularisation. This had important consequences for Christian Democrat parties; many found that their basic prop, the Catholic Church, had had its ascendancy weakened, or had withdrawn entirely from overt political influence. Socioeconomic change and secularisation both posed problems for parties which had commanded a following based upon class or religious loyalty.

At the same time, there was a growing reaction against, and alienation from, the size and power of the state, a critique of both its remoteness from the concerns of ordinary people and its bureaucratic nature. These sentiments contributed to the waves of protest which racked Europe after the late 1960s, to the growing frequency of direct action, and in the late 1980s to the rolling back of the state through, for example, privatisation measures. Out of this turbulence there emerged new parties, as disparate as the West German Greens and the Progress parties of Scandinavia, which espoused new and different concerns. But all, in their different ways, wanted a more participatory form of democracy and an end to the remoteness of the state and its expanding domination of life. It was a theme which was to be taken up by many Conservative parties and then, by the 1990s, to become almost a new received wisdom.

Out of all this social, economic and political flux, there coalesced a new political environment. It was one whose major characteristics were a greater level of electoral change, more emphasis upon issue politics, a pressure upon the homogeneity of political parties and, paradoxically, more pressure upon and more cynicism about government. In many countries the net effect of the new environment was a reduction in the lifespan of governments, which found it harder to maintain their majority, cohesion or privacy of deliberation: in the 1990s governments and politicians in several countries were operating under the cloud of financial scandal. Overall, there were questions about the governability of modern society. At both the mass and elite levels, domestic politics could perhaps be characterised as the politics of uncertainty.

PATTERNS OF PARTY POLITICS

There was, after 1970, a re-emphasis of the political mosaic. While, very generally, the 1970s could be seen as a decade of left popularity, with the 1980s experiencing a new and effective conservative challenge, the national basis of political competition in the 1990s had become, if anything, more distinctive. In the 1970s the only major certainty seemed to be that failure to resolve what public opinion polls and other measurements suggested were important areas of popular concern would end in electoral defeat for the government. By the late 1980s, even that certainty had disappeared, as governments, despite their inability to resolve important economic issues, proved more able to win re-election.

The economic theme was prominent in Britain. By the early 1970s, the post-war boom was over, sterling continued to be under pressure as an international currency, and chronic balance of payments problems persisted. Despite the rapid development of its North Sea oil fields, Britain's economic performance declined further: more pressure upon sterling, climbing unemployment, and inflation twice going over 20 per cent. Even more humiliating was the need of the 1974 Labour government, faced with a breakdown in control of public expenditure, to apply to the IMF for massive financial assistance.

Towards the end of its term of office, the 1966 Labour government, its proclaimed technological revolution a failure, set in motion a political conflict that was to change the face of British politics. It had come to believe that rejuvenation necessitated an effective tripartite collaboration between government, industry and trade unions, along lines developed in other countries. As part of this belief, it sought, unsuccessfully, to bring the trade unions more within the framework of law and to modify the tradition of free collective bargaining. The succeeding Conservative government under Edward Heath, once its attempts to sponsor a dash for growth had produced only higher inflation, turned in the same direction of controlling the unions. Faced eventually with a miners' strike that had effectively crippled the economy, Heath sought an electoral mandate in 1974 on who ran the country, the miners or the government. The result was defeat for the Conservatives. Though lacking a majority, the Labour Party returned to power. It could at least claim to be the only party acceptable to the powerful trade union movement and capable of coming to some kind of arrangement with it. However, the social contracts which it forged with the unions frayed steadily, to collapse finally in the winter of discontent of 1978–79, when widespread and recurring strikes seemed to some to threaten anarchy, and discredited both Labour, which still believed that a rigid control of prices and wages was necessary, and the unions.

Some of the problems which Harold Wilson and, after 1976, James Callaghan had to face were due to their less than firm control of their own party and to Labour's less than firm grip upon government. A slender majority gained in a second election in 1974 soon eroded and, after 1977, the party had to depend upon a pact with the small Liberal Party or support from the various nationalist parties in Scotland and Wales. More important was the changing nature of the Labour Party. Wilson had lifted the ban on party membership for proscribed groups. Partly because this opened membership to more left-wing elements, the party became steadily more radical during Callaghan's reign. By the 1980s the Labour Party had shifted markedly to the left. In 1981 a small group of moderates seceded to form the Social Democrat Party, which subsequently collaborated closely, and eventually merged, with the Liberals. Labour's radicalism continued until a humiliating electoral defeat in 1983, after which a succession of leaders took more than a decade to pull the party back, not just into the political mainstream, but to accept much of the new climate of thinking initiated by Conservative governments.

The Conservatives also broke the consensus. After two electoral defeats in 1974, Heath had to give way. His successor was Margaret Thatcher, and under her leadership the party moved decisively to the right, rejecting Keynesianism and espousing a version of economic liberalism which saw only a limited economic role for government. Having won the general election in 1979, Mrs Thatcher sought to turn convictions into practice. Despite her strong will and her ringing declaration that 'the lady's not for turning', the Conservative government was obliged in 1981 to abandon its intense flirtation with monetarism, an experiment which had severe consequences for the economy and unemployment. But she remained undeterred from pursuing three broad campaigns that were the bedrock of her belief in what was necessary to rebuild British prestige and economic strength: control of inflation, curbing the power of the trade unions, and reducing the economic role of the state. By the mid-1980s, the first two elements of the edifice had largely been achieved, after which the Conservatives stepped up their programme of privatisation. The most symbolic event was perhaps the governmental resistance to, and defeat of, a lengthy miners' strike in 1983–84: revenge for 1974 and a symbol of the vast reduction in trade union influence under Mrs Thatcher.

Despite public opinion polls giving her a low positive rating and indicating a rejection of much of her policy programme, Margaret Thatcher was swept back to power with massive majorities in 1983 and 1987. The first victory might be explained by the euphoria of victory in the 1982 Falklands War with Argentina, whose invading army was successfully ejected from the remote islands by British forces. This could not, however, explain the 1987 victory. What equally counted was that the opposition was divided between a radical and, for many people, unconvincing Labour Party, and a centre–left alliance of Liberals and Social Democrats. Mrs Thatcher fell from power in 1990 not by electoral defeat, but because of internal party unrest over her rigid stance on European integration and total commitment to a highly unpopular local government tax. Nevertheless, her successor as party leader, John Major, duly won a fourth consecutive victory for the Conservatives in 1992 and broadly followed a similar policy line, though by the mid-1990s the government was looking more and more tired and running out of steam. Despite the claim by her critics that Mrs Thatcher's conviction politics had produced something called 'Thatcherism', it was difficult to relate all her behaviour, and that of the Conservative governments, to a single ideological belief system. Nevertheless, her tenure of office decisively shifted the political playing field to the right, and by the 1990s the Labour Party had openly accepted that most of the Conservative innovations of the 1980s could not and should not be reversed.

West Germany also experienced conservative revival. The long CDU occupation of government had ended in 1969 not so much because it lost votes, but because the SPD and the small Free Democrats (FDP) had found sufficient common cause to be able to form a coalition. First under Willy Brandt and then Helmut Schmidt, this coalition was to survive until 1982. Brandt's government was dominated by the need to find a *rapprochement* with Eastern Europe, a quest that culminated with the *Ostpolitik* treaties of 1972. Thereafter, however, economic problems and coalition disagreements weakened Brandt's position, not least because he had a limited interest in and knowledge of the economic field. In 1974 he resigned as a result of a spy scandal involving a senior member of his personal staff.

He was replaced by the more pragmatic Schmidt, a skilful political and economic manager who enjoyed considerable personal popularity, not least because of his success in steering West Germany through the economic turbulence of the 1970s; and this aided the electoral reconfirmation of the coalition in 1976 and 1980. In 1976 the CDU and its sister party in Bavaria, the Christian Social Union (CSU), which had always acted in harmony at the federal level, once again became the largest parliamentary bloc. However, the CDU challenge was weakened by internal party divisions and by the bid by the more right-wing Franz-Josef Strauss, the CSU leader, to become the Chancellor candidate of the two parties. Strauss, committed more to individualism, liberal free market economics and a more aggressive foreign policy towards the East, eventually fulfilled his ambition in 1980. The choice was electorally disastrous for the CDU. Strauss was as unpopular outside his native Bavaria as Schmidt was popular. In addition, his candidacy persuaded the pivotal FDP that it had no alternative but to hold fast to the SPD.

The Strauss factor and the internecine conflicts within and between the CDU and CSU obscured the fact that by 1980 the SPD–FDP coalition was beginning to run out of steam. Tensions were emerging between the two over defence and economic policy, and Schmidt's practical style was alienating many within his own party. By the 1980s the SPD was moving steadily leftwards, partly under the impulse of the new and active Green movement which was displaying an effective ability to compete in the radical left market. An economic downturn after 1980 assisted this radical trend, isolating Schmidt even more within his own party. The coalition eventually collapsed in 1982 as the FDP, alarmed over the direction being taken by the SPD, Schmidt's leadership notwithstanding, indicated a willingness to enter an alliance with the CDU.

That option had become possible because of 1980. Strauss' defeat had demonstrated the limitations of a more unambiguously right alternative. The CDU returned to the safety of the more moderate leadership of Helmut Kohl; this also made a CDU–FDP alliance more possible. The new coalition was reconfirmed in office in 1983 and 1987, despite a relatively colourless leadership and the occurrence of financial scandals and political mistakes. Kohl later received a huge boost from the collapse of Communism in Eastern Europe. As the DDR regime quickly disintegrated at the end of 1989, he took the initiative in pushing for a rapid reunification of the two Germanies. Reunification led to an expanded Federal Republic, and all-German elections in 1990 reconfirmed his leadership, though the CDU performance was better in the ex-DDR than in the old West Germany. The costs of integrating the ex-DDR territory into the Federal Republic after 1990 proved substantially higher than had originally been predicted. This produced resentment in the West at the extra tax burden to be borne, while equal resentment was fanned in the East as unemployment soared and the looked-for economic benefits of reunification were not immediately apparent. While conservative domination was helped by it being the government at the time of the ending of the Cold War, throughout the 1980s and 1990s it was aided by the weakness and divided nature of the opposition. The Greens had continued to grow, and the SPD remained divided over whether it should compete or ally with the Greens, or seek to regain the centre ground.

While weaker in absolute terms, Conservative parties achieved a real and significant advance throughout the Social Democrat bastion of Scandinavia. In the late 1960s, the Nordic Social Democrats shifted somewhat to the left, in response to challenges from their flanks, to advocate further expansion of the state's role in economic affairs: particularly in Denmark and Sweden, there was a desire to build an economic democracy that would parallel and improve the social democracy constructed since the 1940s. Throughout the region, the Social Democrat vote stalled and even faded in the 1970s: it stabilised in the mid-1980s, but never regained entirely all the ground that had been lost. Its decline led to political attention becoming more focused upon the rise of Conservative parties.

Although the Norwegian Labour Party held power from 1973 to 1981, it could only be as a minority government reliant for survival upon left Socialist support. It had been damaged by the contentious EC issue and failed to recover all the ground lost. In 1981 it was replaced by a Conservative-led coalition that dominated government in the early 1980s and sought in some areas to reduce state involvement in public affairs. Conflicts between the non-Socialist parties over financial issues led to the return to power of Labour in 1986, but it remained short of a majority, with continuity in office aided by the inability of its opponents to forge a lasting alliance. In Sweden a milestone was reached in 1976, when the Social Democrats passed into opposition for the first time in forty years. It could only return to power in 1982 as a minority government dependent, as it had been since 1970, upon Communist support. The extent of change was symbolised by a Conservative-led government between 1991 and 1994, and by Social Democrat governments after 1986 moving away from a total commitment to full employment and the cradle-to-grave welfare state.

The picture in Denmark and Finland was more confusing. The former experienced an electoral earthquake in 1972, with extreme political fragmentation. The number of parties doubled overnight, Glistrup's Progress Party emerged for a while as a major challenger, and electoral volatility was very marked. Majority coalition government became even more difficult: the minority Social Democrat governments of the 1970s were replaced in 1982 by a series of long-lasting minority coalitions under Poul Schlüter (the first Conservative premier since 1901) which lasted until 1993 when Schlüter and others resigned as the result of an immigration scandal. In Finland, Kekkonen's centre–left formula persisted through to the 1980s. However, its cohesion had been strained by Agrarian/Centre decline and the inclusion of the Communists after 1966. This basic coalition strategy continued to fray after 1970, and the Communist Party began an internal convulsion that was to erode its strength and split it into two warring factions. As elsewhere, the Conservatives began to ride an electoral wave. However, the Social Democrats held firm and their leader, Mauno Koivisto, won the presidency in 1981, despite the Soviet preference for one of his opponents. In 1987, Koivisto accepted the weakness of the centre–left option and the rise of the Conservatives: he encouraged and accepted the inclusion of the latter in a government coalition with the Social Democrats.

What happened in Scandinavia was not a revolution. Conservative parties advanced everywhere, but equally the Social Democrats remained stronger everywhere. Nevertheless, with other new parties appearing, the right became far stronger than at any time since the war. Its rise introduced more complexity and fluidity into the political systems. On the other hand, while the Conservative wave was in part the result of a heightened popular discontent with the extent of state control, its bureaucratisation, erosion of individual liberty and high levels of taxation, the consensual basis of politics was only marginally breached. The Conservative parties were far from being strong enough by themselves. In most instances they depended upon association with other centre parties, which had their own concerns and wished to maintain their distance from both the left and the right. While it is true that in many policy areas the options pursued were barely distinguishable from those of their Social Democrat predecessors, their greater strength and governmental presence perhaps aided the left more easily to come to terms with the changing economic climate and accept by the late 1980s that the Nordic model of state–economy relations had grown to, perhaps even beyond, its limits.

The consociational coalition pattern which had been claimed to exist in the Low Countries and Austria also seemed to disintegrate under the pressures of change. In Austria the Grand Coalition ended in 1966, while party fragmentation became a major feature of politics in Belgium and the Netherlands. Of the so-called consociational democracies, only in Switzerland did everything seem to continue as before: the semi-permanent coalition of the four largest parties was Western Europe's most durable government.

By the mid-1960s the factors which had engendered the Austrian Grand Coalition in 1945 were no longer relevant. In 1966 the People's Party won an absolute majority and decided to go it alone. Four years later, the balance of power swung to the Socialists who thereafter ruled unchallenged through to 1983. Under the paternalistic and popular chancellorship of Bruno Kreisky, the

Socialists successfully weathered the economic storms of the 1970s, pursuing and intensifying the close governmental relationship with economic interests, and expanding further the already substantial public sector. The transition to single-party government was eased by the retention of much of the consultation and interest patronage of the Grand Coalition era. By the 1980s, however, the economy, especially the public sector, was over-extended. In 1983 the Socialists lost their majority but chose, under Kreisky's successor, to form a coalition with the small conservative Freedom Party. As the latter fell under more extreme right-wing influence, the alliance became more tense, and in 1987 the Grand Coalition was reformed, first to isolate the more nationalist elements in the Freedom Party and, secondly to create in theory, a shared party responsibility for the retrenchment that all agreed must occur. The new Coalition, however, remained lacklustre, plagued by financial scandals affecting the Socialists and the international furore that arose over the election of Kurt Waldheim, a former UN Secretary-General, to the presidency despite revelations and accusations about his wartime role in the German army. In Austria the Kreisky years had been a politics of certainty. The only beneficiary of the more inconclusive years after the mid-1980s appeared to be the growing Freedom Party under its radical and charismatic leader, Jörg Haider.

Confusion seems to have been the hallmark of Dutch and Belgian politics after the early 1960s. The previous stability of the Netherlands had been predicated on the supremacy of religion and the predominance, with their cross-class support, of the three major religious parties. Secularisation had a dramatic impact in the Netherlands, especially on the key Catholic People's Party. Between 1962 and 1973 the latter's vote, along with that of its Protestant allies, collapsed, and several new parties appeared on the scene. While Labour emerged from the turmoil as the largest party, its leftward drift persuaded a moderate faction to secede in 1970. After a period of indecision, the religious parties attempted in 1980 to halt their downward slide by deciding to merge. The new Christian Democratic Appeal was able, through to 1994, to dominate usually centre–right coalitions, which as elsewhere slowly moved towards a more rigorous economic and welfare policy.

The fragmentation that occurred in Belgium was both less complex and potentially more dangerous. The cause was the intensification of the linguistic divide separating Wallonia and Flanders. Under the pressure of the new nationalist parties that had sprung up to espouse the interests and demands of the two language communities, the three dominant parties – Christian Social, Liberal and Socialist – had, by the early 1970s, split into mutually antagonistic French-speaking and Flemish wings. The problem was that a linguistic dimension could be attached to any issue, especially because of the growing economic contrast between a prosperous Flanders and a declining Wallonia. Even minor or extremely localised issues could escalate upwards to topple a government. The picture was further complicated by the differential party strength in the two provinces – the Christian Social Party dominated Flanders, while the Socialists were the strongest force in Wallonia – and by disputes over the status of bilingual Brussels, a predominantly French-speaking enclave within

Flanders. The language issue made coalition formation more arduous and government durability more limited, complicating attempts to tackle the economic problems of high taxation and unemployment, increasing government deficits, and poor investment. Gradually, however, after 1970 Belgium moved towards a territorial devolution of power, but a final constitutional settlement, which effectively created a federal state, was not implemented until 1994: even then, it was accepted that a further look at the situation would be required, and 1999 was set as the date for this.

Further south in Europe, a Conservative wave was much less evident. In Italy the 1970s saw the continued rise of the Communist Party and, in the 1980s, a modest success for the Socialists. Despite the emergence in France of Jean-Marie Le Pen and his National Front movement, a revival of the left was perhaps the major characteristic of French politics. In the new democracies of southern Europe, openly Conservative parties failed to make a mark in Portugal, though by the mid-1980s the country had fallen under the control of a centre–right government that persisted through to 1996. The initial Conservative successes of the late 1970s in Spain and Greece were not sustained after the departure of Suárez and Karamanlis from the party political scene. The Spanish Socialists survived in government through to 1996, but even then proved strong enough to deny their major Conservative rival an absolute parliamentary majority. After 1982, PASOK government rule in Greece was interrupted only briefly between 1990 and 1993.

France had already experienced a Conservative revolution in 1958. It was a decade or more before the various opposition forces were able to come to terms with the new constitutional emphasis upon the presidency and the demotion of parliamentary politics, de Gaulle's own stature and use of the presidential office, and the emergence of a large Gaullist party. By the late 1960s the old party system of the Fourth Republic was dead. The MRP, barely a shadow of its former self, formally dissolved, while the historic Socialist Party, after a derisory 5 per cent of the vote in the 1969 presidential election, also seemed destined for oblivion. France appeared to be faced with a simple and stark choice between Gaullism and the still powerful Communist Party.

In one sense, the turning point was the unrest of 1968. In the subsequent election, it produced a landslide victory for a more conservative Gaullist movement. After de Gaulle resigned in 1969, that conservatism continued under his successor, Georges Pompidou. Under its weight there occurred a reconstitution of both the centre–right and the moderate left. The Gaullists, reorganised in 1976 as the Rally for the Republic (RPR), were faced by a new centre–right alliance, the Union for French Democracy (UDF). On the left, the Communists were opposed after 1971 by a rejuvenated Socialist Party under the leadership of François Mitterrand.

After Pompidou's death in 1974, the Gaullists were torn by internal disputes over the succession. Their disarray enabled Valéry Giscard d'Estaing to forge a broad centre–right coalition that won, but only narrowly, the presidency. In 1981, disagreement between the RPR and UDF contributed to his failure to gain re-election as president. The left also was able to find common cause in the 1970s. Mitterrand's strategy was to seek a *rapprochement* with the Communists as the best way of achieving a left government. In 1972 the two parties agreed upon a joint programme, and in the following two years almost gained parliamentary and presidential victory. In 1978, however, the Communists suddenly abandoned the alliance just before the forthcoming parliamentary elections. The reason was quite simple. Mitterrand had proved to be a popular leader, and his new party had become much more successful than its predecessor. Communist fears about their continued leadership of the left were justified by the election: the Socialists surpassed them for the first time since 1936 and were only marginally edged out of first place by the Gaullists. That trend continued through to the 1980s. In 1981 the buoyant Socialists won control of the National Assembly and Mitterrand was elected to the presidency. The Communist vote continued to decline.

In order to strengthen his base and to avoid opposition on two fronts, Mitterrand persuaded the Communists to join the government as a junior partner. His initial economic strategy was to reverse the strict anti-inflation policy of the Giscard d'Estaing era. It was deficit-led growth that Mitterrand initially sought to revive, but by 1983 he had to accept that the strategy had intensified inflation and national debt, while doing little to check unemployment. Once economic policy was reversed, it was only a matter of time before the Communists, always uneasy about their governmental role and its effect upon their own homogeneity, would decide to leave. The economic about-turn offered them an excuse to do so, which they did in 1984.

In 1986, France moved into a new political era when the RPR and UDF replaced the Socialists in government. For the first time, the Fifth Republic had a president and prime minister of different political persuasions. The new structure, called *cohabitation,* worked better than many had feared. Mitterrand allowed the RPR a more or less free hand in domestic policy, while he still firmly controlled foreign and defence policy. The main significance of *cohabitation* was its confirmation of the importance of the presidency. Mitterrand, not the RPR leader, Jacques Chirac, was regarded internally and abroad as the major figure of French government. That reflected the greatest legacy of the de Gaulle revolution; while a party might be necessary to launch an individual towards the presidency, once elected that individual became divorced from and greater than the party. Immediately upon his re-election in 1988, Mitterrand dissolved parliament, and in the subsequent election the Socialists regained their majority. The next several years, however, were a story of decline, internal dissension and scandal. In disarray, the party lost control of parliament in 1993, forcing the country into a second bout of *cohabitation,* but this time it was accepted as a normal part of politics, with little speculation on a constitutional or political crisis. The Socialist reign finally came to an end in 1995 at the end of Mitterrand's presidency. His successor was the RPR leader, Chirac.

If France had largely thrown off the sickness of the 1950s, the same could not be said of Italy. Governments continued to be short-lived. As long as the PCI remained unacceptable as a government partner, all governments required the presence of the DC. On the other hand, the latter remained faction-ridden, and government formation and survival were frequently dependent upon the jockeying for influence of the various groups within the party. The centre–left option, realised in 1963, was rent with discord between Christian Democrat and Socialist. The smaller parties that were necessary to the option remained suspicious of the motives of their major partners. The net result was that governments continued to limp along, with reforming legislation coming only haltingly and partially.

In the 1970s Italy experienced both economic problems and the terrorism of the Red and Black Brigades, whose activities were directed towards undermining the state. At the same time, secularisation had caught up with the DC. The divorce issue of the early 1970s, which found the party without any political allies, demonstrated the limits of DC and Catholic power, and also the future dangers that might arise from being too closely identified with the Catholic Church. A more obvious challenge was the seemingly inexorable progress of the PCI towards becoming Italy's largest political formation. Anticipating the future and seeking to pacify fears, its leader, Enrico Berlinguer, announced the 'historic compromise', a declaration that the party was willing and able to share power with the DC. Many people believed in the inevitability of such an arrangement, and that the PCI would soon become the largest party. While the 1976 election marked another PCI advance, it was to be the high point for the party. In 1979 the PCI vote fell for the first time since the war, and the losses were not later regained. It was not that the DC had successfully mobilised additional resources; it too continued to have electoral problems. The major beneficiaries were the smaller parties, including some newcomers to the political scene.

The historic compromise might have worked, but even though the PCI persisted with it until 1979, it was never formally accepted by the DC. But in lieu, a different government strategy had to be found and that, as DC fortunes waned, had to be a reconsideration of the centre–left option. Indeed, the importance of the 1976 election had not been just another PCI advance; its outcome meant that for the first time neither a centrist nor a centre–right majority was available. Once the informal 'grand coalition' with the PCI collapsed, a weakened DC had no choice but to negotiate with the Socialists, and to face up to the ambitions of their leader, Benedetto Craxi, who desired the premiership. The centre–left was reconstructed in 1981, with the DC having to concede the premiership for the first time since 1945. In 1983, Craxi achieved his ambition and for the next few years led what proved to be one of Italy's most durable governments. Behind the façade, however, interparty disputes continued, and DC leaders came and went with increasing frequency. The system suddenly exploded in 1991. The ending of the Cold War had discredited the PCI and weakened the DC claim to be the only defender of the Italian faith, but the catalyst was the movement into the open of a financial scandal affecting the Socialists in Milan, Craxi's own power base. From then on, the accusations and allegations spiralled outwards to cover almost every form of corruption and crime, all parties and almost the whole of the Italian political elite. The whole party system disintegrated under the weight of the accusations, incriminations and public disgust. It was symbolic of the old patronage state that both Craxi and Giulio Andreotti, the most powerful DC grandee in the 1970s and 1980s, were indicted on a series of charges in 1993 and 1994. Out of the ashes a new and chaotic party system arose to contest the 1994 elections, with the various groups aligned in centre–left, centre–right and right alliances. Many were alarmed of the potential influence within this radically different political world of both a revivified right movement which had inherited the mantle of the neo-Fascist Social Movement, and the brash and aggressive Northern Leagues which at the extreme wished to pull the richer northern third of the country out of the Italian state.

DILEMMAS OF SOCIAL DEMOCRACY

There was, then, no general Conservative tide across Western Europe after 1970. Rather, the political mosaic, if anything, became more complex. Conservative parties tended to improve their position in northern Europe, but not usually to a hegemonic position; and in Britain and Germany, the respective predominance of the Conservatives and CDU was due as much to the divided nature of the opposition. Southern Europe, by contrast, saw more of a left-wing revival. Over and above party performance, however, the mood of Western Europe had become more conservative, more sceptical about proffered panaceas for economic problems, more dubious about the professed value of high public spending, and more willing to accept a more restricted horizon to government activity and the public sector. Thatcherism may not have been, as some claimed it to be, an ideology of a new right, and not something that received widespread acceptance, even in Britain: nevertheless, some of the ideas proclaimed under its banner – reduced taxation, privatisation, the acceptance of personal responsibility rather than the expectation that the state will provide – seemed to encapsulate and symbolise much of the new mood.

All of this had particular implications for Social Democrat parties over and above their immediate electoral fortunes. Social Democracy was particularly associated with the welfare state: the latter had largely been its creation, and it saw its own future as being closely bound up with its preservation and expansion. The new mood that took root in the 1980s obliged many left parties to reconsider once again the precepts of their existence and the debates about their future that had been a feature of the late 1950s and early 1960s. The effects of the ending of the Cold War after 1989 ensured that these thoughts would be kept at the front of the party mind.

Postwar Social Democracy had justified itself in terms of five basic tenets: a commitment to political liberalism; acceptance of the mixed economy with state intervention used to regulate, but not destroy, capitalism; a belief in Keynesian economics as the basic tool of government steering; the necessity of the welfare state; and a belief in equality. These central tenets encapsulated the first postwar decades. The postwar consensus had essentially been a Social Democratic consensus, as other parties and movements shifted ground to accommodate much of the Social Democrat package. That consensus had been helped by the phenomenon of sustained economic growth; within it, Social Democracy lost ground not so much because its philosophy had been rejected, but because other parties proved more adept at marketing a similar image of the 'good society'.

The more problematic economic fortunes of Western Europe and the eruption of protest that set in after the late 1960s were both a shock and a stimulant to Social Democracy. Not only had it seen, in many countries, its tenets hijacked by other parties; now it faced a set of serious radical challenges. These, along with the growing disillusionment with Keynesianism, led to Social Democracy losing much of its intellectual coherence during the 1970s. It seemed unable to offer new solutions to new problems, to present a forceful defence against a reinvigorated critique of some of its basic premises, a critique that was most effectively presented by the British Conservatives under Margaret Thatcher.

Locked into the belief that they remained both the reality of the present and the hope of the future, the parties found it difficult to reconcile themselves with the new economic situation. A major problem was that Keynesian policies seemed inevitably to lead to increased public expenditure and inflation. With their commitment to full employment and to preserving the existing industrial structure, it was difficult for them to urge wage restraint upon their trade union allies in the more adverse conditions of the 1970s. The favoured strategy had been to offer the unions a share of responsibility in return for restraint. Where successful, as in Scandinavia and Austria, the corporatist structure that evolved gave extra strength not just to economic interests, but also to the image of the Social Democrat parties as successful and effective managers. But in the 1980s that image began to crumble even in those Social Democrat administrations which had previously been successful, with more industrial disputes and economic arguments between the social partners.

Growth had been central to the Social Democrat approach. Once that disappeared, the whole approach was threatened. New arguments appeared, not just from the right, but also from the new radical and ecological left. One major thrust was that there were limits to growth, even perhaps that growth had reached its limits. Growth had been vital for the Social Democrat ambitions on health, education and social welfare. These had entailed an effective redistributive taxation system and a large administrative bureaucracy. After the 1970s, each became an Achilles' heel for the parties. Progressive taxation had originally been justified in terms of redistributing wealth from the rich. By the 1970s, however, the demands of public expenditure and higher wages were steadily pushing many workers into higher tax brackets. The new dilemma was aptly summed up by a Norwegian trade union leader who was heard plaintively to say that progressive taxation had not been meant to hurt 'our people'. The bureaucratic element of the Social Democrat state also came under attack for both its impersonal authoritarianism and its costs, at the extreme as a parasite on the generation of wealth. The new left argued for the democratisation and decentralisation of bureaucracy, the right for its reduction. Both had the same theme: to give more power and responsibility to the grassroots, to the people. Inevitably, the welfare state itself, the central edifice of Social Democracy, also came under critical scrutiny. A more confident right saw it as an obstacle to economic recovery, a prosperous market economy, and the inculcation of individual responsibility and initiative.

While there were great variations in the electoral fortunes of Social Democrat parties, all had to face up to the same dilemmas. Different strategies were employed or expressed as the way forward to revival and a planned future. In the 1970s, one reaction had been, as in Norway, that the economic recession would only be temporary, and to hope that the storm could be weathered without the necessity of changing course. While that strategy soon had to be abandoned, the beliefs underpinning it were so much a part of Social Democracy that emotionally many parties found it impossible to jettison them entirely. Alternatively, the parties could accept the necessity of harsh medicine. This seemed to be more often a consequence of occupying government, but was never popular with the party rank and file, and merely served to exacerbate internal party tensions. In Britain and West Germany it ultimately contributed to party disarray, electoral defeat and a lurch to the left. New environmental arguments, with their demands for restrictions on material growth and infrastructures, served further to undermine old certainties.

The decision by NATO in 1979 to strengthen the military alliance and to install intermediate-range nuclear weapons in Western Europe was a further factor that worsened Social Democrat problems and tensions. It resurrected and strengthened the long-held fears on the left flanks of the parties about militarism, and their anti-American sentiments. Arguments for disarmament, even without a reciprocal Soviet response, gained a firmer hold among many parties, especially in the Netherlands, West Germany, Denmark and Britain. On the other hand, like many of the more left-wing pleas for more state spending and activity, anything that smacked too strongly of pacifism or an anti-NATO position did not prove to be electorally popular and simply compounded the difficulties facing the parties.

With their old tenets no longer certainties, and disturbed by internal arguments, many Social Democrat parties in the 1980s tended to become even more introspective, and for those which had attempted to remain faithful to a radical agenda, electoral defeat forced them to reconsider their options. The future for any party would depend to some extent upon national circumstances. There would be a great difference in opportunity between national contexts where a strong and unified party faced a divided opposition, as in Sweden and Norway, and those where a weaker and possibly divided left faced a more cohesive right. But as they moved into the 1990s, all of them had been obliged, long before the ending of the Cold War indicated a victory for the market economy and liberal democracy, to take cognisance of changing popular conceptions and a more complex society which was more articulate and more middle-class, overall more prosperous yet more uncertain about the future, and more cynical about inflated political promises.

EUROCOMMUNISM

The problems of adjustment faced by Social Democracy perhaps paled in comparison to those faced by the Western European Communist parties. The conventional view of a monolithic bloc slavishly following a Soviet line had never been totally correct. Tito's defection in 1948 had illustrated that there were limits to Soviet control even during the Stalinist era. In Western Europe, the PCI (in Italy) developed an independent line, which it called polycentrism, in the 1950s. The 1956 denunciation of Stalin by Khrushchev provided a powerful impetus for a diversity of opinion within the Communist world, as did the subsequent Sino-Soviet dispute. If there was one event which shattered the efforts of Moscow to hold Western Europe in line with its own perception of a unicentric Communist world, it was the 1968 invasion of Czechoslovakia, which invoked criticism from almost all Western Communist parties. Even the French Communists, the most loyal ally in Western Europe, felt obliged to offer a muted and grudging rebuke. Formally, the need to forge a new relationship was finally made obvious at a conference of European Communist parties convened by the Soviet Union in East Berlin in 1976, which accepted that 'legitimate' criticism was part of life and which, strangely, did not conclude with the traditional symbolic communiqué expressing solidarity with Soviet domestic and foreign policy.

This loosening of Communist strings occurred at more or less the same time as Western economic growth faltered. For the devout Communist, it might have seemed that the long-awaited and predicted crisis of capitalism had finally arrived. While that remained the view of hardliners, the most important consequence of the new situation whereby each party could opt for a national path to Communism was the phenomenon known as Eurocommunism. While the term was used to describe a revolution in the stance of the parties, especially those in France, Italy and Spain in the 1970s, the practices to which it referred had earlier antecedents – like the PCI's polycentric stress on an Italian route to Communism within a pluralist society. And they reflected the unlikelihood of political revolution in Western Europe.

The pace was set, not surprisingly, by the PCI. It possessed by far the largest membership of any Western Communist party, and its appeal had never been restricted to the industrial working classes. It had enjoyed considerable success at the municipal level, where its direction of several local governments had been a model of efficiency and responsibility. It had for long quietly provided the support vital for much DC legislation to succeed, and by the 1970s seemed to be on the threshold of power. This was the background to the 1973 declaration of the historic compromise by Berlinguer. The party advocated strong measures against terrorism of all kinds, stressed the value of EC membership, and even indicated that in government it would honour Italy's NATO commitments. Yet by the end of the decade, it was as far away from power as ever. The DC and Socialists reforged a centre–left alliance, and in 1979 the PCI abandoned the historic compromise. As its support declined in the 1980s, it became more of an opposition party than it had been for some time.

By contrast, the French Communist Party had changed little from the 1940s: a Stalinist party sheltering behind self-imposed isolation, presenting itself as the defender of the working class, though able only to gain the support of a fraction of that class, and intolerant of any divergency of opinion within its own ranks. In 1972 it accepted an alliance with the reconstructed Socialist Party, but soon became uneasily aware that it was being surpassed in popular appeal by its theoretically junior partner. Fearing that it might well be the Socialists who would come to dominate the alliance, the party broke the agreement in 1977, to return to the traditional ghetto where it felt safe. While it did serve in a Socialist government 1981–84, the experience was an unhappy one. Its departure from government did not halt the downward spiral in its support. The French party's flirtation with Eurocommunism had, however, really ended long before its entry into government; participation in government simply confirmed the leadership's belief in the virtues of isolation, even if that meant abandoning any pretence at influencing government.

The Spanish involvement with Eurocommunism was more intense and, perhaps, even more of a failure. After years of oppression and exile under Franco, the Spanish Communists sought to establish their credentials as a responsible party. Ever wary of the power of the military, the party thought the way to power, to a strong electoral base, was to work for an alliance with any opponent of Francoism, even in a government of national concentration. Its leader, Santiago Carrillo, defined perhaps the essence of Eurocommunism when in 1977 he argued that while democracy was not necessarily the same as capitalism, equally, Socialism did not mean Soviet domination: each country and each party had to accept the uniqueness of the national experience and situation. The previous year, at the Berlin conference, Carrillo had lectured the Soviet Union, declaring: 'For years, Moscow was our Rome. We spoke of the Great October Socialist Revolution as if it were our Christmas. That was the period of our infancy; today we have grown up.' The Eurocommunist strategy failed. The Spanish party fared badly in the 1977 election and found it difficult thereafter to raise itself above minor status. The heritage of the left passed decisively to the Socialist Party, which won a majority in 1982.

Similar dramatic statements were not so obvious elsewhere. At the other extreme, the Portuguese Communists remained highly Leninist and revolutionary, but were equally unsuccessful. More typically, the Eurocommunist idea split the smaller Communist parties into warring factions. What Eurocommunism was is more difficult to say. There was an acceptance of pluralist society and the ballot-box, and a more critical attitude towards the Soviet Union. But there were considerable differences between Communist parties. There was, for instance, little in common between Carrillo's views and the more rigid stance of Georges Marchais, the French party leader. In the end, the only thing the three leading exponents of Eurocommunism had in common was the belief that they had an opportunity to share power if they wished to take it.

Eurocommunism was not a new idea. What it did do was to heighten the Communist dilemma. A crisis of capitalism had come and gone, without any real prospects for revolution: the liberal democratic states remained as strong as ever. In addition, it weakened the internal unity of the Communist parties. The attempt to present themselves as another kind of liberal democratic product misfired: electorates stayed with tried and tested brands. Long before Mikhail Gorbachev seemingly undermined their *raison d'être* after 1985, the parties were in trouble. Further efforts to move to a liberal democratic form would not bring any benefits, while to return to the safety of the ghetto seemed certain to bring in its wake a further decline in voters and members, a contraction of the ghetto walls.

The 1980s, therefore, brought few dividends. Electoral decline was evident almost everywhere, and brought disarray in many cases, especially in Finland. When Eurocommunism became fashionable, the Finnish party was already ensconced in government, a member of centre–left coalitions since 1966. But despite the close Finnish ties with the Soviet Union, this party too was exposed to internal dissension and electoral decline. After years of bitter bickering between a 'national' or Eurocommunist majority and a more Stalinist-oriented minority, the party finally split in 1986 into two implacably hostile factions. Even a stream of exhortations of unity by and delegations from Moscow failed to heal the growing breach. The Finnish experience, if not an epitaph, seemed to symbolise the fate of Communism in Western Europe in the 1980s: a group of parties which were more peripheral to the political mainstream than at any time since 1945. Notwithstanding this isolation, they had been sustained through the umbilical cord joining them with Moscow. But already weakened, their fate was finally sealed when Gorbachev effectively severed that link. If the Soviet Union was no longer, after 1988, prepared to prop up the Eastern European regimes militarily, there was little hope for the Communist remnants in the West. In the aftermath of the 1989 revolutions in Eastern Europe and the disintegration of the Soviet Union itself two years later, the parties were swept away into irrelevance, changing their name and image in a desperate attempt at meagre survival.

PARTY GOVERNMENT

Government in Western Europe after 1945 became, even more than in the past, party government. The political parties were the dominant instruments of political rule. The parties were central agencies involved in coordinating and aggregating the variety of interests and political demands, mediating and interpreting social values, and taking political decisions. Their centrality was steadily enhanced by the growth of government power and the extension of politics into ever more areas of life and social activity. Before the late 1960s, few doubts were raised about the ability and durability of responsible party government. The political and economic tumult of the following decade, in generating concern about the effectiveness of political management, problems of economic stability and change, and the future of the welfare state, led to a sharper focus being levelled against party performance.

The greater prevalence of direct action and the appearance of new parties, many concerned only with a narrow band of issues, led some people to believe that parties were losing their integrative ability. The falling levels of party membership also suggested a declining popular acceptance of their role and importance. Heightened electoral volatility and a greater emphasis upon corporatist structures that bypassed the basic electoral link between party and voter were pinpointed as both cause and effect of the decline of party. In retrospect, the worries on both fronts were probably exaggerated. There was greater electoral fluidity in the 1970s, making political and government outcomes less certain, but during the the next two decades this settled down somewhat, in most countries, in a realignment, rather than a dealignment, of electoral forces. In some instances, there was a recoalescence of political forces after the fragmentation of the 1970s, and rapid and substantial electoral shifts were not so much in evidence. Only in Italy did electoral behaviour contribute to a crisis of regime, as a wave of popular hostility over the long series of revelations after 1991 of public corruption swept away the whole of the party system. The corporatist element also did not seem to have undermined the credentials of regimes. The new economic climate demanded, on occasions, hard political decisions which often adversely affected established economic interests. Governments, irrespective of their political colouring, sooner or later demonstrated a greater willingness and ability to take such decisions.

Two popular themes, related yet somewhat contradictory, that surfaced in the 1970s about the future of government were ungovernability and overload. Both arose from interpretations of the more complex and demanding nature of modern society. Ungovernability referred not to a revolutionary attack upon the legitimacy of the political system, but to a possible decline of government effectiveness and a possible withdrawal of consent by the governed. The question of effectiveness was also central to the idea of overload, that governments were increasingly unable to cope with the demands made of them and that the welfare state had embarked upon a road of steadily escalating and open-ended commitments.

Neither developed as a serious danger that threatened to undermine the vitality of the political systems. Parties, of course, could be ineffective in government, but in that case would risk the penalty of defeat in the next election. What had occurred among much of the electorate and of the political elite by the 1990s was the development of both a more realistic attitude about what it was possible for governments to do and a more limited view of what governments should do. On the other hand, this was paralleled by a greater popular scepticism, even perhaps cynicism, about claims by politicians. The electorate might be behaving as consumers in a battle between political supermarkets, but they were perhaps not prepared, without further to-do, to buy all the promotional claims. In part, this might have reflected a growing divorce between the public and political leaderships, in that party politics, especially among those who reached the top, had become a professional occupation like any other. This divorce might be one reason why there seemed to appear a certain complacency, even arrogance, among politicians about their accountability. If there was a dominant feature of the 1990s which had not been present before, it was the public airing of political and party corruption. The scandals which brought down the Italian system after 1991 were paralleled by similar revelations of political and financial corruption among governments and parties in Belgium, France and Spain (earlier scandals having afflicted Austria and West Germany). Along with everything else that had occurred over the previous two decades, it suggested perhaps that Western Europe had not yet found its way towards a new definition of the desirable balance between state and society, between welfare provision and individual responsibility, between bureaucratic paternalism and personal freedom of choice. While the final outcome of this might be uncertain, it seemed clear that it would be contained within a commitment to liberal democracy.

CHAPTER 20

THE ENLARGED COMMUNITY

What is lacking more than anything in European affairs . . . is authority. Discussion is organised: decision is not. By themselves the existing Community institutions are not strong enough. *(Jean Monnet, 1974)*

With the exception of de Gaulle's dramatic press conference vetoing British entry, the meeting of the heads of government of the EC at The Hague in 1969 was the most significant event within the Communities since the Treaty of Rome. It opened the way to enlargement of the club, set down pointers for the need to develop common policies, emphasising particularly the need for deeper integration in foreign and monetary policy, and reaffirmed a faith in ultimate political unity. The fact that the green light was given by the collectivity of the heads of government symbolised where power in the EC had essentially come to lie and indicated how institutionalisation within the organisation would develop in the years to come. However, much of its effort was to come to naught. The 1970s were a period when the EC almost seemed to be marking time, and it would not be until the mid-1980s that the theme of Rome would be taken up again with renewed vigour by those within the EC who had the capacity and authority to direct the organisation and determine its future.

A LOSS OF MOMENTUM

By the mid-1980s the EC had grown from six to twelve members. Britain, Denmark and Ireland joined in 1973, Greece in 1981, and Portugal and Spain in 1986. In each instance, the process of enlargement was awkward and protracted: twelve years before the first expansion was completed, six years in the case of Greece, and eight years for Portugal and Spain. Admittedly, some of the delay could not be directly laid at the EC's doorstep. Nevertheless, the time taken did, to a certain extent, reflect the difficulties and worries expressed about the effect of enlargement upon a going concern; and in many ways the worries were subsequently confirmed. The entry of new members proved to be the beginning of a testing time. The new members were, perhaps inevitably, less European-oriented and less familiar with the at times Byzantine mode of operations of the EC. Some, at least, were in that sense less attuned to the need to accept a certain loss of national independence, which in some situations they would regard as a diminution of national prestige and governmental authority.

The tone was set by Britain which, from the decision of Harold Wilson's 1974 Labour government to seek renegotiation of the terms of entry and have them endorsed by a referendum through to Mrs Thatcher's battles over the budget, seemed to dominate EC headlines. Yet the British position was perhaps a symptom of a more general problem. It acquired notoriety mainly perhaps because of the size of Britain, a country that was, as it were, too important to ignore. In a more quiet, yet equally persistent way, Denmark also attempted to assert a distinctive position for itself; if what it wished to establish had been successful and adopted as a general principle, the character of the EC would have been changed radically. After 1981, Greece followed the British precedent. Immediately after entry, Andreas Papandreou submitted a demand that the terms of accession be renegotiated. What he was, in effect, presenting to the EC was a shopping list of further concessions and financial aid to Greece.

Despite the travails, the new members, or at least their governments (even, perhaps, the 1974 British Labour government), did not seem seriously to entertain the possibility of leaving the EC. There has been only one departure. Greenland, a Danish colony since 1721, had been incorporated into Denmark in 1953. In 1979 it was granted internal autonomy and in 1982 voted in a referendum in favour of withdrawal from the EC, a decision which was finally implemented in 1985. The longer the new members stayed in, the more difficult it would be to consider withdrawal as an option. Hence, while the EC would remain relatively unpopular in countries such as Denmark and Britain, being conveniently placed to be blamed as the scapegoat for all the national ills, especially as the first years of membership coincided with economic downturn, and while political parties in opposition could seek to utilise that disillusionment for their own advantage, the possibility that governments would terminate membership steadily became a more remote option.

It was inevitable that the new members would have different policy concerns, and look for EC action in different economic areas. So, for example, fishery policy acquired a higher and more contentious profile after the first enlargement. In the 1980s, the access of new Mediterranean members meant that products such as olive oil and citrus fruits would become a greater bone of contention, as well as raising more strongly the issue of the regional redistribution of EC resources from the richer north to the poorer south. The Integrated Mediterranean Programmes adopted in 1985 were designed to help the south, over a seven-year period, to fit better into the overall economic design of the EC.

Such issues had to jostle for attention on an already crowded agenda. The enlargement of the 1970s had given the EC a population equivalent to that of the United States or the Soviet Union. Its world trading importance had come to parallel that of America, which increasingly regarded the EC as an economic rival that sought to eliminate competition in its domestic markets by protectionist policies. The EC found that it had to pay considerable attention to its external trading relationships. Internally, there was increased tension between the EC and its member states. On the one hand, national interests were strongly expressed in those bodies populated by government representatives. On the other, the Commission and its bureaucracy, supported by the European Parliament, sought to keep in focus the longer-term commitment to political integration, and endeavoured to achieve harmonisation and standardisation across a range of economic and social policy areas. In this interaction, no state was entirely satisfied, yet all received something of value from the EC, no matter how little. West Germany and Britain were the largest net contributors to the EC budget; both received something tangible in return, West Germany, for example, through the CAP and in trade benefits, and Britain through regional development grants. Yet the question still had to be raised as to whether this crowded agenda was moving the EC directly and swiftly towards the goals of the Treaty of Rome.

Given the fact that enlargement made decision-making more difficult, if only because it simply involved more people sitting round the table, and so made invocations of the Luxembourg Compromise more probable, the degree of coordination and agreement that was achieved after 1972 was quite creditable. But the EC faced problems similar to those experienced by national governments: the demands made upon its resources were almost infinite. Only if the budget was increased, could more flexibility be introduced. The size of the EC budget and, for some states, of the national contributions to it were recurring themes in the 1970s and 1980s. To increase or change the budget meant that the member states would have to grapple with the problem of monetary policy and standardisation, and with the burden of the CAP – where schedules and provisions had been set by the 1969 Hague summit. This interrelated trio of issues never left the political agenda.

A monetary policy had been a long-standing EC aim, and the Werner Report of 1970, commissioned by the Hague summit, pinpointed 1980 as the completion date for full Economic and Monetary Union (EMU) after a three-stage process, the first stage to be in place by 1973. The Report recommended that this should involve the simultaneous harmonisation and coordination of both economic and monetary policy. The ink was barely dry on the Werner Report before its schedule was derailed by the rapid move towards floating currencies. Following upon the 1971 Smithsonian Agreement, and in an effort to keep the EMU timetable on course, the EC attempted to construct a European agreement whereby the margin of permissible fluctuations in the exchange rates of European currencies would be less than those outlined in the broader system. The European structure was described as the snake that would operate within the Smithsonian tunnel, since on a graph it would be seen to 'wriggle' within the broader band. The snake was never successful: Britain participated for only two months, while Italy left soon after when, at the same time, the snake actually floated outside the tunnel. French behaviour was more erratic: France abandoned the snake in 1974; it rejoined the following year, only to leave again in 1976. What was left was a small group of currencies, not all belonging to EC members, clustered around the West German mark. The dream of EMU by 1980 was in tatters.

It was President Giscard d'Estaing of France who, with the backing of Helmut Schmidt, attempted to resurrect the aim of monetary union. Under the urging of a renewed Franco-German axis, the EC states negotiated their way towards the European Monetary System (EMS) agreement of 1978, with implementation to begin the following year. The agreement was for the establishment of a European Currency Unit (ECU) that would stand alongside the national currencies, and of an Exchange Rate Mechanism (ERM). The EMS had several objectives: to make exchange rate adjustments a matter of common concern so as to reach both exchange rate stability and the level of monetary stability necessary for an expansion of world trade; to present a common monetary and exchange policy towards the rest of the world, with a European currency gradually emerging to match the American dollar as a world currency; and to pave the way for full-scale monetary union.

Of these objectives, the final one scarcely left the drawing board – it was to be a decade or more before it would be seriously addressed – while few efforts were made to secure the second, although the ECU made some headway in financial markets. In practice, the EMS was restricted to the first objective, where it had some effect in reducing exchange rate volatility from the levels of the 1970s. The ERM was designed to limit currency fluctuations through EC and domestic intervention when any one currency drifted too far. But that by itself would not be enough to staunch the large capital flows that can occur, as currency speculation by international financial markets in 1992 and 1993 were to demonstrate. That kind of prevention would require policy cooperation, which the EMS was unable to provide.

The member states varied in their attitude towards the scheme and in the extent of their commitment to it. For example, Belgium, Ireland and Italy all wished to retain the right to impose some restrictions on the free movement of private funds within the system, while West Germany debarred its citizens and financial institutions from accepting deposits or liabilities in the new currency unit. Italy retained an exchange rate margin more than twice as wide as those of its fellow members. Most importantly, the EMS lacked a EC-wide scope. While allowing sterling to be part of the basket of currencies that would form the new currency unit, Britain declined to join the ERM, a decision based upon a view of sterling's role as both a petro-currency and international investment currency. Though the justification became less valid in the late 1980s, Britain remained only a partial member of the EMS until 1990, when it entered – albeit for only two years – the ERM. Of the later entrants, Greece followed the British example by not accepting the ERM, while Portugal and Spain preferred to remain completely outside the EMS until 1992 and 1989 respectively. Two decades or so after the original declaration of intent, therefore, the EC had made only limited progress towards the goal of monetary union. The EMS could only be a first step, and almost all the hurdles still had to be overcome.

If Europe lacked a monetary policy, the same could not be said of agriculture:

indeed, some cynics could argue that the Common Agricultural Policy, consuming some two-thirds of the budget, *was* the EC. Set in motion in 1968, with the Hague summit finalising its financial provisions, the CAP was clearly a fully developed EC policy, in that the vast bulk of agricultural produce was subject to the CAP regime. While it was the subject of much satisfaction for many supporters of integration, because it illustrated that a European policy could be constructed, it has also been, ever since its first days, at or near the heart of almost every internal EC dispute. By the 1980s, it could be said to have become a social rather than an economic policy, in that the 'welfare' (and electoral) considerations far outweighed any concern for an efficient agricultural sector. The high levels of industrial unemployment in the 1980s made it appear perhaps even more grotesque. It became a classic study, not only of how difficult it is, at the international level, to set priorities and allocate resources, but also of how, once decisions have been made and structures established, inertia can set in to make any reform extremely difficult.

The CAP has been dominated by national interests, each state being fundamentally concerned about what it receives for itself. When all came to agree in the 1980s on the necessity of reform, none wished that reform to affect adversely whatever benefits it was already receiving. As a result, the overall imbalances in the system had been permitted to continue, with a consequent escalation of both the costs of the programme and the massive surplus produce it generated. For the original Six, the CAP had become an almost holy object: it had been one of their first objectives, and indeed for some thirty years remained almost the only EC common policy. In addition, all received some benefits from it, and all tended to view it more in terms of social justice and politics than as an economic question.

The most vociferous, indeed almost the only, opponent of the EC was Britain, and it was the CAP which lay at the heart of the prolonged British complaints after the mid-1970s about the budget. Along with West Germany, Britain found itself upon entry as one of only two net contributors to the EC budget. The reasons were threefold: Britain was a major world trader and so contributed substantial revenues to the EC from its customs duties; it preferred still to import, for historical reasons, a substantial amount of its food requirements from outside the EC, especially from the Commonwealth; and its small but highly efficient agriculture gained little in the way of EC compensation payments. The CAP provided farmers with guaranteed prices for their products, but the price mechanism was unselective and, to all intents and purposes, automatic. Because it divorced planning and production costs from possible market outcomes, it did not encourage farmers to be economic, nor did its resources all go to the benefit of farmers. The farming population of the EC fell from fourteen to ten million between the mid-1970s and the mid-1980s, yet during the same period real farm incomes also declined. The difference was largely the huge administrative cost of providing cold storage for the surplus produce that arose from the overproduction which the policy itself encouraged. Quite simply, the CAP consumed the bulk of the revenue available to the EC. The latter's budget was not large: 0.5 per cent of EC gross domestic product in 1974, it was only 0.9 per cent by 1985. But the CAP share of the budget steadily increased. If the amount spent on agriculture is taken out of the budget, then what was left to be made available for other programmes, such as the Regional Development Fund, was equivalent to only about 1 per cent of the total spending of national governments. With no end in sight of the ratchet effect on costs, it was the CAP which plunged the EC into a series of budget crises, all threatening bankruptcy, after the late 1970s.

In 1970 it had been agreed that the EC should be financed by its 'own resources'. During an interim period through to 1975, these resources would come from all levies on food imports into the EC, and from an increasing proportion of the tariffs on manufactured goods entering the EC. In 1975 this levy system would be complete, and it would be supplemented by a sum of up to the value of 1 per cent of the value added tax (VAT) in the member states. What the EC needed was a reliable and regular source of income: whatever the level imposed, it was felt that import levies would be too unpredictable. Hence the VAT revenue was to be an essential part of the budget, and the most important element: after 1980 it constituted the bulk of the EC's income.

The implication of 'own resources' was that the EC had to live off its own. It could not amass deficits, or borrow to meet shortfalls. As the CAP inexorably consumed more of the budget, the EC moved to the brink of insolvency towards the end of the 1970s, where it hovered until about 1984. The only way out of the dilemma was to give the EC a guaranteed increase in income: that could come only from an increase in the proportion of VAT revenue contributed by the member states. Britain was strongly opposed to such a move, and indicated that it was prepared to exercise its right of veto unless its own complaints about the size of its contribution to the budget were remedied; and it suggested that the EC ought to put its own house in order and embark upon a radical restructuring of the CAP. Insolvency never actually materialised, and in 1984, when Margaret Thatcher conceded an increase in EC revenues in return for a reduction in Britain's budget contribution, it seemed to have been pushed into the future. However, by 1987 the threat of insolvency had returned; the cause was again the voracious nature of the CAP. And again, the member states, especially the key actors of West Germany and France, were reluctant to grasp the nettle. In the 1988 debates on a budget increase, Britain, for the first time, found a partner, in the shape of the Netherlands, for its argument that budget reviews must embrace a radical review and reining back of the CAP. Insolvency was once again averted by a compromise, and one that did seem to place a limit on CAP expenditure. The problem, however, was that of the structure and logic of the CAP: until those could be tackled, the sheer size of the agricultural component of EC spending would inevitably generate the likelihood of budget crises. The fact that after the mid-1980s the CAP did not occupy as much of the EC limelight as previously was not due to a reconciliation between it and its critics. It did remain unreconstructed, but after 1985 it was the broader issues of economic, monetary and political union which took centre stage.

THE TRIUMPH OF SUMMITRY

For the ardent federalist, the Treaty of Rome had provided the foundations of a European political system. The Commission would be the nucleus of a European government which would be answerable to a European Parliament. According to this scenario, the Council of Ministers would perhaps merely be a body that was necessary during the transitional phase that had to exist before the desired goal was achieved. While the EP was not given any opportunity to develop as a true legislature, the Commission did begin to act very much as an executive. Its first president, Walter Hallstein, could say in 1965 that he could be regarded as a kind of European prime minister.

That structure, or rather the hopes for it, ended with the crisis of the mid-1960s. De Gaulle's actions effectively demoted the Commission as the motor force of progress without necessarily making provision for something to replace it. The process of enlargement after 1969 confirmed that the Commission would be a partner, and perhaps more a junior partner, of national governments. While, along with the EP, the Commission might continue to see itself as the motor of the EC – a point made to the prime minister of Belgium, Leo Tindemans, in 1975 when he was compiling his report on the state and future of the Communities – its ability to initiate cooperation and impose direction had been considerably weakened; in the late 1970s it had to struggle to ensure that its president would have a right to attend or participate in the several intergovernmental forums that had sprung up. The Commission's own ability to act as a collegiate body had also been weakened by enlargement, as it too had to grow in size to incorporate appointees from the new member states. It was further weakened in its dealings with the member states because many of the major economic and monetary issues that came to dominate the agenda fell ouside those areas where, under the Treaty of Rome, it held a brief of exclusive powers.

The EP had never been satisfied with its secondary role. It had always hoped that its disadvantaged position within the EC structure would be rectified. It believed that this might be achieved if it could secure a more democratic base through the direct election of its membership. Even though provision for direct elections had been included in the Treaty of Rome, their introduction was effectively blocked by the national governments until 1974. While some resistance to the idea still persisted, among both governments and national parliaments a distinction was made between electoral base and political power: a popularly elected parliament should not necessarily acquire any expansion of powers, a point made strongly in 1979, for example, by the parliaments in France and Denmark. Hence, while at one level the first direct elections of 1979 were a milestone in the history of the EC, on another they scarcely affected the way in which the organisation worked in practice. It did, in 1982, successfully defer the discharge of the budget as an expression of dissatisfaction over the way in which, in the implementation of the 1980 budget, the Commission had deviated from its amendments and suggestions. But that, perhaps, was indicative of the extent of what the EP could do. It remained very much the poor relation of the EC, far from being a true legislature. It would have to wait until the 1991 Treaty on European Union to receive any significant increase in authority, but still one that fell far short of its own desires.

The degree of national commitment to the EP was low: Denmark's contingent even included members of an anti-EC alliance dedicated towards securing Danish withdrawal from the EC. Attendance at the first two Parliaments was disappointing, not helping the EP's cause: for example, only some 70 per cent of the Euro-MPs attended the debates in 1984 on the EP's most ambitious project, a Draft Treaty on European Union, which it hoped to persuade other EC institutions to accept. Moreover, while the Euro-MPs organised themselves into trans-national party groups, it was a decade or so before it could be said that these had developed something of a sense of common purpose. The peripherality of the EP seemed to be reinforced by the second round of direct elections in 1984. The level of popular interest was lower than in 1979, perhaps partly because the novelty had worn off. The election was not fought on European or EC issues. The parties contested it as national parties, debated national issues, and treated it as an evaluation of the effectiveness and popularity of national governments. It was, in short, a series of national contests: in fact, Luxembourg even arranged to hold its own general election on the same day. These were problems which the EP also failed to overcome in the elections of 1989 and 1994.

Rather than enhancing the role of the Commission and EP, enlargement reinforced the intergovernmental character of the EC. The regular meetings of foreign ministers became more important, and the Council of Ministers acquired an even greater complexity, with a multitude of committees, the membership of which depended upon the issues and national ministries involved. While COREPER could attempt to bring some order to the complexity, it could only organise the agenda: it could not give direction, nor could it prevent the emergence, on occasions, of a European version of interdepartmental bureaucratic rivalry: under its various 'issue guises', the Council could easily pull in several different directions at once. Since the demotion of the Commission, if any order was to be imposed, it could only come from the heads of government.

In 1974 Jean Monnet could comment that 'discussion is organised, decision is not'. The Hague summit of 1969 had been followed by a series of *ad hoc* summit meetings, but only if all heads of government agreed that one should be held. The lack of central direction and coordination demanded that if heads of government were not prepared to delegate decision-making authority to the supranational Commission, they should do so themselves on a regularised basis. The European Council, set up in 1974, with Giscard d'Estaing as the major instigator, was to provide the missing authority. The Council would be composed of the heads of the national governments, and it was agreed that it would meet three times a year (amended in 1986 to twice annually), and that its presidency would rotate across the national capitals every six months. This emphasised that all member states were equal, giving the smaller ones the opportunity to become centres of European, and even world, diplomacy once every few years.

After 1974 the Council became the only body that could set new targets and lay down guidelines for future progress. The EC had entered an era of summitry: its emergence confirmed that the EC had become an intergovernmental organisation. For almost two decades, the Council made no collective pretence at supranationalism: what came out of it, usually after long and intense arguments derived from national interests, was compromise among those interests. The new picture was well summarised in 1981 by Margaret Thatcher, when she said, 'there is no such thing as a separate Community interest; the Community interest is compounded of the national interests of the Ten member states'. The Council, most importantly, was set up by the national leaders themselves, and so was not bound by the EC treaties, nor could it be formally subjected to the influence of either the Commission or the EP. Hence, there seemed to be little concern for adjusting all members to some EC norm; the focus instead seemed to be on adjusting the several national interests closer to each other in order to achieve some minimum overlap.

On the other hand, with the emergence of the European Council the EC acquired a central and potentially powerful body that could set new targets and map the guidelines for future progress. Yet that could come about only if there was a collective political will. In the 1970s that political will seemed to be largely absent. There was, first, inevitable slow progress because of the desire for unanimity in the Council and, secondly, no clear medium for following up the decisions reached by it. In a sense, this seemed to suit its members who in a way appeared to be caught in the cleft stick of needing to demonstrate their own ability to defend national interests and a commitment to further European progress. In many countries, governments could not readily abandon the national interest, if only because their own future depended upon re-election. Certainly, entrenched national interests seemed to intrude whenever the government leaders turned to discuss the fine detail of further progress: hence, their commitment to European union more often seemed to be restricted to general declarations of a belief in European union that both politically and economically were without cost. The dichotomy between rhetorical principle and the problem of practical measures and their implementation (something which in this changed EC could be handled only by the Council, and not the Commission) made the Council a constantly shifting body, giving the EC a certain incoherence as well as flexibility: it typified the tendency whereby the important changes and decisions occurred outside the formal structure of the treaties, almost in an *ad hoc* manner.

Though the rotating Council presidency permitted all states to have an important influence, inevitably the leaders of the larger states carried more weight. In the enlarged EC the motor force became more firmly focused on collaboration between France and the Federal Republic, with Britain acting as the major brake. The roots of Franco-German cooperation lay in the 1963 Treaty of Friendship signed by de Gaulle and Adenauer. The two states developed a network of formal consultations and meetings at all levels, including biannual conversations of the heads of the two governments. The two were not always in harmony: they differed sharply, for example, during the aftermath of the 1973 oil crisis. But on EC matters, if the two states were in accord, then generally the EC advanced further. Beginning with the Hague summit of 1969, many of the important steps taken by the EC – enlargement, renegotiation of Britain's terms of entry, the EMS – were due to joint agreement and initiatives from France and West Germany.

Although this high level of collaboration persisted through to the early 1990s in the raher more formal relationship forged after 1982 between François Mitterrand and Helmut Kohl, the apogee of Franco-German leadership was reached in the late 1970s in the close relationship that developed between Giscard d'Estaing and Schmidt. Neither had a particularly strong emotional commitment to the EC, but both regarded collaboration on Europe as the best means of also maximising returns from membership for their countries. Their collaboration was based on a close personal friendship and a similar background in economic and monetary matters, an experience not shared by most of their colleagues on the Council. In addition, each headed his government for a relatively long period (Schmidt, 1974–82, Giscard d'Estaing, 1974–81) at a time when, in almost all the other member states, the premiership changed hands more frequently.

While the two leaders did attempt to keep their partners informed of their ideas and plans, they did not always succeed in dispelling suspicions about an exclusive two-man club. Criticisms of their behaviour mounted towards the end of the decade. It was perhaps Margaret Thatcher who most directly challenged the Schmidt–Giscard leadership in her arguments over the budget. While she perhaps underestimated the value which both France and West Germany attached to their relationship, it is also correct that at times Giscard d'Estaing and Schmidt gave the impression that they regarded the Council as their private preserve. The arrival of Mrs Thatcher marked a more persistent British voice in the Council and the EC after the relative lack of interest of the previous Labour government, a voice that would often stand alone in the debates and discussions. While the influence of Schmidt and Giscard d'Estaing arose from a specific combination of political and personal circumstances, the Franco-German understanding remained central to the development of the EC, and integral to the renewed drive for integration and union that began in the mid-1980s. The two states had developed a community of interest, the preservation of which both regarded as important for the future course of the EC and for the overall stability of Western Europe.

BRITAIN: A EUROPEAN MAVERICK?

Though Britain had not joined in the movement towards European integration in the 1950s, the European debate, to a considerable extent, had revolved around the British position. Once Harold Macmillan had reversed British policy in 1961, it again returned as a central theme. The view that had coalesced in the later 1950s and one reiterated later by de Gaulle, that Britain was a European maverick, seemed to be confirmed after the EC's enlargement in 1973. For the next two decades, Britain was to be the problem child of the EC.

The terms of entry had been negotiated by the strongly European Edward Heath in the face of a growing popular rejection of the EC. And the Labour Party had also rejected the terms, if not the principle, of entry, promising that a future Labour government would not only demand renegotiation of the terms, but would also – a revolutionary step for British politics – if the renegotiation proved successful, test the public mood through a referendum. These two issues were taken up by Harold Wilson after he returned as premier in 1974. Though irritated by the demand for renegotiation, Britain's partners conceded the point. In 1975, they accepted that the British financial contributions would be linked to the relative value of gross national product in the EC, with a clawback if the contributions exceeded a certain level. The subsequent referendum, with all party leaderships urging acceptance, provided a satisfactory majority in favour of continued membership.

That, however, was not the end of the matter. In a changed world economic climate, the EC was blamed by large sections of the British population for at least some of the country's economic ills (as it also was in Denmark). It is true that the picture had changed from the assumptions before entry that Britain would benefit from the projected Regional Development Fund. That optimism had been dashed in part by the 1973 economic crisis. That had placed pressure on the West German budget, making West Germany, the major paymaster of the EC, reluctant to go along with an ambitious regional development progrmme. Simultaneously, ideological opposition on the left of the Labour Party hardened, placing the party leadership in a very difficult position. Popular disenchantment with the EC, however, did give British governments sustenance in their arguments with their European partners over financial issues, arguments which persisted until at least 1984. The essence of the British dispute with the EC was the perception by Britain that it bore an unfair share of the EC budget, and that since it did not benefit greatly from the CAP, the return it received was inadequate.

The roots of the dispute lay in the 1970 EC decision that it ought to have its own financial resources. Since the CAP was by far and away the most expensive EC item, the 'own resources' were essentially a way of funding the programme. The two British complaints were therefore interrelated. Although transitional arrangements had been accepted for the three new entrants, to last until 1980, Britain regarded its contribution to the budget, settled by the automatic system, to be too great compared to what it received under the CAP compensatory system, especially as it was being imposed upon what was one of the poorer members of the EC.

Only part of the British argument was correct. In terms of its gross national product, and compared to the overall pattern of payment by the member states, the British contribution was not excessively out of line. Because, however, it was a major world trader and an important food importer with an efficient agriculture, Britain was a major contributor to EC earnings through customs duties, but received little intervention money from the CAP. It was the gap between payment and receipt that produced a conviction in Britain that it was the largest net contributor to the EC budget.

The question of adjusting the budget mechanism was first raised by the Labour government during the renegotiation of the accession treaty. It rumbled on acrimoniously throughout the 1970s, surfacing again during the discussions on the EMS. After the election of the Conservatives in 1979, it became perhaps *the* European issue. Labour's strategy had been to argue for a reduction in the scale of the British contribution. This may not have been so astute a strategy given that the contribution was not grossly disproportionate to that of other members; but it did, perhaps, fit in with Labour's more minimal interest for participation in the EC. Under the Conservative government, the British focus shifted to the returns that the country received from the EC. After 1979, European Council meetings were dominated by confrontation on the British demand for a more just return, or what Margaret Thatcher, to the great annoyance of the rest, referred to as 'our money'.

When the issue was raised in 1980, the European Council eventually agreed upon a rebate formula that was to last until 1983. The Conservative government returned to the attack in 1982, shortly before the 1980 formula was due to expire. In 1981 the Commission had attempted to cut the knot, suggesting that net beneficiary countries should return some of their receipts for redistribution to Britain. West Germany and France, however, were insistent that rebates, if any, should come from the EC budget and not be paid directly by the other members: it might be regarded as a first British penetration of its opponents' armour. In 1982, the principle of a British rebate was accepted: it would be linked to the difference between the British share of the EC's gross national product and the proportionate value of its share of the budget. This was not enough for Britain: the acrimony became more bitter and the voices more strident. Yet despite all the pressure and her isolation within the Council, Margaret Thatcher remained unmoved. She continued to insist upon a rebate, linking it to what she regarded as a necessary reform of the CAP, a proposal strongly resented by many members. At that time, Denmark, France and Ireland in particular rejected any idea of placing a ceiling on agricultural expenditure.

The crisis boiled over in May 1982, when Britain exercised a veto on proposed higher target prices for food. In exasperation, the other nine set aside the Luxembourg Compromise of 1966, refusing to accept the veto, and voting for an increase in food prices. Despite the angry words, the shock of what had happened forced the two sides to withdraw somewhat from the brink. The British reaction was quite muted, possibly in part because of the need for EC support for its Falklands policy. For the other side, their action could be regarded as a dangerous precedent for the future, considering that each state had special national interests which, under certain circumstances, it would wish to defend. A one-year settlement, less than what Britain wanted, was proposed and accepted. Finally, at the Fontainebleau summit in 1984, a long-term annual corrective mechanism for a budget rebate for Britain was accepted and immediately implemented.

In terms of the effort which Britain devoted to its budget grievances, it is questionable whether the cost was worth it. Britain had known before entry that a deficit of this order was probable; in terms of total British expenditure, the amount of money involved was not very great; and British farmers did receive some benefits from the CAP. On the other hand, Britain had expected much greater returns through regional policy and grants. Britain certainly conceded a great deal of goodwill by its aggressive diplomacy, especially under Mrs Thatcher. It failed to appreciate, or chose to ignore, the great significance which the original Six, especially France, attached to the CAP. The policy was regarded by France as the major economic benefit it derived from Europe. West Germany was the other important member that Britain had to win over. West Germany was willing to concede some adjustments to keep Britain in the EC, since its major economic benefit from membership was an industrial common market, of which the large British market was an important element. On the other hand, however, the Franco-German relationship was central to West German perceptions, and no government in Bonn was willing to sacrifice that.

Among the other members, there was perhaps a lack of appreciation of the British mood: the British public was cynical about, even fearful of, the EC; the British economy was much weaker than that of most of its partners. To stand up to the EC may have been for Margaret Thatcher a further tactic for the regeneration of British pride. At a more individual level, she was also perhaps irked by the dismissive and patronising treatment of her by Schmidt and Giscard d'Estaing after her election to the premiership.

While on one level the British issue may have been rather trivial, on another it was very important. The CAP was, if one is allowed deliberately to mix metaphors, both white elephant and sacred cow. Despite its cost and inefficiency, it was one of the few concrete symbols of what the EC had achieved. As such, the commitment to it among the original members was very high, as was the need of funding it, even though it threatened EC solvency throughout the 1980s. A common critique of Britain was that its argument was merely utilitarian and concerned only with national interest. That was a reasonable point; certainly, the terms on which entry had been sold to the British electorate were highly utilitarian. Though it may have been the weakness of British industry which prevented it from taking a fuller advantage of membership, British governments would still have to be seen to be securing something from the EC. On the other hand, Mrs Thatcher was right about the imbalance in the budget, and without her the CAP might not have had a stricter regime imposed upon it in the 1980s.

In pursuing such a policy, Britain was, in fact, not behaving very differently from other member states. Utilitarianism had always been a prominent characteristic of the EC. It was an integral part of the behaviour of Denmark and, later, of Greece. It had always been a necessary part of French policy, and of French conflicts with other members, such as the 'wine war' with Italy in the mid-1970s. Under Schmidt, West German policy had also moved in the same direction. Britain's reputation as a maverick may have been due first to the not altogether concealed suspicion, even hostility, which the Labour governments of Wilson and Callaghan displayed towards Europe. Later, it may have been because of the personality of Margaret Thatcher and the issue on which she chose to fight. But essentially, Britain was too important to be ignored or to be simply dismissed as a 'new boy'. That each member state has been tempted towards utilitarian attitudes is corroborated by evidence from areas where the EC as an entity has had some control. Every member state has been subjected to investigation by the Commission and the Court of Justice for infringement of EC regulations. All have been found wanting on numerous occasions, yet Britain has been far from the worst offender: that 'honour' has gone to Italy. At any rate, with the Fontainebleau settlement of 1984, the EC could hope that the British issue had been finally resolved. With the concurrence of Mrs Thatcher in 1985 on the agreement to aim for a single internal market by the end of 1992, a European Council decision that relaunched at last a drive towards closer integration, and the later British entry into the ERM, it seemed that Britain's isolation was at an end. However, as the EC after the late 1980s took up a renewed drive towards both monetary and political union, Britain again moved apart from its partners. The arguments of the 1990s between Britain and the rest over the future direction and structure of the EC illustrated, perhaps, that the budget disputes of earlier years had, on a deeper level than that of the merely utilitarian, been symptomatic of a more profound division, one which essentially revolved around the value and trust which one placed in the historic notion of the nation-state.

THE SLOW RETURN TO UNION

The essential objective of the Treaty of Rome had been spelled out in its preamble: to achieve 'an ever closer union among the European peoples'. Some considerable economic progress had been made by the original Six during the first decade, though the planned common market did not come about on schedule. Political progress had been even more painful, with de Gaulle and the issue of enlargement as stumbling blocks. It was the 1969 Hague summit which prepared the ground for further advances: agreement was reached on enlargement; a structure was accepted for the CAP; and consideration was given to the question of economic and monetary union (EMU). Behind all these issues, there lurked the shadow of political integration, the ultimate objective of the Rome treaty.

The momentum unleashed at The Hague carried through to the Paris summit meeting of 1972. On the political front, it led to the Davignon Report (named after Viscount Etiènne Davignon of Belgium). It proposed that the EC should look first at policy areas where the states already possessed an identifiable commonality of interest, and recommended that the first steps should be in foreign policy. The report was immediately accepted and implemented. It led to European Political Cooperation (EPC), essentially a concept of inter-governmental cooperation rather than a structure or formal institution. The system was held by a second Davignon Report in 1973 to have been successful.

EPC focused primarily upon three kinds of broad initiative: the adoption of common foreign policy statements and policies by, after 1975, the European Council; sanctions against undemocratic regimes; and the adoption of a single EC representation in international forums and conferences, most successfully in the UN. Though it had its drawbacks and disappointments, EPC was largely a success story, perhaps in part because of its more diffuse nature. Equally, however, it did not mean integration.

The question of EMU was a logical extension of the existing customs union. Its details were provided in another report in 1970, prepared by Pierre Werner, the Luxembourg premier. The Werner Report argued for a simultaneous harmonisation of economic, fiscal and budgetary policy, to be achieved in a three-stage programme by a reinforced centralised decision-making capacity in monetary policy. The broad objectives of the Report were accepted by the heads of government in 1971. Though prospects became more dubious with the final disintegration of the Bretton Woods structure, increased monetary instability and rising inflation, the goal was endorsed again at the Paris summit of 1972, a meeting which attempted to pull the several ideas about progress together. Paris was important for two reasons: it was the first meeting of the government leaders of the enlarged EC, and the final outcome was a formal commitment to a European Union. The timetable mapped out was ambitious and reasonably detailed. A Regional Development Fund was to be established by 1973, as was an environmental policy. A programme of social action was to be launched in 1974, and there was to be a commitment to an energy policy. A common external policy *vis-à-vis* GATT and the developing world was also to be established. The capstone was the agreement that EMU should be complete by 1980, with the commitment to a transformation of 'the whole complex of their relations into a European Union before the end of the present decade'. Summitry was also institutionalised at Paris, with the decision to meet three times annually. The participants also committed themselves to direct elections to the EP. The rhetoric was heady, but the overarching concept of union still remained sufficiently vague to satisfy the diverse interests of all the participants. While a Regional Development Fund and the Lomé Convention, linking the EC to developing countries, were both set up in 1975, and direct elections held in 1979, the other initiatives were slow to develop. Most importantly, the EMU never got off the ground, though the EMS was established in 1979, and the 'end of the present decade' came and went without any obvious progress on European union. Paris, in fact, proved to be the peak of the new optimism generated a few years earlier at The Hague.

The commitment to an ultimate union was an all-embracing one. For it to be turned into reality, the several threads of the past, and the members' hopes for the future, would need to be interwoven into a seamless garment. Given the rise of summitry, that task could only belong to the heads of government. In 1974, they invited Leo Tindemans, the prime minister of Belgium, to consult with the national capitals on the degree of political cooperation and integration thought possible or desirable. His report, issued in 1976, illustrated the difficulty of matching reality with rhetoric. While Tindemans himself stressed that the cautious tone of the report was because he wanted to be realistic, not utopian, he nevertheless recommended a common foreign policy and defence collaboration, more common policies, and a popularly elected legislature. More controversially, perhaps, was the suggestion that the EC might accept a rate of integration in economic and financial areas that would vary from country to country, that the end goals might be more easily achieved if the EC did not insist that all members, in all policy areas, should move in total tandem with each other. The notion of a two-speed Europe was something that was viewed with deep suspicion by the less committed states of Britain and Denmark. While the idea was never formally discussed and quietly disappeared, it was a weapon that some members might be tempted to wield against recalcitrant states, and it resurfaced again in 1984 and, later, in the mid-1990s.

On the whole, the Tindemans Report did not advance the cause of union very far. Indeed, while it did reaffirm the Paris decisions, in suggesting a more realistic approach of concentrating upon the minimum concrete steps that might be possible, the report may well have helped to diminish further whatever momentum remained from the hopes of 1972. In fact, the European Council displayed little interest in the report; it merely expressed 'great interest' in it. The same fate befell a similar report in 1979 by a so-called Committee of Three Wise Men appointed by the Council the previous year to review the institutional machinery of the EC. The Committee's recommendations for a strengthening of the supranational element of the EC and a curtailment of national sovereignty were simply not acted upon. It was difficult not to conclude that, despite its rhetoric, the European Council in the late 1970s was not strongly committed to the notion of deeper integration.

The Commission and the EP may still have had union as their major ambition, but they also remained muted on the topic for some time. There was a widespread feeling in the EC around 1980 that a new initiative on political integration was needed to halt a seeming drift: even Britain supported this view in principle. However, the next major attempted push came as the result of an initiative taken outside the formal EC institutional structure. Known as the Genscher–Colombo Plan, after the West German and Italian foreign ministers, it was perhaps less of a plan than an attempt to spur the EC, and especially the Council, into action.

What Hans-Dietrich Genscher and Emilio Colombo argued for in their Draft European Act of 1981 was not new; even so, it was not particularly welcomed by the Council, since at the heart of the scheme lay the suggestion that the role of the EC institutions should be made more explicit, especially that of the Council, which had emerged outside the formal institutional framework of Rome. One particular implication, an increase in the EC budget, inevitably aroused British opposition. Greece and Denmark rejected out of hand any possibility of further restrictions on their own ability to formulate and apply national policies. France, too, was hesitant about any endorsement, and even Genscher's own premier, Schmidt, baulked at some of the consequences: he had already hinted on several occasions that West Germany could not continue indefinitely as the paymaster of the EC. In the end, the Genscher–

Colombo drive went the same way as the Tindemans Report. Its ideas were diluted into a straightforward declaration of intent without any specific proposals, deadlines or timetables. Once again, rhetoric triumphed over action.

Genscher and Colombo were nevertheless correct in their belief that something had to be done to reassert Europe's position in the world. Economically, the inability to achieve monetary cooperation was weakening Europe in the face of a strengthening American dollar. A concerted action might have helped to combat inflation and unemployment, which were beginning to bite ever harder across the EC. Politically, Europe's relationship with the United States had worsened in the aftermath of the acrimony surrounding the Carter presidency; and Europeans were also becoming alarmed by the hawkish stand of Ronald Reagan.

While the Genscher–Colombo Plan had no direct impact, it was important in keeping the idea of union and political cooperation before the power centre of the EC. It contributed to the new round of discussions upon which the governments embarked in 1982, even though these resulted only in yet another general statement, grandiosely entitled the Solemn Declaration on European Union, made by the European Council in Stuttgart in 1983. On the other hand, Genscher and Colombo had a EC ally whose importance had potentially increased. With its popular base now rooted in direct elections, the EP was anxious to demonstrate that its credentials were now backed by some muscle. With what it could regard as a popular mandate behind it, the EP was not content with a secondary supportive role. Even before the Genscher–Colombo round had begun, the EP, under the urging and leadership of Altiero Spinelli, a veteran federalist and ex-Commissioner (1972–76), had launched a thorough review of the EC with a view to producing a new, forthright and specific blueprint for political union. Its endeavours culminated in a Draft Treaty on European Union, not just a revamping of Rome, but a completely new document that was intended to endow the EC with the supranational authority which had steadily dissipated over the previous decades. The Draft Treaty proposed a single institutional framework that would encompass all levels of cooperation, as well as making the institutions more efficient and democratically accountable.

Perhaps only a starry-eyed idealist would have believed that the Draft Treaty could be sold to the European Council as a finished product: it wanted too much too quickly. The EP was still held at arm's length by the national governments, and it had still to establish itself as a positive force at the electoral level. The next round of direct elections in 1984 provided the EP with an opportunity to sell itself and its ideas to the electorate, and to mobilise public opinion. Even by the standards of the 1979 election, the 1984 experience was disappointing. In particular, the European package did not figure prominently anywhere: the elections were fought as distinctive national campaigns on national issues, something that would also characterise all future EP elections. The Draft Treaty would become another historical archive.

On the other hand, the Draft Treaty exercise was not perhaps entirely in vain. It added to the weight of documentation arguing for reform and progress, and its broad-ranging approach did present the choices to be made very clearly. It indicated at least some possibilities that might reasonably be achieved, and it helped to keep the question of union on the agenda. The EP reconfirmed its role as the conscience of the original EC ideal, worrying away around the edges of the existing system. In that respect, the efforts of Spinelli and his colleagues were one factor that persuaded the European Council itself to consider a revision of the original treaties.

That revision began as another item at the important Fontainebleau summit of 1984. The EC had seemingly drifted for a number of years, despite innovations like the EMS. It was encumbered with a range of unresolved issues which the European Council hitherto had been unable or reluctant to resolve: the budget arguments with Britain, the financing of the EC, the costs of the CAP, French objections to the membership of Spain and Portugal. Under the prodding of its host, François Mitterrand, the Council swept these away at Fontainebleau, making it more possible to focus on the future. The members agreed to look again at how they might condense the many and varied views on integration into a set of proposals that would be politically manageable and acceptable. Two committees were established. One, a Committee for a People's Europe, was charged with examining how the EC might develop practical symbols that would help nurture the growth of a European identity at the mass level, an area barely touched to date by the EC. Clearly, however, any such symbolic gestures could come to fruition only in the long term. The other committee was to look at political change. Its conclusions on institutional reform trod familiar ground, focusing as they did on the strengthening of the supranational element and a reduction of the authority of the Council of Ministers and the national governments. The Milan summit of 1985, at which these proposals were considered, was an ill-tempered affair, and seemingly did not advance matters very far. Countries like Britain and Denmark tended at least to be reasonably consistent in the wariness with which they approached the topic of union. For others, however, rhetorical commitment seemingly still tended to be demoted whenever an issue of national interest arose. For example, Helmut Kohl could, in 1984, ringingly declaim to the West German parliament: 'Who is prepared to follow us on the way to European political union with the stated objective of a United States of Europe?' Yet within a year, and only days before the Milan summit was due to review the future, West Germany chose to exercise its veto, for the first time in EC history, on the question of increasing the price of cereals. Rhetoric and action seemed to remain as far apart as ever.

Nevertheless, the Fontainebleau decisions had emphasised how the question of union had been taken up again by the only body that had the ability to turn dream into reality, and the Milan meeting was far from inconclusive. Out of these two years there emerged a commitment to establish a single internal market – an original objective of Rome nearly three decades earlier – and a proposal for an intergovernmental conference on further integration. It was this conference, which met towards the end of 1985, which pushed the EC towards the Single European Act (SEA) which, finally ratified in 1987, was a fundamental revision of the founding treaties. Its major objective was to prepare the way for the establishment, by the end of 1992, of a genuine internal market, 'an area without frontiers in which the free movement of goods, persons, services and capital is ensured', with, as far as possible, decisions to achieve this market being taken by qualified majority voting, and with the Commission reporting on interim progress in 1988 and 1990. Inevitably, there were numerous objections. For example, France, Greece and Ireland wondered about such a rigid deadline, while Denmark and Greece again confirmed resistance to any loss of national sovereignty that might be implied in the suggestion for more majority voting.

It would have been reasonable to assume in 1985 that the national divisions within the European Council would be reproduced at the intergovernmental conference, and perhaps also that if past history was any guide, the end result would, at most, be cosmetic change. In the end, the member states were to surprise everyone, including perhaps themselves, by launching a process of what were to be the most decisive changes in the structure of the EC since Rome. One important factor in this change was the active role of the Commission. In 1985 the European Council charged the Commission with the task of preparing the way for 1992 and the internal market. It was a chore which the Commission entered into with gusto, producing a White Paper which listed some 300 separate measures relating to physical, fiscal and technical barriers to trade which would have to be taken, and a timetable for each. It was the first time that the Commission had essentially been let off the leash that had been imposed upon it after the disputes of the 1960s. In addition, it was a new Commission whose members were all strongly committed to further integration, not least its new president, Jacques Delors, who used the new-found 'freedom' of the Commission to reassert it as a motor force for closer union.

While very much a compromise, the scope of the SEA was far-reaching, and its implications enormous. At its heart lay the commitment to a fully integrated internal market by the end of 1992, but it also covered institutional reform and European Political Cooperation (EPC). In other words, as well as dealing with measures that were deemed necessary for completing the common market, it referred to new policy objectives, new forms of decision-making and legislative processes within the EC, and extending the foreign policy scope of EPC to cover even matters of defence and security – Ireland's policy of neutrality notwithstanding. In retrospect, it is difficult perhaps to understand how some could fail to appreciate how far the significance of all this would or could extend. It would inevitably focus attention not just on isolated instances of national discrimination, but ultimately on the whole range of national systems of taxation and law, the plethora of national standards and regulations in a range of policy areas, and national social welfare and security systems. At the extreme it implied the abolition of all internal frontier controls – whether of goods or people. This implication had been accepted by five – all bar Italy – of the original Six which in June 1985 signed the Schengen Agreement, a commitment to create a border-free zone among themselves.

Because the SEA involved a revision of the founding treaties of the EC, it had to be sent to the national parliaments for ratification. Initially, only nine states ratified the Act without further ado. Italy complained that the Act was insufficient, but indicated that it was withholding its signature in protest over Denmark's hostility to the plan. Ratification was also delayed in Greece, ostensibly as a symbolic protest against the isolation of, and pressure upon, Denmark. It was the latter upon which the fate of the SEA hinged. In the discussions on the SEA, Denmark had reserved its position on almost everything, mainly, however, because its minority government could not be certain of a parliamentary majority in Copenhagen. Since the early 1970s, Danish minority governments had had to be drawn from a more fragmented party system, and they found it exceedingly difficult to control the legislature. In particular, the Danish parliament had asserted its right to supervise and virtually lay down the conditions of Danish EC participation and policy, and it rejected the SEA. In exasperation, the Conservative premier, Poul Schlüter, sought to bypass his opponents by calling a referendum, where he made it clear that what was at stake was not the Act, but Denmark's continued membership of the EC: a negative vote, he said, 'would be interpreted as our first step towards leaving' the EC. Despite the economic card, Schlüter managed to gain only a small majority in the 1986 referendum. It was, however, sufficient for Denmark to sign the Act. The final implementation of the SEA in 1987 was delayed for a few months because of a court ruling in Ireland that the government should have held a referendum to amend the Constitution before it could sign the Act, in order to adjust the country's constitutional position of neutrality to the SEA reference to cooperation on European security. With that obstacle easily passed, the Act duly came into force.

The SEA did not advance political union very far, nor did it constitute a major overhaul of the institutional balance of power within the EC. But there was more to the SEA than its detail. It was a significant step, and one which had been initiated and approved by the European Council, the body which in the 1980s ultimately held the key to any further integration. Over and above the text of the Act, 1992 became the symbol of something significant that all assumed would occur, though what that something might be remained a matter of interpretation. What counted was that all the member states accepted that 1992 would mark the beginning of something new, and their beliefs and behaviour after 1986 were conditioned accordingly. Despite variation of opinion, all accepted that an internal market might mean economic integration; but once that had been accepted by all as an objective, there were those who asked how this could be achieved without a similar degree of monetary and, ultimately, political union. Powerful voices in the European Council, spearheaded by a more formal, but no less effective, Franco-German unity of thought between Mitterrand and Kohl, joined forces with a reinvigorated Commission to push for the ultimate goal. Under the strong leadership of Jacques Delors, the Commission utilised to the full its powers under the 1992 objectives and the SEA to become the most activist Commission in the EC's history. And within the Commission Delors came to enjoy a predominance equalled in the past only by Hallstein: he used his authority and influence throughout the whole of the EC and beyond the narrow provisions of the SEA to become, in effect, the leading spokesman not just for 1992 but also for what should come afterwards. Through dint of some forward planning and some happenstance, between Fontainebleau and the SEA the EC found itself embarked on an accelerated route towards more intensive union, a route which led directly to the European Council discussions at Maastricht in December 1991, discussions which produced the Treaty on European Union and transformed the EC into the European Union (EU).

CHAPTER 21

THE IMPROBABLE DECADE

Our days of weakness are over.   (*Ronald Reagan, 1984*)

Our earth is a ship on which we are the passengers . . . and it cannot be allowed to be wrecked. There will be no second Noah's Ark.
        (*Mikhail Gorbachev*, Perestroika, *London, 1987, p. 12*)

Almost before they began, the 1980s were labelled 'the dangerous decade', which people feared, after the sea-change in super-power and international relations at the end of the 1970s, would be a new ice age in which the risk of confrontation between the United States and the Soviet Union would be much greater than at any time for several decades. Certainly, for a while, those fears seemed to be confirmed. The early years of the decade were not auspicious, as talks between the two powers stuttered and then broke down. By 1983 American-Soviet relations, though not bedevilled by a serious crisis of the proportions of Cuba, were at their lowest ebb since the Stalin era. Yet within a few years the climate had again changed abruptly. The new Cold War, if that is what it was, thawed so rapidly that towards the end of the decade there was a broad feeling that a more genuine and realistic détente was not just possible, but even more probable than ever before. That renewed confidence was still based on assumptions about the durability of the bipolar world. Few imagined that the shift in climate would culminate in the *annus mirabilis* of 1989, a year which saw the end of Soviet hegemony in Eastern Europe, the first stage of a process that within two years would see the disintegration of the Soviet Union itself, and the ending of the Cold War.

In the Soviet Union the long reign of Leonid Brezhnev finally ended with his death in 1982. During his rule the Soviet system had been stabilised after the ebullient gyrations of Khrushchev. The Soviet Union pushed hard for both détente and an expansion of Soviet military power. The first objective had been dashed by Nixon's resignation, the later insistence by Carter of tying détente to progress on human rights within the Soviet Union, and, after 1980, the more hardline stance of Reagan. The latter aim, however, had seemingly been achieved, though perhaps at an increasing cost to the domestic economy.

Despite a belligerent foreign policy, the Soviet Union had become a more conservative state, more cautious overall, and suffering from a domestic economic sclerosis caused by a stifling of necessary initiative and reform by an insistence upon conservative Communist orthodoxy.

Although a more institutionalised procedure had been adopted for determining the succession, there was no heir-apparent to Brezhnev. He was followed by two short-lived leaders, both elderly and ill, with the second, a devoted Brezhnev protégé, clearly being a stop-gap appointment. It was the election of Mikhail Gorbachev to the leadership in 1985 which heralded the injection of a new dynamism into the Soviet Union; he seemed to acknowledge more openly the deficiencies of the Soviet economic system and the burdens of its defence budget. For Gorbachev, one way of improving the economy was to seek real disarmament gains. His slogans for internal reform, *glasnost* (openness) and *perestroika* (reconstruction) became two of the few Russian words widely used as common parlance in Western commentaries. Gorbachev's attempts to reform the Communist system by making it more open politically and economically while still retaining the supremacy of the Communist Party were to lead, however, to the destruction of the system itself.

Gorbachev was faced by Ronald Reagan, elected as American president in 1980, who had earlier stated that there was an arms race, but that only the Soviet Union was competing in it. In his first term in office, Reagan vigorously attempted to raise American prestige and military strength. This more hawkish attitude, certainly in terms of a reaffirmed commitment to Western Europe, at first gratified European leaders. Satisfaction later turned to alarm with the realisation that Reagan was ready and willing, unilaterally if necessary, to defend American interests. The 1983 invasion of Grenada to overthrow a left-wing regime in the island, the bombing raid on Libya in 1985 as a response to what the United States saw as Libyan direction and funding of international terrorism, and the decision in 1987 to despatch American warships to patrol and, if necessary, to take action in the Persian Gulf were but three acts which did not entirely meet with the approval of Western Europe.

By the late 1980s, however, the Soviet-American dialogue had been resumed at the highest levels, hinting at the prospect of a real disarmament. Some of the implications of this dialogue worried Western European leaders, for the super-powers had agreed that disarmament should begin with the removal of intermediate-range nuclear weapons from the continent, that is, the very weapons that the leaders had only recently argued were necessary for its protection. Over the previous decade, Western European worries about the American capacity for leadership had compounded their continuing concern about an American decoupling from Europe. After 1985, the Western leaders were also forced to ponder the implications of what might develop from the more skilful diplomacy that was being waged by Gorbachev. The particular dilemmas might have been new, but that Western Europe was faced with a dilemma was not new. Ever since the 1940s, Western Europe had been in a constant state of agitation, albeit for different reasons at different times, about the relationship between the super-powers, and about how that relationship impinged upon its own interests and future. That agitation did not cease after the retreat of the Soviet Union from Eastern Europe in the late 1980s, not least because it led to a reunited Germany. After the initial exhilaration of 1989 and 1990, Western Europe was forced to realise that while the political cartography of Europe may be changing, defence and security problems had not evaporated. That was underlined by the final disintegration of the Soviet Union in 1991. Now there lay not one, but three nuclear powers to the east: Russia, Ukraine and Khazakhstan. Russia may have been a wounded giant in economic and political turmoil, but it remained at least a latent super-power. These were the circumstances which led to the debates about whether NATO was no longer necessary, whether it should extend its membership eastwards, and what role the United States should play in the future security of the continent. That the continent had no contingency plan for what it might do without the United States, indeed that Western Europe would find it extremely difficult to achieve effective military and security cooperation without American involvement was underlined by the European failure to achieve a satisfactory political and military solution to the turmoil and violence that accompanied the disintegration of Yugoslavia after 1991.

THE REASSERTION OF THE UNITED STATES

A flexing of American muscle began with the election of Ronald Reagan to the presidency. Reagan had won that election not least because of his criticism of the concessions of previous years. American reassertion, however, began with the much-maligned Jimmy Carter. After 1977, his pursuance of human rights, which extended to communicating openly with dissidents within the Soviet Union, might conceivably be interpreted as the first stage of recuperation. The policy might be said to have had two objectives: to regain a moral ascendancy for the United States, and to demonstrate to his own increasingly conservative and worried country that détente had not been, and need not be, a one-way street. Carter's 'conversion' to a sterner line, and his disillusionment with the Soviet Union, came too late to save him: he was swamped by the adverse events of 1979 and 1980.

Nevertheless, what Carter did was to provide a platform upon which Reagan could build. As distinct from human rights, Reagan concentrated on reasserting American military and strategic interests. His convincing victory in 1980 gave him a mandate for reconstructing American military strength, and for launching the largest programme of American defence expenditure ever seen in peacetime, in order, to quote from a 1982 communiqué from the American Joint Chiefs of Staff, that 'in the dangerous years ahead it will be essential that any potential aggressor realize that the US has the capability for a global response with the appropriate weapons of our choice regardless of where the aggression occurs'. As part of this programme, Reagan became a committed supporter of the installation in Western Europe of intermediate-range nuclear weapons and the modernisation of NATO, so much so that deployment became identified as his policy. He was less interested in following up the other part of the 1979 twin-track decision, that the West should actively negotiate with the Soviet Union about reducing or eliminating these weapons from Europe. While he did agree to begin negotiations at the end of 1981, within the SALT framework, this perhaps was partly to pacify Western European apprehension about the missiles and to make their installation easier.

Reagan had reverted to the conception of Communism held by the United States in the late 1940s and early 1950s: strategic and nuclear considerations could not be divorced from the ideological struggle. Hence it was insufficient for the United States simply to counteract what it regarded as a military imbalance. It also had to be active on political, economic and ideological fronts: Communism had to be contained everywhere in all its aspects. This led to an aggressive campaign by the United States to limit and destroy what was claimed to be Soviet-sponsored terrorism and subversion. This American response was particularly vigorous in the Western hemisphere. Reagan strenuously backed the centre–right government in El Salvador in its bloody struggle against left-wing guerrillas, even providing it with military advisers in 1981. Soon afterwards, he gave succour to the rebel 'Contras' in their fight against the Sandinista regime established in neighbouring Nicaragua in 1979. The most forceful example of an American military response near its own borders was the 1983 invasion of Grenada.

The Reagan administration was not averse to pursuing similar tactics elsewhere, though with mixed success. There was the abortive attempt in 1983 to link up with UN peacekeeping forces to sustain a pro-Western regime in, and the territorial integrity of, Lebanon. More successful perhaps was the bombing raid on Libya, a retaliatory measure against a regime that was accused by the United States of sponsoring and funding terrorism across the world, especially against American interests and citizens. And in 1987 he despatched American naval forces to the Persian Gulf to safeguard, by military means if necessary, the vital oil-bearing shipping lanes caught in the middle of a seemingly endless war between Iran and Iraq. These and similar actions indicated a belief that American military intervention was both a necessary and efficacious method of defending and furthering American interests.

Reagan was a skilled orator, highly effective at communicating appeals to patriotism. The new assertiveness was also apparent at the ideological level. Reagan pursued an aggressive rhetorical campaign against the Soviet Union, accusing it, in the forum of the UN, of fomenting world revolution, and branding it as an 'evil empire' with 'dark purposes'. Two events in particular during the early 1980s buttressed him in his belief that terrorism was an integral element of Soviet policy: the indications of Soviet-Bulgarian complicity in an assassination attempt on the Polish Pope, John Paul II, and the shooting down by the Soviet Union of an unarmed South Korean airliner which had strayed into Soviet airspace, with the loss of 269 lives.

This view of the world also meant that direct sanctions against the Soviet Union were a necessary complement to the strategy of military preparedness. While Reagan lifted the grain embargo imposed upon the Soviet Union by Carter, so fulfilling his 1980 campaign promise to American farm interests, he continued to pursue and intensify an embargo on the export of high-technology products, the definition of which was broadly conceived to cover anything deemed to be integral to American and Western security. The embargo embraced the whole Soviet bloc, and was occasionally supplemented by more general sanctions against a particular state: for example, American sanctions were deployed against Poland in 1981 in response to the declaration of martial law and the regime's move to break up the independent Solidarity trade union movement. And Reagan constantly urged his European allies to follow the American lead, most notably, if without much success, in attempting to stop the construction of a pipeline that would relay Siberian natural gas from the Soviet Union to Western Europe. Reagan's extension, in 1982, of the ban on licence exports for American equipment to cover that produced by American subsidiary companies abroad merely irritated Western Europe, which treated the pipeline agreement as a strictly commercial enterprise, and refused to accept the American view that East–West economic relations were an adjunct of the political and military competition.

It was not that the Reagan administration was averse to détente. It was interested in maintaining the SALT talks and remained committed to the CSCE process: the latter had begun to work for confidence-building measures between NATO and the Warsaw Pact, and in 1986 a first agreement, the Stockholm Accord, was reached on the verification and aerial inspection of planned military exercises. In addition, the MBFR talks were proceeding at their usual leisurely pace. And in 1982 the United States agreed to begin the Strategic Arms Reduction Talks (START) in Geneva, even though the Soviet Union had clearly made START conditional upon an American acceptance of its own views on intermediate-range nuclear weapons. However, détente had to take place under what the United States perceived to be a proper military balance, and on its own terms. Hence Reagan continued to put forward his own proposals for détente, but their more practical aspects tended to be obscured by his more resolute actions and strident rhetoric.

But by 1984 it seemed as if the two super-powers had been driven even further apart. Most of the surviving bilateral discussions on disarmament had broken down, and new initiatives seemed to have been abandoned indefinitely. In addition, a new issue had surfaced to alienate the two from each other. This was Reagan's 1983 launch of his Strategic Defence Initiative (SDI), which soon became popularly known as the Star Wars programme. Basically, SDI was a proposal for an effective space-based ballistic missiles defence system, a further way for Reagan of redressing the nuclear imbalance. While perhaps more propaganda and science fiction than potential reality, SDI rapidly became an article of faith to Reagan, while for the Soviet Union its abandonment became a *sine qua non* of any developments on détente.

By 1984, the United States had definitely cast aside the shadow of Vietnam. Reagan's domestic prestige was high, and he won another convincing election victory in that year. Yet within two years, his administration was embroiled in a scandal involving the sale of arms to Iran and the channelling of the profits to the Contra rebels in Nicaragua. The revelations assumed the proportions of a Watergate, and similarly threatened to discredit the president and his administration. Perhaps partly because of his new domestic problems, Reagan's interest in a satisfactory deal with the Soviet Union, as something that could be a lasting achievement of his presidency, increased. In 1986 he agreed to a summit meeting with the new Soviet leader, Mikhail Gorbachev, in Reykjavik. The summit was not entirely successful because the United States did not seem to be sufficiently prepared to respond to, or counter, the several proposals which Gorbachev had brought with him to Iceland. Yet within a year, some of the Reykjavik ideas had been embraced by the United States, which subsequently seemed to be rushing headlong towards détente and disarmament to the extent of ignoring and alarming its European allies, most of whom had been perturbed by what they regarded as American adventurism. But after 1986 European attention turned from Washington towards Moscow, to consider with a mix of disbelief, worry and hope the consequences of the internal reforms being attempted by Gorbachev. Although it was to be some years before the Soviet Union itself would collapse, the reassertion of American interests by Reagan and the accumulation of Soviet problems had by the late 1980s left the United States in a dominant position as a world power.

THE DECLINE OF THE SOVIET EMPIRE

In the 1970s, the Soviet Union had had four major concerns. On two, it could be reasonably satisfied: the German issue had been resolved, and through alliances it had established its own version of containment around China. These had complemented its aims of stabilising the arms race without conceding any advantages it may have acquired in that area, while continuing to create and benefit from opportunities that might arise for extending its political and ideological influence outside Europe. It was the latter two objectives which led to the American reaction, so rebounding against the Soviet Union. In the 1980s the Soviet Union sought to preserve the advantages it had gained during the previous decade. It believed that its massive military and strategic expansion had been justified in order to achieve parity with the United States. In a sense, it was still seeking acknowledgement of the super-power status which it felt it had been denied by American policy ever since 1945. As for the Western accusations of disparity in conventional and strategic weapons, the Soviet Union argued that it had to be viewed in a broader perspective: it was necessary to compensate for the American policy of containment, which had resulted in the encirclement of the Soviet Union by a chain of 'unfriendly' states, many of which provided homes for American bases.

The events of the late 1970s forced Brezhnev and the Soviet Union to re-evaluate their détente strategy: the conclusion was that it had just about run its natural course. A more prickly United States persuaded the Soviet Union that little was to be lost either by cracking down hard on its own dissidents or by seeking to buttress its influence in Afghanistan. Both reactions were part and parcel of its claim to have a right to be treated as a super-power, and resentment about external criticisms of its right to act like one. Afghanistan, however, was to be an Achilles' heel, a Soviet version of Vietnam. The Soviet Union became locked into a conflict which it could not lose, but from which it could not extricate itself without considerable loss of face. Although to stay in Afghanistan involved an economic burden, a steady loss of life and world disapprobation, for the conservative leadership around the ailing Brezhnev there was no choice. It was not until the late 1980s that the Soviet Union accepted the inevitable: Gorbachev, who had earlier described Afghanistan as a 'bleeding wound', eventually withdrew Soviet forces in 1989. It was retreat without victory, a psychological blow to Soviet Communism as devastating as withdrawal from Vietnam had been for the United States.

However, that lay in the future. As the improbable decade began, the Soviet Union was obliged to focus more closely upon the old battleground of Europe, where it faced renewed political and military challenges. It was not surprising that the human rights aspect of the Helsinki Final Act raised hopes in Eastern Europe. While the Soviet Union might hope that its allies would, like itself, not allow dissident pressure to get out of hand, its desire for a reasonable accord with the West, not least in terms of trading links, made it more circumspect about direct intervention. Its worries were well-founded. Helsinki was costly to the Soviet Union, as human rights groups emerged everywhere in Eastern Europe. The most prominent of these, such as Charter 77 in Czechoslovakia, survived strong state persecution to become a major critic of social, political and economic policy; their views and the imprisonment of their members were widely reported in the Western media. However, perhaps the most serious challenge to its control of Eastern Europe that the Soviet Union had to face in the early 1980s was only partly inspired by the human rights campaign. In response to the severe economic difficulties being experienced throughout Eastern Europe, a new trade union movement had sprung up in Poland in 1980. Protesting against inept and heavy-handed political and economic management, and beginning among the shipyard workers of Gdansk, the new Solidarity organisation spread like wildfire to become a genuine mass movement which, rooted as it also was in the Catholic religion, acquired the symbolism and trappings of nationalist yearning. Because Solidarity was based in the working class and called itself an independent trade union, it posed difficult management problems for a Socialist state which called itself a workers' democracy. The Polish government seemed to be incapacitated, helpless against the Solidarity tide of political pressure and strikes.

The political implications of Solidarity were alarming for the Soviet Union. Once again, it faced the possibility of an unravelling of its defensive structure and ideological hegemony in Eastern Europe. While the Soviet interest demanded counteraction, direct intervention under the Brezhnev Doctrine was inadvisable. While there was increased disillusionment with the United States, the Soviet Union still hoped for progress on, or at least stabilisation of, détente; and the Solidarity cause, particularly its human rights aspect, was strongly backed by the United States. The Soviet dilemma was how to bring back order to Poland without incurring Western penalties. It was the Polish military which came to the rescue. In 1981 the army, undoubtedly with Soviet knowledge and approval, declared martial law and proceeded to disband Solidarity. Despite the immediate and expected Western retaliation of protests and sanctions, the Soviet Union and Poland remained unswayed.

Nevertheless, the events of 1981 were an augury of the problems that would emerge in Eastern Europe in the 1980s. Solidarity continued to survive and agitate as an underground organisation, and the army coup had effectively demoted the Polish Communist Party from its leading role. The new government proved equally incapable of resolving the continuing economic problems of poor investment, management and growth. These, however, were common to the whole of Eastern Europe, and it was something that the Soviet Union itself could do little about. As a result of *Ostpolitik*, the Soviet Union had encouraged its Eastern European satellites to forge closer economic and trading links with the West, but by the early 1980s their uncompetitive situation had placed them deeply in debt to the West. While the Soviet Union still believed that politically its allies should reject the capitalist West and remained unwilling to tolerate any radical reform, it could not itself, crippled as it was by its own planning inefficiencies and escalating defence spending, come to their assistance: it already bore most of the costs of the Warsaw Pact and provided Eastern Europe with much of the raw materials it required. Its European satraps had, in fact, become, even more than before, a handicap rather than a buffer zone against a possible Western invasion. It was a dilemma, perhaps, that could only be resolved by Moscow as part of a recognition that the Soviet command system was, over the long term, proving incapable of meeting the economic challenge of the capitalist West: it was a recognition that eventually came with the appointment of Gorbachev as leader of the Soviet Union.

The Soviet response to Reagan's rearmament programme of the early 1980s came on two fronts. As well as trying to persuade the United States that its fears were without foundation, the Soviet Union persisted in its time-honoured strategy of attempting to exploit and widen national differences within the Atlantic alliance. Western Europe had to be persuaded not to support the American arms build-up. The Soviet Union had probably never given up the dream of divorcing Western Europe from the United States, and in the late 1970s Soviet efforts in this direction became more blatant. An effective propaganda campaign, targeted against Western Europe, had been waged in 1978 against Carter's proposal to develop the neutron bomb. The exercise was repeated even more vigorously after 1979 over the NATO plans for modernisation and the installation of intermediate-range nuclear weapons in Western Europe. For the Soviet Union, NATO's twin-track proposal introduced a greater degree of uncertainty, even, perhaps in its implications for arms control and European security, invalidating the central tenet of its own foreign policy – that economic and strategic advantage would accrue from détente through arms control. Hence, the response was a more threatening posture, of indicating a possible Soviet withdrawal from those elements of the arms control talks which still survived. Simultaneously, it strenuously sought to encourage the Western European anti-nuclear and peace movements to demonstrate against NATO's rearmament and refurbishment.

The exercise was to be a futile one and, perhaps, self-defeating. Certainly, the Western peace movements were extremely vocal and succeeded in establishing an umbrella cross-national organisation. Moreover, the notion of peace proved to be attractive and contagious on the European left. Unilateral nuclear disarmament, even neutrality, acquired a stronger foothold in several Social Democrat parties, most significantly in those of Britain and West Germany. In Scandinavia, it led to the resurrection, though without concrete results, of the idea of a Nordic nuclear-free zone, first offered to Denmark and Norway by the Soviet Union in 1958, and revived periodically thereafter. The Nordic Social Democrats who pursued the idea, however, wanted a zone that would be guaranteed by the super-powers in times of war, as well as of peace, something that was unacceptable to a great power.

However, unilateralism failed to appeal to other parties, or to the bulk of Western opinion which, while desirous of peace and afraid of nuclear war, still preferred to endorse a nuclear NATO as the most effective defence against what it perceived to be the major enemy. This was particularly true in the most important NATO countries. The Soviet campaign raised scarcely a ripple in Italy, largely ignored even by the PCI. In Britain the newly unilateralist Labour Party, in the 1983 and 1987 elections, went down to its worst defeats and lowest levels of popular support since the 1930s. In West Germany the SPD became a weak and divided opposition after electoral defeat in 1983. Even the election of a Socialist government in France gave the Soviet Union little joy. François Mitterrand was forthright on the need for Western readiness and united strength.

The Soviet problem was that, while it had wanted to establish an effective détente, it refused to accept the legitimacy of Western worries over its own military expansion. During the two years before his death, Brezhnev was unable to offer any new thinking on foreign policy and disarmament, while his two successors, Yuri Andropov and Konstantin Chernenko, who each ruled for about a year, had too little time, even if they had the inclination, to pursue new initiatives. It was the appointment of Mikhail Gorbachev in 1985 as the new Soviet leader which brought a breath of fresh air to the Kremlin, presenting the West with new, yet strangely familiar, dilemmas.

From the outset, Gorbachev stressed that his first priority was to overhaul the creaking Soviet economy through a reorganisation of economic management. He had concluded that this could be achieved only by allowing a greater expression of individual freedom and opinion in several previously closed areas of public life. In early 1986 he first employed the two phrases of *glasnost* and *perestroika* – openness and restructuring – which came to symbolise the direction of his domestic policy, a policy which he planned would result in a more open society led by a more publicly accountable Communist Party. The sustenance of military expenditure seemed to have a low ranking on his list of priorities. Gorbachev took up the theme of détente while still criticising American militarism, particularly Reagan's SDI project. But behind his stance, perhaps, there lay a greater honesty about the implications of an accelerated arms race for the less efficient Soviet economy and for the growing economic burden of an Eastern Europe whose reliability in the event of a war could well be doubtful, as well as an acceptance of the fact that if the Soviet Union wished to prevent a rearmament of Western Europe, it had to demonstrate a positive commitment to reduce its own arsenal. The first few months of Gorbachev's rule were reminiscent of Khrushchev's whirlwind actions of the late 1950s. Soviet proposals and ideas flowed so fast that the West had difficulty in assimilating them, let alone responding to them. This was particularly true of the United States, still basking in the assertiveness of President Reagan. It was to be a few years before the West would accept him, as Mrs Thatcher was later to put it, as a man with whom it could do business.

In 1986, the leaders of the two super-powers met in Reykjavik, in the first summit for many years. The propaganda victory largely went to the Soviet Union. The United States did not seem to possess a coherent brief with which it could negotiate on, or rebut, the numerous Soviet proposals. Perhaps the most significant Soviet offer at Reykjavik was the so-called Double Zero Option, the withdrawal from Europe not only of all intermediate-range, but also all short-range, nuclear missiles. This was a dramatic advance on the original American proposal (the Zero Option) of 1981 for the removal of intermediate-range missiles. The suggestion seemed to take the United States by surprise, but the principle was accepted by both sides who also agreed that subsequent negotiations would proceed independently of any concessions earlier demanded by the Soviet Union on the American decision to develop SDI. By the time Reagan's successor, George Bush, held a summit meeting with Gorbachev in late 1989, the extent of international relaxation had passed far beyond the boundaries of what, only three years earlier, had been deemed possible.

By the late 1980s, the United States had entered accelerated arms reduction talks with the Soviet Union. While Reagan still regarded SDI as non-negotiable, it soon disappeared from the agenda, and by 1987 he seemed to be attempting to outbid Gorbachev on the speed and extent of proposed disarmament. Several further factors about the new Soviet leader may have been influential in persuading both the United States and Western Europe of the sincerity of his intentions. First, he seemed to acknowledge Western fears about Soviet aims: the missile offers were meant to allay those fears. Secondly, he seemed to indicate a retrenchment of Soviet interventionism throughout the world, most especially in Afghanistan. Finally, the West came to accept that his foreign policy seemed to be linked to a determination to reduce the huge Soviet defence burden in order to reconstruct the ossified domestic economy. The new openness which had been indicated by the Soviet acceptance of Western aid and assistance in two major disasters that occurred shortly after Gorbachev's accession to power – a major earthquake in Armenia and an explosion at a nuclear plant (the world's worst nuclear disaster) at Chernobyl in Ukraine in 1986 – made Western Europe more ready to believe in the sincerity of his intentions.

In both Gorbachev's own actions, and certainly in the reactions of the West, the concepts of *glasnost* and *perestroika* were transferred also to the international stage, no more so than in Europe where by 1989 Gorbachev had begun to talk of a Common European Home. While it is unclear exactly what he took it to mean, it seemed to refer, at least in part, to a new European-wide security system that would aid his own domestic authority – under some pressure from Communist hardliners – and also accommodate a Europe where countries with different political and socioeconomic systems could coexist with each other within a framework of common European values. Indeed, by 1989 the West's concern was not whether Gorbachev was sincere, but whether he could survive as Soviet leader.

The most dramatic impact of the new Soviet line came in Eastern Europe, where Gorbachev also urged the regimes to reform their economic systems and introduce a degree of liberalisation in order to secure the loyalty of their citizens. The annual summit of the Warsaw Pact in the summer of 1989 declared that no member had the right to dictate events in another country, an implicit rejection of the Brezhnev Doctrine. It had, in fact, become apparent that Gorbachev was not prepared to give the Eastern European regimes the guarantee of Soviet military support and intervention in the event of internal unrest. His visit to East Berlin later in the year to participate in the celebrations for the fortieth anniversary of the DDR regime was a strained affair, as he criticised the regime for failing to take account of the views of its citizens. But pressures had been building up in some parts of Eastern Europe even before 1989. Poland, as always, had remained restive and a problem. Solidarity continued to be active, by 1988 even displaying its banners openly. In 1989 its leaders were invited to participate in a series of discussions on the worsening economic situation, and it was re-legalised. The regime committed itself to a multiparty election in June, as a result of which a non-Communist coalition government was formed. Gorbachev described this historic event as an 'internal affair'. In a more quiet way Hungary had by 1989 gone even further down the path of economic and political reform.

It was Hungary which in a sense precipitated the hectic final months of the year by opening its western borders with Austria in the early summer. This opened up a route to the West which, over the coming months, was followed by thousands of East Germans. Protests by the DDR were ignored by both the Soviet Union and Hungary. Unrest escalated in the DDR as the regime, too late, offered some reforms, but without relinquishing single-party control. On the evening of 9–10 November, the world watched in amazement as the beleaguered and crumbling regime threw open the greatest symbol of the Cold War, with thousands of East Germans flocking through the Berlin Wall to see the western side of the city for the first time in almost thirty years. It was not enough. The regime was simply swept away in the space of a few days, to be followed soon after by those in Czechoslovakia and in Bulgaria. Finally, riots broke out in Romania; the brutal dictatorship of Nikolai Ceauşescu was toppled overnight, with the dictator himself being summarily executed on Christmas Day. It is unclear whether or how far the Soviet Union sought to control this flood of events, but once it had decided not to intervene, a decade which had begun so ominously had ended in the inconceivable. Communism survived only in those countries where indigenous forces had brought it to power:

Albania and Yugoslavia, as well as the Soviet Union itself. But its survival there was to be only some two years, with the further disintegration of Yugoslavia and the Soviet Union producing many new states on maps of the world.

WESTERN EUROPEAN DILEMMAS

After a glacial beginning, the speed of change in super-power relations during the 1980s was such that it left Western Europe struggling to keep pace and to assimilate what the various proposals would mean for its own security and future. It re-emphasised several long-standing dilemmas, as well as creating some new ones. At the beginning of the decade, Western European governments were concerned about American impotence and were urging sterner American action against perceived Soviet imperialism, even in the European theatre, where détente still remained a Soviet priority. Western Europe was gratified when President Reagan took up the clarion call. Within a few years, this gratification turned to alarm over what Western Europe saw as American brinkmanship, based upon an unsophisticated view of the world. By the closing years of the decade, alarm itself had been replaced by a disquiet over the pace of the new détente. While that may have been originally welcomed by Western Europe, there were fears that it might, in a sense, abandon the continent to its own resources, first because the United States seemed determined to outbid the Soviet Union in what was on offer, and later because of uncertainty about the consequences of the contraction of the Soviet imperium.

The first part of the decade was dominated by arguments over NATO's twin-track decision. Installation of the missiles was something which military commanders urgently wanted. In 1981, the supreme NATO commander, General Bernard Rogers, reiterated why it was deemed so important when he said: 'As a result of the relentless Soviet accumulation of military power and NATO's inadequate and oft-times faltering response, the very credibility of our deterrent is in jeopardy.' The NATO view was strongly backed by Reagan. In Europe, however, only Margaret Thatcher's Conservative government in Britain seemed to remain an undeviating supporter (though strongly backed from the wings by President Mitterrand of France), rejecting Soviet offers of talks on arms control. In addition, the issue raised little public controversy in Italy, another receiving country for the missiles, where even the PCI did not oppose installation.

Greater problems arose in West Germany, Belgium and the Netherlands. In West Germany, Helmut Schmidt, struggling to maintain control over his SPD and concerned about the growing appeal of the anti-nuclear Green Party, shifted ground to urge more talks. However, after 1982 the new CDU government of Helmut Kohl resolutely reaffirmed the NATO commitment, joining Margaret Thatcher in refusing to be deviated off course by the vocal peace movement that existed in both countries, or by the anti-nuclear stance of the opposition SPD and Labour parties. The second thoughts that emerged in Belgium were perhaps only in part due to anti-nuclear sentiment: they also arose from the general frailty of coalition governments still labouring under the

political impact of the division between the country's two language communities. The most awkward problems had to be faced by the Netherlands, which
lay at the heart of the peace movement that enjoyed much support across all
the parties. The struggle was long and bitter, with much external pressure
being exerted upon the Dutch government. After several postponements, the
missiles were eventually deployed in 1985, two years later than the original
deadline. By then the peace movements had passed their peak, and their
support swiftly dissipated after deployment.

While Western European governments welcomed the renewed American
commitment to the continent, they were to be perturbed by what they saw as
American adventurism, just as they had been by Soviet exploits in the 1970s.
While Reagan saw the détente of the past decade as illusory and dangerous,
Western Europe had appreciated its benefits in trade and exchanges. Once
again, Europe's specific regional interests were in conflict with American global and strategic perceptions. Thus the American intervention in Grenada was
not looked upon favourably in Europe, though perhaps reluctantly accepted
as something deemed necessary to American interests. The same was not true
of the American bombing raid on Libya, which much of Western Europe, apart
from the British Conservative government, condemned as a dangerous and
foolhardy action that would do nothing to solve the question of international
terrorism. Again, the regional interest was dominant: the raid angered the Arab
world, and Western Europe fretted over the possible impact on its reliance on
Middle Eastern oil. The fact that Libyan terrorist activities seemed to subside
after the raid did not persuade Western Europe to revise its opinion.

The raid itself was perhaps less important as an act than as a symbol of an
American policy that Western Europe found both fascinating and disagreeable.
The one major exception to this general mood was Britain, where Mrs Thatcher
proved to be President Reagan's most loyal ally, supporting the action staunchly.
To some extent, this might be regarded as a debt which had to be redeemed
for American political and logistical support for Britain's Falklands War of
1982. However, while British and American views of the world were not entirely in harmony, on détente they did seem to share a similar belief. Like
Reagan, Mrs Thatcher saw a policy of strength as being the best strategy for
defence and peace.

Reagan's SDI scheme was greeted with a great deal of scepticism in Western
Europe. Though it was argued that SDI would be even more expensive and
riskier than the current delicate balance of mutually assured destruction, Western
Europe was more concerned with the implications that lay closer to home: an
operating SDI might persuade the United States to contemplate withdrawing
from Europe; it might increase the chances of a limited nuclear war in Europe;
and it might increase the technology gap between the United States and Western
Europe. Only the Conservative government in Britain, perhaps, tended to accept
the plan as something that was intrinsically valuable. The general scepticism,
however, was linked to the persisting worry that, despite American assurances
to the contrary, SDI might be a first step towards an uncoupling of the defence
of the United States from that of Western Europe, as well as, of course, to the

possibility of SDI obliging the Soviet Union to respond in kind, with a consequent heightening of super-power tension.

Paradoxically, the rapid change from Cold War to détente after 1985 did
little to reduce Western European concern. Still torn between the desires for
both an effective détente on the continent and an effective American military
guarantee, Western Europe, which had earlier resisted American requests for
even limited sanctions against the Soviet Union, urged President Reagan to
respond positively and quickly to the new initiatives emanating from Moscow.
The three major powers, Britain, France and West Germany, were, however,
rather more cautious in their evaluation of the new situation.

Ironically, the one item of disarmament which the two super-powers seemed
to agree actually offered the greatest opportunities was on the very weapons
which Western Europe and NATO had urged to be part of the Western ar-
moury. The Soviet espousal of the Double Zero Option in turn led to the
United States and the Soviet Union seemingly competing with each other
on the speed with which they wanted an agreement on intermediate-range
weapons, while simultaneously discussing strategic weapons reductions. The
Geneva talks were resumed, with both sides increasing the weight and importance of their representatives there. The real possibility of an accord on
intermediate and other weapons was popularly hailed in the West as a great
breakthrough. In Western European military and conservative political circles, there was considerably less jubilation, especially among the NATO high
command. Quite simply, the intermediate talks would, if successful, result
in only a minimal reduction in the arms race: the vast super-power strategic
arsenals would hardly be disturbed. In that sense, the elimination of theatre
weapons had primarily a symbolic value. More to the point, it could leave
Western Europe exposed once again to the massive conventional superiority of the Soviet Union, against which there would only be the American
strategic deterrent. The question of whether the United States would actually
risk a total nuclear war if that were the only way to halt a conventional conflict
on the continent would once again be on the agenda.

The Reagan–Gorbachev talks of the late 1980s culminated in the historic
intermediate missile treaty signed by the two leaders in Washington in 1987,
a treaty which agreed to the removal of intermediate missiles from Europe. A
step towards the world that was to be in the 1990s, it nevertheless highlighted
the fundamental dilemmas of Western Europe. Essential to the strategic thinking of both super-powers, and the prime beneficiary of détente, there was little
that Western Europe could do by itself in intervening between Moscow and
Washington. While a continuation of a harmonious American-Soviet dialogue
was essential for European détente, Western Europe could recall that it was
the seeming success of such a dialogue that brought it to the critical position
of the late 1970s. That did underline that détente and reliance upon American
protection did not necessarily go hand in hand. Western Europe wanted both,
but perhaps it was impossible for it to be satisfied simultaneously on both
fronts.

By the 1980s both the super-powers had discovered that they could not control the flow of events in other parts of the world. In Europe, however, the illusion, and perhaps even the reality, of such control had persisted in greater strength: Western Europe was too inextricably intertwined with both and central to their interests. It had to fit in with their conceptions of each other, with the American concern with what the Soviet Union was doing, and with the Soviet reaction to what the United States was. At the same time, Western Europe had a vested interest in seeking to disentangle European affairs from the wider global competition. One inevitable consequence of this unenviable position was the view that Western Europe should not simply wait upon an American lead, but also actively seek some accommodation with the East on its own initiative: by 1988, for example, the EC had reached an agreement on mutual recognition with COMECON and a series of trade agreements.

However, while the iron curtain may have been penetrated at many points, until the momentous events of 1989 it remained a phrase which symbolised the very real division of Europe into two parts. Behind that division lay the two contrasting world pictures of Washington and Moscow. The rapid course of events in the 1980s, through to the crumbling of the Communist bloc, was a reminder that any détente, to be successful, cannot only be unilateral, and that its success cannot be ensured until the two sides speak the same language. And for Western Europe, it would have to be the same language as it spoke itself. What could be achieved had perhaps already been achieved with, for example, the agreements in the 1970s which seemingly had *de facto* resolved the German issue. One noteworthy point about the 1980s was that the German issue and the status of Berlin were not areas of contention; nor were they used as pressure points to raise the temperature of international competition.

Equally, however, the Western European input into any international dialogue depended on how far it was able to speak with one voice. In the late 1980s, President Reagan might express the desire that the Western alliance would become a partnership of two equal continents, but that merely paraphrased similar statements by most of his predecessors. The dream remained impossible as long as the nuclear and financial weight of the alliance rested in American hands. While Western Europe might desire a commensurate share of nuclear decision-making, it was rarely willing to increase its own economic input into the alliance. No member state approached the 4 per cent annual increase in expenditure which the NATO command had calculated in the early 1980s as being necessary for achieving a viable threshold of conventional defence.

Apart from the questions of expenditure, one of the problems of NATO remained the great diversity of opinion that faced the United States among its allies. The differences of opinion that emerged with more force in the 1970s still persisted. After the Washington treaty, West Germany alarmed its allies by changing tack to press for a similar agreement on short-range weapons, since they inevitably would have the two Germanies as their targets. Some small states, most notably Denmark, still preferred a minimal (according to its critics, a non-existent) role: similar problems, but of a lesser magnitude, occurred with Norway and the Netherlands. The problems of the Mediterranean flank also endured, with only Italy being placid and consistently loyal. Turkey occasionally voiced its resentment at the perceived lack of appreciation of its contribution to the alliance, while Greek unhappiness persisted after its return to the NATO fold in 1980. On the other hand, Spain joined the alliance, but not its command structure, in 1986. In general, the southern members of NATO, except Italy, seemed to regard NATO's main purposes to be the provision of income since, unlike the northern members, they were direct recipients of military aid.

All of this was simply a further illustration that the United States and Western Europe had different perceptions of the world in general and of NATO in particular. That gap might, to some extent, be counterbalanced if Western Europe could agree upon a common defence strategy and policy. Few efforts in that direction had been made in the past; those that were, like EDC, made little progress. However, the breakneck speed with which the United States and the Soviet Union approached détente in the late 1980s brought home with greater force, as did the subsequent Soviet retreat from Eastern Europe – and at least to the major European states – that they might well possess a common defence concern that could be more effectively pursued through organised collaboration. Thus Britain and France resisted suggestions that their nuclear forces be included in the inventory of armaments being drawn up by the super-powers, and began to talk directly with each other about possible closer collaboration; West Germany and France agreed on bilateral military cooperation, including a joint brigade. The EC expressed an interest in a common security policy. And when Britain, France, Belgium and Italy sent naval forces to the Persian Gulf in 1987, West Germany, which argued that it was constitutionally forbidden to deploy its forces outside Europe, agreed to cover the gaps in Europe left by its allies. Above all, the almost forgotten Western European Union was resurrected from the historical archives, to become a forum for discussions on European defence. It is perhaps somewhat ironical that it was the likelihood of a more extensive détente which relaunched the idea of a Europeanisation of Western European defence. WEU had a ready-made structure which could serve as the institutions through which a Western European, as distinct from an Atlantic, defence policy might be reached. This and other issues were to persist into the 1990s as Western Europe faced up to a new life without not just the Communist threat, but also a Soviet Union, and perhaps even without an American presence with its guidance and protection.

CHAPTER 22

ALTERED STATES

We are leaving an unfair but stable world, for a world we hope will be more just, but which will certainly be more unstable.

(*François Mitterrand, 1990*)

The unravelling of the Eastern bloc continued apace after the Communist regimes had been swept from power at the end of 1989. The installation of new democratic governments from the Baltic to the Black Sea brought to an end the Soviet security and economic systems. COMECON collapsed as a functioning entity almost overnight. With Soviet acquiescence, the new governments agreed to the dismantling of the Warsaw Pact by April 1991, with its political dissolution to occur twelve months later, although in the event it was not to be until 1994 that the last Soviet troops left the former Pact territories.

While Western Europe celebrated its seeming victory in the Cold War, its attention remained focused on the East, with a mix of fascination and trepidation at the events occurring in Moscow. Gorbachev's policies may have made him a hero in Western eyes; his domestic popularity, by contrast, had plummeted. He continued to insist that the Soviet Union would remain faithful to Communism, that the party would be the major agency of his desired changes, and that it must remain the dominant organisation once his policies of reconstruction had taken root. Ironically, much of the resistance to *glasnost* and *perestroika* lay within the Communist Party itself. In order to bolster his own authority and capacity to direct change, Gorbachev had the newly elected legislature, the Congress of People's Deputies – the first multi-party assembly elected by open competition in the Soviet Union – appoint him to a restyled presidency in March 1990. The move served to isolate him even further. It was opposed by conservatives who feared it would further weaken Soviet influence or their own prestige and security within the party and state hierarchies. At the same time, neither the presidency nor Gorbachev himself was capable of satisfying the demands and expectations that the reform process had unleashed, since the central organ of change delegated by Gorbachev – the party – was utterly incapable of either supervising radical socioeconomic change or of reforming itself. Gorbachev's relaxation of central authority and control had not only simply fuelled popular pressure for more reform; it had fostered unrest across the numerous national minorities scattered throughout the Soviet Union. Several of the constituent Soviet republics sought extensive autonomy at the least from Moscow. At their head were the three Baltic republics of Estonia, Latvia and Lithuania, whose annexation by the Soviet Union in 1940 had never been recognised by the West: they would be content with nothing less than full independence. Symbolically, the Lithuanian Communists broke with the Soviet party at the end of 1990, strongly condemning past Soviet policies.

Gorbachev, without any allies, was forced into a more and more impossible balancing act between a conservative opposition, whose strength lay within the party, hostile to any change, and radical reformists for whom his erstwhile ally, Boris Yeltsin, had become the leading symbol and spokesman. Under the reform programme, Yeltsin had successfully won election in 1990 as Chairman of the Russian Republic on a platform of radical economic and political reform mixed with Russian nationalism, and the following year he dramatically announced his resignation from the Communist Party and from all Soviet positions at a session of the People's Congress. In 1991 Gorbachev was briefly deposed by a clumsy and abortive hardline coup. While its failure did much to further discredit the party, Gorbachev did not benefit from it. The praise and popularity went to Yeltsin, who had publicly denounced the coup. Gorbachev continued to insist upon the centrality of the party, but was clearly increasingly incapable of directing affairs. The Baltic states withstood his bluff and threats, quickly gaining independence. Their effective and surprisingly peaceful secession marked the beginning of the end. By the end of 1991 Gorbachev occupied an office that had little or no authority. His resignation symbolised the breaking up of the Soviet Union, as the constituent republics, one after another, formally declared their independence and indicated an intention to establish a competitive liberal democracy and a market economy.

The Soviet Union had survived for little more than a year after the meeting of the CSCE in November 1990 where the signatories had, in the Charter of Paris (sometimes called the Charter for a New Europe), declared that 'the era of confrontation and division of Europe has ended', agreeing to work together for the promotion and defence of democracy, human rights and a free market economy. The Charter was formally held to mark the end of the Cold War. This may have brought the curtain down on the Europe created out of the ashes of war in 1945, but what was to take its place was much less certain. There was, in the early 1990s, much talk of pan-European cooperation, and suggestions that a central role could be played by the CSCE. But it was clear by 1991, as the Soviet Union hurtled towards oblivion, that the dominant international organisations would, in their different orbits, be those long-established Western ones – NATO and the EC – which had demonstrated a healthy pedigree and viability. Again, however, what their future roles and outcomes would be were also matters of debate. Security and defence, cooperation and integration would be central themes of the new Europe.

THE NEW SECURITY CONUNDRUM

One of the most common phrases heard in the first euphoric days was the 'peace dividend'. A hangover from the Cold War days, it expressed the belief that if only the defence burden could be reduced though arms control and disarmament, then the money previously spent by governments on security could be more profitably utilised in other policy areas. This was to be a pipe-dream. First, although the Soviet Union may have disappeared, Russia survived as a major power: one could not assume that it would never in the future pose a threat to Western security. In addition, there could well be problems in other parts of the world where the West might need adequate defence to protect its own interests.

By the mid-1990s some of the objectives of the old arms control talks had been achieved. All Western European states had cut back on their defence expenditure. In particular, the United States had begun to scale down its massive European commitment. The dividend, however, did not necessarily appear. Under the new economic regime of fiscal realism that dominated a Western Europe increasingly concerned about excessive and escalating public spending, governments took the opportunity of reducing defence budgets as a way of reducing their overall expenditure. In addition, the closing of military bases – including American installations everywhere and British garrisons in Germany – along with the reduction or cancellation of orders for military equipment, threw some local economies into disarray and drove defence industries into at times desperate cost-cutting measures and intensified competition to sell their products.

The notion of a peace dividend soon disappeared from common parlance, and so did the idea that the only major pan-European organisation, the CSCE, would provide a structure for the new Europe. Its major contribution, perhaps, came at its Paris meeting in November 1990 when the member states formally declared the end of the division of Europe and agreed to establish new structures for settling disputes by peaceful means. The following year the CSCE agreed to set up a permanent headquarters and a more extensive inter-governmental organisation, with the aim of creating an all-European security system. These proposals were formalised in 1992 in the Helsinki Document, which set out a reinforcement of the institutional framework and outlined new bodies that would work for conflict prevention and provide crisis management. In 1994 the CSCE renamed itself the Organisation for Cooperation and Security in Europe (OCSE).

That perhaps was the limit of what the CSCE could do within the new European architecture. Its value admittedly lay in its comprehensive membership linking East with West, especially in having the Soviet Union and, later, Russia, as a member, and it did in the early 1990s play a valuable, but perhaps subordinate, role in phasing out the Cold War. Its weakness was that it was a product of the Cold War, as a forum where all members of the conflicting blocs could meet. The new democratic governments of Eastern Europe no longer saw themselves as being different from the West: indeed, they wanted to be part of the West. Therefore, as far as the human rights aspect of the CSCE was concerned, they would now look to the Council of Europe, where acknowledgement of human rights was the essential criterion for membership. The economic provisions of the CSCE had only ever existed on paper: the new governments soon declared that their long-term aim was to join the Western economic nexus, particularly the EC. And as for security, they saw the West as their security, and wanted guarantees from the West in the event of any possible Soviet or Russian threat: the eastward extension of NATO inevitably therefore came on to the agenda.

Indeed, that issue had already appeared at the end of 1989 with the move towards German reunification. For West Germany, reunification had been an objective ever since 1949. *Ostpolitik* had been a means, not an end; as Helmut Schmidt said in 1977: 'For us in Germany the German question remains open: we are called to achieve the reunification of Germany.' Its possibility re-emerged with the breaking of the Berlin Wall, the subsequent collapse of the DDR regime, and the West German reluctance and constitutional inability to staunch the westward flow of East German citizens into the Federal Republic.

There were, in 1989–90, many opponents of the Communist regime in the DDR who did not wish reunification. The popular mood, however, was strongly in favour, as was the government reaction in the Federal Republic. With a general election due towards the end of 1990, no West German party felt able to resist the siren call of unification. The Kohl government also felt obliged to keep an eye on the Soviet Union and the increasingly difficult situation of Gorbachev. There were concerns in Bonn in 1990 that Gorbachev might not survive and that if he fell, his replacement might try to reassert Soviet power. Hence, there were fears that the window of opportunity offered by the collapse of the DDR regime might close at any time, that West Germany could not afford the luxury of a more long-term perspective, that the choice was between immediate action and the possibility of losing the chance for a very long period of time.

Kohl's policy was laid down within days of the fall of the Berlin Wall in a ten-point programme which outlined a gradual and staged process of unification through a democratisation of the DDR and the establishment of confederal structures between the two states. However, this strategy was almost immediately negated by the Kohl government itself because of its heavy involvement in the campaign in early 1990 for the first multi-party elections in the DDR, and also by its continuing provision of special treatment of Germans from the DDR seeking to settle in the Federal Republic. The rapidity of developments in the DDR and the outcome of the 1990 multi-party election made it clear that reunification was almost unstoppable. The focus of discussion switched to how that could be achieved constitutionally and economically. Monetary union was established in July 1990, with formal unification coming three months later.

Reunification, however, could not be a matter for the two Germanies alone. There were some in the West who were alarmed by the prospect of a new German colossus in Central Europe, and the attitude of the ailing Soviet Union also had to be considered. However, Gorbachev was in a weak bargaining position, and essentially could engage only in damage limitation. The Soviet attitude shifted after a visit to Moscow in February 1990 by Kohl and Genscher, possibly because of a reiterated West German commitment of substantial financial aid for the reconstruction of the Soviet economy. In the same month an international meeting in Canada accepted the notion of the Two Plus Four Talks between the two Germanies and the four major wartime Allies (who would consult with their partners in NATO and other international forums) to deal with the external aspects of reunification, the final agreement on which would be presented to the CSCE for endorsement.

There were two major issues. One was the Western insistence that a re-united Germany must be part of NATO, a demand eventually conceded by the Soviet Union. In return, it was agreed that no NATO forces would be stationed in DDR territory. West Germany also agreed to a transitional period after formal unification, during which Soviet troops would remain in the DDR, with the costs of their continued presence there and of their eventual resettlement in the Soviet Union being borne by the Bonn government. The second issue was the German-Polish border, since the West had never formally accepted the post-1945 Oder–Neisse line. The latter was, however, quickly endorsed, with West Germany formally renouncing any claims to the lands east of the line.

A Treaty on the Final Settlement with Respect to Germany was signed by the Two Plus Four participants in September 1990. It also provided for the staged withdrawal of Soviet forces from DDR territory by 1994, and imposed limits on the size of German armed forces and on the kinds of weapons they could possess. The issue of Berlin was settled a few weeks later in New York when the four wartime Allies signed an agreement that ended their rights and responsibilities in Germany. It was the last act of the Second World War, although the last Allied troops did not leave the city until 1994. The reunited Germany formally came into being in October 1990, less than one year after the world saw the opening of the Berlin Wall; it was, however, less a merger of two independent states and more the absorption of the DDR into an expanded Federal Republic.

The new Germany, with Berlin to be again the capital by 1995 (a date later deferred until 2000), was by far the largest state in Europe, its prominence heightened after the Soviet collapse at the end of 1991. Although the proven democratic record of West Germany over the years muted alarm over reunification, it did not entirely eliminate concern. Reunification raised again the question of what to do with Germany, and people spoke of the choice between a German Europe and a European Germany. The concern intensified debates over European integration and the continent's security.

German reunification advanced the borders of NATO, if not NATO forces, to the Oder–Neisse line. However, countries to the east, like Poland and Hungary, did not see this eastward expansion as a threat. Indeed, their ambition was to join NATO: they did not accept CSCE as an adequate alternative. NATO's major dilemmas were twofold. First, there was the question of how much preparedness and force was necessary in the altered state of Europe, and how this could be reconciled with strong pressures for reductions in national defence budgets. A first reduction was undertaken in the Conventional Forces in Europe treaty of 1990, something which effectively concluded talks originally launched between NATO and the Warsaw Pact, which dealt with the issue of arms surpluses. The vast array of armaments situated along the Central Front was to be wound down, with NATO material being scrapped or transferred to the organisation's poorer southern members.

This issue was part of a broader dilemma. The old Soviet threat had gone, with no clear or predictable challenge immediately observable. Equally, the end of the Cold War had made nonsense of NATO's whole forward defence strategy, the core of which had been the large troop and material concentrations in Germany. It was not, however, only a military rethink that was necessary. The problem of adaptation was more a political problem, a question of how to re-evaluate the goals of the alliance and the basic treaty obligations of its members. For many of the European participants, the attitude of the United States was crucial, for they wished to preserve NATO as an Atlantic alliance. Others thought that the demise of the Soviet Union offered Western Europe the opportunity to develop its own defence strategy and security alliance under, for example, the auspices of the EC: the old idea of taking WEU and making it the security branch of a more integrated EC was back on the table. In addition, NATO had to face up to the desire for membership from Eastern Europe, and the hostility of the Soviet Union and, after 1991, Russia to that very notion.

Whether NATO could or should survive and still have a purpose was based on the presumption of an uncertain world, and that NATO might be usefully engaged to maintain peace in volatile situations outside its designated area of operation, including territories once controlled by the Soviet Union. Despite actions such as the 1991 Gulf War where NATO states were involved as members of a UN task force – where their experience of collaboration within NATO proved to be a valuable asset in logistical and strategic planning – the first real test of its ability to act, and the first real demonstration of the lack of a credible alternative, came in Europe, in the morass of war that engulfed Yugoslavia in 1991. The eruption of conflict began in mid-1991 with the formal secession from the Yugoslav state of Slovenia and Croatia, and the recognition, upon West German insistence that went against the more cautious approach to the impending break-up of Yugoslavia favoured by its partners, of Croatia by the EC.

The subsequent conflict between Croatia and the rump Yugoslavia led by Serbia, and the later three-sided civil and ethnic war that engulfed Bosnia-Hercegovina was initially regarded by the United States as a European problem, and one that should be resolved by the Europeans themselves. The task of brokering a political settlement was taken up by the EC, operating in conjunction with the UN, with some enthusiasm. The experience, however, demonstrated how far Western Europe still had to go before it could speak with a common and authoritative voice in a serious international crisis, and how difficult it was for the EC to direct or monitor a peacekeeping operation. The

Yugoslav and Bosnian imbroglio simply underlined the fact of American pre-dominance. It was the eventual intervention of the United States which gave hope for an end to the Bosnian conflict. In April 1994 a Contact Group was formed to coordinate discussion and strategy on a settlement to the armed conflict. Along with Britain, France and Germany, it directly involved the United States and Russia. It was American efforts which finally forced the warring parties to a territorial settlement in Bosnia-Hercegovina at a peace conference in Dayton, Ohio in November 1995, the honouring of which would be ensured by NATO ground forces. NATO air forces, however, had already been in action since early 1993, enforcing an exclusion zone that banned military flights in Bosnian airspace. The NATO input had been requested by the UN. When NATO fighters shot down Serbian military aircraft in February 1994, it was the first ever combat action undertaken by NATO. More than anything else, the Yugoslavian tragedy demonstrated not just that NATO had a continued value and purpose, but also that the success of these still depended upon the United States remaining at the heart of the alliance.

That value and that purpose were almost certainly not disputed by the new democratic governments of Eastern Europe which, shortly after their inauguration, began to agitate for some kind of formal relationship with, and ultimate membership of, NATO. The Eastern dimension fed into the debates about the future role of the organisation. In May 1991 NATO agreed to a Rapid Reaction Corps, inaugurated the following year and to be fully operational by 1995. The Corps was to be a small rapid deployment force that could be mobilised quickly to intervene in localised disputes outside the traditional NATO area. The logic behind this development was to be applied in Bosnia.

More generally, NATO's aims and objectives were amended in the 1991 Rome Declaration on Peace and Cooperation to take account of the post-Cold War situation in Europe: the document attempted to define the future role of NATO in terms of continent-wide security structures and a partnership with the countries of Eastern Europe. At the same time NATO admitted that Eastern European membership was a possibility, but presumably only in the long term. In reality, NATO's objective seemed to be to delay the question of Eastern European membership, to which Russia was utterly hostile, as long as possible. A first step was taken in 1992 with the formation of the North Atlantic Cooperation Council, a body which would link NATO not only with Eastern European states, but also with the successor states to the Soviet Union, which had come together in a Commonwealth of Independent States (CIS). The Council was intended to provide some security for Eastern Europe and a mechanism for peacekeeping. Little more than a sop, its purpose and value were unclear since it seemed to duplicate and confuse the role of the CSCE. NATO later developed a planned Partnership for Peace agreement, through which the Eastern European states and Russia would individually be linked to the organisation. Most accepted the proposal, but made it clear that they regarded the commitment as a step towards full membership. By 1996 NATO's delaying tactics seemed to be running out of options for a decision on Eastern Europe. The problem facing it was to extend the notion of a European security system that would have NATO as its central element, but would nevertheless be acceptable to a hostile and nervous Russia. This was in part why the West welcomed Russian involvement in the Bosnian peacekeeping operation after 1995. As part of the exercise, a full-ranking Russian general was seconded to NATO headquarters in Belgium where he had direct access to NATO's supreme military commander. While this secondment was useful in coordinating the efforts in the Balkans, its greater significance perhaps was to demonstrate to Russia the essential defensive nature of NATO and its effective levels of interstate cooperation.

One further problem was the relationship between NATO and the ambitions of the EC to develop a common defence and security policy, possibly through a utilisation of WEU, a notion to which France in particular was strongly committed. A possible linkage between Eastern European participation and the notion of a European peacekeeping structure without American leadership was made in 1996 when, after three years of discussion, NATO approved the formation of a multinational military force, probably to be placed under the aegis of WEU, that could be used by European governments. The principle behind the notion of combined joint task forces was to have a kind of mix-and-match force that could be adapted to suit different kinds of challenge without the involvement of American ground troops, though it was agreed that such units would be able to draw upon American support, such as intelligence, communications and airlift potential. It was also made clear that the project offered the possibility of incorporating non-NATO troops, such as those from Eastern Europe, into the mix-and-match structure.

All of these moves represented attempts to provide answers to the reform of NATO, which all members accepted as a necessary consequence of the changing needs that had emerged after the ending of the Cold War. However, while they might introduce a greater degree of flexibility into the organisation, the major questions still had to be resolved. These inevitably related to the eastwards expansion of NATO, strongly urged by Germany, and its future relationship with Russia. They also related to the future role of the United States and the extent to which the latter would stand back from European joint task forces, should these emerge. Equally, while the idea of an EC-directed security policy and force had its supporters in Western Europe, others were adamant that NATO must remain as the ultimate guarantor of security. However, as the drawn-out Bosnian episode demonstrated, Western Europe has a long way to go before it can seriously consider dispensing with a NATO under American leadership.

By contrast to the debates and hesitations over NATO expansion, in non-military matters East and West came together more readily after the shredding of the iron curtain. After 1989 the Council of Europe steadily welcomed more and more Eastern states as members: in 1996 the hitherto unbelievable occurred when Russia joined the organisation. In addition, there was a flourishing of several regional groupings of states, bringing together national and local authorities, that straddled the previous East–West divide: the Donauländer grouping (1990); Black Sea Economic Cooperation (1991); the Council of Baltic

Sea States (1992); the Central European Initiative (1992); the Barents Euro-Arctic Council (1993). None of these, however, while valuable in their own right and objectives, was a substitute for the ultimate political and economic goals of the new Eastern regimes. The EC was their political and economic beacon, just as NATO was their security beacon. There, however, they came up against not just how far their own economies would need to change in order to cope with EC membership, but also the EC's own dreams of a closer union, for which further enlargement would be a distraction, even a danger.

THE ROAD TO MAASTRICHT

By the end of the 1980s the EC was in the throes of its preparations for the launch of the single internal market. The objective of 1992, according to the Commission, was the idea of a 'Europe without frontiers', a concept which in its implications went far beyond a mere economic community. The consensus reached among the member states in the mid-1980s on the virtues of a single market was broken because of a renewed debate over the broader future direction and structure of the EC. Under the strong leadership of Jacques Delors, the Commission utilised to the full its powers under the Single European Act (SEA) to become the most activist Commission in the EC's history. A close confidant of Mitterrand and holding a view of the future that was largely shared by the French president and the West German chancellor, Kohl, Delors used his authority and influence throughout the whole of the EC and beyond the narrow provisions of the SEA to become the most prominent spokesman not just for 1992 but also for what should come after 1992. The objective was to sustain an accelerating programme of integration that would spread beyond the single market to incorporate a major EC reorganisation that would have as its centrepiece further steps towards monetary and political union.

Three initiatives were particularly important in the late 1980s: on EMU, the budget and the Social Charter. In each of these areas the essential argument was between those who wanted a maximisation of integration and full union as quickly as possible – for whom Delors became the principal advocate – and those who desired the economic single market, but little else. The major proponent of the latter viewpoint was the British government of Mrs Thatcher.

The effectiveness of the budgetary decisions taken by the European Council at Fontainebleau in 1984 had proved to be short-lived: within a few years the threat of insolvency seemed to be returning. In 1987 Delors took the initiative in reconstructing a package which proved on the whole to be acceptable to the European Council. Even Britain accepted the principle of the package, restricting its concern to an emphasis upon the need for more effective and binding discipline. Most importantly, the CAP was to be amended so that spending on it would be based upon a more realistic market balance between supply and demand, with any increase in expenditure pegged, at a maximum, to the rate of growth of the EC's own resources. Equally, however, the proposed reforms were linked to the internal market programme, for which the Council accepted that some decisions had to be taken immediately, and it was accepted that the new level of resourcing must also take account of the 'proportionality of contributions in accordance with the relative prosperity of member states'.

One way or another, the budget issue had been a dominating theme of EC discussions and arguments for almost two decades. The decisions taken in 1984, along with the subsequent developments that culminated in the Delors package, did eventually remove the budget from centre-stage. Arguments over resourcing and allocation would continue, at times with as much vehemence as in the past, but after 1987 they were increasingly overshadowed by new questions that arose from the renewed drive towards further integration, questions which divided those who saw 1992 as an end from those who regarded it as almost a second beginning.

One of those new themes was the Social Charter, a proposal for a minimum set of workers' and citizens' rights, which Mrs Thatcher labelled as 'Marxist'. For Delors, the internal market had to be seen to benefit workers as well as businesses. Fundamentally, the Charter was little more than a set of not particularly revolutionary principles, setting out to codify in general terms much of what the EC had already begun to do in the social sector. It referred to living and working conditions, freedom of movement, training and opportunities, sex equality, and health and safety. As such, much of the Social Chapter appeared fairly anodyne, but it was nevertheless strongly rejected by Britain when it came up for European Council approval in 1989, and when the EC eventually discussed a revision of the founding treaties at Maastricht, Britain successfully gained an opt-out from its provisions.

However, the most significant of Delors' initiatives was his return to EMU. Monetary policy had, by and large, been something of a missing element from the SEA, but inevitably the logic of 1992 demanded that it be addressed. Delors took up again the quest for EMU, including those ingredients essential for it to be truly effective – a single central bank and a single European currency – after being requested to consider the problem by the European Council in 1988. His 1989 report saw progress to EMU as a three-stage process, with greater harmonisation, if not inflexibility, of currency movement, within the ERM as the first step. The European Council, despite British objections, agreed that the starting point of the first stage would be in July 1990. The battle seemed to have been won when Mrs Thatcher, against her instincts, was persuaded in October 1990 to take Britain into the ERM.

However, Mrs Thatcher and the British Conservatives never lost their uneasiness about both the speed at which events were occurring and the end goal which seemed to have been accepted by most other European leaders. Her major riposte came in late 1988 in a major speech at Bruges when, though stressing the British commitment to the EC, she concluded her critique with the statement that 'Working more closely together does not require powers to be centralised in Brussels or decisions to be taken by an appointed bureaucracy. . . . We have not successfully rolled back the frontiers of the state in Britain, only to see them recognised at a European level, with a European super-state exercising a new dominance from Brussels.'

Both Delors and Thatcher had legitimate views of Europe. The difference was that one was looking beyond 1992 to some kind of political federation or union, while the other would be content with a more strictly economic internal market flanked by heightened cooperation among the member states on a host of other issues. It was a debate whose roots lay far back in the past, yet because the essential parameters of the debate had shifted further away from intergovernmentalism towards supranationalism through the accumulation of common practices of the past decades, Mrs Thatcher was, if for no other reason, on weaker ground than, for instance, de Gaulle had been twenty years earlier. From Fontainebleau to the SEA events had transpired to give the Commission, backed by much of the European Council, a new momentum. While what the post-1992 world would or should look like might be in dispute, the weight of leadership, especially that of Kohl and Mitterrand, was solidly behind Delors. From the SEA through to the 1991 Maastricht debates on constructing a new and more extensive political framework for the EC, a bruised and usually isolated Britain seemed to be waging a lonely and futile rearguard action against an integrationist juggernaut.

The drive, however, continued. In 1989 the EC leaders agreed upon the establishment of an Intergovernmental Conference (IGC) that would discuss and construct an edifice for monetary union. By the end of 1990 the argument seemed to have been settled. The first EMU stage was in place, Britain had entered the ERM, and the European Council had set the beginning of 1994 as the start of the second EMU phase. Earlier in 1990, moreover, Mitterrand and Kohl, among others, had returned to the attack, proposing political union by 1993, and the IGC on EMU was supplemented by a parallel IGC that would consider a revision of the EC treaties in order to achieve 'the transformation of the Community from an entity mainly based on economic integration and political co-operation into a union of a political nature, including a common foreign and security policy'. The two IGCs would feed into the European Council meeting scheduled to meet in Maastricht at the end of 1991.

Mrs Thatcher's 1981 assertion that there was no separate EC interest had, despite the rhetoric of integration, largely been accurate. However, between 1988 and 1990 the speed of events challenged the Thatcher assertion: to a greater or lesser extent all the member states bar Britain had come round to the view that there was a separate Community interest. The bandwagon of union steadily gained further momentum among the European political elites, and as the EC moved into 1991, outside Britain almost everyone – whether enthusiastically for it or fatalistically resigned to it – seemed to have accepted union as a *fait accompli* and to believe that the European Council meeting in Maastricht would need only to rubber-stamp the transformation of the EC and its founding treaties.

With the forced resignation as premier of Mrs Thatcher in late 1990, all twelve member states seemed at last to be pulling together since the new British prime minister, John Major, declared that his intention was to place Britain 'at the very heart of Europe'. At the same time, external events had transpired to ensure that EC introspection about its future would not be a matter only of internal concern. The EFTA states, alarmed that the internal market might be injurious to their own economies, had entered into intensive economic negotiations with the EC, and in 1989 the two sides began work on a framework for a European Economic Area (EEA), a gigantic free trade area rather than a customs union with a common external tariff, within which the EFTA countries would gain access to the single market, but largely on the EC's terms. Agreement was reached in 1991, with the EEA scheduled to be launched in 1993. When the EEA eventually began to operate, it was, however, a shadow of its original intentions. Of the EFTA states, Switzerland had been obliged to withdraw from the proposed structure when its acceptance was rejected by a popular referendum in December 1992. Of the remainder, all but Iceland had, even before the talks reached their climax, come to the conclusion that while the EEA might meet some of their economic concerns, it could not provide the complete economic answer. Accordingly, Austria, Finland, Norway and Sweden eventually submitted formal applications for EC membership, making the EEA possibly only a temporary arrangement. The EC had also drawn similar conclusions. In 1990 the European Council produced a list of states which it considered to be eligible for accelerated membership, with entry to the EC by 1995. The list was restricted to the EFTA states, and negotiations began fairly soon afterwards. In 1995 EC membership was expanded to fifteen, with the accession of Austria, Finland and Sweden: as a result of yet another negative popular referendum, ratification of membership did not occur in Norway.

The EC and its plans for the 1990s could equally not but be affected by the dramatic collapse of the Communist regimes in Eastern Europe. The consequent reunification of Germany and the aspirations of the new democratic regimes forced the EC to have an eastern policy for almost the first time – and precisely when it would perhaps have preferred not to have to do so. The new regimes wanted not only economic aid for their market reforms, but also an association with, and ultimate membership of, the EC. In short, Eastern Europe posed the same kind of dilemma as EFTA, but on a larger and more complex scale. While it was quite clear that it would be some time before the Eastern economies would reach a position where they could be accommodated within the market-oriented structures of the EC, their ambitions fuelled further the debate over the future of integration between those who thought priority should be given to enlargement, and those who wanted first to push on with a tighter union among the existing members. The latter, however, were in the driving seat, and indeed the events in Eastern Europe simply made them even more detemined to push harder for a political union.

Within this broader context one decisive factor that kept the Maastricht head of steam going was that France and Germany had arrived at a common position by different routes. Ever since 1945 French European policy had been largely driven by the question of how it could control Germany. After 1990 a stronger and united Germany – everyone at the time grossly underestimated the economic drain on German resources of the ex-DDR territories – possibly less reliant on the United States and the EC, and facing a weakened Soviet Union, might, it was feared, choose to operate more independently of its neighbours. For Mitterrand and the French leadership, there seemed to be no alternative but to continue down the integration road, locking Germany so tightly within a political union that its independence of action would be greatly circumscribed. Equally, for Kohl, German reunification had made closer union more imperative. To reassure France and others that the new Germany would remain a good neighbour, he repeated the old arguments that potential dangers could best be avoided if Germany was incorporated into a more integrated European political system.

In any case, events subsequent to the ending of the bipolar world within which the EC had grown up made it possible to believe, for the first time since 1945, that the historical dream of a European union – not just a restricted EC or a Western Europe – could be on the verge of realisation. While it was broadly accepted within the EC that that dream would, even in the best of circumstances, take some considerable time to come to fruition, by 1991 both the personal beliefs of the EC's leading figures and *Realpolitik* had seemingly turned the planned Maastricht session into an odd hybrid of a foregone conclusion and an overwhelming necessity, despite words of warning from Britain and others. It was clear to the leaders who would assemble at Maastricht in December 1991 that their decisions would be scrutinised by and would affect the external world in a way that would not have been thought possible a few years earlier. Even so, the final stretches of the road to Maastricht and what would be found there would not be so obvious as some had expected.

AN EVER CLOSER UNION?

The opening of the 1990s saw the EC well on course towards the single market, with most of the necessary directives approved and in place. The two IGCs opened in December 1990. That on further political integration already had a draft plan on which it could work. Political union would entail consideration of how to reinforce democratic legitimacy in the EC – something that would involve, *inter alia*, strengthening the European Parliament, introducing a common foreign and security policy, and establishing a European citizenship and structure of civil and workers' rights. The IGC on EMU was seemingly less contentious. By the second half of 1991 the finance ministers had more or less completed some additional finishing touches to the 1989 Delors Plan. With the first stage already in position, they agreed that the second stage would commence in 1994, with the final transition to full EMU coming three years later. However, they also insisted that eligibility to participate in the final stage would depend upon a member state meeting strict budgetary, inflation and monetary criteria.

In December 1991 the EC leaders assembled in Maastricht in a mood of high anticipation and tension. Their task was to finalise a treaty framework for a European Union, incorporating political union and EMU, determine a timetable for their implementation, and launch the EC along a new security dimension. Kohl's view was that Maastricht was 'crossing the Rubicon. There is no going back.' Because of the high stakes involved, the theatricals were also explosive, with Britain in particular being intransigent. John Major may have wished to be at the heart of Europe, but his vision still differed markedly from that of most of his counterparts, and the British determination to resist, which at one stage threatened to jeopardise the whole proceedings, enforced several compromises.

Most importantly, British insistence led to the deletion of references to federalism: the finally agreed text described the EU as only 'a new stage in the process of creating an ever closer union among the peoples of Europe', a phrase capable of many interpretations. In addition, Britain's refusal to concede the Social Charter led not only to it opting out of the social dimension, but to the social dimension being appended to the treaty only as a Protocol where implementation would depend upon intergovernmental cooperation across the other member states. However, EC competence was strengthened in several areas, including the environment, education, health and consumer protection. A new Cohesion Fund was established to assist the development of the poorer southern members, and the notion of 'union citizenship' was introduced, but this was not clearly defined in a legal sense. On the other hand, the degree of institutional reform extending the force of supranationalism was limited: the stress was on the notion of subsidiarity, that decisions should be taken at the lowest possible level of institutional authority, with the EC acting only in areas where desired objectives could not be achieved at the national level by the member states. The EU that emerged in the final Treaty on European Union was a structure of three distinct pillars. At its heart lay the old EC, somewhat augmented in authority. Paralleling it were two separate pillars, one for a Common Foreign and Security Policy and the other for Justice and Home Affairs: these two pillars were to be intergovernmental only in character, with no formal role in them for any of the supranational EC institutions. Effectively, then, the European Council became the only body which formally could seek to coordinate the activities of all three pillars. The overall outcome was less than what many had hoped for, but the ability of Delors and others to force the pace had peaked in the run-up to Maastricht. At the summit, the leaders reverted more to the customary convention of compromise, quite often in terms of the lowest possible common denominator. The final result was less clear than many had hoped for.

If caution, confusion and compromise were characteristic of the political arena, the same was not true of EMU, though here, too, utilitarian national considerations also came into play. For the pro-union forces it had perhaps always been EMU that offered a more effective route to integration. The leaders essentially accepted the earlier IGC recommendations on EMU, as regards the timetable, the new central institutions that would be created, and the stringent criteria on economic performance that member states would need to meet in order to be eligible for inclusion in EMU. The European Council would decide by the end of 1996 whether sufficient states (a majority was necessary) had met the criteria, but if no date for the third stage had been set by the end of 1997, EMU would occur come what may in January 1999. Even here, the ranks were also broken. Britain argued for and gained a special Protocol to the treaty allowing it to opt out of the final stage.

After the conclusion of Maastricht, leaders claimed that the package would benefit everyone, with union passing 'the point of no return'. These were brave words which skated over a rather more confused reality. Lacking much of the clarity of the Treaty of Rome, the Maastricht document essentially reflected unanimity at a more generalised level, not least because Britain had successfully opted out of the social dimension, removed all references to federalism, gained provisional exemption from full EMU, and resisted all proposals to give the EP substantial extra powers. But national interests had come to the fore almost everywhere, and the treaty probably satisfied no one. It fell far short of the previous claims made for it, while nevertheless advancing Europe further along the integrationist road than many sceptics would have wished – but it was doubtful whether it had led the EC beyond the Rubicon.

The ink was barely dry on the draft treaty before it ran into problems. A first serious criticism came from an unexpected source when in February 1992 the powerful German Bundesbank, lying at the heart of the EMS, expressed grave reservations about the feasibility of a single currency, and hence of EMU. That was paralleled by widespread public concern in Germany, primarily about the possible demise of the mark. But Kohl was forced to concede that the powerful regional governments within the country should have representation and a say in almost all aspects of EU affairs, and an ultimately unsuccessful legal challenge against the constitutionality of the treaty meant that Germany was the last member state to ratify the treaty, doing so in late 1993. Not unexpectedly, the ratification process also proved to be long and arduous in Britain, mainly because of opposition among Conservative backbenchers. The treaty was finally ratified in July 1993 only when the struggling Major government invoked a vote of confidence to force the rebels to heel.

However, the major challenge to the Maastricht settlement came from Denmark, where the constitution required that any transfer of sovereignty to a supranational authority receive the assent of five-sixths of the parliament or, failing that, a parliamentary majority endorsed by a referendum. Hitherto, Danish governments had avoided unnecessary conflict by divorcing economic cooperation within the EC from any implications of political union. That was no longer possible since, in 1992, union was the issue. Inevitably, the decision went to a referendum where a tense campaign resulted in a narrow rejection of the treaty, producing consternation, disbelief and disarray throughout the EC. The response that the treaty was not renegotiable simply did not sound credible. Unaccustomed to popular revolts, the leaders in a sense were almost forced to make up rules as they went along. The Danish referendum was but one indication that the European electorates were less enthusiastic about the implications of union. A further pointer came in France where the Danish result had prompted Mitterrand to declare a referendum on the treaty. While there were good domestic reasons for the decision – he hoped to boost his own flagging popularity and capitalise on the divisions over Europe within the opposition centre-right parties – it is fair to assume he anticipated a decisive vindication of Maastricht. In the event, a vehement campaign in September 1992 resulted in only a narrow victory of 51 per cent. Mitterrand's claim that the result demonstrated that France was 'still capable of inspiring Europe' sounded rather hollow.

An emergency meeting of the European Council was called in the summer of 1992 to discuss ratification and the concurrent problems afflicting EMU: the leaders were forced to admit that the EC had to become more open and receptive to public opinion. At the same time Denmark listed the various options that were open to it. While accepting that the treaty was not negotiable, with a casuistic flourish the government said it supported 'amending the Treaty without changing it'. By the end of the year the European Council had accepted clauses that would permit Denmark to opt out of currency union, any future common defence policy, any institutionalisation of European citizenship, and several of the judicial arrangements, as well as giving guarantees that the high Danish standards in social and environment policies would not be subverted by harmonisation and convergence. With these promises, the Danish government was able to achieve a small majority in a second referendum, a result, however, which was followed by the most extensive riots experienced by the country since 1945.

It would have been surprising if difficulties in pushing through the political aspects of union had not surfaced – but with the exemptions gained by Denmark joining those ceded to Britain, the treaty became even less revolutionary and cohesive, and when the EU eventually formally came into existence in November 1993, the event was virtually unnoticed, almost as if everyone was too exhausted or embarrassed to acknowledge it. However, given the deals struck at Maastricht, it was EMU which offered a more direct route to union. In tandem with the ratification difficulties, the EC experienced a potentially more devastating monetary crisis.

As part of the preparations for full EMU, the ERM had become more rigid. However, the new inflexibility imposed upon the participants because of the rigid criteria set for EMU qualification paid little regard to national economic strength or to international assessments of the worth of individual currencies. In September 1992 and again the following year massive speculation on the world's money markets afflicted several European currencies. The blanket refusal by the EC to reconsider the ERM central currency rates did not convince the markets. The tide of speculation could not easily be staunched. The worst affected countries, Britain and Italy, were forced to drop out of the ERM and allow their currencies to float downwards, while other states were obliged to devalue. After the second crisis in August 1993 the ERM band restrictions were loosened: despite brave words from the EC, the new bands were so broad that most currencies had in effect returned to the floating world of the 1970s. By the middle of the decade, many observers had also commented that other economic problems, such as sluggish growth and high unemployment, were a consequence of the rigidity of the EMU criteria which, for example, were keeping interest rates very high. Nevertheless, the EU remained committed to EMU by 1999 at the latest, even though there was a question-mark over how many member states would meet the criteria: the consensus of opinion seemed to indicate that there would be very few. By the middle of the decade the EU seemed to have regained some of its confidence about the future, even though the border-free commitment of the Schengen Agreement, embracing the majority of the member states, was still not fully operational. Along with its reiteration of the inevitability of EMU by 1999, it had returned to the theme of further change. A new IGC in 1996 would consider the future political direction of the EU, not only further institutional change, but also the desire of some to create a common defence and security policy.

The Maastricht treaty had referred to the possibility of WEU becoming the future defence arm of the EU. This argument, pushed most forcefully by France, remained a matter of contention, with several members, including Britain, resisting it and insisting that NATO was the proper and most effective defence alliance for Western Europe. Certainly, while the degree of EU collaboration in foreign policy remained high, major crises in the 1990s – before and during the 1991 Gulf War and from 1992 onwards over what to do about the consequences of the disintegration of Yugoslavia – demonstrated that there were limits to effective consensus. These crises seemed to indicate that when a major issue arose which closely affected the EU, it could do little but follow a more minimalist collective line dictated by a mix of political expediency and an awareness of its lack of effective political and military muscle. Given, however, the generally more sensitive nature of national emotions in international affairs, doubts persisted in many quarters as to whether these would be or could be subsumed in a common EU defence policy and structure.

The EU future, therefore, remained uncertain. Debates over enlargement, supranationalism, common policies – all themes revolving around more and what kind of integration – would almost certainly persist as they had done ever since 1950. On the other hand, and despite the innumerable squabbles, the EU has achieved a great deal and membership – even of the sceptical and suspicious Britain – has locked the countries in an ever firmer embrace. Even at the height of their disputes with the rest, the most reluctant governments have not seriously raised the question of withdrawal. Mrs Thatcher, perhaps the most trenchant opponent of supranationalism, nevertheless always stressed, when premier, that Britain would remain an equal and loyal member of the EC. More and more, perhaps, some threads have become too interwoven to be unravelled. The EC, now transformed into the EU, has become a fact of Western European life, and like most lives it has developed through a layering of experiences, a series of accretions – some mutually reinforcing, some tectonically abrasive – which have bound the members ever more closely together. Maastricht and its consequences should perhaps be viewed as just part of an ongoing story, rather than as either a revolution or a failure.

This slower and sometimes wildly erratic movement may perhaps have more accurately reflected and accommodated reality than the grand dramatic gestures which have surfaced at regular intervals, though undoubtedly those have served the purpose of keeping alive the issue of where integration ought to be going. In 1983, Helmut Schmidt described the EC as 'the core of that part of Europe in which we live and which provides the political chance to shape the future of our societies'. As the EU approaches the millennium, the dramatic changes of the previous decade have given it the opportunity of becoming the core of a wider Europe. And no matter what form the EU takes, those states who choose or are obliged to remain outside will not be able to avoid addressing their relationship with it. In the exhilarating moments of 1989 that marked the downfall of the Soviet empire in Eastern Europe, the EC leaders issued a communiqué that stated 'the Community is and must remain a point of reference and influence. It remains the corner-stone of a new European architecture and, in its will to openness, a mooring for future European equilibrium.' Maastricht only partially and indirectly addressed the design of that new European architecture. What is clear is that if the long-term goal of unification is to be achieved, the issues of deepening and widening, of preserving national uniqueness and creating a more integrated EU, must be tackled simultaneously for the EU's central place in the whole European firmament to be confirmed and consolidated.

CHAPTER 23

REQUIESCAT IN PACE:
COLD WAR WESTERN EUROPE

Whoever deals with Europe deals with the world's worst fire hazard. Repeatedly it bursts into flames. . . . After each past conflagration, the structure has been rebuilt substantially as before. (*John Foster Dulles, 1947*)

All the family quarrels have been sorted out. The family is now going to grow and we can think of the future. (*Jacques Delors, 1985*)

The outlook for Europe in the aftermath of the Second World War appeared bleak. In 1947, Sir Winston Churchill, never one for understatement, asked: 'What is Europe now?' His own answer was: 'A rubble heap, a charnel house, a breeding ground of pestilence and hate.' Behind the hyperbole lay a certain grim reality. Two major military conflicts, separated by severe economic depression and political instability and violence, had culminated in a scenario where there were no European victors. To the historic nationalist competition of the past, there would be added the new ideological and political competition of the two victors of the war, the United States and the Soviet Union. In Europe, the new reality was symbolised by the *de facto* partition of the continent, of Germany, and of Berlin. The lines that were drawn after the defeat of Hitler's Reich were to remain very largely undisturbed across almost half a century, even if there were few at the time who appreciated the seemingly permanent nature of the shift that had taken place. If Europe were to continue to be a fire hazard, it would be because of the predilections and imperatives of Soviet and American interests, not because of Europe's own behaviour.

The name of the game in the first postwar years seemed to be survival: survival in the face of looming economic collapse and military threat. Yet the decades since 1945, taken together, were not particularly bad for Western Europe. The turning point came in 1948 and 1949, with the psychological boost of Marshall Aid, the Truman Doctrine and the formation of NATO. The American guarantee which these actions implied helped to set Western Europe firmly on the road to recovery. Within a generation, it tripled its wealth: 1948 marked the beginning of an era of rapid economic growth and unprecedented levels of prosperity that extended across most segments of society. While the decades of uninterrupted economic expansion, and the belief that this would continue in the future, made Western Europe ill-prepared to react swiftly and positively to the economic turmoil of the 1970s and the greater uncertainty of the subsequent two decades, it was nevertheless in a much stronger position to tackle problems of economic transformation and structural adjustment than it had been three decades earlier. Despite the stresses and the seemingly stubborn persistence of both inflation and unemployment after the 1970s, Western Europe did not relive, nor did it expect to relive, the economic collapse of the 1930s. While high levels of unemployment, particularly of long-term unemployment, prevailed through to the 1990s, Western European economies continued to function at a high level, and most individuals saw their standard of living continue to rise. But while Western Europe's wealth may have increased, in global terms its relative position had declined. Between 1945 and 1970, for example, its increase in industrial production was just over one-half of that of the United States and a small fraction of that of Japan. The rise of new and vibrant Asian economies, such as those of Singapore and South Korea, after the 1980s represented a further challenge to its relative position.

The economic transformation of Western Europe after the late 1940s was paralleled by a strengthening of the commitment to liberal democracy. Challenges from the extreme left and the far right were, in general, stifled through lack of support. Terrorism failed in its objective of demonstrating what it argued was the inherent repressive nature of the state, as a prelude to its collapse through revolution. And even though the apparent consensus of the 1950s subsequently weakened under the twin impact of 1968 and 1973, no major political actors or significant groups of people rejected the principles of parliamentary democracy. On the other hand, governments after the 1970s found their freedom of action more circumscribed: a more educated, more articulate, and more demanding electorate, coupled with the accumulated expectations placed upon government, made the management of the state by parties more complex and unpredictable.

Economic growth and domestic political stability stood in stark contrast to the political status of Western Europe in the world. Europe may have remained a central stage for world politics, but the Western European states were no longer leading players. Germany was divided, and the influence of the other two major Western states, Britain and France, diminished rapidly in almost every way. Western Europe was trapped by the Cold War, the meeting place of East and West, and constrained by the boundaries set in 1945. The area lay at the heart of the Cold War, yet that very centrality not only gave rise to tension, but also, in a sense, provided a certain stability. Four decades of super-power tension and competition did not give rise to a European conflict. Soviet hegemony remained confined to the areas that had passed within its sphere by 1948. It honoured its acceptance of a neutral status for Austria, tolerated an independent status for Finland, and after 1949 took no direct action to seek the ejection of the Western Allies from Berlin. Reciprocally, the West also did not transgress the guidelines of 1945. Voices of protest may have been raised about East Germany in 1953, Hungary in 1956, Berlin in 1961, Czechoslovakia in 1968, and Poland in 1981, but the United States remained careful not to move beyond a verbal assault on Soviet hegemony in Eastern Europe. Quite simply, the United States and Western Europe could do nothing about Eastern Europe, short of seeking a resolution through military, and almost certainly nuclear, conflict. Similarly, the Soviet Union's reach towards Western Europe was blocked as long as the area sheltered underneath the American protective umbrella.

Western Europe became, in essence, a client of the United States, a status which, in the late 1940s, the countries themselves had been desperate to have formalised. In the last resort, Western European independence relied upon the American guarantee. Despite the increasing complexity of world politics, bipolarity remained a fact of life in Europe through to the 1990s. It was a condition sealed in the 1960s by the consolidation of a balance of terror between the two super-powers. On the one hand, once the immediate threat of a Soviet invasion appeared to recede, Western Europe became more restive over, and resentful of, American predominance and the American tendency to see Europe as no more than one part of its own global perceptions. On the other hand, despite its expressions of resentment and irritation, Western Europe was unable to dispense with the United States. The Soviet Union consistently demonstrated that it would not tolerate any undermining of its strategic interests in Eastern Europe: any relaxation of East–West relations had definite limits. While the Western European states may have fretted under American leadership, they were not united enough or strong enough to stand up to the Soviet Union alone. In addition, because of American nuclear power, Western Europe did not feel the need to maintain massive defensive forces of its own; it received its security relatively cheaply. Without the ability and/or the will to provide by itself an adequate level of conventional or nuclear defence, Western Europe was not able to offer any substitute for American leadership.

Its unease pushed Western Europe in two contradictory directions. On the one side, it generated a strong desire for an effective détente on and demilitarisation of the continent, and the view that the basic division of Europe should not prevent the development and consolidation of mutually beneficial relationships and links across the divide. Paralleling this yearning, there was a real fear that one day the United States might decouple itself from Europe, leaving the continent to fend for itself. This fear was ever present, irrespective of whether the United States was pursuing a belligerent or accommodating policy towards the Soviet Union. The dilemma of détente versus military protection dogged Western Europe after 1945. It was part of the Cold War, and would remain insoluble as long as the basic conditions of 1945 survived.

Perhaps it was in the defence and security arena that the ending of the Cold War had its greatest impact upon Western Europe. With the collapse of the Soviet Union and its empire, the parameters which had hitherto constrained Western Europe were no longer there. While Russia would survive as a major nuclear power, and one suffering from domestic political and economic instability, the defensive urge had dissipated. The 'peace dividend' demanded a winding down of military preparedness, most importantly of the American commitment. For Western Europe, one issue may not have changed: the need to retain some kind of American presence in Europe. However, it was equally apparent that Western Europe would need to accept a larger share of whatever its future defence needs might be. In turn, this required a more coherent defence and security structure and level of cooperation in addition to, or possibly standing apart from, whatever NATO might become. This was part of the reasoning which led the EC towards seeking a common defence and security policy. On the other hand, the evidence of the early 1990s was not reassuring. Western Europe floundered in its attempts to find a resolution to the conflicts in the former Yugoslavia, and a possible end to the bloodshed in Bosnia emerged only with the eventual involvement of the United States and NATO.

Paralleling American military strength after 1945 was American economic dominance. Western Europe became part of an American-led world trading system, upon which the European countries have become totally dependent. None can shut itself off from the world picture and a world economy which still, perhaps, fundamentally revolves around the United States. Its fulcrum, under both the fixed exchange rate and floating arrangements, was the American dollar. The United States, in effect, became a kind of world bank whose policies and practices have had a direct and intimate effect upon the world economy. As such, it has had important consequences for Western European economies and monetary policies. However, in the 1990s, Western Europe, in the guise of the EC, emerged more visibly as a competitor and rival to the United States, partly as a consequence of its own economic integration and partly because of relative American economic decline. This had little to do with the ending of the Cold War, but the loosening of the defence imperative after 1989 did perhaps increase Western Europe's determination to stand up to the United States in economic affairs. The number of disputes between the two sides of the Atlantic did seem to increase in the 1980s, and the at times bitter arguments within the 1986–94 GATT talks that eventually culminated in the creation of a new World Trade Organisation might well be indicative of a new norm.

Economic development, political change and technological advance have combined to make Western Europe both smaller and more dependent upon both internal cooperation and external factors. It was reduced status and interdependence which persuaded some people that more intense and formal cooperation would be both valuable and necessary. The Western European states became entangled in a web of international and European organisations, some dating back to the 1940s, others of more recent origin. The filaments of the organisational web seem to be forever spreading; they have been supplemented by the increasing permeability of national frontiers through, for example, the multiplication of multinational corporations, the growth of mass tourism and the spread of the electronic media.

Within this complex of cooperation, the EC emerged as the most ambitious attempt at economic and political union. Despite its several failures over the years, the economies of its members have become steadily more interlocked, and the longer the processes of cooperation and harmonisation survive, the greater the degree of interdependence and the more difficult it would be to prise them apart. The penetration of the European fabric by the EC has been sufficiently deep for the member governments and national groups increasingly to define their own interests and to plot their actions upon the supposition of the EC's permanency and the importance of the EC level of decision-making.

On the debit side, the EC remains far from being a political union. The diverse mosaic of the several states, in all their political, historical and cultural variety, has in many ways remained the bedrock of EC life. Indeed, the states and their governments embedded themselves even deeper with the vast expansion of their regulatory and supervisory duties and obligations that together constituted the welfare state. Until the late 1980s the grand rhetoric on political union, on a United States of Europe, that regularly punctuated the EC's existence, was never reflected in practice. Gesture and principle may be important, but what the EC was able to achieve was due at least as much to a slow process of accretion within which national self-interest played a not so small role. The ending of the Cold War was instrumental in obliging the EC to look again at itself, at its external relations, and to consider its future. However, as some of the furore over the Maastricht treaty indicated, the European electorates could no longer be taken for granted. To some extent, the success of the EC since the 1950s was due to skilful elite leadership, in part perhaps because of the parameters imposed upon the continent by the Cold War and the fact that the ultimate guarantee of continued independence was provided by the United States. After 1989 and 1991 a more exposed EC would more obviously stand or fall by its own actions, but as the organisation moved into the closing years of the twentieth century its endeavours were still focused on how to turn itself into a more effective political system, into a new form of 'state'. Yet the logic of union would seem to demand that Europe would need to acquire some of the attributes of a 'nation'. That aspect of political development has been something the EC has rarely addressed, but for the EU to become a genuine union, citizenship would need to mean something more than the simplistic legal formula of Maastricht. That would seem to be at least one of the major challenges to be broached in the years to come.

Nevertheless, notwithstanding these and many other concerns, the member states – even the most recent additions – have become locked more closely in a single organisation. Over the years countries have taken their stands on issues more and more in relation to the EC which, furthermore, became a major repository of liberal parliamentary democracy, shining in particular as a beacon to the new democratic regimes of Eastern Europe after 1989. Every other state and organisation has had increasingly to acknowledge the importance of the EC, and even to seek some form of accommodation with them. In the altered state of the world in the 1990s, even more than ever before, the EC represented the most obvious cornerstone of whatever new architectural design might emerge on the continent.

Two prominent features of the EC's evolution have been the stabilising influence of close Franco-German cooperation and the growing weight of the Federal Republic. If France lost its acknowledged and undisputed leadership of Europe after the mid-1960s, it was only slowly and reluctantly that West Germany appeared willing to take up at least part of the mantle. But with the strongest European economy behind it, and occupying a geopolitical position so crucial to European stability, West Germany was central to EC development. During the confused period after the 1973 oil crisis, West Germany began to assert a political authority more commensurate with its economic status. The shift was undoubtedly facilitated by the freeing of much of its political energy after the agreements reached in the early 1970s with its eastern neighbours: the *Ostpolitik* agreements, in a sense, marked the coming of age of West Germany, confirming as they did, at least for the then foreseeable future, the permanency of post-1945 political boundaries. In turn, the growing importance of West Germany perhaps made it even more imperative for its western neighbours, especially France, to ensure that West Germany was locked into a Western European collaborative world.

For the Federal Republic, its role within an enlarged EC was an important factor in its changing foreign and economic policies. While the realities of the Cold War world and its defence and economic commitments tied West Germany firmly to the United States and Western Europe, its geographical location and historical memories meant that it could not totally deny or accept partition. The search for an accommodating relationship with the DDR and the rest of Eastern Europe was, after 1969, balanced by the emphasis that the success of *Ostpolitik* could be secured only within the context of an integrated EC and an Atlantic alliance. It was these considerations which made West Germany so important to so much of European politics, and a decisive element in whether the continent remained a fire hazard.

The European world may have been turned upside down by the disintegration of the Soviet Union and its empire, yet in this regard the European logic remained unaffected by the events in Eastern Europe. The reunification of Germany, the democratisation of Eastern Europe, and the political and economic desires of the new Eastern regimes simply reconfirmed the centrality of Germany to any integrative and security ventures on the continent: in short, the imperatives of geopolitical and geoeconomic location were underlined further. The question of what to do with Germany, the status of Berlin, the defence of Western Europe, and Western European integration – these were the great challenges of the Cold War decades. It was in the Federal Republic that they met. The future route of the EU and the extent of its possible future enlargement, the future place of NATO in European security, and the new European architecture are challenges that Western Europe will have to face as it moves into the next century. And as with the issues of the Cold War years, it is in Germany that these challenges will converge.

BIBLIOGRAPHY

The following bibiliography is merely selective and is intended to offer the reader a reasonably extensive guide to further reading on the themes and developments reviewed in the preceding chapters. Books published in foreign languages and articles in academic journals, etc. have been excluded. However, the books listed below will provide references to these and many other sources, including official papers and documents.

I. GENERAL HISTORIES AND SURVEYS

Barzini, L. *The Impossible Europeans*, London, Weidenfeld & Nicolson, 1983.

Blacksell, M. *Post-War Europe: A Political Geography*, Folkstone, Dawson, 1977.

Boltho, A., ed. *The European Economy: Growth and Crisis*, Oxford, Oxford University Press, 1982.

De Carmoy, G. and Story, J. *Western Europe in World Affairs*, London, Greenwood, 1986.

Flora, P., ed. *Growth to Limits: The Western European Welfare States since World War II*, Berlin, de Gruyter, 1986, 2 vols.

Frost, G. and McHallam, A., eds. *In Search of Stability: Europe's Unfinished Revolution*, London, Adamantine Press, 1992.

Godson, J., ed. *The Transatlantic Crisis*, London, Alcove Press, 1974.

Grosser, A. *The Western Alliance: European–American Relations since 1945*, London, Macmillan, 1980.

Hettne, B., ed. *Europe: Dimensions of Peace*, London, Zed Books, 1988.

Hine, R.C. *The Political Economy of European Trade*, Brighton, Wheatsheaf, 1985.

Jackson, J.H. *The Postwar Decade*, London, Gollancz, 1961.

Joll, J. *Europe since 1870: An International History*, London, Penguin, 1976.

Kindleberger, C.P. *Europe's Postwar Growth*, Cambridge, Mass., Harvard University Press, 1967.

Landes, D.S., ed. *Western Europe: The Trials of Partnership*, Lexington, Mass., Lexington Books, 1977.

Laqueur, W. *Europe since Hitler*, London, Weidenfeld & Nicolson, 1970.

Lewis, P.G. *Central Europe Since 1945*, London, Longman, 1994.

Mayne, R. *Postwar: The Dawn of Today's Europe*, London, Thames and Hudson, 1983.

Postan, M.M. *An Economic History of Western Europe 1945–1964*, London, Methuen, 1967.

Sampson, A. *The New Europeans*, London, Hodder & Stoughton, 1968.

Van Ham, P. *The EC, Eastern Europe and European Unity: Discord, Collaboration and Integration since 1947*, London, Pinter, 1993.

Vaughan, R. *Twentieth Century Europe*, London, Croom Helm, 1978.

Wallace, W. *The Transformation of Western Europe*, London, Chatham House, 1990.

Williams, A. *The Western European Economy: A Geography of Postwar Developments*, London, Hutchinson, 1987.

Young, J.W. *Cold War Europe 1945–1989*, London, Arnold, 1991.

II. INTERNATIONAL POLITICS AND ORGANISATIONS

1. General histories and surveys

Archer, C. *Organizing Western Europe*, London, Arnold, 1994.

Curtis, M. *Western European Integration*, New York, Harper and Row, 1965.

Degenhardt, H.W. *Treaties and Alliances of the World*, London, Longman, 1986.

Palmer, M. and Lambert, J. *European Unity*, London, Allen & Unwin, 1968.

Rittberger, V., ed. *International Regimes in East–West Politics*, London, Pinter, 1990.

2. International economy

Acheson, A.L.K. and Chant, J.F. *Bretton Woods Revisited*, London, Macmillan, 1972.

Cohen, B.J. *The International Political Economy of Monetary Relations*, Cheltenham, Elgar, 1993.

Dam, K.W. *The GATT: Law and International Economic Organisation*, London, UCP, 1970.

Greenaway, D. *International Trade Policy*, London, Macmillan, 1983.

Jackson, J.H. *Restructuring the GATT System*, London, Pinter, 1990.

Kock, K. *International Trade Policy and the GATT, 1947–1967*, Stockholm, Almqvist & Wiksell, 1969.

Lieber, R.J. *Oil and the Middle East War: Europe in the Energy Crisis*, Cambridge, Mass., Harvard Center for International Affairs, 1976.

McGovern, D. *International Trade Regulation, GATT, the United States and the European Community*, Exeter, Exeter University Press, 1982.

Merlini, C. *Economic Summits and Western Decision-Making*, London, Croom Helm, 1984.

Putnam, R. and Bayne, N. *Hanging Together: Cooperation and Conflict in the Seven-Power Summits*, London/Beverly Hills, Sage, 1987.

Solomon, R. *The International Monetary System, 1945–1976*, New York, Harper and Row, 1977.

Tew, R. *The Evolution of the International Monetary System 1945–1981*, London, Hutchinson, 1981.

3. The Cold War: general histories and surveys

Ambrose, S.E. *Rise to Globalism*, London, Penguin, 1988.

Balfour, M. *The Adversaries: America, Russia and the Open World 1941–62*, London, Routledge, 1962.

Berger, C. *The Korean Knot: A Military–Political History*, Philadelphia, Pennsylvania University Press, 1957.

Bowker, M. and Smith, R., eds. *From Cold War to Collapse*, Cambridge, Cambridge University Press, 1992.

Bown, C. and Mooney, P.J. *Cold War to Détente 1945–85*, London, Heinemann, 1986.

Crockatt, R. and Smith, S., eds. *The Cold War Past and Present*, London, Allen & Unwin, 1987.

Deporte, A.W. *Europe between the Superpowers*, New Haven, Yale University Press, 1986.

Dibb, P. *The Soviet Union: The Incomplete Superpower*, London, Macmillan, 1986.

Dockrill, M. *The Cold War, 1945–63*, London, Routledge, 1988.

Edmonds, R. *Soviet Foreign Policy: The Brezhnev Years*, London, Oxford University Press, 1985.

Gaddis, J.L. *The Long Peace*, New York, Oxford University Press, 1987.

Halle, L.J. *The Cold War as History*, London, Chatto & Windus, 1967.

Halliday, F. *The Making of the Second Cold War*, London, Verso, 1984.

Hoffman, S. *Primacy or World Order: American Foreign Policy since the Cold War*, New York, McGraw-Hill, 1978.

Hoffman, S. *Dead Ends: American Foreign Policy in the New Cold War*, Cambridge, Mass., Ballinger, 1983.

Ingram, K. *A History of the Cold War*, London, Finlayson, 1955.

La Feber, W. *America, Russia and the Cold War, 1945–1971*, New York, Wiley, 1972.

Loth, W. *The Division of the World 1941–1955*, London, Routledge, 1988.

Luard, E., ed. *The Cold War: A Reappraisal*, London, Thames and Hudson, 1964.

Mackintosh, J.M. *Strategy and Tactics of Soviet Foreign Policy*, London, Oxford University Press, 1962.

Nogee, J.L. and Donaldson, R.H. *Soviet Foreign Policy since the Second World War*, New York, Pergamon, 1988.

Pipes, R. *Soviet Strategy in Europe*, London, Macdonald, 1976.

Rees, D. *Korea: The Limited War*, London, Macmillan, 1964.

Rees, D. *The Age of Containment*, London, Macmillan, 1967.

Seaburg, P. *The Rise and Decline of the Cold War*, New York, Basic Books, 1967.

Smith, J. *The Cold War 1945–1965*, Oxford, Blackwell, 1989.

Spanier, J. *American Foreign Policy since the Second World War*, New York, Praeger, 1985.

Terry, S.M., ed. *Soviet Policy in Eastern Europe*, New Haven, Yale University Press, 1984.

Ulam, A.B. *The Rivals: American and Russia since World War II*, New York, Viking, 1971.

Weisberger, B.A. *Cold War, Cold Peace*, New York, American Heritage, 1984.

3.1. Origins

Clemens, D.S. *Yalta*, New York, Oxford University Press, 1970.

Davis, L.E. *The Cold War Begins*, Princeton, Princeton University Press, 1974.

Edmonds, R. *The Big Three*, London, Penguin, 1991.

Elliott, M. *Pawns of Yalta*, Urbana, University of Illinois Press, 1982.

Feis, H. *Between Peace and War, the Potsdam Conference*, Princeton, Princeton University Press, 1960.

Feis, H. *From Trust to Terror: The Onset of the Cold War 1945–1950*, New York, Norton, 1970.

Gaddis, J. *The United States and the Origins of the Cold War 1941–1947*, New York, Columbia University Press, 1972.

McNeill, W.H. *America, Britain and Russia: Their Co-operation and Conflict, 1941–1946*, London, Oxford Univerity Press, 1953.

Thomas, H. *Armed Truce*, London, Hamilton, 1986.

Yergin, D. *Shattered Peace*, London, Deutsch, 1978.

Young, J.W. *France, the Cold War and the Western Alliance 1944–49*, London, Pinter, 1990.

3.2. The German question

Backer, J.H. *The Decision to Divide Germany*, Durham, NC, Duke University Press, 1978.

Calleo, D. *The German Problem Reconsidered*, London, Cambridge University Press, 1978.

Catudal, H.M. *The Diplomacy of the Quadripartite Agreement on Berlin*, Berlin, Berlin-Verlag, 1978.

Clay, L.D. *Decision in Germany*, London, Heinemann, 1950.

Conlan, W.H. *Berlin: Beset and Bedevilled*, New York, Fountainhead Press, 1963.

Davison, W.P. *The Berlin Blockade*, Princeton, Princeton University Press, 1958.

Fritsch-Bournazel, R. *Europe and German Reunification*, Oxford, Berg, 1992.

Galante, P. and Miller, P. *The Berlin Wall*, New York, Doubleday, 1965.

Gednin, J. *The Hidden Hand: Gorbachev and the Collapse of East Germany*, Washington DC, American Enterprise Institute, 1992.

Gimbel, J. *The American Occupation of Germany*, Stanford, Stanford University Press, 1968.

Golay, J. *The Founding of the Federal Republic of Germany*, Chicago, University of Chicago Press, 1958.

Hahn, W. *Between Westpolitik and Ostpolitik*, London, Sage, 1975.

Hämäläinen, P.K., ed. *Uniting Germany*, Aldershot, Dartmouth, 1994.

Hancock, M.D. and Welsh, H.A., eds. *German Unification*, Boulder, Westview, 1994.

Hendry, I.D. and Wood, M.C. *The Legal Status of Berlin*, Cambridge, Grotius, 1987.

Kurz, H.D., ed. *United Germany and the New Europe*, Cheltenham, Elgar, 1993.

Larrabee, F.S., ed. *The Two German States and European Security*, London, Macmillan, 1989.

Merkl, P.H. *The Origins of the West German Republic*, New York, Oxford University Press, 1963.

Minnerup, G. *The German Question after the Cold War*, London, Pinter, 1993.

Robson, C.B. *Berlin: Pivot of German Destiny*, Chapel Hill, University of North Carolina Press, 1960.

Smith, J.E. *The Defense of Berlin*, Baltimore, Johns Hopkins University Press, 1963.

Sowden, J.K. *The German Question 1945–1973*, Bradford, Bradford University Press, 1975.

Speier, H. *Divided Berlin*, New York, Praeger, 1961.

Stent, A. *From Embargo to Ostpolitik*, Cambridge, Cambridge University Press, 1981.

Tusa, A. and Tusa, J. *The Berlin Blockade*, London, Hodder & Stoughton, 1988.

Willis, F.R. *The French in Germany 1945–1949*, Stanford, Stanford University Press, 1955.

Windsor, P. *City on Leave: A History of Berlin 1945–1962*, London, Chatto & Windus, 1963.

Zink, H. *The United States in Germany*, Princeton, Princeton University Press, 1957.

3.3. Détente

Ashton, S.R. *In Search of Détente*, London, Macmillan, 1989.

Steibel, G. *Détente: Promises and Pitfalls*, New York, Crane, Russak, 1975.

Stevenson, R.W. *The Rise and Fall of Détente*, London, Macmillan, 1985.

Van Oudenaren, J. *Détente in Europe*, Durham, NC, Duke University Press, 1991.

3.4. Conference on Security and Cooperation in Europe (CSCE)

Freeman, J. *Security and the CSCE Process*, London, Macmillan, 1991.

Mastny, V. *The Helsinki Process and the Reintegration of Europe*, London, Pinter, 1992.

Möttölä, K., ed. *Ten Years After Helsinki: The Making of the European Security Region*, Boulder, Westview, 1986.

Sizoo, J. and Jurrjens, R. *CSCE Decision-Making*, The Hague, Nijhoff, 1984.

3.5. End

Armstrong, D. and Goldstein, E., eds. *The End of the Cold War*, London, Cass, 1991.

Buzan, B., Kelstrup, M., Lemaitre, P., Tromer, E. and Waever, O. *The European Security Order Recast*, London, Pinter, 1990.

Cox, M., ed. *Beyond the Cold War*, Lanham, Md, University Press of America, 1990.

Hogan, M.J., ed. *The End of the Cold War*, Cambridge, Cambridge University Press, 1992.

Jackson, R.J., ed. *Europe in Transition: The Management of Security after the Cold War*, London, Adamantine Press, 1992.

Ullman, R.H. *Securing Europe*, London, Adamantine Press, 1991.

Zeman, Z.A.B. *The Making and Breaking of Communist Eastern Europe*, Oxford, Clarendon, 1991.

4. NATO: general histories and surveys

Alford, J. and Hunt, K, eds. *Europe in the Western Alliance*, London, Macmillan, 1988.

Baylis, J. *Anglo-American Defence Relationships, 1939–1984*, London, Macmillan, 1984.

Burrows, P. and Edwards, G. *The Defence of Western Europe*, London, Butterworth, 1982.

Chipman, J. *NATO's Southern Allies: Internal and External Challenges*, London, Routledge, 1988.

Cimbala, S.J. *NATO Strategies and Nuclear Weapons*, London, Pinter, 1989.

Cleveland, H. *NATO: The Transatlantic Bargain*, New York, Harper and Row, 1970.

Flynn, G., ed. *The Internal Fabric of Western Security*, London, Croom Helm, 1981.

Flynn, G., ed. *NATO's Northern Allies*, London, Croom Helm, 1985.

Freedman, L., ed. *The Troubled Alliance*, London, Heinemann, 1983.

Louis, W.R. and Bull, H., eds. *The Special Relationship: Anglo-American Relations since 1945*, Oxford, Clarendon, 1989.

Osgood, R. *NATO: The Entangling Alliance*, Chicago, University of Chicago Press, 1962.

Park, W. *Defending the West: A History of NATO*, Brighton, Wheatsheaf, 1986.

Serfaty, S. *Fading Partnership: America and Europe after 30 Years*, New York, Praeger, 1979.

Smith, M. *Western Europe and the United States: The Uncertain Alliance*, London, Allen & Unwin, 1984.

Stromseth, J.E. *The Origins of Flexible Response*, London, Macmillan, 1988.

4.1. Formation and early years

Acheson, D.G. *Present at the Creation*, New York, Signet, 1970.

Cook, D. *Forging the Alliance, NATO 1945 to 1950*, London, Secker and Warburg, 1989.

De Staercke, A., ed. *NATO's Anxious Birth*, London, Hurst, 1985.

Henderson, N. *The Birth of NATO*, London, Weidenfeld & Nicolson, 1982.

Ireland, T.P. *Creating the Entangling Alliance*, London, Aldwych, 1981.

Kaplan, L.S. *The United States and NATO: The Formative Years*, Lexington, Ky, University of Kentucky Press, 1984.

Risto, O., ed. *Western Security: The Formative Years*, Oslo, Universitetsforlaget, 1985.

Smith, J., ed. *The Origins of NATO*, Exeter, Exeter University Press, 1990.

4.2. Future developments

Peterson, J. *Europe and America in the 1990s*, Cheltenham, Elgar, 1993.

Wyllie, J.H. *European Security in the New Political Environment*, London, Longman, 1995.

5. Decolonisation

Dalloz, J. *The Indo-China War*, Dublin, Gill & Macmillan, 1990.

Darwin, J. *Britain and Decolonialisation*, London, Macmillan, 1988.

Epstein, L.D. *British Politics in the Suez Crisis*, London, Pall Mall, 1964.

Holland, R.F. *European Decolonisation*, London, Macmillan, 1985.

Pickles, D. *Algeria and France*, London, Methuen, 1963.

Thomas, H. *The Suez Affair*, London, Weidenfeld & Nicolson, 1967.

III. EUROPEAN INTEGRATION

1. Integration before 1957

1.1. General reviews and histories

Arter, D. *The Politics of European Integration in the Twentieth Century*, Aldershot, Dartmouth, 1993.

Beloff, M. *The United States and the Unity of Europe*, New York, Random House, 1963.

Brinkley, D. and Hackett, C., eds. *Jean Monnet: The Path to European Unity*, London, Macmillan, 1991.

Lindberg, L. *The Political Dynamics of European Economic Integration*, Stanford, Stanford University Press, 1963.

Monnet, J. *Memoirs*, London, Collins, 1978.

Schmitt, H.A. *The Path to European Union*, Baton Rouge, Louisiana State University Press, 1962.

Stirk, P.M.R. and Willis, D., eds. *Shaping Postwar Europe*, London, Pinter, 1991.

Urwin, D.W. *The Community of Europe*, London, Longman, 1995.

Vaughan, R. *Post-War Integration in Europe*, London, Edward Arnold, 1976.

Zurcher, A.J. *The Struggle to Unite Europe 1940–1958*, New York, New York University Press, 1958.

1.2. Resistance movements

Delzell, C.F. *Mussolini's Enemies: The Italian Anti-Fascist Resistance*, Princeton, Princeton University Press, 1961.

Hawes, S. and White, R., eds. *Resistance in Europe 1939–1945*, London, Penguin, 1976.

Heydecker, J.J. and Leeb, J. *The Nuremberg Trials*, Westport, Greenwood, 1975.

Smith, M.L. and Stirk, P.M.R., eds. *Making The New Europe*, London, Pinter, 1990.

Wilkinson, J.D. *The Intellectual Resistance in Europe*, Cambridge, Mass., Harvard University Press, 1981.

1.3. Benelux

De Vries, J. *Benelux, 1920–1970*, London, Fontana, 1975.

Meade, J.E. *Negotiations for Benelux*, Princeton, Princeton Studies in International Finance, 1957.

Riley, R.C. and Ashworth, G.J. *Benelux: An Economic Geography*, London: Chatto & Windus, 1975.

1.4. Marshall Plan and OEEC

Carew, A. *Labour under the Marshall Plan*, Manchester, Manchester University Press, 1987.

Diebold, W. *Trade and Payments in Western Europe*, New York, Council on Foreign Relations, 1952.

Gimbel, J. *The Origins of the Marshall Plan*, Stanford, Stanford University Press, 1976.

Hoffman, S. and Maier, C. *The Marshall Plan*, Boulder, Westview, 1985.

Hogan, M.J. *The Marshall Plan*, London, Cambridge University Press, 1987.

Milward, A.W. *The Reconstruction of Western Europe 1945–51*, London, Methuen, 1984.

Price, H.B. *The Marshall Plan and its Meaning*, Ithaca, Cornell University Press, 1955.

Wexler, I. *The Marshall Plan Revisited*, Westport, Greenwood, 1983.

1.5. Council of Europe

Beddard, R. *Human Rights and Europe*, London, Sweet & Maxwell, 1973.

Haas, E.B. *Consensus Formation in the Council of Europe*, Berkeley/Los Angeles, University of California Press, 1960.

Hurd, V.D. *The Council of Europe*, New York, Manhattan Press, 1958.

Robertson, A.H. *The Council of Europe*, London, Stevens, 1961.

1.6. From Schuman Plan to EEC

Aron, R. and Lerner, D. *France Defeats EDC*, New York, Praeger, 1957.

Diebold, W. *The Schuman Plan*, New York, Praeger, 1959.

Furniss, E.S. *France: Troubled Ally*, New York, Doubleday, 1960.

Fursdon, E. *The European Defence Community*, London, St Martin's Press, 1980.

Haas, E.B. *The Uniting of Europe: Political, Social and Economic Forces 1950–1957*, Stanford, Stanford University Press, 1968.

Lister, L. *Europe's Coal and Steel Community*, New York, Twentieth Century Fund, 1960.

Mason, H.L. *The European Coal and Steel Community*, The Hague, Nijhoff, 1955.

McGeehan, R. *The German Rearmament Question*, Urbana, University of Illinois Press, 1971.

Milward, A.S., Brennan, C. and Romero, F. *The European Rescue of the Nation-State*, London, Routledge, 1992.

Spierenburg, D. and Poidevin, R. *The History of the High Authority of the European Coal and Steel Community*, London, Weidenfeld & Nicolson, 1994.

2. The European Communities

2.1. General histories

Duignan, P. and Gann, L.H. *The United States and the New Europe 1945–1993*, Oxford, Blackwell, 1994.

Pryce, R., ed. *The Dynamics of European Union*, London, Croom Helm, 1987.

Urwin, D.W. *The Community of Europe*, London, Longman, 1995.

Weigall, D. and Stirk, P., eds. *The Origins and Development of the European Community*, Leicester, Leicester University Press, 1992.

2.2. General studies

Barbour, P., ed. *The European Union Handbook*, London, Fitzroy Dearborn, 1996.

Butler, R. *Europe: More Than a Continent*, London, Heinemann, 1986.

Church, C.H. and Phinnemore, D. *European Union and European Community*, Hemel Hempstead, Harvester Wheatsheaf, 1994.

Dinan, D. *Ever Closer Union?*, London, Macmillan, 1994.

Lintner, V. and Mazey, S. *The European Community: Economic and Political Aspects*, London, McGraw-Hill, 1991.

Lodge, J., ed. *The European Community and the Challenge of the Future*, London, Pinter, 1993.

Nicoll, W. and Salmon, T. *Understanding the New European Community*, London, Philip Allan, 1994.

Nugent, N. *The Government and Politics of the European Union*, London, Macmillan, 1994.

Serfaty, S. *Understanding Europe: The Politics of Unity*, London, Pinter, 1992.

Tugendhat, C. *Making Sense of Europe*, London, Penguin, 1986.

Williams, A.M. *The European Community*, Oxford, Blackwell, 1991.

2.3. The early years

Beloff, N. *The General Says No*, London, Penguin, 1963.

Bodenheimer, S. *Political Union: A Microcosm of European Politics 1960–1966*, Leiden, Sijthoff, 1967.

Camps, M. *Britain and the European Community 1955–63*, Princeton, Princeton University Press, 1964.

Camps, M. *What Kind of Europe?*, London, Chatham House, 1965.

Camps, M. *European Unification in the Sixties: From the Veto to the Crisis*, New York, McGraw-Hill, 1966.

Hallstein, W. *United Europe: Challenge and Opportunity*, London, Oxford University Press, 1962.

Hallstein, W. *Europe in the Making*, London, Allen & Unwin, 1972.

Lindberg, L. and Scheingold, S. *Europe's Would-be Polity*, Englewood Cliffs, Prentice-Hall, 1970.

Morgan, R. *European Integration since 1955*, London, Batsford, 1972.

Newhouse, J. *Collision in Brussels: The Common Market Crisis of 30 June 1965*, London, Faber, 1967.

Silj, A. *Europe's Political Puzzle: A Study of the Fouchet Negotiations and the 1963 Veto*, Cambridge, Mass., Harvard University Press, 1967.

Willis, F.R. *France, Germany and the New Europe 1945–1967*, London, Oxford University Press, 1968.

2.4. Enlargement

Allen, H. *Norway and Europe in the 1970s*, Oslo, Universitetsforlaget, 1979.

Kitzinger, U.W. *Diplomacy and Persuasion: How Britain Joined the Common Market*, London, Thames and Hudson, 1973.

Nicolson, F. and East, R. *From the Six to the Twelve: The Enlargement of the European Communities*, London, Longman, 1987.

Pinder, J. *The European Community and Eastern Europe*, London, Chatham House, 1991.

Schonfield, A. *Europe: Journey to an Unknown Destination*, London, Penguin, 1973.

Seers, D. and Viatsos, C., eds. *The Second Enlargement of the EEC*, London, Macmillan, 1982.

Tsoukalis, L. *The European Community and its Mediterranean Enlargement*, London, Allen & Unwin, 1981.

Van Ham, P. *The EC, Eastern Europe and European Unity*, London, Pinter, 1993.

2.5. Institutions

Brown, L.N. and Jacobs, F.G. *The Court of Justice of the European Communities*, London, Sweet & Maxwell, 1989.

Bulmer, S. and Wessels, W. *The European Council*, London, Macmillan, 1987.

Fitzmaurice, J. *The European Parliament*, Farnborough, Saxon House, 1978.

Jacobs, F. and Corbett, R. *The European Parliament*, London, Longman, 1990.

Kirchner, E.J. *Decision Making in the European Community: The Council Presidency and European Integration*, Manchester, Manchester University Press, 1992.

Lasok, K.P.E. *The European Court of Justice*, London, Butterworths, 1993.

Morgan, A. *From Summit to Council*, London, Chatham House, 1976.

O'Nuallain, C., ed. *The Presidency of the European Council of Ministers*, London, Croom Helm, 1985.

Robinson, A. and Webb A. *The EP in the EC Policy Process*, London, PSI, 1985.

2.6. Policies

Allen, D., Rummel, R. and Wessels, W. eds. *European Political Cooperation*, London, Butterworths, 1982.

Cecchini, P., Catinat, M. and Jacquemin, A. *The European Challenge: The Benefits of a Single Market*, Brussels, European Commission, 1987.

Coffey, P. *The European Monetary System*, The Hague, Nijhoff, 1984.

Fennell, R. *The Common Agricultural Policy of the Community*, London, Granada, 1988.

George, S. *Politics and Policy in the European Community*, Oxford, Oxford University Press, 1991.

Harrop, J. *The Political Economy of Integration in the European Community*, Cheltenham, Elgar, 1992.

Hill, C., ed. *National Foreign Policies and European Political Cooperation*, London, Allen & Unwin, 1983.

Ludlow, P. *The Making of the European Monetary System*, London, Butterworths, 1982.

Kruse, D.C. *Monetary Integration in Western Europe*, London, Butterworths, 1980.

Nuttall, S.J. *European Political Co-operation*, Oxford, Clarendon, 1992.

Sherman, H., ed. *Monetary Implications of the 1992 Process*, London, Pinter, 1990.

Tsoukalis, L. *The New European Economy: The Politics and Economics of Integration*, Oxford, Oxford University Press, 1991.

Wallace, H., Wallace, W. and Webb, C., eds. *Policy-Making in the European Community*, Chichester, Wiley, 1989.

2.7. Relations with member states

Bulmer, S. and Paterson, W.E. *The Federal Republic of Germany and the European Community*, London, Allen & Unwin, 1987.

Bulmer, S., George, S. and Scott, A., eds. *The United Kingdom and EC Membership Evaluated*, London, Pinter, 1992.

George, S. *An Awkward Partner, Britain in the European Community*, Oxford, Oxford University Press, 1990.

George, S. *Britain and European Integration since 1945*, Oxford, Blackwell, 1991.

Morgan, R. and Bray, C., eds. *Partners and Rivals in Western Europe: Britain, France and Germany*, Aldershot, Gower, 1986.

Simonian, H. *The Privileged Partnership: Franco-German Relations in the European Community 1969–1984*, Oxford, Clarendon, 1985.

Wallace, W., ed. *Britain in Europe*, London, Heinemann, 1980.

Willis, F.R. *Italy Chooses Europe*, Oxford, Oxford University Press, 1971.

3. EFTA

Benoit, E. *Europe at Sixes and Sevens*, New York, Columbia University Press, 1961.

Corbet, H. and Robertson, D., eds. *Europe's Free Trade Experiment*, Oxford, Oxford University Press, 1970.

Jamar, J. and Wallace, H., eds. *EEC–EFTA: More Than Just Good Friends?*, Bruges, Catherine Press, 1988.

Meyer, F.V. *The European Free Trade Association*, New York, Praeger, 1960.

Pedersen, T. *The Wider Western Europe*, London, RIIA, 1988.

Wallace, H. *The Wider Western Europe: Reshaping the EC–EFTA Relationship*, London, Pinter, 1992.

4. Nordic cooperation

Anderson, S.V. *The Nordic Council*, Seattle, University of Washington Press, 1967.

Archer, C., ed. *Scandinavia and European Integration*, Aberdeen, Aberdeen University Press, 1973.

Friis, H., ed. *Scandinavia between East and West*, Ithaca, Cornell University Press, 1950.

Haskel, B. *The Scandinavian Option*, Oslo, Universitetsforlaget, 1976.

Miljan, T. *The Reluctant Europeans*, London, Hurst, 1977.

Solem, E. *The Nordic Council and Scandinavian Integration*, New York, Praeger, 1977.

Sundelius, B. *Managing Transnationalism in Northern Europe*, Boulder, Westview, 1978.

Turner, B. and Nordqvist, G. *The Other European Community*, London, Weidenfeld & Nicolson, 1982.

Wendt, F. *Cooperation in the Nordic Countries*, Stockholm, Almqvist & Wiksell, 1981.

IV. NATIONAL HISTORIES AND POLITICS

1. Comparative and general

Cheles, L. *et al.*, eds. *The Far Right in Western and Eastern Europe*, London, Longman, 1995.

Cox, A., ed. *Politics, Policy and the European Recession*, London, Macmillan, 1982.

Dahl, R.A., ed. *Political Oppositions in Western Democracies*, New Haven, Yale University Press, 1966.

Gillespie, R. and Paterson, W.E., eds. *Rethinking Social Democracy in Western Europe*, London, Cass, 1993.

Gutteridge, W., ed. *The New Terrorism*, London, Mansell, 1986.

Hanley, D.L., ed. *Christian Democracy in Europe*, London, Pinter, 1993.

Ionescu, G. *Centripetal Politics*, London, Hart-Davis, 1975.

Irving, R.E.M. *The Christian Democratic Parties of Western Europe*, London, Allen & Unwin, 1979.

Kaltefleiter, W. and Pfalzgraff, R.L., eds. *The Peace Movements in Europe and the United States*, London, Croom Helm, 1985.

Kindersley, R., ed. *In Search of Eurocommunism*, London, Macmillan, 1981.

Kolinsky, E., ed. *Opposition in Western Europe*, London, Croom Helm, 1987.

Kolinsky, M. and Paterson, W.E., eds. *Social and Political Movements in Western Europe*, London, Croom Helm, 1976.

Krejci, J. and Velimsky, V. *Ethnic and Political Nations in Europe*, London, Croom Helm, 1981.

Lijphart, A. *Democracy in Plural Societies*, New Haven, Yale University Press, 1978.

Lodge, J., ed. *The Threat of Terrorism*, Brighton, Wheatsheaf, 1988.

Machin, H., ed. *National Communism in Western Europe*, London, Methuen, 1983.

McInnes, N. *The Communist Parties of Western Europe*, London, Oxford University Press, 1975.

O'Ballance, E. *Terrorism in the 1980s*, London, Arms and Armour Press, 1989.

Padgett, S. and Paterson, W.E. *A History of Social Democracy in Postwar Europe*, London, Longman, 1991.

Pfalzgraff, R.L. and Dougherty, J.E., eds. *Shattering Europe's Defense Consensus*, New York, Pergamon, 1985.

Rochon, T.R. *Mobilizing for Peace: The Antinuclear Movements in Western Europe*, Princeton, Princeton University Press, 1988.

Rose, C. *Campaigns against Western Defence: NATO's Adversaries and Critics*, London, Macmillan, 1985.

Urwin, D.W. and Paterson, W.E., eds. *Politics in Western Europe Today*, London, Longman, 1990.

Watson, M., ed. *Contemporary Minority Nationalism*, London, Routledge, 1990.

Wolinetz, S.B., ed. *Parties and Party Systems in Liberal Democracies*, London, Routledge, 1988.

2. Austria

Bader, W. *Austria between East and West 1945–55*, Stanford, Stanford University Press, 1966.

Cronin, A.J. *Great Power Politics and the Struggle over Austria 1945–55*, Ithaca, Cornell University Press, 1986.

Sully, M.A. *A Contemporary History of Austria*, London, Routledge, 1990.

Whitnah, D.R. and Erickson, E.L. *The American Occupation of Austria*, London, Greenwood, 1985.

3. Britain

Bartlett, C.J. *A History of Postwar Britain 1945–1974*, London, Longman, 1977.

Beer, S.H. *Britain Against Itself*, New York, Norton, 1982.

Calvocoressi, P. *The British Experience, 1945–1975*, London, Bodley Head, 1978.

Gamble, A. *Britain in Decline*, London, Macmillan, 1990.

Hennessy, P. *Never Again: Britain 1945–1951*, London, Vintage, 1993.

Hennessy, P. and Seldon, A., eds. *Ruling Performance: British Governments from Attlee to Thatcher*, Oxford, Blackwell, 1987.

Kavanagh, D. *Thatcherism and British Politics*, Oxford, Oxford University Press, 1990.

Kavanagh, D. and Morris, P. *Consensus Politics from Attlee to Thatcher*, Oxford, Blackwell, 1989.

Layton-Henry, Z.A. *The Politics of Race in Britain*, London, Allen & Unwin, 1984.

McGarry, J. and O'Leary, B. *Explaining Northern Ireland*, Oxford, Blackwell, 1995.

Morgan, K.O. *Labour in Power, 1945–51*, Oxford, Oxford University Press, 1984.

Nairn, T. *The Break-Up of Britain*, London, New Left Books, 1981.

Pelling, H. *The Labour Governments, 1945–51*, London, Macmillan, 1984.

Rose, R. *Governing without Consensus*, London, Faber, 1971.

Sissons, M. and French, P., eds. *Age of Austerity*, London, Hodder & Stoughton, 1963.

Smith, D. *The Rise and Fall of Monetarism*, London, Penguin, 1987.

Stafford, G.B. *The End of Economic Growth?: Growth and Decline in the U.K. since 1945*, Oxford, Robertson, 1981.

4. France

Ambler, J.S. *The French Army in Politics*, Columbus, Ohio State University Press, 1966.

Ardagh, J. *France Today*, London, Penguin, 1988.

Avril, P. *Politics in France*, London, Penguin, 1969.

Charlot, J. *The Gaullist Phenomenon*, London, Allen & Unwin, 1971.

Crawley, A. *De Gaulle*, London, Collins, 1969.

Crozier, B. *De Gaulle: The Statesman*, London, Eyre Methuen, 1973.

Frears, J.F. *France in the Giscard Presidency*, London, Allen & Unwin, 1981.

Graham, B.D. *The French Socialists and Tripartism 1944–1947*, London, Weidenfeld & Nicolson, 1965.

Hanley, D.L. and Kerr, A.P. *May '68: Coming of Age*, London, Macmillan, 1989.

Hanley, D.L., Kerr, A.P. and Waites, N.H. *Contemporary France: Politics and Society since 1945*, London, Routledge, 1984.

Hartley, A., *Gaullism*, London, Routledge & Kegan Paul, 1972.

Johnson, R.W. *The Long March of the French Left*, London, Macmillan, 1981.

Kolodziej, E. *French International Policy under de Gaulle and Pompidou*, Ithaca, Cornell University Press, 1974.

Larkin, M. *France since the Popular Front*, Oxford, Oxford University Press, 1988.

Mazey, S. and Nenman, M., eds. *Mitterrand's France*, London, Croom Helm, 1987.

Rioux, J.-P. *The Fourth Republic 1944–1958*, Cambridge, Cambridge University Press, 1987.

Seale, P. and McConville, M. *French Revolution 1968*, London, Penguin, 1968.

Williams, P. *Crisis and Compromise*, London, Longman, 1972.

Wright, G. *The Reshaping of French Democracy*, London, Methuen, 1950.

5. Germany

Ardagh, J. and Schmitz, K. *Germany and the Germans*, London, Hamilton, 1987.

Balfour, M. *West Germany: A Contemporary History*, London, Croom Helm, 1982.

Bark, D.L. and Gress, D.R. *A History of West Germany*, Oxford, Blackwell, 1989, 2 vols.

Becker, J. *Hitler's Children*, Philadelphia, Lippincott, 1977.

Dahrendorf, R. *Society and Democracy in Germany*, London, Weidenfeld & Nicolson, 1968.

Derbyshire, I. *Politics in Germany*, Edinburgh, Chambers, 1991.

Graf, W. *The German Left since 1945*, Cambridge, Oleander, 1976.

Hanrieder, W. *West German Foreign Policy, 1949–1963*, Stanford, Stanford University Press, 1967.

Paterson, W.E. and Smith, G., eds. *The West German Model*, London, Cass, 1981.

Prittie, T. *The Velvet Chancellors*, London, Muller, 1979.

Turner, H.A. *The Two Germanies since 1945*, New Haven, Yale University Press, 1987.

6. Ireland

Hussey, G. *Ireland Today*, London, Penguin, 1995.

Lee, J.J. *Ireland 1912–1985*, Cambridge, Cambridge University Press, 1989.

Keogh, D. *Twentieth Century Ireland*, Dublin, Gill & Macmillan, 1994.

O'Brien, C.C. *States of Ireland*, London, Hutchinson, 1972.

7. Italy

Allum, P. *Italy – Republic without Government?*, London, Weidenfeld & Nicolson, 1973.

Grindrod, M. *The Rebuilding of Italy*, London, RIIA, 1955.

Haycraft, J. *Italian Labyrinth*, London, Secker and Warburg, 1985.

Hine, D. *Governing Italy*, Oxford, Clarendon, 1993.

Kogan, N. *A Political History of Postwar Italy*, New York, Praeger, 1983.

Mammarella, G. *Italy after Fascism*, Montreal, Casalini, 1964.

Sassoon, D. *Contemporary Italy*, London, Longman, 1986.

8. Low Countries

Fitzmaurice, J. *The Politics of Belgium*, London, Hurst, 1983.

Gladdish, K. *Governing from the Centre*, London, Hurst, 1991.

Lijphart, A. *The Politics of Accommodation*, Berkeley/Los Angeles, University of California Press, 1968.

9. Scandinavia

Arter, D. *Politics and Policy-Making in Finland*, Brighton, Wheatsheaf, 1987.

Childs, M.W. *Sweden: The Middle Way on Trial*, New Haven, Yale University Press, 1980.

Elder, N., Thomas, A.H. and Arter, D. *The Consensual Democracies*, Oxford, Robertson, 1982.

Fitzmaurice, J. *Politics in Denmark*, London, Hurst, 1981.

Graubard, S.R., ed. *Norden – The Passion for Equality*, Oslo, Norwegian University Press, 1986.

Milner, H. *Sweden: Social Democracy in Practice*, Oxford, Oxford University Press, 1989.

Wisti, F. *et al. Nordic Democracy*, Copenhagen, Det Danske Selskab, 1981.

10. Southern Europe

Arango, E.R. *Spain: From Repression to Renewal*, Boulder, Westview, 1985.

Clogg, R. *A Short History of Modern Greece*, Cambridge, Cambridge University Press, 1986.

Featherstone, K. and Katsoudas, D.K., eds. *Political Change in Greece: Before and After the Colonels*, London, Croom Helm, 1987.

Gallagher, T. *Portugal: A Twentieth Century Interpretation*, Manchester, Manchester University Press, 1983.

Gunther, R., Sari, G. and Shabad, G. *Spain After Franco*, Berkeley/Los Angeles, University of California Press, 1986.

Koyman, M. *Revolution and Counter-Revolution in Portugal*, London, Merlin, 1987.

O'Ballance, E. *The Greek Civil War, 1944–49*, London, Faber, 1966.

Opello, W. *Portugal's Political Development*, Boulder, Westview, 1985.

Payne, S.G. *Basque Nationalism*, Reno, University of Nevada Press, 1975.

Payne, S.G. *The Franco Regime, 1936–1975*, Madison, University of Wisconsin Press, 1987.

Preston, P. *The Triumph of Democracy in Spain*, London, Methuen, 1986.

Pridham, G. *Securing Democracy*, London, Routledge, 1990.

Pridham, G., ed. *The New Mediterranean Democracies*, London, Cass, 1984.

Williams, A., ed. *Southern Europe Transformed*, New York, Harper and Row, 1984.

Woodhouse, C.M. *The Rise and Fall of the Greek Colonels*, London, Granada, 1985.

11. Switzerland

Linder, W. *Swiss Democracy*, London, St Martin's Press, 1994.

Steinberg, J. *Why Switzerland?*, Cambridge, Cambridge University Press, 1976.

MAPS

1. Cold War Europe

Member of NATO

(France and Spain, though both members
are not part of NATO's military
command structure, France since 1966,
Spain since accession in 1984.)

Member of Warsaw Pact
(formally ended 1991)

0   150 mls

0   150 km

FINLAND

Helsinki

Moscow

USSR

Warsaw

OLAND

KIA

GARY

RUMANIA   Yalta

lgrade

LAVIA

BULGARIA

BANIA   Istanbul

GREECE   TURKEY

Athens

Nicosia

CRETE (Gr.)   CYPRUS

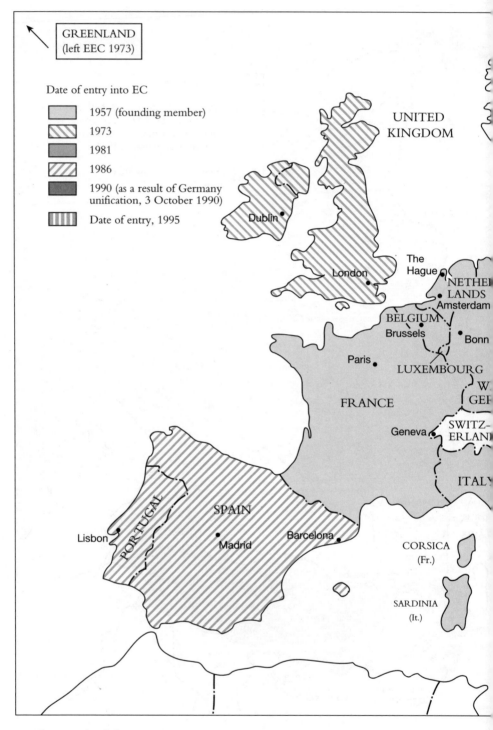

2. The growth of the European Economic Community

3. Modern Europe

INDEX